READING SOCIAL RESEARCH

READING SOCIAL RESEARCH
STUDIES IN INEQUALITIES AND DEVIANCE

JEFFREY C. DIXON | ROYCE A. SINGLETON, JR.

College of the Holy Cross

Los Angeles | London | New Delhi
Singapore | Washington DC

Los Angeles | London | New Delhi
Singapore | Washington DC

FOR INFORMATION:

SAGE Publications, Inc.
2455 Teller Road
Thousand Oaks, California 91320
E-mail: order@sagepub.com

SAGE Publications Ltd.
1 Oliver's Yard
55 City Road
London EC1Y 1SP
United Kingdom

SAGE Publications India Pvt. Ltd.
B 1/I 1 Mohan Cooperative Industrial Area
Mathura Road, New Delhi 110 044
India

SAGE Publications Asia-Pacific Pte. Ltd.
3 Church Street
#10-04 Samsung Hub
Singapore 049483

Acquisitions Editor: David Repetto
Editorial Assistant: Lauren Johnson
Production Editor: Laura Stewart
Copy Editor: Jackie Tasch
Typesetter: C&M Digitals, Ltd.
Proofreader: Stefanie Storholt
Cover Designer: Gail Buschman
Marketing Manager: Erica DeLuca
Permissions Editor: Karen Ehrmann

Printed in the United States of America

Library of Congress Cataloging-in-Publication Data

Reading social research : Studies in inequalities and deviance/edited by Jeffrey C. Dixon, Royce A. Singleton, Jr.

p. cm.
Includes bibliographical references.

ISBN 978-1-4522-4201-9 (pbk.)

1. Social sciences—Research. 2. Research—Evaluation.
I. Dixon, Jeffrey C. II. Singleton, Royce, A., Jr.

H62.R354 2013
300—dc23   2012017341

This book is printed on acid-free paper.

12 13 14 15 16 10 9 8 7 6 5 4 3 2 1

CONTENTS

PREFACE

What should students learn in an introductory research methods course? In addition to learning about fundamental methodological concepts and approaches, students should be able to identify and evaluate these concepts and approaches in reports of actual research. Indeed, when we analyzed syllabi from nearly 100 courses in methods of social research, this was the most common learning objective, listed by 60 percent of the instructors. As one instructor put it, at the end of the course, students should be able to "read original research and accurately describe the researcher's questions, methodology, and findings, and . . . critically assess the author's methods and conclusions."

With this aim in mind, we ourselves have always assigned several research articles in our methods courses. Having done this, however, we know how difficult it is to find articles that are excellent examples of research and still accessible to undergraduates. The few existing readers tend to contain articles that, although accessible, are not consistently empirically rigorous. By contrast, we want our students to be able to read and understand recent articles that are exemplars of methodological concepts and approaches. The problem is that such articles tend to be too complex and too long.

This book, a collection of 20 articles and book excerpts, is our answer to the problem. The collection is comprehensive, covering a broad range of methodological approaches and topics found in most courses in social research methods and in many research methods textbooks (e.g., Babbie, 2013; Schutt, 2012; Singleton & Straits, 2010). The selections represent some of the latest and best work in sociology; are exemplary applications of research methods; and are highly abridged and accessible to undergraduates.

We selected readings based on several criteria. First, we chose examples of *empirical research*; therefore, we excluded literature reviews, strictly theoretical papers, commentaries, and pieces on how to conduct research. Second, selections represent research *exemplars*, which tend to be found in leading journals such as *American Sociological Review*. Third, the proposed topics, as well as many of the readings, are based on the authors' content analyses of curricula and research methods syllabi from the top 50 research universities and the top 50 liberal arts colleges in the *US News & World Report* 2011 national rankings. Fourth, reading selections focus explicitly on the key sociological dimensions of race/ethnicity, class, gender, deviance and crime, which should pique students' interest. Finally, we tried to balance quantitative and qualitative selections throughout the reader.

As we abridged each article, we made sure that readers could clearly follow the researcher's report from problem statement to literature review to methods, results, and conclusions. Wanting to make the anthology affordable, we tried to keep readings as short as possible by deleting nonessential elaborations, most footnotes, and some parts of the analysis. We also included only tables and figures that were essential to the results and that could be understood with little or no statistical knowledge. In the end, the abridgments retain the sophisticated logic and analysis that made these selections important contributions to the social science literature. They clearly demonstrate key methodological concepts and approaches while drawing students in with interesting and provocative topics and findings.

Besides the careful abridgment of articles, the reader contains several other features designed to facilitate students' comprehension of the readings and research methodology:

• Brief introductions to each unit present key methodological concepts as well as one or more examples/illustrations of that topic and note how the unit readings are related to the topic and one another.

• Following the unit introduction, we offer web links to other material, as appropriate, such as professional codes of ethics, the American Association of Public Opinion Research's (AAOPR) discussion of random sampling, supplementary articles, and relevant data and computer programs that students can use.

• For each reading, a brief introduction places the research in the context of theory and methods and asks students to consider how the reading illustrates a concept or approach.

• At the end of each abridged article, we include questions that check students' understanding of the methodology. To further enhance the usefulness of the questions, we provide answers on a website for the book.

• We also include a glossary of the major terms used in the book.

REFERENCES

Babbie, E. (2013). *The practice of social research* (13th ed.). Belmont, CA: Wadsworth.

Schutt, R. K. (2012). *Investigating the social world: The process and practice of research* (7th ed.). Thousand Oaks, CA: Sage.

Singleton, R. A., Jr., & Straits, B. C. (2010). *Approaches to social research* (5th ed.). New York: Oxford University Press.

ACKNOWLEDGMENTS

The content analysis of syllabi, upon which reading selections are partly based, was made possible by a Ruettgers Grant for the development of teaching resources through the College of the Holy Cross for which Meg Flanighan provided research assistance. Part of the work, too, was done during Dixon's junior research leave from the College of the Holy Cross (fall 2011). This book would not have been possible without the willingness of methods instructors to share their syllabi and ideas with us. Our colleagues at the College of the Holy Cross provided helpful thoughts and comments. Also, John Lang alerted us to possible selections and a website devoted to examples of sociological research (http://scatter.wordpress.com/2011/08/28/a-beautiful-method/#more-5498). Reviewers at Sage Publications provided valuable suggestions on our prospectus and reading selections. We thank Dave Repetto at SAGE, who was willing to take this project on and was extremely helpful and patient throughout the process. We also thank Kate Blehar of Behar Design for creating the figures in Unit I and for helping to develop the cover. Finally, we would like to thank our wives, Zeynep Mirza-Dixon and Nancy Singleton, for their suggestions, love and support. Although we have not always incorporated suggestions from all of those above, we are grateful for the time that they took to give them. This book is certainly better for it.

INTRODUCTION

One of the best ways to learn about research methods is to read reports of empirical studies. This book consists of a collection of 20 such studies, carefully chosen to represent a broad range of approaches and methods of contemporary social research. Organized in 10 units, selected journal articles and book excerpts illustrate the relationship between theory and research, the ethical and political dimensions of research, methods of selecting cases and measuring concepts, and various ways of gathering and analyzing data. Each unit introduces the methodological topic, provides Web resources related to the topic, presents two reading selections, and then poses questions to assess your understanding of the researchers' methodology.

Although designed primarily as an introduction to research methods, this book also has a secondary goal: to expose readers to substantive topics fundamental to, and at the forefront of, sociology and other social sciences. Through rigorous empirical research, sociology and related disciplines formulate and answer questions about the social world. As we selected examples of methodological topics and approaches, we focused on studies addressing questions in the areas of race/ethnicity, gender/sexuality, social class, deviance, and crime.

Race remains one of the most important determinants of life chances and personal well-being. Social scientists continue to examine issues of racial segregation and discrimination and racial differences in nearly every aspect of social life. In this book, you will find reading selections that address several questions about race:

Given that information about the race of respondents routinely appears in a variety of sociological studies (Snipp, 2003), it is important to examine how researchers determine a person's racial identity. Many studies rely on a question from the U.S. decennial Census, but Selection 5 asks: Does the standard Census question about a person's race adequately capture the lived experience of race?

Selection 10 addresses a question of employment discrimination, asking if employers are less likely to hire black than white applicants, given equivalent credentials and work experience. Selection 17 further asks: Is there a difference between what employers say they will do and what they actually do when it comes to hiring black and white ex-criminal offenders?

In addition to racial discrimination, racial segregation remains an obstacle to personal well-being and equal life chances. African Americans and other racial and ethnic minorities continue to live in segregated neighborhoods, which often are located in economically depressed areas with high crime rates and other social problems. Selection 2 addresses the issue of police surveillance in a predominantly black and largely poor ghetto, asking: What is it like for young black men to be wanted by law enforcement authorities or otherwise "on the run"?

One way of measuring change in the racial climate is to trace media images of racial groups over time. Selection 15 asks: What does the portrayal of blacks in U.S. children's picture books reveal about changes in race relations in the mid- to late-twentieth century?

Research on gender has burgeoned in the last third of the 20th century. As women entered the labor market in increasing numbers and as their level of education surpassed that of men, researchers have examined issues of employment discrimination, sexual harassment, and the household division of labor, among others. At the same time, changing gender norms influenced research on sexuality, and researchers began to examine sexual orientation as another basis of inequality. Reading selections address several of these topics:

> Studies have shown that employment outside the home tends to have little impact on the amount of housework that women perform (Lachance-Grzela & Bouchard, 2010). Research on the gender gap in household labor is beset, however, by problems in estimating the amount of housework that husbands and wives do. Selection 6 asks: How accurate are self-reports on the time spent on housework? What do survey questions reveal about the household division of labor?

> The women's movement has raised consciousness about sexual harassment and sexual abuse. Selection 13 examines one form of harassment, unwelcome sexual advances, asking: What strategies do women use to thwart men who make unwanted advances in bars and nightclubs?

> Selection 18 addresses a consequence of abuse, namely, what is the impact of physical and sexual abuse on patterns of marriage and cohabitation among women in low-income families?

> Beginning with the gay rights movement in the 1970s and most recently with the debate on the recognition and legal sanctioning of same-sex marriage, homosexuality has been very much in the news and a focal point of social research. Two selections address questions related to homosexuality: Do attitudes toward adoption by gay and lesbian parents affect the interpretation of research on the developmental outcomes for children raised by lesbigay parents? (Selection 4) How much did Americans' attitudes toward homosexuality change in the last quarter of the 20th century? (Selection 12)

Social class forms yet another axis that defines inequality (Grusky & Ku, 2008). Research has examined many facets and consequences of class or economic inequality. Two selections mentioned above, which focus on black men in a poor ghetto (Selection 2) and women in low-income families (Selection 18), cross-cut class inequality. Other readings also address issues of inequality.

> As homelessness increased nationally in the 1980s, researchers examined its prevalence and causes. Selection 20 asks: Given the stigma of being homeless, how do homeless people shape personal identities that provide them with a modicum of self-worth and dignity?

> In the wake of dramatic new federal welfare legislation in the 1990s, which was designed to accelerate the transition from work to welfare, researchers examined the challenges faced by low-income single mothers. Selection 14 asks: Given that neither welfare nor low-wage work is sufficient to meet the needs of low-income single mothers, what strategies do they use to make ends meet?

> According to Bruce Western and Becky Pettit (2010), "from 1980 to 2008, the U.S. incarceration rate climbed from 221 to 762 per 100,000" (p. 9). This growth in the prison population, they argue, is profoundly linked to inequality, with economic disadvantage both a cause and consequence of penal confinement. Selection 16 examines how unemployment and welfare spending, among other factors, are related to the rate of prison growth in five Western nations.

Sociologists also have a longstanding interest in deviance, or actions that violate social norms, including formal laws and informal norms of acceptable behavior. Several selections address current issues in crime and deviance, including many already noted (Selections 2, 10, 16, and 17).

> Complementing Selection 16, Selection 10 also examines one of the economic penalties exacted by incarceration, asking: Given equivalent credentials and work experience, are persons with a criminal record less likely to be hired than those without a record?

> Erroneous criminal convictions uncovered by DNA testing and other new techniques have led

legal scholars and social researchers to examine procedural errors in the prosecution of crimes (Lucas, Graif, & Lovaglia, 2006). Selection 9 asks: Why are prosecutors more likely to intentionally use illegal or improper methods in prosecuting a serious crime, such as murder, than a less serious crime, such as assault?

Although college drinking was once viewed as a harmless rite of passage, it became reframed in the 1990s as a public health problem partly as the result of studies of binge drinking (Dowdall, 2009). A key study was a national survey reported in Selection 11, which brought attention to the prevalence of heavy episodic drinking and its negative personal consequences. Selection 19 addresses a question raised by this early research: Is alcohol consumption related to the academic performance of college students?

Knowing the answers to the research questions posed in these readings is important for understanding the social world. But it also is important to understand how the researchers arrived at the answers—in other words, to understand the process and elements of social research. And therein lies a more practical reason for the readings: You can learn how to critically evaluate research claims and apply this knowledge in your everyday life. Moreover, these readings provide models for you to follow in conducting your own research, whether in the course you are currently taking; on a thesis, capstone, or other academic research; or on a current or future job project. Let us elaborate on both of these points.

Being able to critically evaluate research is very important because you are exposed to numerous evidentiary claims in everyday life: "The latest scientific research has found this . . ." or "evidence shows that . . ." In order to evaluate such claims, we need to better understand the research behind them. Understanding the process of measurement, for example, is central to critically evaluating claims. After reading this book, you may start to ask how "this" or "that" was actually defined and measured. And, you'll know from the reading selections on race and housework in Unit III that different measurements

can yield different findings. Reading selections also discuss sampling and allude to the problem of overgeneralization, which you may encounter in everyday life. Your friend may tell you, "I'm sure that most Americans oppose this policy because all of my friends do." After reading the unit on sampling, you'll understand that claims based on a selective sample of opinions cannot be generalized to "most Americans." To make claims about a population or simply about the group of people being studied, researchers and everyday folks alike need to be systematic in how they select samples and think carefully about whether "most Americans" have an equal chance of being selected and heard.

Employers want critical-thinking and research skills, too. *The Chronicle of Higher Education* cites a recent study suggesting that there is a gap between employers' expectations and applicants' critical thinking skills (Johnson, 2011; for the original report, see: http://www.acics.org/events/content.aspx?id=4718). Critical thinking and analytical reasoning skills (such as the ability to evaluate scientific and other claims) are second in importance only to communication skills in a survey asking select employers what colleges should place *more* emphasis on (Hart Research Associates, 2010, p. 9). Moreover, this same report indicates that "employers see a positive benefit in educational innovations that foster active learning and research skills" (p. 7). Of the employers they surveyed, 81% said it would help a lot or a fair amount if colleges ensured "that students develop the skills to research questions in their field and develop evidence-based analyses" (p. 8). In the postindustrial, service-based economy of the United States (discussed in Selection 1), it is likely that you will need research and data analysis skills to land a job and do well in it.

As you read this book, don't forget that you are not just learning methods: You are learning something about social life; you are learning material that can applied to everyday life; and you are learning research skills that employers say that they want.

REFERENCES

Dowdall, G. (2009). *College drinking: Reframing a social problem*. Westport, CT: Praeger.

Grusky, D. B., & Ku, M. C. (2008). *Social stratification: Class, race, and gender in sociological perspective*. Boulder, CO: Westview.

Hart Research Associates. (2010). Raising the bar: Employers' views on college learning in the wake of the economic downturn. Retrieved August 15, 2012, from http://www.aacu.org/leap/documents/2009_EmployerSurvey.pdf

Johnson, L. (2011, December 5). Employers say college graduates lack job skills. *Chronicle of Higher Education*. Retrieved August 15, 2012, from http://chronicle.com/article/Employers-Say-College/130013/

Lachance-Grzela, M., & Bouchard, G. (2010). Why do women do the lion's share of housework? A decade of research. *Sex Roles, 63,* 767–780.

Lucas, J. W., Graif, C., & Lovaglia, M. J. (2006). Misconduct in the prosecution of severe crimes: Theory and experimental test. *Social Psychology Quarterly, 69,* 97–107.

Snipp, C. M. (2003). Racial measurement in the American census: Past practices and implications. *Annual Review of Sociology, 29,* 563–588.

Western, B., & Pettit, B. (2010). Incarceration and social inequality. *Daedalus, 139*(3), 8–19.

UNIT I

FROM THEORY TO RESEARCH AND BACK

Research ideas do not just fall from the sky. Every step of the research process, from the development of hypotheses to drawing conclusions, is informed by **social theories**. A social theory, put simply, is a set of abstract statements describing how the social world works. As more and more research is conducted, and as the research environment changes, social theories may gain or lose favor, undergo modifications, or fade away altogether (Kuhn, 1962; Popper, 1959). Thus, scientific research involves a constant interplay between theory and research: Social theories influence research, and research influences social theories.

Social Theory ◄────► Research

The interplay between social theories and research occurs in one or both of two ways. One way is through **deduction,** which basically refers to moving from the abstract to the more specific. Deduction is like walking through one large door and then walking through progressively smaller doors (see Figure I.1). Sometimes, researchers deduce hypotheses, represented by the second door in Figure I.1, from theories, represented by the first door in Figure I.1. When derived from a theory, a **hypothesis** is a more *specific* statement

of what the researcher expects to find. These hypotheses are then tested on observations, or data, which are represented by the third door in Figure I.1.

Consider research related to rational choice theory, which assumes that people are rational and that they make decisions on the basis of their own self-interest. The social world, according to this theory, is made up of people seeking to maximize their gains and minimize their losses. Fullerton and Dixon (2010) deduced from rational choice theory—that is, *hypothesized*—that older people would be more likely than younger people to support spending on social security. This hypothesis follows from the theory: Older people are generally closer to the age at which they can draw financial benefits from social security.

A hypothesis concerns the relationship between an **independent variable**—that is, the variable that influences the outcome—and the **dependent variable**, which is the outcome that is influenced. (Here is one way to remember this: **I**ndependent = **I**nfluences, whereas **d**ependent = influence**d**). In Fullerton and Dixon's (2010) research, the independent variable is age (older versus younger), and the dependent variable is opinion toward social security spending (e.g., support versus oppose). The hypothesis is that as age ↑, support for social security ↑. Analyzing

FIGURE I.1   Deduction

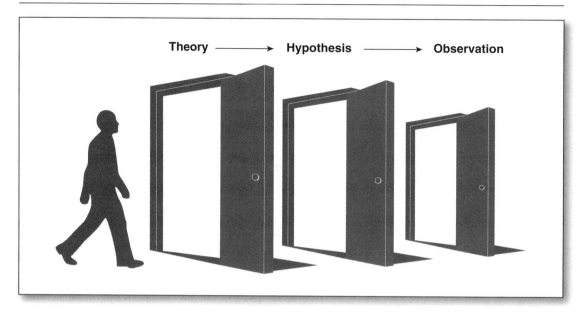

Theory ⟶ Hypothesis ⟶ Observation

survey data—or observations—between 1984 and 2008, Fullerton and Dixon found support for their hypothesis.

In contrast to deduction, induction generally refers to moving from the specific to the more general. In this way, it is like walking through one small door and then walking through progressively larger doors (see Figure I.2). In contrast to deduction, induction may begin with observations, which are represented by the first door in Figure I.2. In the process of research, induction may mean generalizing from more specific observations to larger theoretical meanings (see the second and third doors of Figure I.2, respectively).

Although Fullerton and Dixon (2010) generally found support for their hypothesis, their data were not fully consistent with rational choice theory. For example, they found that while people generally become more supportive of social security as they age, middle-aged people were most supportive of social security. They concluded from this observation and others that even though older people may find it in their immediate self-interest to support social security, rational choice theory needs to be modified in

this case because it is actually in *"everyone's interest"* to support social security (p. 664, emphasis added). And, in fact, their research is part of a continuing line of criticism of rational choice theory, which has largely fallen out of favor among sociologists today.

The two selections in this unit illustrate the connection between theory and research. The first selection highlights how researchers *deduce* hypotheses from theories—in this case, from modernization theory. Based on an ethnographic study of young black men in Philadelphia, the second selection shows how researchers *induce* broader theoretical meanings from their observations. As you read these selections, pay attention to the relationships among social theories, hypotheses, and observations.

References

Fullerton, A. S., & Dixon, J. C. (2010). Generational conflict or methodological artifact? Reconsidering the relationship between age and policy attitudes in the U.S., 1984–2008. *Public Opinion Quarterly* 74(4), 643–673.

FIGURE I.2   Induction

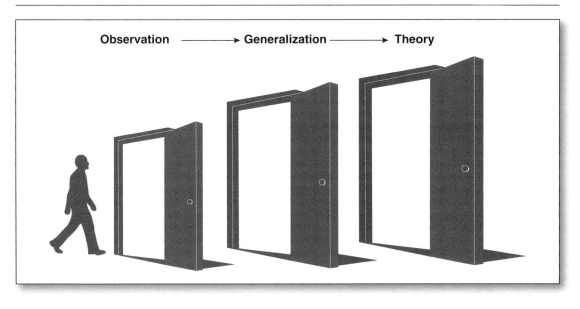

Observation ⟶ Generalization ⟶ Theory

Kuhn, T. (1962). *The structure of scientific revolutions.* Chicago: University of Chicago Press.

Popper, K. (1959). *The logic of scientific discovery.* London: Hutchinson & Co.

RESOURCES

The American Sociological Association (ASA), Section on Theory:

http://www.asatheory.org/

- The ASA is American sociologists' national professional organization. Its website has links to theory journals and various theory-related websites; click on the Resources tab and then scroll to the middle and bottom of the page.

Marxist Internet Archive:

http://www.marxists.org/

- The researchers of the first selection draw heavily on the work of Karl Marx, a prominent sociological theorist, and you can find many of his writings at this very popular website. The site also includes writings by Max Weber, another prominent theorist whose work is featured in the first selection, and these writings are available at http://www.marxists.org/reference/archive/weber/index.htm

The World Values Survey (WVS):

http://worldvaluessurvey.org/

- This website provides a link allowing you to download the very data that the researchers in our first selection use, along with more recent data and other resources.

The FBI's Uniform Crime Reports (UCR):

http://www.fbi.gov/about-us/cjis/ucr

- Widely used in research in criminology, the FBI's UCR is referenced in the second reading selection in this unit. Under the Stats & Services tab on this website, you can find data on crime, law enforcement, and other related areas.

Selection 1

Are societies' cultural values shaped by economic modernization, religious traditions, or both? Karl Marx and Max Weber, major figures in the development of sociological theory, advanced different theories in the 19th and early 20th centuries to answer this question. In this selection, Ronald Inglehart and Wayne E. Baker use contemporary survey data on cultural values from around the world to address this ongoing theoretical debate. Specifically, they are interested in understanding the sources of (1) "survival" values, which emphasize basic human survival, and (2) "traditional" values, which emphasize the role of religion and the family. When you read this selection, pay attention to the relationship among social theories, hypotheses, and results. After you complete the selection, you should understand how the authors deduced hypotheses from modernization theory and how their results suggest modifications to this theory.

MODERNIZATION, CULTURAL CHANGE, AND THE PERSISTENCE OF TRADITIONAL VALUES

RONALD INGLEHART AND WAYNE E. BAKER

The last decades of the twentieth century were not kind to modernization theory, once widely considered a powerful tool for peering into the future of industrial society. Modernization theory's most influential proponent, Karl Marx, claimed that economically developed societies show the future to less developed societies (Marx 1973). His prophecies have had enormous impact, but as the twenty-first century begins, few people anticipate a proletarian revolution or trust a state-run economy. Furthermore, although theorists from Marx to Nietzsche to Lerner to Bell predicted the decline of religion in the wake of modernization,

Source: "Modernization, Cultural Change, and the Persistence of Traditional Values," by Ronald Inglehart and Wayne E. Baker," *American Sociological Review*, Vol. 65, No. 1, Looking Forward, Looking Back: Continuity and Change at the Turn of the Millenium (Feb., 2000), pp. 19-51.

religion and spiritual beliefs have not faded. Instead, social and political debate about religious and emotionally charged issues such as abortion and euthanasia have grown increasingly salient (DiMaggio, Evans, and Bryson 1996; Hunter 1991; Williams 1997), and a resurgence of fundamentalist Islam has established a major cleavage in international politics.

Nevertheless, a core concept of modernization theory seems valid today: Industrialization produces pervasive social and cultural consequences, from rising educational levels to changing gender roles. Industrialization is seen as the central element of a modernization process that affects most other elements of society. Marx's failures as a prophet are well documented, but he correctly foresaw that industrialization would transform the world. When he was writing *Das Kapital* (1867), only a handful of societies were industrialized; today, there are dozens of advanced industrial societies, and almost every society on Earth is at some stage of the industrialization process.

Our thesis is that economic development has systematic and, to some extent, predictable cultural and political consequences. These consequences are not iron laws of history; they are probabilistic trends. Nevertheless, the probability is high that certain changes will occur, once a society has embarked on industrialization. We explore this thesis using data from the World Values Surveys. These surveys include 65 societies and more than 75 percent of the world's population. They provide time-series data from the earliest wave in 1981 to the most recent wave completed in 1998, offering new and rich insights into the relationships between economic development and social and political change.

MODERNIZATION OR THE PERSISTENCE OF TRADITIONAL VALUES?

The central claim of modernization theory is that economic development is linked with coherent and, to some extent, predictable changes in culture and social and political life. Evidence from around the world indicates that economic development tends to propel societies in a roughly predictable direction: Industrialization leads to occupational specialization, rising educational levels, rising income levels, and eventually brings unforeseen changes—changes in gender roles, attitudes toward authority and sexual norms; declining fertility rates; broader political participation; and less easily led publics.

But cultural change does not take the simple linear path envisioned by Marx, who assumed that the working class would continue to grow until a proletarian revolution brought an end to history. In 1956, the United States became the world's first society to have a majority of its labor force employed in the service sector. During the next few decades, practically all OECD (Organization for Economic Cooperation and Development) countries followed suit, becoming "post-industrial" societies, in Bell's (1973) terms. These changes in the nature of work had major political and cultural consequences (Bell 1973, 1976; Dahrendorf 1959). In marked contrast to the growing materialism linked with the industrial revolution, the unprecedented existential security of advanced industrial society gave rise to an intergenerational shift toward postmaterialist and postmodern values (Inglehart 1977, 1990, 1997). While industrialization was linked with an emphasis on economic growth at almost any price, the publics of affluent societies placed increasing emphasis on quality-of-life, environmental protection, and self-expression. Cultural change in postindustrial society was moving in a new direction. Accordingly, we suggest that economic development gives rise to not just one, but two main dimensions of cross-cultural differentiation: a first dimension linked with early industrialization and the rise of the working class; a second dimension that reflects the changes linked with the affluent conditions of advanced industrial society and with the rise of the service and knowledge sectors.

The shift from preindustrial to industrial society wrought profound changes in people's daily experiences and prevailing worldviews (Bell 1973; Inglehart 1997; Spier 1996). Preindustrial life, Bell (1976) argues, was a "game against nature" in which "one's sense of the world is conditioned by the vicissitudes of the elements— the seasons, the storms, the fertility of the soil, the amount of water, the depth of the mine seams, the droughts and the floods" (p. 147). Industrialization brought less dependence on nature, which had been seen as inscrutable, capricious, uncontrollable forces or anthropomorphic spirits. Life now became a "game against fabricated nature" (Bell 1973:147), a technical, mechanical, rationalized, bureaucratic world directed toward the external problem of creating and dominating the environment. As human control of the environment increased, the role ascribed to religion and God dwindled. Materialistic ideologies arose with secular interpretations of history, and secular utopias were to be attained by human engineering operating through rationally organized bureaucratic organizations.

The emergence of postindustrial society seems to be stimulating further evolution of prevailing worldviews, but it is moving in a different direction. Life in postindustrial societies centers on services. Less effort is focused on producing material objects, and more effort is focused on communicating and processing information. Most people spend their productive hours dealing with other people and symbols. Increasingly, one's formal education and job experience help develop the potential for autonomous decision-making (Bell 1973, 1976). Thus, the rise of postindustrial society leads to a growing emphasis on self-expression (Inglehart 1997). The hierarchical organizations of the industrial age required (and allowed) little autonomous judgment, whereas service and knowledge workers deal with people and concepts, operating in a world in which innovation and the freedom to exercise individual judgment are essential. Self-expression becomes central. Furthermore, the historically unprecedented wealth of advanced industrial societies, coupled with the rise of the welfare state, mean that an increasing share of the population grows up taking survival for granted. Their value priorities shift from an overwhelming emphasis on economic and physical security toward an increasing emphasis on subjective well-being and quality of life (Inglehart 1977, 1997). Thus, cultural change is not linear; with the coming of postindustrial society, it moves in a new direction.

Different societies follow different trajectories even when they are subjected to the same forces of economic development, in part because situation-specific factors, such as cultural heritage, also shape how a particular society develops. Weber ([1904] 1958) argued that traditional religious values have an enduring influence on the institutions of a society. Following this tradition, Huntington (1993, 1996) argues that the world is divided into eight major civilizations or "cultural zones" based on cultural differences that have persisted for centuries. These zones were shaped by religious traditions that are still powerful today, despite the forces of modernization. The zones are Western Christianity, the Orthodox world, the Islamic world, and the Confucian, Japanese, Hindu, African, and Latin American zones.

Scholars from various disciplines have observed that distinctive cultural traits endure over long periods of time and continue to shape a society's political and economic performance. For example, Putnam (1993) shows that the regions of Italy in which democratic institutions function most successfully today are those in which civil society was relatively well developed in the nineteenth century and even earlier. Fukuyama (1995) argues that a cultural heritage of "low-trust" puts a society at a competitive disadvantage in global markets because it is less able to develop large and complex social institutions. Hamilton (1994) argues that, although capitalism has become an almost universal way of life, civilizational factors continue to structure the organization of economies and societies: "What we witness with the development of a global economy is not increasing uniformity, in the form of a universalization of Western culture, but rather the continuation of civilizational diversity through the active reinvention and reincorporation of non-Western civilizational patterns" (p. 184). Thus, there are striking cross-cultural variations in the organization of capitalist production and associated managerial ideologies (DiMaggio 1994; Guillén 1994).

THE EVIDENCE

Data

Our main data source is the World Values Surveys, the largest investigation ever conducted of attitudes, values, and beliefs around the world. This study carried out three waves of representative national surveys: in 1981–1982, 1990–1991, and 1995–1998. It covers 65 countries on all six inhabited continents, and contains more than 75 percent of the world's population. These societies have per capita annual gross national products ranging from $300 to more than $30,000, and their political systems range from long-established stable democracies to authoritarian states.

We use the most recent data for the 65 countries. The number of respondents interviewed in these surveys averages about 1,400 per country.

Measures

Our thesis implies that economic development is linked with a broad syndrome of distinctive value orientations [or dimensions]. Two dimensions reflect cross-national polarization between *traditional* versus *secular–rational* orientations toward authority; and *survival* versus *self-expression* values. Each society can be located on a global map of cross-cultural variation based on these two dimensions (Inglehart 1997:81–98).

We use the term "traditional" in a specific sense here. Although the full range of "traditions" is diverse, a mainstream version of preindustrial society having a number of common characteristics can be identified. All of the preindustrial societies for which we have data show relatively low levels of tolerance for abortion, divorce, and homosexuality; tend to emphasize male dominance in economic and political life, deference to parental authority, and the importance of family life, and are relatively authoritarian; most of them place strong emphasis on religion. Advanced industrial societies tend to have the opposite characteristics.

Table 1.1 lists the 10 items that tap the traditional versus secular–rational dimension and the survival versus self-expression dimension. The items in each dimension are highly intercorrelated.

The survival/self-expression dimension taps a syndrome of trust, tolerance, subjective well-being, political activism, and self-expression that emerges in postindustrial societies with high levels of security. At the opposite extreme, people in societies shaped by insecurity and low levels of well-being tend to emphasize economic and physical security above all other goals, and feel threatened by foreigners, by ethnic diversity and by cultural change. This leads to an intolerance of gays and other outgroups, an insistence on traditional gender roles, and an authoritarian political outlook.

FINDINGS AND DISCUSSION

Global Cultural Map, 1995–1998

Figure 1.1 shows the location of 65 societies on the two dimensions [from] Table 1.1. The vertical axis on our global cultural map corresponds to the polarization between traditional authority and secular-rational authority associated with the process of industrialization. The horizontal axis depicts the polarization between survival values and self-expression values related to the rise of postindustrial society. The boundaries around groups of countries in Figure 1.1 are drawn using Huntington's (1993, 1996) cultural zones as a guide.

Cross-cultural variation is highly constrained. If the people of a given society place a strong emphasis on religion, that society's relative position on many other variables can be predicted—from attitudes toward abortion, level of national pride (highly religious nations rank high on national pride), the desirability of more respect for authority (religious nations place much more emphasis on respect for authority), to attitudes toward childrearing.

Economic development [also] seems to have a powerful impact on cultural values: The value

TABLE 1.1   Items Characterizing Two Dimensions of Cross-Cultural Variation: Nation-Level Analysis

Dimension and Item
Traditional vs. Secular-Rational Values
TRADITIONAL VALUES EMPHASIZE THE FOLLOWING:
God is very important in respondent's life.
It is more important for a child to learn obedience and religious faith than independence and determination.
Abortion is never justifiable.
Respondent has strong sense of national pride.
Respondent favors more respect for authority.
(SECULAR-RATIONAL VALUES EMPHASIZE THE OPPOSITE)
Survival vs. Self-Expression Values
SURVIVAL VALUES EMPHASIZE THE FOLLOWING:
Respondent gives authority to economic and physical security over self-expression and quality-of-life.
Respondent describes self as not very happy.
Respondent has not signed and would not sign a petition.
Homosexuality is never justifiable.
You have to be very careful about trusting people.
(SELF-EXPRESSION VALUES EMPHASIZE THE OPPOSITE)

Source: Nation-level and individual-level data from 65 societies surveyed in the 1990–1991 and 1995–1998 World Values Surveys.

systems of rich countries differ systematically from those of poor countries. Figure 1.1 reflects a gradient from low-income countries in the lower left quadrant, to rich societies in the upper right quadrant. Figure 1.2 redraws Figure 1.1, showing the economic zones into which these 65 societies fall. All 19 societies with an annual per capita gross national product over $15,000 rank relatively high on both dimensions and fall into a zone at the upper right-hand corner. This economic zone cuts across the boundaries of the Protestant, ex-Communist, Confucian, Catholic, and English–speaking cultural zones. All societies with per capita GNPs below $2,000 fall into a cluster at the lower left of Figure 1.2, in an economic zone that cuts across the African,

FIGURE 1.1   Locations of 65 Societies on Two Dimensions of Cross-Cultural Variation: World Values Surveys, 1990–1991 and 1995–1998

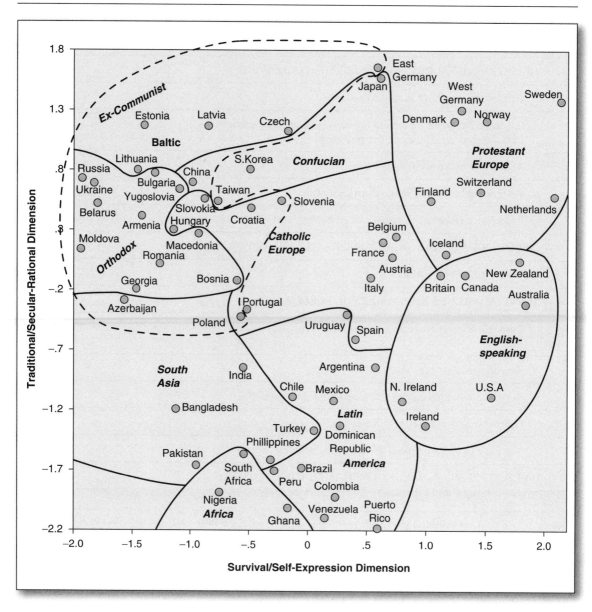

South Asian, ex–Communist, and Orthodox cultural zones. The remaining societies fall into two intermediate cultural-economic zones. Economic development seems to move societies in a common direction, regardless of their cultural heritage. Nevertheless, distinctive cultural zones persist two centuries after the industrial revolution began.

GNP per capita is only one indicator of a society's level of economic development. As Marx argued, the rise of the industrial working class was a key event in modern history. Furthermore, the changing nature of the labor force defines three distinct stages of economic development: agrarian society, industrial society, and postindustrial society (Bell 1973, 1976). Thus, another set of boundaries could be superimposed on the societies in Figure 1.1: Societies with a high percentage of the labor force in agriculture would fall near the bottom of the map, societies with a high percentage of industrial workers would fall near the top, and societies with a high percentage in the service sector would be located near the right-hand side of the map.

The traditional/secular-rational dimension is associated with the transition from agrarian society to industrial society. The shift from an agrarian mode of production to industrial production seems to bring with it a shift from traditional values toward increasing rationalization and secularization. Nevertheless, a society's cultural heritage also plays a role. Thus, all four of the Confucian-influenced societies have relatively secular values, regardless of the proportion of their labor forces in the industrial sector. The former Communist societies also rank relatively high on this secularization dimension, despite varying degrees of industrialization. Conversely, the historically Roman Catholic societies display relatively traditional values when compared with Confucian or ex-Communist societies with the same proportion of industrial workers.

The survival/self-expression dimension is linked with the rise of a service economy. While the traditional/secular-rational values dimension and the survival/self-expression values dimension reflect industrialization and the rise of postindustrial society, respectively, this is only part of the story. Virtually all of the historically Protestant societies rank higher on the survival/self-expression dimension than do all of the historically Roman Catholic societies, regardless of the extent to which their labor forces are engaged in the service sector. Conversely, virtually

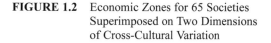

FIGURE 1.2 Economic Zones for 65 Societies Superimposed on Two Dimensions of Cross-Cultural Variation

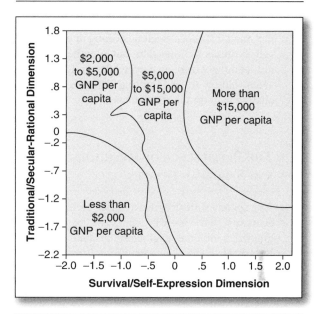

Note: All but one of the 65 societies shown in Figure 1.1 fit into the economic zones indicated here; only the Dominican Republic is mislocated.

Source: GNP per capita is based on the World Bank's Purchasing Power Parity estimates as of 1995, in U.S. dollars (World Bank 1997:214–15).

all of the former Communist societies rank low on the survival/self-expression dimension. Changes in the GNP and occupational structure have important influences on prevailing worldviews, but traditional cultural influences persist.

Figure 1.1 indicates that the United States is not a prototype of cultural modernization for other societies to follow, as some modernization writers of the postwar era naively assumed. In fact, the United States is a deviant case, having a much more traditional value system than any other advanced industrial society. On the traditional/secular-rational dimension, the United States ranks far below other rich societies, with levels of religiosity and national pride comparable to those found in developing societies. The phenomenon of American exceptionalism has been discussed by Lipset (1990, 1996), Baker (1999), and others; our results support their argument. The United States does rank among the most advanced societies along the survival/ self-expression dimension, but even here, it does not lead the world, as the Swedes and the Dutch seem closer to the cutting edge of cultural change than do the Americans.

The Persistence of Religious and Spiritual Beliefs

As a society shifts from an agrarian to an industrial economy and survival comes to be taken for granted, traditional religious beliefs tend to decline. Nevertheless, as the twenty-first century opens, cleavages along religious lines remain strong.

The subjective importance of religious beliefs has changed little in most advanced industrial democracies. For example, the World Values Surveys asked, "How important is God in your life?" (This variable is a particularly effective indicator of overall religiosity and was a component of the traditional/secular-rational values dimension). The percentage choosing "10," the highest score on the question's 10-point scale, declined only slightly in advanced industrial democracies (see Table 1.2). Although the publics in the overwhelming majority of these societies reported lower rates of church attendance, only about half of these societies show declining emphasis on the importance of God, and the mean change is a decline of only 1 percentage point. Religious feeling holds up even more strongly in the rest of the world. In all six of the ex-Communist societies for which we have time-series data, the importance attached to God increased. A similar pattern held in most of the developing and low-income societies: The importance of God in one's life increased in five of the eight societies, and in one of the societies in which it did not increase (Nigeria), it remained at an extremely high level.

TABLE 1.2   Percentage Rating the "Importance of God in Their Lives" as "10" on a 10-Point Scale, by Country and Year

Country	1981	1990- 1991	1995- 1998	Net Change
Advanced Industrial Democracies[a]				
Australia	25	-	21	−4
Belgium	9	13	-	+4
Canada	36	28	-	−8
Finland	14	12	-	−2
France	10	10	-	0
East Germany	-	13	6	−7
West Germany	16	14	16	0
Great Britain	20	16	-	−4
Iceland	22	17	-	−5

Country	1981	1990- 1991	1995- 1998	Net Change
Advanced Industrial Democracies[a]				
Ireland	29	40	-	+11
Northern Ireland	38	41	-	+3
Italy	31	29	-	–2
Japan	6	6	5	–1
Netherlands	11	11	-	0
Norway	19	15	12	–7
Spain	18	18	26	+8
Sweden	9	8	8	–1
Switzerland	-	26	17	–9
United States	50	48	50	0
Ex-Communist Societies[b]				
Belarus	-	8	20	+12
Bulgaria	-	7	10	+3
Hungary	21	22	-	+1
Latvia	-	9	17	+8
Russia	-	10	19	+9
Slovenia	-	14	15	+1
Developing and Low-Income Societies[c]				
Argentina	32	49	57	+25
Brazil	-	83	87	+4
Chile	-	61	58	–3
India	-	44	56	+12
Mexico	60	44	50	–10
Nigeria	-	87	87	0
South Africa	50	74	71	+21
Turkey	-	71	81	+10

[a]Eleven of 19 advanced industrial democracies declined; mean change = -1.

[b]Of ex-Communist societies, 6 of 6 increased; mean change = +6.

[c]Of developing and low-income societies, 5 of 8 increased; mean change = +6.

CONCLUSION

Evidence from the World Values Surveys demonstrates both massive cultural change and the persistence of distinctive traditional values. Economic development is associated with pervasive, and to some extent predictable, cultural changes. Industrialization promotes a shift from traditional to secular-rational values, while the rise of postindustrial society brings a shift toward more trust, tolerance, well-being, and postmaterialist values. Economic collapse tends to propel societies in the opposite direction. If economic development continues, we expect a continued decline of institutionalized religion. The influence of traditional value systems is unlikely to disappear, however, as belief systems exhibit remarkable durability and resilience. Empirical evidence from 65 societies indicates that values can and do change, but also that they continue to reflect a society's cultural heritage.

Modernization theorists are partly right. The rise of industrial society is linked with coherent cultural shifts away from traditional value systems, and the rise of postindustrial society is linked with a shift away from absolute norms and values toward a syndrome of increasingly rational, tolerant, trusting, postindustrial values. Economic development tends to push societies in a common direction, but rather than converging, they seem to move on parallel trajectories shaped by their cultural heritages. We doubt that the forces of modernization will produce a homogenized world culture in the foreseeable future.

We propose several modifications of modernization theory. First, modernization does not follow a linear path. The rise of the service sector and the transition to a knowledge society are linked with a different set of cultural changes from those that characterized industrialization. Moreover, protracted economic collapse can reverse the effects of modernization, resulting in a return to traditional values, as seems to be happening in the former Soviet Union.

Second, the secularization thesis is oversimplified. Our evidence suggests that it applies mainly to the industrialization phase—the shift from agrarian society to industrial society that was completed some time ago in most advanced industrial societies. This shift was linked with major declines in the role of the church, which led Marx and others to assume that, in the long run, religious beliefs would die out. The shift from agrarian to urban industrial society reduces the importance of organized religion, but this is counterbalanced by growing concerns for the meaning and purpose of life. Religious beliefs persist, and spiritual concerns, broadly defined, are becoming more widespread in advanced industrial societies.

Third, cultural change seems to be path dependent. Economic development tends to bring pervasive cultural changes, but the fact that a society was historically shaped by Protestantism or Confucianism or Islam leaves a cultural heritage with enduring effects that influence subsequent development. Even though few people attend church in Protestant Europe today, historically Protestant societies remain distinctive across a wide range of values and attitudes. The same is true for historically Roman Catholic societies, for historically Islamic or Orthodox societies, and for historically Confucian societies.

Fourth, it is misleading to view cultural change as "Americanization." Industrializing societies in general are *not* becoming like the United States. In fact, the United States seems to be a deviant case, as many observers of American life have argued (Lipset 1990, 1996)—its people hold much more traditional values and beliefs than do those in any other equally prosperous society (Baker 1999). If any societies exemplify the cutting edge of cultural change, it would be the Nordic countries.

Finally, modernization is probabilistic, not deterministic. Economic development tends to transform a given society in a predictable direction, but the process and path are not inevitable. Many factors are involved, so any prediction must be contingent on the historical and cultural context of the society in question.

Nevertheless, the central prediction of modernization theory finds broad support: Economic development is associated with major changes in prevailing values and beliefs:

The worldviews of rich societies differ markedly from those of poor societies. This does not necessarily imply cultural convergence, but it does predict the general direction of cultural change.

REFERENCES

Baker, Wayne E. 1999. *North Star Falling: The American Crisis of Values at the New Millennium.* School of Business, University of Michigan, Ann Arbor, MI. Unpublished manuscript.

Bell, Daniel. 1973. *The Coming of Post-Industrial Society.* New York: Basic Books.

———. 1976. *The Cultural Contradictions of Capitalism.* New York: Basic Books.

Dahrendorf, Ralf. 1959. *Class and Class Conflict in Industrial Society.* Stanford, CA: Stanford University Press.

DiMaggio, Paul. 1994. "Culture and Economy." Pp. 27–57 in *The Handbook of Economic Sociology,* edited by N. J. Smelser and R. Swedberg. Princeton, NJ: Princeton University Press.

DiMaggio, Paul, John Evans, and Bethany Bryson. 1996. "Have Americans' Social Attitudes Become More Polarized?" *American Journal of Sociology* 102:690–755.

Fukuyama, Francis. 1995. *Trust: The Social Virtues and the Creation of Prosperity.* New York: Free Press.

Guillén, Mauro. 1994. *Models of Management: Work, Authority, and Organization in a Comparative Perspective.* Chicago, IL: University of Chicago Press.

Hamilton, Gary G. 1994. "Civilizations and Organization of Economies." Pp. 183–205 in *The Handbook of Economic Sociology,* edited by N. J. Smelser and R. Swedberg. Princeton, NJ: Princeton University Press.

Hunter, James Davison. 1991. *Culture Wars: The Struggle to Define America.* New York: Basic Books.

Huntington, Samuel P. 1993. "The Clash of Civilizations?" *Foreign Affairs* 72(3):22–49.

———. 1996. *The Clash of Civilizations and the Remaking of World Order.* New York: Simon and Schuster.

Inglehart, Ronald. 1977. *The Silent Revolution: Changing Values and Political Styles in Advanced Industrial Society.* Princeton, NJ: Princeton University Press.

———. 1990. *Culture Shift in Advanced Industrial Society.* Princeton, NJ: Princeton University Press.

———. 1997. *Modernization and Postmodernization: Cultural, Economic, and Political Change in 43 Societies.* Princeton, NJ: Princeton University Press.

Lipset, Seymour Martin. 1990. "American Exceptionalism Reaffirmed." *Toqueville Review* 10:23–45.

———. 1996. *American Exceptionalism.* New York: Norton.

Marx, Karl. 1973. *Foundations of the Critique of Political Economy.* New York: Vintage Books.

———. 1867. *Das Kapital: Kritik der politischen Ökonomie.* Vol. 1. Hamburg, Germany: O. Meissner.

Putnam, Robert. 1993. *Making Democracy Work: Civic Traditions in Modern Italy.* Princeton, NJ: Princeton University Press.

Spier, Fred. 1996. *The Structure of Big History: From the Big Bang until Today.* Amsterdam, Holland: Amsterdam University Press.

Weber, Max. [1904] 1958. *The Protestant Ethic and the Spirit of Capitalism.* Translated by T. Parsons. Reprint, New York: Charles Scribner's Sons.

Williams, Rhys H., ed. 1997. *Cultural Wars in American Politics.* New York: Aldine de Gruyter.

World Bank. 1997. *World Development Report.* New York: Oxford University Press.

QUESTIONS

1. According to Marx's modernization theory, industrialization brings about predictable cultural and social changes. Give one example of these changes. What economic development, shown first in the United States, suggests that cultural change did not follow the "simple linear path envisioned by Marx"?

2. Explain how each of the following social forces challenges modernization theory: (a) the emergence of post-industrial society and (b) the enduring influence of traditional religious values.

3. What do the authors hypothesize about the effects of economic development on (a) traditional versus secular values and (b) survival versus self-expression values? That is, as

economic development increases, how will each of these values change?

4. Look back at Figure 1.2. The "survival/self-expression" dimension of cultural values is at the bottom of this figure, running horizontally. On this dimension, lower numbers represent greater survival values, whereas higher numbers represent greater self-expression values (which are the opposite of survival). Looking at the left-hand side of the figure, or vertically, you'll see that this is the "traditional/secular-rational" dimension of cultural values. Here, lower numbers represent more traditional values, whereas higher numbers represent more secular-rational values (which are the opposite of tradition). Knowing this, do the results in Figure 1.2 support the researchers' hypotheses, if we assume that gross national product (GNP) is a good measure of economic development?

5. In light of the researchers' results, what revisions do they propose to modernization theory? How does this illustrate the connection between research and theory?

Selection 2

What is it like for young black men to be wanted by law enforcement authorities or otherwise "on the run"? In this selection, Alice Goffman answers this question by drawing on observational data in a predominantly black and largely poor ghetto in Philadelphia. Goffman details the strategies that these men use to avoid authorities and others, as well as the consequences of these strategies; she also spells out what her study theoretically means for society as a whole. As you read this selection, pay attention to the theoretical meaning that Goffman infers or induces from her findings.

ON THE RUN: WANTED MEN IN A PHILADELPHIA GHETTO

ALICE GOFFMAN

The number of people incarcerated in the United States has grown seven times over the past 40 years, and this growth has been concentrated among Black men with little education (Garland 2001; Western 2006). For Black men in recent birth cohorts, the experience of incarceration is now typical: 30 percent of those with only high school diplomas have been to prison, and 60 percent of those who did not finish high school have prison records by their mid–30s (Pettit and Western 2004). One in four Black children born in 1990 had a father imprisoned (Wildeman 2009). Such "mass imprisonment" (Garland 2001) transmits social and economic disadvantage, to be sure. African American former felons face significant discrimination in the labor market, as well as health costs, obstacles to housing, and large-scale disenfranchisement (Hammett, Harmon, and Rhodes 2002; Pager 2007; Rubenstein and Mukamal 2002; Uggen and Manza 2002; Western 2006). Moreover, imprisoned and formerly imprisoned men have difficulties participating in sustained ways in the lives of their families (see Nurse 2002; Western, Lopoo, and McLanahan 2004). Their partners and children consequently become socially and economically disadvantaged in the process (for reviews, see Comfort 2007; Hagan and Dinovitzer 1999).

Expansions in incarceration have been accompanied by increases in policing and

Source: "On the Run: Wanted Men in a Philadelphia Ghetto," by Alice Goffman, 2009, *American Sociological Review,* 74, 339–357. Copyright 2009 by Sage Publications.

supervision in poor communities. While the police were scarcely present in the ghetto decades ago, today, police helicopters can regularly be heard overhead, cameras now monitor people on the streets, and large numbers of young men—including many who have never been convicted of felonies—have pending cases in the criminal courts, are on probation, released on bail, issued low-level warrants, and are routinely chased, searched, questioned, and arrested by the police. How does this affect daily life in poor Black communities?

This article, building on prior work pertaining to the urban poor, as well as broader conceptions of power in the modern era (e.g., Foucault 1979), draws on six years of fieldwork with a group of poor African American young men in Philadelphia. In doing so, it offers an extended ethnographic look at life in the policed and surveilled ghetto that has taken shape in the era of mass imprisonment.

THE URBAN POOR AND POLICING

In Philadelphia, the number of police officers increased by 69 percent between 1960 and 2000, from 2.76 officers for every 1,000 citizens to 4.66 officers.[1] The Philadelphia Adult Probation and Parole Department supervised more than 60,000 people in 2006. These people paid the city more than 10 million dollars in restitution, fines, court costs, and supervisory fees that year. In Philadelphia, 12,000 people violated the terms of their probation or parole and were subject to warrants for their arrest (Philadelphia Adult Probation and Parole Department 2007). Even more people were issued bench warrants for missing court or for unpaid court fees, or arrest warrants for failure to turn themselves in for a crime. Such surveillance, policing, and supervision raise important sociological questions about the role of the state in managing poverty and maintaining racial inequality (Wacquant 2001). They also raise questions about the nature and consequences of modern surveillance and power.

Foucault (1979) suggested that the modern era would increasingly be characterized by surveillance and that state monitoring of citizens would become increasingly complete. Building on ethnographic insights, my conclusions highlight ways in which contemporary surveillance may indeed be taking the forms Foucault described in his analysis of panoptic power. Yet my conclusions also suggest that the consequences of such surveillance for everyday life may differ from those envisioned by Foucault. Rather than encouraging self-monitoring, the forms of supervision and policing found in the neighborhood I observed foster a climate of fear and suspicion in which people are pressured to inform on one another. Young men do not live as well-disciplined subjects, but as suspects and fugitives, with the daily fear of confinement.

FIELDWORK, THE 6TH STREET BOYS, AND NEIGHBORHOOD CONTEXT

When I was an undergraduate at the University of Pennsylvania, I tutored a high school student, Aisha (names of people and streets are fictitious). I began to get to know some of her friends and neighbors, and in the fall of 2002 I moved into an apartment in the poor to working-class Black neighborhood in which she lived. At this point, Aisha's mother had begun referring to me as her "other daughter" and Aisha and I became "sisters" (Anderson 1978; Stack 1974). When Aisha's cousin Ronny, age 15, came home from a juvenile detention center, Aisha and I started hanging out with him in a neighborhood about 10 minutes away called 6th Street. Ronny introduced me to Mike, who was 21, a year older than I was. When Mike's best friend Chuck, age 18, came home from county jail, we began hanging out with him too.

When I first started spending time with Ronny and Mike on 6th Street, their neighbors and relatives remarked on my whiteness and asked me to account for my presence. Ronny introduced me as Aisha's "sister," and I mentioned that I lived nearby. After a few months, Mike decided to "take me under his wing" and began referring to me as "sis." Bit by bit, other young men in the group started introducing me to others as their cousin or as a "homie" who "goes way back."

The five blocks known as 6th Street are 93 percent Black, according to a survey of residents that Chuck and I conducted in 2007. At the busiest intersection, men and boys stand outside offering bootleg CDs and DVDs, stolen goods, and food to drivers and passersby. The main commercial street includes a bullet-proofed Chinese food store selling fried chicken wings, "loosie" cigarettes, condoms, baby food, and glassines for smoking crack. The street also includes a check-cashing store, hair dresser, payday loan store, Crown Fried Chicken restaurant, and a pawnshop. On the next block, a Puerto Rican family runs a corner grocery.

Of the 217 households surveyed, roughly one fourth received housing vouchers. In all but two households, members reported receiving some type of government assistance in the past three years.

Chuck, Mike, and Ronny were part of a loose group of about 15 young men who grew up around 6th Street and were joined by the fact that they were, for the most part, unemployed and trying to make it outside of the formal economy. They occasionally referred to their group as "the 6th Street Boys" when distinguishing themselves from other street-corner groups, and five of them had "6th Street" tattooed on their arms. Among the 15 young men, eight were 18 or 19 years old when I met them, four were in their early 20s, and one was age 23. Ronny was 14 and Reggie was 15. Six years later, Mike was the only one to have graduated from high school. Alex worked steadily in his father's heating and air-conditioning repair shop, and four others occasionally found seasonal construction jobs or low-skilled jobs at places like Taco Bell and McDonald's. By 2002, the crack trade was in decline, as it was in other parts of the country (Jacobs 1999). Seven of the young men worked intermittently as low-level crack dealers; others sold marijuana, Wet (PCP and/or embalming fluid), or pills like Xanax. Some of the men occasionally made money by robbing other drug dealers. One earned his keep by exotic dancing and offering sex to women.

Between January 2002 and August 2003, I conducted intensive observation "on the block," spending most of my waking hours hanging out on Chuck's back porch steps, or along the alley way between his block and Mike's block, or on the corner across from the convenience store. In the colder months, we were usually indoors at Chuck's and a few other houses in the area. I also went along to lawyers' offices, court, the probation and parole office, the hospital, and local bars and parties. By 2004, some of the young men were in county jails and state prisons; for the next four years I spent between two and six days a week on 6th Street and roughly one day a week visiting members of the group in jail and prison. I also kept in touch by phone and through letters.

The young men agreed to let me take field notes for the purpose of one day publishing the material, but I generally did not ask direct questions and most of what is contained here comes from observations I made or conversations I heard.[2] Over the course of this research I also interviewed two lawyers, a district attorney, three probation officers, two police officers, and a federal district court judge.

On Being Wanted

By 2002, curfews were established around 6th Street for those under age 18 and video cameras had been placed on major streets. During the first year and a half of fieldwork, I watched the police stop pedestrians or people in cars, search them, run their names to see if any warrants came up, ask them to come in for questioning, or make an arrest at least once a day, with five exceptions. I watched the police break down doors, search houses, and question, arrest, or chase suspects through houses 52 times. Police helicopters circled overhead and beamed search lights onto local streets nine times. I noted blocks taped off and traffic redirected as police searched for evidence or "secured a crime scene" 17 times. I watched the police punch, choke, kick, stomp on, or beat young men with night sticks 14 times during this first year and a half.

People with warrants out for their arrest for failure to turn themselves in when accused of a crime understand that the police may employ a number of strategies in attempting to locate them. In an interview, two police officers explained that when they are looking for a suspect, they access Social Security records, court records, hospital admission records, electric and gas bills, and employment records. They visit a suspect's "usual haunts" (e.g., his home, his workplace, and his street corner) at the times he is likely to be there, threatening his family or friends with arrest, particularly when they have their own lower–level warrants or are on probation or have a pending court case. The police also use a sophisticated computer mapping program that tracks people who have warrants or are on probation, parole, or released on bail. The police round up these potential informants and threaten them with jail time if they do not provide information about the suspect they are looking for.

In the 6th Street neighborhood, a person was occasionally "on the run" because he was a suspect in a shooting or robbery, but most people around 6th Street had warrants out for far more minor infractions. In the survey that Chuck and I conducted in 2007, of the 217 households that make up the 6th Street neighborhood, we found 308 men between the ages of 18 and 30 in residence. Of these men, 144 reported that they had a warrant issued for their arrest because of either delinquencies with court fines and fees or for failure to appear for a court date within the past three years.

Young men worried that they would be picked up by the police and taken into custody even when they did not have a warrant out for their arrest. Those on probation or parole, on house arrest, and who were going through a trial expressed concern that they would soon be picked up and taken into custody for some violation that would "come up in the system." Even those with no pending legal action expressed concern that the police might "find some reason to hold them" because of what they had done, who or what they knew, or what they carried on their person. In this sense, being "on the run" covers a range of circumstances. I use the term to mean anyone whose claim to a life outside of confinement is not secure or legitimate and who may be taken into custody if they

encounter the authorities. People "on the run" make a concerted effort to thwart their discovery and apprehension.

PATHS TO PRISON AND STRATEGIES OF EVASION

Once a man finds that he may be stopped by the police and taken into custody, he discovers that people, places, and relations he formerly relied on, and that are integral to maintaining a respectable identity, get redefined as paths to confinement. I am concerned here with the kinds of relations, localities, and activities that threaten a wanted man's freedom, with the techniques he commonly employs to reduce these risks, and with some of the contingencies associated with these techniques.

Hospitals

Alex and his girlfriend, Donna, both age 22, drove to the hospital for the birth of their son. I got there a few hours after the baby was born, in time to see two police officers come into the room and arrest Alex. He had violated his parole a few months before by drinking alcohol and had a warrant out for his arrest. As an officer hand-cuffed him, Donna screamed and cried, and as they walked Alex away she got out of the bed and grabbed hold of him, moaning, "Please don't take him away. Please I'll take him down there myself tomorrow I swear, just let him stay with me tonight." The officers told me they had come to the hospital with a shooting victim who was in custody and, as was their custom, ran the names of the men on the visitors list. Alex came up as having a warrant out for a parole violation, so they arrested him along with two other men on the delivery room floor.

Alex spent a year back upstate on the parole violation. Just after his son's first birthday he was re-released on parole, with another year left to complete it. He resumed work at his father's heating and air-conditioning repair shop, stopped smoking marijuana, and typically came home before his curfew. Three weeks before Alex was due to complete his parole sentence, he was on his way home from 6th Street when a man with a hooded sweatshirt covering his face stepped quickly out from behind the side of a store and walked Alex, with a gun in his back, into the alley. Alex said the man took his money and pistol-whipped him three times, then grabbed the back of his head and smashed his face into a concrete wall.

Alex called Mike and me to come pick him up. When we arrived, Alex was searching on the ground for the three teeth that had fallen out, and the blood from his face and mouth was streaming down his white T-shirt and onto his pants and boots. His jaw and nose were swollen and looked as if they might be broken. I pleaded with him to go to the hospital. He refused, saying that his parole officer might hear of it and serve him a violation for being out past curfew, for fighting, for drinking, or any other number of infractions.

That night, Alex called his cousin who was studying to be a nurse's assistant to come stitch up his face. In the morning, he repeated his refusal to avail himself of medical care:

> All the bullshit I done been through [to finish his parole sentence], it's like, I'm not just going to check into emergency and there come the cops asking me all types of questions and writing my information down and before you know it I'm back in there [in prison]. Even if they not there for me some of them probably going to recognize me then they going to come over, run my shit [run a check on his name] . . . . I ain't supposed to be up there [his parole terms forbade him to be near 6th Street, where he was injured]; I can't be out at no two o'clock [his curfew was ten]. Plus they might still got that little jawn [warrant] on me in Bucks County [for court fees he did not pay at the end of a trial two years earlier]. I don't want them running my name, and then I got to go to court or I get locked back up.

The Police

Like going to hospitals, using the police was risky. After Mike completed a year in prison he was released on parole to a halfway house. When his mother went on vacation, he invited a man he met in prison to her house to play video games. The next day Mike, Chuck, and I went back and found his mother's stereo, DVD player, and two televisions were gone. A neighbor told us he had seen the man taking these things out of the house in the early morning.

Mike called the police and gave them a description of the man. When we returned to the block, Reggie and Steve admonished Mike about the risks he had taken:

> *Reggie:* And you on parole! You done got home like a day ago! Why the fuck you calling the law for? You lucky they ain't just grab [arrest] both of you.

> *Steve:* Put it this way: They ain't come grab you like you ain't violate shit, they ain't find no other jawns [warrants] in the computer. Dude ain't pop no fly shit [accused Mike of some crime in an attempt to reduce his own charges], but simple fact is you filed a statement, you know what I'm saying, gave them niggas your government [real name]. Now they got your mom's address in the file as your last known [address], so the next time they come looking for you they not just going to your uncle's, they definitely going to be through there [his mother's house].

Mike returned to the halfway house a few days later and discovered that the guards were conducting alcohol tests. He left before they could test him, assuming he would test positive and spend another year upstate for the violation. Three days later the police found him at his mother's house and took him into custody. He mentioned that he thought their knowledge of his new address must have come from the time he reported the robbery.

While people on probation or parole may make tentative use of the police, men with warrants typically stay away. During the first year and a half I spent on 6th Street, I noted 24 instances in which members of the group contacted the police when they were injured, robbed, or threatened. These men were either in good standing with the courts or had no pending legal constraints. I did not observe any person subject to a warrant call the police or voluntarily make use of the courts during the six years I spent there. Indeed, young men with warrants seemed to see the authorities only as a threat to their safety. This has two important implications.

First, steering clear of the police means that wanted men tend not to use the ordinary resources of the law to protect themselves from crimes perpetrated against them. This can lead a person to become the target of those who are looking for someone to rob. Second, wanted people's inability to turn to the police when harmed can lead young men to use violence to protect themselves or to get back at others.

Family and Friends

Like going to the hospital or using the police, even more intimate relations—friends, family, and romantic partners—may pose a threat and thus have to be avoided or at least carefully navigated.

I witnessed women call the police on their boyfriends or kin to punish them or get back at them. Mike and Marie's relationship witnessed just such a tension. They had a son when they were seniors in high school and a daughter two years later. When Mike and Marie were 22, and their children were 1 and 3 years old, Mike began openly seeing another woman, Tara. Mike claimed that he and Marie had broken up and he could do as he wished, but Marie did not agree to this split and maintained they were still together and that he was in fact cheating. ("He don't be telling me we not together when he laying in the bed with me!") Mike provoked expressions of jealousy (called "stunting") as he began riding past Marie's block with Tara on the back of his ATV motorbike. Marie seemed infuriated at the insult of her children's father riding through her block with another woman for all of her family and neighbors to see.

Tara said she wanted to fight Marie and almost did so one afternoon. Marie stood outside her house, with six relatives in back of her, waving a baseball bat and shouting, "Get your kids, bitch. I got mine!" (Meaning that she had more claim to Mike than Tara did because they

shared two children.) One of Tara's girlfriends and I held her back while she took off her earrings and screamed, "I got your bitch, bitch!" and "I'm going to beat the shit out this fat bitch."

One afternoon when Mike was sitting on a neighbor's steps, a squad car pulled up and two police officers arrested him. He had a bench warrant out for missing a court date. He said later that he never even thought to run, assuming the police were there to pick up the men standing next to him who had recently robbed a convenience store. As Mike sat in the police car, Marie talked at him through the window in a loud voice:

> You not just going to dog [publicly cheat on or humiliate] me! Who the fuck he think he dealing with? Let that nigga sit for a minute [stay in jail for a while]. Don't let me catch that bitch up there either [coming to visit him in jail].

Although Marie did call the cops and get Mike taken into custody that day, she was the first person to visit in county jail.

While family members, partners, or friends of a wanted man occasionally call the police on him to control his behavior or to punish him for a perceived wrong, close kin or girlfriends also link young men to the police because the police compel them to do so. Reggie, age 17, was stopped by the police for "loitering" on the corner and allowed the police to search him. When the police officer discovered three small bags of crack in the lining of his jeans, Reggie started running. The cops lost him in the chase, and an arrest warrant was issued for possession of drugs with intent to distribute.

Reggie told me that the police raided his house the next night at 3:00 a.m. He left through the back door and ran through the alley before they could catch him. The officers came back the next night, breaking open the front door (which remains broken and unlocked to this day), and ordered Reggie's younger brother and his grandfather to lie facedown on the floor with their hands on their heads while they searched the house. An officer promised Reggie's mother that if she gave up her son, they would not tell Reggie she had betrayed him. If she did not give

Reggie up, he said he would call child protective services and have her younger son taken away because the house was infested with roaches, covered in cat shit, and unfit to live in.

I was present two nights later when the police raided the house for the third time. An officer mentioned they were lucky the family owned the house: if it was a Section 8 building they could be immediately evicted for endangering their neighbors and harboring a fugitive. (Indeed, I had seen this happen recently to two other families.) The police found a gun upstairs that Reggie's mother could not produce a permit for; they cuffed her and took her to the police station. When her youngest son and I picked her up that afternoon, she said they told her she would be charged for the gun unless she told them where to find Reggie.

Reggie's mother begged him to turn himself in, but Reggie refused. His grandfather, who owned the house, told Reggie's mother that he would no longer allow her to live there with her kids if she continued to hide her son from the police:

> This ain't no damn carnival. I don't care who he is, I'm not letting nobody run through this house with the cops chasing him, breaking shit, spilling shit, waking me up out of my sleep. I'm not with the late night screaming and running. I open my eyes and I see a nigga hopping over my bed trying to crawl out the window. Hell no! Like I told Reggie, if the law run up in here one more time I be done had a stroke. Reggie is a grown-ass man [he was 17]. He ain't hiding out in my damn house. We going to fuck around and wind up in jail with this shit. They keep coming they going to find some reason to book my Black ass.

Reggie's grandfather began calling the police when he saw Reggie in the house, and Reggie's mother told him that he could no longer stay there.

BEING WANTED AS A MEANS OF ACCOUNTING

Once a man is wanted, maintaining a stable routine, being with his partner and family, going to work, and using the police may link him to the authorities and lead to his confinement. While legal entanglements may exacerbate these difficulties, being wanted also serves as a way to save face and to explain inadequacies.

[As an example,] warrants serve as an important explanation for not having a job. Steve had a warrant out for a few weeks when he was 21, and repeatedly mentioned how he could not get work because of this warrant:

> If I had a whip [car] I'd go get me a job up King of Prussia [a mall in a neighboring county] or whatever. But I can't work nowhere in Philly. That's where niggas be fucking up. You remember when Jason was at McDonald's? He was like, "No, they [the police] ain't going to see me, I'm working in the back." But you can't always be back there, like sometimes they put you at the counter, like if somebody don't show up, you know what I mean? How long he worked there before they [the police] came and got him? Like a week. They was like, "Um, can I get a large fry and your hands on the counter because your Black ass is booked!" And he tried to run like shit, too, but they was outside the jawn [the restaurant] four deep [four police officers were outside] just waiting for him to try that shit.

Although Steve now and then invoked his warrant as an explanation for his unemployment, the fact was that Steve did not secure a job during the six years I knew him, including the times when he did not have a warrant.

Being wanted serves as an excuse for a wide variety of unfulfilled obligations and expectations. At the same time, it is perhaps only because being wanted is in fact a constraining condition that it works so well as a means of accounting for failure. Having a warrant may not be the reason why Steve, for example, did not look for work, but it was a fact that police officers did go to a man's place of work to arrest him, and that some of the men experienced this first-hand. In the context of their ongoing struggles, what they said amounted to reasonable "half-truths" (Liebow 1967) that could account for their failures, both in their own minds and in the minds of others who had come to see their own lives in similar terms.

DISCUSSION

Systems of policing and supervision that accompanied the rise in imprisonment have fostered a climate of fear and suspicion in poor communities—a climate in which family members and friends are pressured to inform on one another and young men live as suspects and fugitives, with the daily fear of confinement.

Young men who are wanted by the police find that activities, relations, and localities that others rely on to maintain a decent and respectable identity are transformed into a system that the authorities make use of to arrest and confine them. The police become dangerous to interact with, as does showing up to work or going to places like hospitals. Instead of a safe place to sleep, eat, and find acceptance and support, mothers' homes are transformed into a "last known address," one of the first places the police will look for them. Close relatives, friends, and neighbors become potential informants.

One strategy for coping with these risks is to avoid dangerous places, people, and interactions entirely. A young man thus does not attend the birth of his child, nor seek medical help when he is badly beaten. He avoids the police even if it means using violence when he is injured or becoming the target of others who are looking for someone to rob. A second strategy is to cultivate unpredictability—to remain secretive and to "dip and dodge." To ensure that those close to him will not inform on him, a young man comes and goes in irregular and unpredictable ways, remaining elusive and untrusting, sleeping in different beds, and deceiving those close to him about his whereabouts and plans. If a man exhausts these possibilities and gets taken into custody, he may try to avoid jail time by informing on the people he knows.

Whatever the strategy, a man finds that as long as he is at risk of confinement, staying out of prison and participating in institutions like family, work, and friendship become contradictory goals; doing one reduces his chance of achieving the other. Staying out of jail becomes

aligned not with upstanding, respectable action, but with being an even shadier character.

Contemporary theories of social stratification and political sociology argue that the criminal justice system has become a vehicle for passing on disadvantage (Western 2006) and "an instrument for the management of dispossessed and dishonored groups" (Wacquant 2001:95). The findings presented here confirm these important theses, but my fieldwork also suggests that those so managed are hardly hapless victims, immobilized in webs of control. Instead, men and women on 6th Street evade and resist the authorities, at times calling on the state for their own purposes, to make claims for themselves as honorable people, and to exercise power over one another.

CONCLUSIONS AND THEORETICAL IMPLICATIONS

Young men on the run in Philadelphia can tell us something about how power operates in contemporary society. Indeed, the policing of the modern ghetto may be usefully juxtaposed to the influential theory of power Foucault outlines in *Discipline and Punish* (1979). Taking the prison as an example, Foucault suggests that modern punishment is organized not on the principle of occasional fear-inspiring public brutality, but on a panoptic system of inspection, surveillance, and graded rewards and punishments. The law is enforced systematically: individuals are carefully monitored and examined and files are kept on them.

At first glance, the Philadelphia neighborhood I studied, with its video cameras on street lamps, frequent police stops and searches, and monitoring of residents through probation, parole, and house arrest, seems to resemble the panoptic fortress town Foucault envisioned in *Discipline and Punish* (1979). Yet the ghetto cannot be placed under the general umbrella of the panopticon. A different form of power exists there, and with different results for the people involved.

Foucault suggests that in prisons, authorities accomplish cooperation through "constant, uninterrupted supervision" and a system of graded punishments and rewards. People are coaxed into compliance through careful training, examining, and monitoring, through minute attention to the movements and gestures of the body. Eventually, subjects come to internally monitor themselves (Garland 2001).

In comparison to prisons, the monitoring and supervision of ghetto residents is incomplete. Enclosed spaces make near perfect surveillance and enforcement possible: people can live unlawfully only if they do not get caught or if the authorities look the other way (Sykes [1958] 2007). In spaces like the 6th Street neighborhood, however, many people break the law without the authorities knowing; many others are known to be in violation but the authorities do not have the resources or the ability (or, to be more cynical, the desire) to locate them all and bring them to justice.

Surveillance and supervision in the ghetto are incomplete not only because people are widely able to break the rules and to evade the authorities, but also because the forms of supervision do not strive to be all-encompassing in the first place. Residents of the neighborhood I studied do not find that their movements are tightly controlled and regimented, as they would be in a prison; they do not eat, sleep, and live together under the watchful gaze of one central authority, nor is their privacy and personal property permanently denied them (Foucault 1979; Goffman 1961; Sykes [1958] 2007). Supervision around 6th Street is based not on constant observation and disciplining, but on a kind of checkpoint or flashpoint system, whereby certain people are only occasionally (if not randomly) monitored, searched, observed, or dispossessed.

These occasional examinations (the urine test during a probation meeting, the stop and frisk on a street corner, the raid of a house, or the running of a driver's name in the police database to see if any warrants come up) are put to use not—as Foucault envisioned—to dole out a range of small punishments and rewards in the interest of

correction and training, but to identify people who may qualify for prison and to bring those people into the hands of the state.

This form of power—occasional, incomplete, and for the purpose of identifying candidates for extreme sanction—does not seem to produce orderly subjects. Self-discipline and the internalization of norms makes little sense in a context in which following the rules (e.g., appearing in court, showing up to probation meetings, or turning oneself in when accused) may *hasten* one's removal to prison.

A final point of comparison: Foucault argues that power based on fear (the public hangings) was replaced in the modern era by power based on observation, examination, and discipline. In the 6th Street neighborhood, one indeed finds monitoring and supervision, but this monitoring does not put an end to fear. In fact, the lives of residents are organized precisely around fear, that is, the fear of being sent to jail.

By studying the ghetto ethnographically, we can see how the forms of power Foucault envisioned operating in a panopticon actually pan out when applied to a neighborhood. People in the modern policed ghetto do not live as tightly controlled and disciplined subjects. Rather, they are living as semilegal or illegal people, coping with the daily threat of capture and confinement. The life of a suspect or a fugitive is quite different from the life of a captive, even though broadly speaking, the same forms of power—observation, examination, the keeping of files—may sustain them both.

Rather than placing the ghetto, along with the rest of society, under a "generalized panopticism" (Garland 1990:146), the 6th Street situation suggests an alternative form of power. In cases where a state (or some other power) is in the business of severely sanctioning a group of people we will see one group of people who are charged with administering the sanction and another group who are receiving it. If the sanction is confinement in a prison, workhouse, or mental asylum, we may see a group of people living as inmates or subjects as described by Foucault's panopticon. But we will also see, outside of these institutions, an apparatus charged with identifying, catching, and judging likely candidates, and a group of people living with the risk of sanction and trying to avoid it, as fugitives.

Instead of thinking of residents of the modern ghetto as inmates of prisons or other panoptic places, we might compare ghetto residents to other semilegal or illegal people who qualify for some sanction and who are trying to avoid it: undocumented immigrants who are at risk of being deported, Jews living in Nazi Germany who may be sent to concentration camps, draft-dodgers or deserters from the army who may be imprisoned or shot, escaped slaves who may be found and sent back to the plantations, or communists in the United States and Europe when the party was illegal. It is with these groups that residents of the modern ghetto may find some common experience. It is this kind of social situation that should be taken into account if we are to fully grasp the effects of policies like mass incarceration.

NOTE

1. Data on the number of police officers in Philadelphia is taken from the Federal Bureau of Investigation, Uniform Crime Reports (1960 through 2000). Population estimates of Philadelphia are taken from the U.S. Bureau of the Census.

2. I use quotes when I wrote down what people said as they spoke (by typing it directly onto a laptop or by using a cell phone text message). I omit the quotes when I noted what people said after an event or conversation, and I paraphrase when I wrote down what people said at the end of the day in my field notes. Since I did not use a tape recorder, even the speech in quotes should be taken only as a close approximation.

REFERENCES

Anderson, Elijah. 1978. *A Place on the Corner.* Chicago, IL: University of Chicago Press.

Comfort, Megan. 2007. "Punishment Beyond the Legal Offender." *Annual Review of Law and Social Science* 3:271–96.

Foucault, Michel. 1979. *Discipline and Punish.* New York: Vintage.

Garland, David. 1990. *Punishment and Modern Society.* Chicago, IL: University of Chicago Press.

——. 2001. "Introduction: The Meaning of Mass Imprisonment." Pp. 1–3 in *Mass Imprisonment: Social Causes and Consequences,* edited by D. Garland. London, UK: Sage.

Goffman, Erving. 1961. *Asylums.* New York: Anchor Books.

Hagan, John and Ronit Dinovitzer. 1999. "Collateral Consequences of Imprisonment for Children, Communities, and Prisoners." *Crime and Justice* 26: 121–62

Hammett, Theodore M., Mary P. Harmon, and William Rhodes. 2002. "The Burden of Infectious Disease among Inmates of and Releasees from U.S. Correctional Facilities, 1997." *American Journal of Public Health* 92(11):1789-94.

Liebow, Elliot. 1967. *Tally's Corner.* Boston, MA: Little, Brown.

Nurse, Anne. 2002. *Fatherhood Arrested.* Nashville, TN: Vanderbilt University Press.

Pager, Devah. 2007. *Marked: Race, Crime, and Finding Work in an Era of Mass Incarceration.* Chicago, IL: University of Chicago Press.

Pettit, Becky and Bruce Western. 2004. "Mass Imprisonment and the Life–Course: Race and Class Inequality in U.S. Incarceration." *American Sociological Review* 69:151–69.

Philadelphia Adult Probation and Parole Department. 2007. *2006 Annual Report.* Retrieved March 2009 (http://fjd.phila.gov/pdf/report/2006appd.pdf).

Rubenstein, Gwen and Debbie Mukamal. 2002. "Welfare and Housing–Denial of Benefits to Drug Offenders." Pp. 37–49 in *Invisible Punishment: The Collateral Consequences of Mass Imprisonment,* edited by M. Mauer and M. Chesney–Lind. New York: New Press.

Stack, Carol. 1974. *All Our Kin.* New York: Harper Colophon Books.

Sykes, Gresham. [1958] 2007. *Society of Captives.* Princeton, NJ: Princeton University Press.

Uggen, Chris and Jeff Manza. 2002. "Democratic Contradiction? Political Consequences of Felon Disenfranchisement in the United States." *American Sociological Review* 67(6):777–803.

Wacquant, Loïc. 2001. "Deadly Symbiosis: When Ghetto and Prison Meet and Mesh." *Punishment & Society* 3(1):95–133.

Western, Bruce. 2006. *Punishment and Inequality in America*. New York: Russell Sage Foundation.

Western, Bruce, Leonard Lopoo, and Sara McLanahan. 2004. "Incarceration and the Bonds between Parents in Fragile Families." Pp. 21–45 in *Imprisoning America*, edited by M. Patillo, D. Weiman, and B. Western. New York: Russell Sage Foundation.

QUESTIONS

1. What, exactly, does Goffman mean when she refers to the "surveillance" of the ghetto?

2. How did Goffman gain access to and observe young black men in Philadelphia?

3. Many of the men whom Goffman observed were "on the run." Explain how even men who are not suspects in a crime may be "on the run."

4. Briefly describe how ghetto surveillance may threaten the freedom of black men in the context of (a) hospitals, (b) the police, and (c) family and friends.

5. What do the experiences of these young black men in Philadelphia theoretically tell us about surveillance in the ghetto more generally and how it differs from prison surveillance?

UNIT II

ETHICS AND POLITICS OF RESEARCH

The studies you read about in this volume illustrate the methodological choices that researchers make as they design and carry out their research. As you will see, researchers choose procedures which, given available resources such as time and money, will yield the most scientifically valid and credible evidence. Indeed, questions about each selection ask you to critique the study largely on this basis. Methodological choices, however, depend on more than purely scientific and practical considerations; they also depend on ethical and political concerns.

Being ethical means acting in morally responsible ways. In this sense, social researchers are expected to report findings honestly and to treat research participants with respect and protect them from harm. For many years, it was left to individual investigators, using their personal standards of morality, to deal with ethical issues arising from their research (Sieber, 1982, p. 4). However, following the revelation of atrocities committed by Nazi scientists, as well as several other studies of questionable ethics in the 1960s and 1970s, the federal government and professional organizations such as the American Sociological Association developed ethical codes for the conduct of social research. Nowadays, investigators are expected to evaluate research plans and procedures in terms of generally accepted ethical principles.

According to these ethical principles, social scientists should:

1. Consider the welfare of participants so that the research maximizes benefits and minimizes possible harm

2. Obtain participants' **informed consent** by giving them the opportunity to make a voluntary and informed decision about whether to take part in the research

3. Respect individuals' right to privacy by gathering information **anonymously** or by taking measures to protect its **confidentiality**

4. Use **deception** as a last resort, but when it is used, sensitively debrief participants to correct any misconceptions about the research

One controversial study that predated the codification of professional ethical principles was Stanley Milgram's (1974) famous "shock" experiments on obedience to authority. Some social scientists criticized the experiments on ethical grounds. In the first selection, Milgram defends his methods against these critics.

Political considerations also invariably enter into the research process. As much as social scientists would like to believe that their research is objective and unbiased, politics—in terms of both personal beliefs and larger structural forces—may influence what researchers choose to study, how they study it, and how they interpret findings. In the wake of the women's movement in the 1970s, for example, many scholars pointed out the impact of sexism on social research. They noted that gender differences often were ignored; studies of one sex, usually males, were presented as if they were applicable to both sexes; and problems were selected and findings interpreted from a male-dominant perspective (Eichler, 1988; Keller, 1982).

Politics is especially likely to affect support for and the use of research findings on controversial topics such as sexual relations and sexual orientation. A case in point is a study on Americans sexual behaviors and attitudes (you will read about the sampling procedure used in this study in Selection 7, "Sex in America"). Carried out in the early 1990s, the study was intended in part to help fight AIDS by providing information about the transmission of the disease, who was most at risk for getting AIDS through sexual contact, and how people could be persuaded to change risky behaviors (Michael, Gagnon, Laumann, & Kolata, 1994, p. 26). Initially, the researchers sought support from the federal government and were awarded a grant from the National Institute of Child Health and Development. When Senator Jesse Helms got wind of it, however, he introduced an amendment to an appropriations bill that prohibited the institute from funding the study. Sex surveys,

> Helms argued, are not really intended "to stop the spread of AIDS. The real purpose is to compile supposedly scientific facts to support the left-wing liberal argument that homosexuality is a normal, acceptable life-style. . . . As long as I am able to stand on the floor of the U.S. Senate," he added, "I am never going to yield to that sort of thing, because it is not just another life-style; it is sodomy." (Fausto-Sterling, 1992, p. 30)

The research was ultimately funded by private philanthropic organizations and conducted (see Selection 7), but not without political turmoil along the way.

An extremely controversial political issue today is homosexual parenting. Many Americans oppose homosexual marriage, and a few U.S. states directly or indirectly prohibit adoption of children by same-sex couples. In the second selection, Judith Stacey and Timothy Biblarz consider how political ideology affects research on homosexual parenting. Their analysis illustrates the interpretive bias of both opponents and supporters of homosexual parenthood.

REFERENCES

Eichler, M. (1988). *Nonsexist research methods: A practical guide.* Boston: Allen and Unwin.

Fausto-Sterling, A. (1992). Why do we know so little about human sex? *Discover, 13*(6), 28–30.

Keller, E. F. (1982). Feminism and science. *Signs, 7,* 589–602.

Michael, R. T., Gagnon, J. H., Laumann, E. O., & Kolata, G. (1994). *Sex in America: A definitive survey.* Boston: Little, Brown.

Milgram, S. (1974). *Obedience to authority: An experimental view.* New York: Harper and Row.

Sieber, J. E. (1982). Ethical dilemmas in social research. In J. E. Sieber (Ed.), *The ethics of social research: Surveys and experiments* (pp. 1–29). New York: Springer-Verlag.

RESOURCES

AAPOR Code of Professional Ethics and practice:

http://www.aapor.org/AAPOR_Code_of_Ethics/4249.htm

- All professional associations for the social sciences have an ethical code of conduct. This code, from the American Association for Public Opinion Research (AAPOR), is particularly useful for those doing surveys.

American Sociological Association Code of Ethics:

http://www.asanet.org/about/ethics.cfm

- This link introduces the ASA Code of Ethics, presents the Preamble and General Principles from the ASA Code, and contains links to the ASA Code and to resources for teaching ethics.

Code of Federal Regulations:

http://www.hhs.gov/ohrp/humansubjects/guidance/45cfr46.html

- The Department of Health and Human Services provides federal regulations for the protection of human subjects, which apply to all research involving human subjects that is supported directly or indirectly by the federal government. All institutions covered by the policy (which includes virtually all U.S. colleges and universities) must establish an Institutional Review Board (IRB) to assure compliance with the policy.

Human Participation Protection Education:

http://phrp.nihtraining.com/users/login.php

- This free online tutorial on the rights and welfare of human participants in research satisfies the NIH human subjects training requirement for obtaining federal funds. Users can print a certificate of completion on completing the course.

Selection 3

Between 1960 and 1963, Stanley Milgram carried out a program of research at Yale University to understand people's willingness to obey orders from an authority, even if it meant harming another human being. When participants arrived at Milgram's laboratory, they met another ostensible participant. Both were told that they would be taking part in an experiment designed to assess the impact of punishment on learning. One of them, the real subject, would play the role of teacher; the other, a confederate of the experimenter, would play the role of the learner. The experimenter represented the authority figure. When the learner (confederate) provided an incorrect answer, the experimenter ordered participants (the teachers) to deliver to learners what participants thought were dangerous and increasingly high levels of electric shock. The teachers did not know that learners were not actually shocked. To the participants, this was a highly stressful conflict situation: Should they obey the experimenter in administering the shocks, or should they refuse to continue the experiment?

The results of the study were alarming; under most conditions, participants obeyed the authority fully, despite signs of the learner's discomfort and pleas to stop. Milgram also reported that many participants showed obvious signs of stress including sweating, trembling, and occasionally nervous laughter. In the following excerpt from the Appendix of his book, Milgram presents an ethical defense of his research program. As he points out, participants were carefully debriefed at the conclusion of the study, and the impact of their participation was thoroughly assessed. As you read his defense, ask yourself: Was his research ethically justified?

PROBLEMS OF ETHICS IN RESEARCH

STANLEY MILGRAM

For some critics, the chief horror of the experiment was not that the subjects obeyed but that the experiment was carried out at all. Among professional psychologists a certain polarization occurred. The experiment was both highly praised and harshly

Source: Appendix I {pp. 193-200} from *Obedience to Authority: An Experimental View* by Stanley Milgram. Copyright © 1974 by Stanley Milgram. Reprinted by permission of HarperCollins Publishers.

criticized. In 1964, Dr. Diana Baumrind (1964) attacked the experiments in the *American Psychologist*, in which I later published this reply:

> In a recent issue of *American Psychologist*, a critic raised a number of questions concerning the obedience report. She expressed concern for the welfare of subjects who served in the experiment, and wondered whether adequate measures were taken to protect the participants.
>
> At the outset, the critic confuses the unanticipated outcome of an experiment with its basic procedure. She writes, for example, as if the production of stress in our subjects was an intended and deliberate effect of the experimental manipulation. There are many laboratory procedures specifically designed to create stress (Lazarus, 1964), but the obedience paradigm was not one of them. The extreme tension induced in some subjects was unexpected. Before conducting the experiment, the procedures were discussed with many colleagues, and none anticipated the reactions that subsequently took place. Foreknowledge of results can never be the invariable accompaniment of an experimental probe. Understanding grows because we examine situations in which the end is unknown. An investigator unwilling to accept this degree of risk must give up the idea of scientific inquiry.
>
> Moreover, there was every reason to expect, prior to actual experimentation, that subjects would refuse to follow the experimenter's instructions beyond the point where the victim protested; many colleagues and psychiatrists were questioned on this point, and they virtually all felt this would be the case. Indeed, to initiate an experiment in which the critical measure hangs on disobedience, one must start with a belief in certain spontaneous resources in [people] that enable them to overcome pressure from authority.
>
> It is true that after a reasonable number of subjects had been exposed to the procedures, it became evident that some would go to the end of the shock board, and some would experience stress. That point, it seems to me, is the first legitimate juncture at which one could even start to wonder whether or not to abandon the study. But momentary excitement is not the same as harm. As the experiment progressed there was no indication of injurious effects in the subjects; and as the subjects themselves strongly endorsed the experiment, the judgment I made was to continue the investigation.
>
> Is not the criticism based as much on the unanticipated findings as on the method? The findings were that some subjects performed in what appeared to be a shockingly immoral way. If, instead, every one of the subjects had broken off at "slight shock," or at the first sign of the learner's discomfort, the results would have been pleasant, and reassuring, and who would protest?
>
> A very important aspect of the procedure occurred at the end of the experimental session. A careful postexperimental treatment was administered to all subjects. The exact content of the dehoax varied from condition to condition and with increasing experience on our part. At the very least, all subjects were told that the victim had not received dangerous electric shocks. Each subject had a friendly reconciliation with the unharmed victim, and an extended discussion with the experimenter. The experiment was explained to the defiant subjects in a way that supported their decision to disobey the experimenter. Obedient subjects were assured of the fact that their behavior was entirely normal and that their feelings of conflict or tension were shared by other participants. Subjects were told that they would receive a comprehensive report at the conclusion of the experimental series. In some instances, additional detailed and lengthy discussions of the experiments were also carried out with individual subjects.
>
> When the experimental series was complete, subjects received a written report which presented details of the experimental procedure and results. Again, their own part in the experiments was treated in a dignified way and their behavior in the experiment respected. All subjects received a follow up questionnaire regarding their participation in the research, which again allowed expression of thoughts and feelings about their behavior.
>
> The replies to the questionnaire confirmed my impression that participants felt positively toward the experiment. In its quantitative aspect (see Table 3.1), 84% of the subjects stated they were glad to have been in the experiment; 15% indicated neutral feelings; and 1.3% indicated negative feelings. To be sure, such findings are to be interpreted cautiously, but they cannot be disregarded.
>
> Further, four-fifths of the subjects felt that more experiments of this sort should be carried out, and 74% indicated that they had learned something of

TABLE 3.1 Excerpt from Questionnaire Used in a Follow-up Study of the Obedience Research

Now that I have read the report, and all things considered . . .	*Defiant*	*Obedient*	*All*
1. I am very glad to have been in the experiment	40.0%	47.8%	43.5%
2. I am glad to have been in the experiment	43.8%	35.7%	40.2%
3. I am neither sorry nor glad to have been in the experiment	15.3%	14.8%	15.1%
4. I am sorry to have been in the experiment	0.8%	0.7%	0.8%
5. I am very sorry to have been in the experiment	0.0%	1.0%	0.5%

Note: Ninety-two percent of the subjects returned the questionnaire. The characteristics of the nonrespondents were checked against the respondents. They differed from the respondents only with regard to age; younger people were overrepresented in the nonresponding group.

personal importance as a result of being in the study.

The debriefing and assessment procedures were carried out as a matter of course, and were not stimulated by any observation of special risk in the experimental procedure. In my judgment, at no point were subjects exposed to danger and at no point did they run the risk of injurious effects resulting from participation. If it had been otherwise, the experiment would have been terminated at once.

The critic states that, after he has performed in the experiment, the subject cannot justify his behavior and must bear the full brunt of his actions. By and large it does not work this way. The same mechanisms that allow the subject to perform the act, to obey rather than to defy the experimenter, transcend the moment of performance and continue to justify his behavior for him. The same viewpoint the subject takes while performing the actions is the viewpoint from which he later sees his behavior, that is, the perspective of "carrying out the task assigned by the person in authority."

Because the idea of shocking the victim is repugnant, there is a tendency among those who hear of the design to say "people will not do it." When the results are made known, this attitude is expressed as "if they do it they will not be able to live with themselves afterward." These two forms of denying the experimental findings are equally inappropriate misreadings of the facts of human social behavior. Many subjects do, indeed, obey to the end, and there is no indication of injurious effects.

The absence of injury is a minimal condition of experimentation; there can be, however, an important positive side to participation. The critic suggests that subjects derived no benefit from being in the obedience study, but this is false. By their statements and actions, subjects indicated that they had learned a good deal, and many felt gratified to have taken part in scientific research they considered to be of significance. A year after his participation one subject wrote: "This experiment has strengthened my belief that man should avoid harm to his fellow man even at the risk of violating authority."

Another stated: "To me, the experiment pointed up . . . the extent to which each individual should have or discover firm ground on which to base his decisions, no matter how trivial they appear to be. I think people should think more deeply about themselves and their relation to their world and to other people. If this experiment serves to jar people out of complacency, it will have served its end."

These statements are illustrative of a broad array of appreciative and insightful comments by those who participated.

The 5-page report sent to each subject on the completion of the experimental series was specifically designed to enhance the value of his experience. It laid out the broad conception of the experimental program as well as the logic of its design. It described the results of a dozen of the experiments, discussed the causes of tension, and attempted to indicate the possible significance of the experiment. Subjects responded enthusiastically; many indicated a desire to be in further experimental research. This report was sent to all subjects several years ago. The care with which it was prepared does not support the critic's assertion that the experimenter was indifferent to the value subjects derived from their participation.

The critic fears that participants will be alienated from psychological experiments because of the intensity of experience associated with laboratory procedures. My own observation is that subjects more commonly respond with distaste to the "empty" laboratory hour, in which cardboard procedures are employed, and the only possible feeling upon emerging from the laboratory is that one has wasted time in a patently trivial and useless exercise.

The subjects in the obedience experiment, on the whole, felt quite differently about their participation. They viewed the experience as an opportunity to learn something of importance about themselves, and more generally, about the conditions of human action.

A year after the experimental program was completed, I initiated an additional follow-up study. In this connection an impartial medical examiner, experienced in outpatient treatment, interviewed 40 experimental subjects. The examining psychiatrist focused on those subjects he felt would be most likely to have suffered consequences from participation. His aim was to identify possible injurious effects resulting from the experiment. He concluded that, although extreme stress had been experienced by several subjects, "none was found by this interviewer to show signs of having been harmed by his experience. . . . Each subject seemed to handle his task (in the experiment) in a manner consistent with well-established patterns of behavior. No evidence was found of any traumatic reactions." Such evidence ought to be weighed before judging the experiment.

A concern with human dignity is based on a respect for [a person's] potential to act morally. The critic feels that the experimenter *made* the subject shock the victim. This conception is alien

to my view. The experimenter tells the subject to do something. But between the command and the outcome there is a paramount force, the acting person who may obey or disobey. I started with the belief that every person who came to the laboratory was free to accept or to reject the dictates of authority. This view sustains a conception of human dignity insofar as it sees in each man a capacity for choosing his own behavior. And as it turned out, many subjects did, indeed, choose to reject the experimenter's commands, providing a powerful affirmation of human ideals.

The experiment is also criticized on the grounds that "it could easily effect an alteration in the subject's . . . ability to trust adult authorities in the future.". . . However, the experimenter is not just any authority: He is an authority who tells the subject to act harshly and inhumanely against another man. I would consider it of the highest value if participation in the experiment could, indeed, inculcate a skepticism of this kind of authority. Here, perhaps, a difference in philosophy emerges most clearly. The critic views the subject as a passive creature, completely controlled by the experimenter. I started from a different viewpoint. A person who comes to the laboratory is an active, choosing adult, capable of accepting or rejecting the prescriptions for action addressed to him. The critic sees the effect of the experiment as undermining the subject's trust of authority. I see it as a potentially valuable experience insofar as it makes people aware of the problem of indiscriminate submission to authority.

Yet another criticism occurred in Dannie Abse's play, *The Dogs of Pavlov,* which appeared in London in 1971 and which uses the obedience experiment as its central dramatic theme. At the play's climax, Kurt, a major character in the play, repudiates the experimenter for treating him as a guinea pig. In his introduction to the play, Abse especially condemns the illusions employed in the experiment, terming the setup "bullshit," "fraudulent," "cheat." He allowed my rejoinder to appear in the foreword to his book. I wrote to him:

Misinformation is employed in the experiment; illusion is used when necessary in order to set the stage for the revelation of certain difficult-to-get-at truths; and these procedures are justified for one reason only: they are, in the end, accepted and endorsed by those who are exposed to them. . . .

When the experiment was explained to subjects they responded to it positively, and most felt it was an hour well spent. If it had been otherwise, if subjects ended the hour with bitter recriminatory feelings, the experiment could not have proceeded.

This judgment is based, first, on the numerous conversations I have had with subjects immediately after their participation in the experiment. Such conversations can reveal a good deal, but what they showed most was how readily the experience is assimilated to the normal frame of things. Moreover, subjects were friendly rather than hostile, curious rather than denunciatory, and in no sense demeaned by the experience. This was my general impression, and it was later supported by formal procedures undertaken to assess the subjects' reaction to the experiment.

The central moral justification for allowing a procedure of the sort used in my experiment is that it is judged acceptable by those who have taken part in it. Moreover, it was the salience of this fact throughout that constituted the chief moral warrant for the continuation of the experiments.

This fact is crucial to any appraisal of the experiment from an ethical standpoint.

One further point: the obedient subject does not blame himself for shocking the victim, because the act does not originate in the self. It originates in authority, and the worst the obedient subject says of himself is that he must learn to resist authority more effectively in the future.

That the experiment has stimulated this thought in some subjects is, to my mind, a satisfying . . . consequence of the inquiry. An illustrative case is provided by the experience of a young man who took part in a Princeton replication of the obedience experiment, conducted in 1964. He was fully obedient. On October 27, 1970, he wrote to me:

"Participation in the 'shock experiment' . . . has had a great impact on my life. . . ."

"When I was a subject in 1964, though I believed that I was hurting someone, I was totally unaware of why I was doing so. Few people ever realize when they are acting according to their own beliefs and when they are meekly submitting to authority. . . .To permit myself to be drafted with the understanding that I am submitting to authority's demand to do something very wrong would make me frightened of myself. . . . I am fully prepared to go to jail if I am not granted Conscientious Objector status. Indeed, it is the only course I could take to be faithful to what I believe. My only hope is that members of my board act equally according to their conscience. . . ."

He inquired whether any other participants had reacted similarly, and whether, in my opinion, participation in the study could have this effect.

I replied:

"The experiment does, of course, deal with the dilemma individuals face when they are confronted with conflicting demands of authority and conscience, and I am glad that your participation in the study has brought you to a deeper personal consideration of these issues. Several participants have informed me that their own sensitivity to the problem of submission to authority was increased as a result of their experience in the study. If the experiment has heightened your awareness of the problem of indiscriminate submission to authority, it will have performed an important function. If you believe strongly that it is wrong to kill others in the service of your country, then you ought certainly to press vigorously for CO status, and I am deeply hopeful that your sincerity in this matter will be recognized."

A few months later he wrote again. He indicated, first, that the draft board was not very impressed with the effect of his participation in the experiment, but he was granted CO status nonetheless. He writes:

"The experience of the interview doesn't lessen my strong belief of the great impact of the experiment on my life. . . ."

". . . You have discovered one of the most important causes of all the trouble in this world. . . . I am grateful to have been able to provide you with a part of the information necessary for that discovery. I am delighted to have acted, by refusing to serve in the Armed Forces, in a manner which people must act if these problems are to be solved.

"With sincere thanks for your contribution to my life. . . ."

REFERENCES

Baumrind, D. 1964. Some thoughts on the ethics of research: After reading Milgram's "Behavioral study of obedience." *American Psychologist*, 19, 421–423.

Lazarus, R. 1964. A laboratory approach to the dynamics of psychological stress. *American Psychologist*, 19, 400–411.

QUESTIONS

1. What measures did Milgram take to protect the welfare of his subjects and to ascertain that they had not been harmed by their participation?

2. A guiding ethical principle of current scientific research is that "risks to subjects are reasonable in relation to anticipated benefits." Briefly describe Milgram's assessment of the risks and benefits of participating in the obedience experiment.

3. How did Milgram respond to the following criticisms? (a) Obedient subjects will be harmed psychologically because they will not be able to justify their repugnant actions to themselves. (b) Participation in the experiment will undermine future trust in authority.

4. What was Milgram's ultimate ethical justification for carrying out his research?

5. What do you think is Milgram's weakest defense of his study? What else, if anything, should he have done to protect participants' rights and welfare? (Consider the four principles outlined in the introduction to this unit.)

Selection 4

Polls indicate a sharp divide in American society on attitudes toward homosexual relations and rights. In 2011, 39% of the American public believed that gay or lesbian relations are "morally wrong" and 48% opposed the legal recognition of same-sex marriages (http://www.gallup.com/poll/1651/Gay-Lesbian-Rights.aspx#2). A particularly contentious issue concerns parenting; in 2009, 54% of Americans thought that homosexual couples should have the legal right to adopt a child and 44% thought that they should not (http://www.gallup.com/poll/1651/Gay-Lesbian-Rights.aspx#2). Such opinions matter in the courts and in social research. Even though few states prohibit adoption by gay or lesbian parents, decisions to grant adoption often depend on beliefs about homosexuals and the value of traditional heterosexual marriage. In this selection, Judith Stacey and Timothy Biblarz show how the interpretation of research findings is affected by attitudes on both sides of the parenting issue. Much of the article evaluates the claim of most studies that "there are no differences in developmental outcomes between children raised by lesbigay parents and those raised by heterosexual parents" (Stacey & Biblarz, 2001, p. 159).

(How) Does the Sexual Orientation of Parents Matter?

Judith Stacey

Timothy J. Biblarz

As the new millennium begins, struggles by nonheterosexuals to secure equal recognition and rights for the new family relationships they are now creating represent some of the most dramatic and fiercely contested developments in Western family patterns.

It is not surprising, therefore, that social science research on lesbigay family issues has

Source: "(How) Does the Sexual Orientation of Parents Matter?" by Judith Stacey and Timothy J. Biblarz, *American Sociological Review,* Vol. 6. No.2 (Apr/2001), pp. 159-183.

become a rapid growth industry that incites passionate divisions. For the consequences of such research are by no means "academic," but bear on marriage and family policies that encode Western culture's most profoundly held convictions about gender, sexuality, and parenthood. As advocates and opponents square off in state and federal courts and legislatures, in the electoral arena, and in culture wars over efforts to extend to nonheterosexuals equal rights to marriage, child custody, adoption, foster care, and fertility services, they heatedly debate the implications of a youthful body of research, conducted primarily by psychologists, that investigates if and how the sexual orientation of parents affects children.

This body of research, almost uniformly, reports findings of no notable differences between children reared by heterosexual parents and those reared by lesbian and gay parents, and it finds lesbigay parents to be as competent and effective as heterosexual parents. Lawyers and activists struggling to defend child custody and adoption petitions by lesbians and gay men, or to attain same-gender marriage rights and to defeat preemptive referenda against such rights have drawn on this research with considerable success (cf. Wald 2000). Although progress is uneven, this strategy has promoted a gradual liberalizing trend in judicial and policy decisions. However, backlash campaigns against gay family rights have begun to challenge the validity of the research.

In 1997, the *University of Illinois Law Review Journal* published an article by Wardle (1997), a Brigham Young University law professor, that impugned the motives, methods, and merits of social science research on lesbian and gay parenting. Wardle charged the legal profession and social scientists with an ideological bias favoring gay rights that has compromised most research in this field and the liberal judicial and policy decisions it has informed. He presented a harshly critical assessment of the research and argued for a presumptive judicial standard in favor of awarding child custody to heterosexual married couples. The following year, Wardle

drafted new state regulations in Utah that restrict adoption and foster care placements to households in which all adults are related by blood or marriage. In March 2000, a paper presented at a "Revitalizing Marriage" conference at Brigham Young University assailed the quality of studies that had been cited to support the efficacy of lesbigay parenting (Lerner and Nagai 2000). Characterizing the research methods as "dismal," Lerner and Nagai claimed that "the methods used in these studies were sufficiently flawed so that these studies could not and should not be used in legislative forums or legal cases to buttress any arguments on the nature of homosexual vs. heterosexual parenting" (p. 3).

We depart sharply from the views of Wardle on the merits and morals of lesbigay parenthood as well as on analysis of the child development research. We agree, however, that ideological pressures constrain intellectual development in this field. In our view, it is the pervasiveness of social prejudice and institutionalized discrimination against lesbians and gay men that exerts a powerful policing effect on the basic terms of psychological research and public discourse on the significance of parental sexual orientation. The field suffers less from the overt ideological convictions of scholars than from the unfortunate intellectual consequences that follow from the implicit hetero-normative presumption governing the terms of the discourse—that healthy child development depends upon parenting by a married heterosexual couple. While few contributors to this literature personally subscribe to this view, most of the research asks whether lesbigay parents subject their children to greater risks or harm than are confronted by children reared by heterosexual parents. Because anti-gay scholars seek evidence of harm, sympathetic researchers defensively stress its absence.

We take stock of this body of psychological research from a sociological perspective. We analyze the impact that this hetero-normative presumption exacts on predominant research strategies, analyses, and representations of findings.

The inescapably ideological and emotional nature of this subject makes it incumbent on scholars to acknowledge the personal convictions they bring to the discussion. Because we personally oppose discrimination on the basis of sexual orientation or gender, we subject research claims by those sympathetic to our stance to a heightened degree of critical scrutiny and afford the fullest possible consideration to work by scholars opposed to parenting by lesbians and gay men.

THE CASE AGAINST LESBIAN AND GAY PARENTHOOD

A few psychologists subscribe to the view that homosexuality represents either a sin or a mental illness and continue to publish alarmist works on the putative ill effects of gay parenting (e.g., Cameron and Cameron 1996; Cameron, Cameron, and Landess 1996). Even though the American Psychological Association expelled Paul Cameron, and the American Sociological Association denounced him for willfully misrepresenting research (Cantor 1994; Herek 1998, 2000), his publications continue to be cited in amicus briefs, court decisions, and policy hearings. For example, the chair of the Arkansas Child Welfare Agency Review Board repeatedly cited publications by Cameron's group in her testimony at policy hearings, which, incidentally, led to restricting foster child placements to heterosexual parents (Woodruff 1998).

Likewise, Wardle (1997) draws explicitly on Cameron's work to build his case against gay parent rights. Research demonstrates, Wardle maintains, that gay parents subject children to disproportionate risks; that children of gay parents are more apt to suffer confusion over their gender and sexual identities and are more likely to become homosexuals themselves; suffer greater risks of depression and other emotional difficulties; and that the social stigma and embarrassment of having a homosexual parent unfairly ostracizes children and hinders their relationships with peers. Judges have cited Wardle's article to justify transferring child custody from lesbian to heterosexual parents.

Wardle extrapolates (inappropriately) from research on single-mother families to portray children of lesbians as more vulnerable to everything from delinquency, substance abuse, violence, and crime, to teen pregnancy, school dropout, suicide, and even poverty. In short, the few scholars who are opposed to parenting by lesbians and gay men provide academic support for the convictions of many judges, journalists, politicians, and citizens that the sexual orientation of parents matters greatly to children, and that lesbigay parents represent a danger to their children and to society. Generally, these scholars offer only limited, and often implicit, theoretical explanations for the disadvantages of same-sex parenting—typically combining elements of bio-evolutionary theory with social and cognitive learning theories (e.g., Blankenhorn 1995). Cameron et al. (1996) crudely propose that homosexuality is a "learned pathology" that parents pass on to children through processes of modeling, seduction, and "contagion." The deeply rooted hetero-normative convictions about what constitutes healthy and moral gender identity, sexual orientation, and family composition held by contributors to this literature hinders their ability to conduct or interpret research with reason, nuance, or care.

THE CASE FOR LESBIAN AND GAY PARENTHOOD

Perhaps the most consequential impact that heterosexism exerts on the research on lesbigay parenting lies where it is least apparent—in the far more responsible literature that is largely sympathetic to its subject. It is easy to expose the ways in which the prejudicial views of those directly hostile to lesbigay parenting distort their research (Herek 1998). Moreover, because anti-gay scholars regard homosexuality itself as a form of pathology, they tautologically interpret any evidence that children may be more likely to engage in homoerotic behavior as evidence of harm. Less obvious, however, are the ways in which heterosexism also hampers research and analysis among those who explicitly support lesbigay parenthood. With rare exceptions, even the most sympathetic proceed from a highly defensive posture that accepts heterosexual parenting as the gold standard and investigates whether lesbigay parents and their children are inferior.

This sort of hierarchical model implies that *differences* indicate *deficits* (Baumrind 1995). Instead of investigating whether (and how) differences in adult sexual orientation might lead to meaningful differences in how individuals parent and how their children develop, the predominant research designs place the burden of proof on lesbigay parents to demonstrate that they are not less successful or less worthy than heterosexual parents. Too often scholars seem to presume that this approach precludes acknowledging almost any differences in parenting or in child outcomes. A characteristic review of research on lesbian-mother families concludes:

> [A] rapidly growing and highly consistent body of empirical work has failed to identify significant differences between lesbian mothers and their heterosexual counterparts or the children raised by these groups. Researchers have been unable to establish empirically that detriment results to children from being raised by lesbian mothers. (Falk 1994:151)

Given the weighty political implications of this body of research, it is easy to understand the social sources of such a defensive stance. As long as sexual orientation can deprive a gay parent of child custody, fertility services, and adoption rights, sensitive scholars are apt to tread gingerly around the terrain of differences. Unfortunately, however, this reticence compromises the development of knowledge not only in child development and psychology, but also within the sociology of sexuality, gender, and family more broadly. For if homophobic theories seem crude, too many psychologists who are sympathetic to lesbigay parenting seem hesitant to theorize at all.

This reticence is most evident in analyses of sexual behavior and identity—the most politically

sensitive issue in the debate. Virtually all of the published research claims to find no differences in the sexuality of children reared by lesbigay parents and those raised by nongay parents—but none of the studies that report this finding attempts to theorize about such an implausible outcome. Yet it is difficult to conceive of a credible theory of sexual development that would not expect the adult children of lesbigay parents to display a somewhat higher incidence of homoerotic desire, behavior, and identity than children of heterosexual parents. For example, biological determinist theory should predict at least some difference in an inherited predisposition to same-sex desire; a social constructionist theory would expect lesbigay parents to provide an environment in which children would feel freer to explore and affirm such desires.

In fact, the only "theory" of child development we can imagine in which a child's sexual development would bear no relationship to parental genes, practices, environment, or beliefs would be an arbitrary one. Yet this is precisely the outcome that most scholars report, although the limited empirical record does not justify it.

Rethinking the "no differences" doctrine, some scholars urge social scientists to look for potentially beneficial effects children might derive from such distinctive aspects of lesbigay parenting as the more egalitarian relationships these parents appear to practice (Patterson 1995; also see Dunne 2000). While we welcome research attuned to potential strengths as well as vulnerabilities of lesbigay parenting, we believe that knowledge and policy will be best served when scholars feel free to replace a hierarchical model, which assigns "grades" to parents and children according to their sexual identities, with a more genuinely pluralist approach to family diversity.

RECONSIDERING THE PSYCHOLOGICAL FINDINGS

We examined the findings of 21 psychological studies (listed at the bottom of Table 4.1) published between 1981 and 1998 that we considered best equipped to address sociological questions about how parental sexual orientation matters to children. One meta-analysis of 18 such studies (11 of which are included among our 21) characteristically concludes that "the results demonstrate no differences on any measures between the heterosexual and homosexual parents regarding parenting styles, emotional adjustment, and sexual orientation of the child(ren)" (Allen and Burrell 1996:19). To evaluate this claim, we selected for examination only studies that: (1) include a sample of gay or lesbian parents and children and a comparison group of heterosexual parents and children; (2) assess differences between groups in terms of statistical significance; and (3) include findings directly relevant to children's development. The studies we discuss compare relatively advantaged lesbian parents (18 studies) and gay male parents (3 studies) with a roughly matched sample of heterosexual parents. Echoing the conclusion of meta-analysts Allen and Burrell (1996), the authors of all 21 studies almost uniformly claim to find no differences in measures of parenting or child outcomes. In contrast, our careful scrutiny of the findings they report suggests that on some dimensions—particularly those related to gender and sexuality—the sexual orientations of these parents matter somewhat more for their children than the researchers claimed.

The empirical findings from these studies are presented in Table 4.1. Table 4.1 summarizes findings on the relationship between parental sexual orientation and three sets of child "outcome" variables: (1) gender behavior/gender preferences, (2) sexual behavior/sexual preferences, and (3) psychological well-being. Positive signs (+) indicate a statistically significant higher level of the variable for lesbigay parents or their children, while negative signs (-) indicate a higher level for heterosexual parents or their children. Zero (0) indicates no significant difference.

Children's Gender Preferences and Behavior

The first panel of Table 4.1 displays findings about the relationship between the sexual orientation of parents and the gender preferences and behaviors of their children. The findings demonstrate that, as we would expect, on some measures meaningful differences have been observed in predictable directions. For example, lesbian mothers in R. Green et al. (1986) reported that their children, especially daughters, more frequently dress, play, and behave in ways that do not conform to sex-typed cultural norms. Likewise, daughters of lesbian mothers reported greater interest in activities associated with both "masculine" and "feminine" qualities and that involve the participation of both sexes, whereas daughters of heterosexual mothers report significantly greater interest in traditionally feminine, same-sex activities (also see Hotvedt and Mandel 1982). Similarly, daughters with lesbian mothers reported higher aspirations to nontraditional-gender occupations (Steckel 1987). For example, in R. Green et al. (1986), 53 percent (16 out of 30) of the daughters of lesbians aspired to careers such as doctor, lawyer, engineer, and astronaut, compared with only 21 percent (6 of 28) of the daughters of heterosexual mothers.

Sons appear to respond in more complex ways to parental sexual orientations. On some measures, like aggressiveness and play preferences, the sons of lesbian mothers behave in less traditionally masculine ways than those raised by heterosexual single mothers. However, on other measures, such as occupational goals and sartorial styles, they also exhibit greater gender conformity than do daughters with lesbian mothers (but they are not more conforming than sons with heterosexual mothers) (R. Green et al. 1986; Steckel 1987). Such evidence, albeit limited, implies that lesbian parenting may free daughters and sons from a broad but uneven range of traditional gender prescriptions. It also suggests that the sexual orientation of mothers interacts with the gender of children in complex ways to influence gender preferences and behavior. Such findings raise provocative questions about how children assimilate gender culture and interests—questions that the propensity to downplay differences deters scholars from exploring.

TABLE 4.1   Findings on the Associations between Parents' Sexual Orientations and Selected Child Outcomes: 21 Studies, 1981 to 1998

Variable Measured	Direction of Effect
Gender Behavior/Preferences:	
Girls' departure from traditional gender role expectations and behaviors—in dress, play, physicality, school activities, occupational aspirations (Hoeffer 1981; Golombok et al.. 1983; R. Green et al. 1986; Steckel 1987; Hotvedt and Mandel 1982).	0/+
Boys' departure from traditional gender role expectations and behaviors—in dress, play, physicality, school activities, occupational aspirations (Hoeffer 1981; Golombok et al. 1983; R. Green et al. 1986; Steckel 1987; Hotvedt and Mandel 1982).	0/+
Boys' level of aggressiveness and domineering disposition (Steckel 1987).	-
Child wishes she/he were the other sex (Green et al. 1986).	0
Sexual Behavior/Sexual Preferences	
Young adult child has considered same-sex sexual relationship(s); has had same-sex sexual relationship(s) (Tasker and Golombok 1997).	+
Young adult child firmly self-identifies as bisexual, gay, or lesbian (Tasker and Golombok 1997).	0
Boys' likelihood of having a gay sexual orientation in adulthood, by sexual orientation of father (Bailey et al. 1995).	(+)
Girls' number of sexual partners from puberty to young adulthood (Tasker and Golombok 1997).	+
Boys' number of sexual partners from puberty to young adulthood (Tasker and Golombok 1997).	(-)
Quality of intimate relationships in young adulthood (Tasker and Golombok 1997).	0
Have friend(s) who are gay or lesbian (Tasker and Golombok 1997).	+
Self-Esteem and Psychological Well-Being	
Children's self-esteem, anxiety, depression, internalizing behavioral problems, externalizing behavioral problems, total behavioral problems, performance in social arenas (sports, friendships, school), use of psychological counseling, mothers' and teachers' reports of children's hyperactivity, unsociability, emotional difficulty, conduct difficulty, other behavioral problems (Golombok, Spencer, and Rutter 1983; Huggins 1989; Patterson 1994; Flaks et al. 1995; Tasker and Golombok 1997; Chan, Raboy, and Patterson 1998; Chan, Brooks, et al. 1998).	0
Daughters' self-reported level of popularity at school and in the neighborhood (Hotvedt and Mandel 1982).	+

Mothers' and teachers' reports of child's level of affection, responsiveness, and concern for younger children (Steckel 1987).	+
Experience of peer stigma concerning own sexuality (Tasker and Golombok 1997).	+
Cognitive functioning (IQ, verbal, performance, and so on) (Flaks et al. 1995; R. Green et al. 1986).	0
Experienced problems gaining employment in young adulthood (Tasker and Golombok 1997).	0

Sources: The 21 studies considered in Table 4.1 are, in date order: Hoeffer (1981); Kweskin and Cook (1982); Miller, Jacobsen, and Bigner (1982); Rand, Graham, and Rawlings (1982); Golombok, Spencer, and Rutter (1983); R. Green et al. (1986); M. Harris and Turner (1986); Bigner and Jacobsen (1989); Hotvedt and Mandel (1982); Huggins (1989); Steckel (1987); Bigner and Jacobsen (1992); Jenny, Roesler, and Poyer (1994); Patterson (1994); Bailey et al. (1995); Flaks et al. (1995); Brewaeys et al. (1997); Tasker and Golombok (1997); Chan, Raboy, and Patterson (1998); Chan, Brooks, et al. (1998); and McNeill, Rienzi, and Kposowa (1998).

+ = significantly higher in lesbigay than in heterosexual parent context.

0 = no significant difference between lesbigay and heterosexual parent context.

− = significantly lower in lesbigay than heterosexual parent context.

( ) = borders on statistical significance.

0/+ = evidence is mixed.

Consider, for example, the study by R. Green et al. (1986) that, by our count, finds at least 15 intriguing, statistically significant differences in gender behavior and preferences among children (4 among boys and 11 among girls) in lesbian and heterosexual single-mother homes. Yet the study's abstract summarizes: "Two types of single-parent households [lesbian and heterosexual mothers] and their effects on children ages 3–11 years were compared. . . . No significant differences were found between the two types of households for boys and few significant differences for girls" (p. 167).

Children's Sexual Preferences and Behavior

The second panel of Table 4.1 shifts the focus from children's gender behavior and preferences to their sexual behavior and preferences, with particular attention to thought-provoking findings from the Tasker and Golombok (1997)

study, the only comparative study we know of that follows children raised in lesbian-headed families into young adulthood and hence that can explore the children's sexuality in meaningful ways. A significantly greater proportion of young adult children raised by lesbian mothers than those raised by heterosexual mothers in the Tasker and Golombok sample reported having had a homoerotic relationship (6 of the 25 young adults raised by lesbian mothers—24 percent—compared with 0 of the 20 raised by heterosexual mothers). The young adults reared by lesbian mothers were also significantly more likely to report having thought they might experience homoerotic attraction or relationships. The difference in their openness to this possibility is striking: 64 percent (14 of 22) of the young adults raised by lesbian mothers report having considered same-sex relationships (in the past, now, or in the future), compared with only 17 percent (3 of 18) of those raised by heterosexual mothers. Of course, the fact that 17 percent of those raised by heterosexual mothers also report some openness to same-sex relationships, while 36 percent of those raised by lesbians do not, underscores the important reality that parental influence on children's sexual desires is neither direct nor easily predictable.

If these young adults raised by lesbian mothers were more open to a broad range of sexual possibilities, they were not statistically more likely to self-identify as bisexual, lesbian, or gay. To be coded as such, the respondent not only had to currently self-identify as bisexual/lesbian/gay, but also to express a commitment to that identity in the future. Tasker and Golombok (1997) employ a measure of sexual identity with no "in-between" categories for those whose identity may not yet be fully fixed or embraced. Thus, although a more nuanced measure or a longer period of observation could yield different results, Golombok and Tasker (1996) choose to situate their findings within the "overall no difference" interpretation:

> The commonly held assumption that children brought up by lesbian mothers will themselves grow up to be lesbian or gay is not supported by the findings of the study: the majority of children who grew up in lesbian families identified as heterosexual in adulthood, and there was no statistically significant difference between young adults from lesbian and heterosexual family backgrounds with respect to sexual orientation. (p. 8)

This reading, while technically accurate, deflects analytic attention from the rather sizable differences in sexual attitudes and behaviors that the study actually reports.

Children's Mental Health

Given historic social prejudices against homosexuality, the major issue deliberated by judges and policymakers has been whether children of lesbian and gay parents suffer higher levels of emotional and psychological harm. Unsurprisingly, therefore, children's "self-esteem and psychological well-being" is a heavily researched domain. The third panel of Table 4.1 shows that these studies find no significant differences between children of lesbian mothers and children of heterosexual mothers in anxiety, depression, self-esteem, and numerous other measures of social and psychological adjustment. The roughly equivalent level of psychological well-being between the two groups holds true in studies that test children directly, rely on parents' reports, and solicit evaluations from teachers. The few significant differences found actually tend to favor children with lesbian mothers (see Table 4.1). Given some credible evidence that children with gay and lesbian parents, especially adolescent children, face homophobic teasing and ridicule that many find difficult to manage (Tasker and Golombok 1997; also see Bozett 1989:148; Mitchell 1998), the children in these studies seem to exhibit impressive psychological strength.

Similarly, across studies, no relationship has been found between parental sexual orientation and measures of children's cognitive ability. Moreover, to our knowledge no theories predict such a link. Thus far, no work has compared children's *long-term* achievements in education, occupation, income, and other domains of life.

No Differences of Social Concern

The findings summarized in Table 4.1 show that the "no differences" claim does receive strong empirical support in crucial domains. Children [of lesbigay parents] display no differences from heterosexual counterparts in psychological well-being or cognitive functioning. Because every relevant study to date shows that parental sexual orientation per se has no measurable effect on the quality of parent-child relationships or on children's mental health or social adjustment, there is no evidentiary basis for considering parental sexual orientation in decisions about children's "best interest." In fact, given that children with lesbigay parents probably contend with a degree of social stigma, these similarities in child outcomes suggest the presence of compensatory processes in lesbigay-parent families. Exploring how these families help children cope with stigma might prove helpful to all kinds of families.

HOW THE SEXUAL ORIENTATION OF PARENTS MATTERS

We have identified psychological research on the effects of parental sexual orientation and have challenged the predominant claim that the sexual orientation of parents does not matter at all. We argued instead that despite the limitations, there is suggestive evidence and good reason to believe that contemporary children and young adults with lesbian or gay parents do differ in modest and interesting ways from children with heterosexual parents. Most of these differences, however, are not causal, but are indirect effects of parental gender or selection effects associated with heterosexist social conditions under which lesbigay-parent families currently live.

First, our analysis of the psychological research indicates that the effects of parental gender trump those of sexual orientation (Brewaeys et al. 1997; Chan, Brooks, et al. 1998; Chan, Raboy, and Patterson 1998; Flaks et al. 1995). A diverse array of gender theories (social learning theory, psychoanalytic theory, materialist, symbolic interactionist) would predict that children with two same-gender parents, and particularly with co-mother parents, should develop in less gender-stereotypical ways than would children with two heterosexual parents. There is reason to credit the perception of lesbian co-mothers in a qualitative study (Dunne, 2000) that they "were redefining the meaning and content of motherhood, extending its boundaries to incorporate the activities that are usually dichotomized as mother and father" (p. 25). Children who derive their principal source of love, discipline, protection, and identification from women living independent of male domestic authority or influence should develop less stereotypical symbolic, emotional, practical, and behavioral gender repertoires. Indeed, it is the claim that the gender mix of

parents has no effect on their children's gender behavior, interests, or development that cries out for sociological explanation.

Second, because homosexuality is stigmatized, selection effects may yield correlations between parental sexual orientation and child development that do not derive from sexual orientation itself. For example, social constraints on access to marriage and parenting make lesbian parents likely to be older, urban, educated, and self-aware—factors that foster several positive developmental consequences for their children. On the other hand, denied access to marriage, lesbian co-parent relationships are likely to experience dissolution rates somewhat higher than those among heterosexual co-parents (Bell and Weinberg 1978; Weeks, Heaphy, and Donovan 2001, chap. 5). Not only do same-sex couples lack the institutional pressures and support for commitment that marriage provides, but qualitative studies suggest that they tend to embrace comparatively high standards of emotional intimacy and satisfaction (Dunne 2000; Sullivan 1996; Weeks et al. 2001). Thus, a higher dissolution rate would be correlated with but not causally related to sexual orientation, a difference that should erode were homophobia to disappear and legal marriage be made available to lesbians and gay men.

Most of the differences in the findings discussed above cannot be considered deficits from any legitimate public policy perspective. They either favor the children with lesbigay parents, are secondary effects of social prejudice, or represent "just a difference" of the sort democratic societies should respect and protect. Apart from differences associated with parental gender, most of the presently observable differences in child "outcomes" should wither away under conditions of full equality and respect for sexual diversity. Indeed, it is time to recognize that the categories "lesbian mother" and "gay father" are historically transitional and conceptually flawed, because they erroneously imply that a parent's sexual orientation is the decisive characteristic of her or his parenting. On the contrary, we propose that homophobia and discrimination are the chief reasons why parental sexual orientation matters at all. Because lesbigay parents do not enjoy the same rights, respect, and recognition as heterosexual parents, their children contend with the burdens of vicarious social stigma. Likewise, some of the particular strengths and sensitivities such children appear to display, such as a greater capacity to express feelings or more empathy for social diversity (Mitchell 1998; O'Connell 1994), are probably artifacts of marginality and may be destined for the historical dustbin of a democratic, sexually pluralist society.

Even in a utopian society, however, one difference seems less likely to disappear: The sexual orientation of parents appears to have a unique (although not large) effect on children in the politically sensitive domain of sexuality. The evidence, while scanty and underanalyzed, hints that parental sexual orientation is positively associated with the possibility that children will be more likely to attain a similar orientation—and theory and common sense also support such a view. Children raised by lesbian co-parents should and do seem to grow up more open to homoerotic relationships. This may be partly due to genetic and family socialization processes, but what sociologists refer to as "contextual effects" not yet investigated by psychologists may also be important. Because lesbigay parents are disproportionately more likely to inhabit diverse, cosmopolitan cities—Los Angeles, New York and San Francisco—and progressive university communities—such as Santa Cruz, Santa Rosa, Madison, and Ann Arbor (Black, Gates, et al. 2000)—their children grow up in comparatively tolerant schools, neighborhoods, and social contexts, which foster less hostility to homoeroticism.

We recognize the political dangers of pointing out that recent studies indicate that a higher proportion of children with lesbigay parents are themselves apt to engage in homosexual activity. In a homophobic world, anti-gay forces deploy such results to deny parents custody of their own children and to fuel backlash movements opposed to gay rights. Nonetheless, we believe that denying this probability capitulates to

heterosexist ideology and is apt to prove counterproductive in the long run. It is neither intellectually honest nor politically wise to base a claim for justice on grounds that may prove falsifiable empirically. Moreover, the case for granting equal rights to nonheterosexual parents should not require finding their children to be identical to those reared by heterosexuals. Nor should it require finding that such children do not encounter distinctive challenges or risks, especially when these derive from social prejudice. The U.S. Supreme Court rejected this rationale for denying custody when it repudiated discrimination against interracially married parents in *Palmore v. Sidoti* in 1984: "[P]rivate biases may be outside the reach of the law, but the law cannot, directly or indirectly, give them effect" (quoted in Polikoff 1990:569–70). Inevitably, children share most of the social privileges and injuries associated with their parents' social status. If social prejudice were grounds for restricting rights to parent, a limited pool of adults would qualify.

One can readily turn the tables on a logic that seeks to protect children from the harmful effects of heterosexist stigma directed against their parents. Granting legal rights and respect to gay parents and their children should lessen the stigma that they now suffer and might reduce the high rates of depression and suicide reported among closeted gay youth living with heterosexual parents. Thus, while we disagree with those who claim that there are no differences between the children of heterosexual parents and children of lesbigay parents, we unequivocally endorse their conclusion that social science research provides no grounds for taking sexual orientation into account in the political distribution of family rights and responsibilities.

It is quite a different thing, however, to consider this issue a legitimate matter for social science research. Planned lesbigay parenthood offers a veritable "social laboratory" of family diversity in which scholars could fruitfully examine not only the acquisition of sexual and gender identity, but the relative effects on children of the gender and number of their parents as well as of the implications of diverse biosocial routes to parenthood. Such studies could give us purchase on some of the most vexing and intriguing topics in our field, including divorce, adoption, step-parenthood, and domestic violence, to name a few. To exploit this opportunity, however, researchers must overcome the hetero-normative presumption that interprets sexual differences as deficits, thereby inflicting some of the very disadvantages it claims to discover. Paradoxically, if the sexual orientation of parents were to matter less for political rights, it could matter more for social theory.

REFERENCES

Allen, Mike and Nancy Burrell. 1996. "Comparing the Impact of Homosexual and Heterosexual Parents on Children: Meta-Analysis of Existing Research." *Journal of Homosexuality* 32:19–35.

Bailey, J. Michael, David Bobrow, Marilyn Wolfe, and Sarah Mikach. 1995. "Sexual Orientation of Adult Sons of Gay Fathers." *Developmental Psychology* 31:124–29.

Baumrind, Diana.1995. "Commentary on Sexual Orientation: Research and Social Policy Implications." *Developmental Psychology* 31:130–36.

Bell, Alan P. and Martin S. Weinberg. 1978. *Homosexualities: A Study of Diversity among Men and Women*. New York: Simon and Schuster.

Bigner, Jerry J. and R. Brooke Jacobsen. 1989. "Parenting Behaviors of Homosexual and Heterosexual Fathers." *Journal of Homosexuality* 18:73–86.

———. 1992. "Adult Responses to Child Behavior and Attitudes toward Fathering: Gay and Nongay Fathers." *Journal of Homosexuality* 23:99–112.

Black, Dan A., Gary Gates, Seth Sanders, and Lowell Taylor. 2000. "Demographics of the Gay and Lesbian Population in the United States: Evidence from Available Systematic Data Sources." *Demography* 37:139–54.

Blankenhorn, David. 1995. *Fatherless America: Confronting Our Most Urgent Social Problem*. New York: Basic Books.

Bozett, Frederick W. 1989. "Gay Fathers: A Review of the Literature." Pp. 137–62 in *Homosexuality and the Family*, edited by F. W. Bozett. New York: Haworth Press.

Brewaeys, A., I. Ponjaert, E. V. Van Hall, and S. Golombok. 1997. "Donor Insemination: Child Development and Family Functioning in Lesbian Mother Families." *Human Reproduction* 12:1349–59.

Cameron, Paul and Kirk Cameron. 1996. "Homosexual Parents." *Adolescence* 31:757–76.

Cameron, Paul, Kirk Cameron, and Thomas Landess. 1996. "Errors by the American Psychiatric Association, the American Psychological Association, and the National Educational Association in Representing Homosexuality in Amicus Briefs about Amendment 2 to the U.S. Supreme Court." *Psychological Reports* 79:383–404.

Cantor, David. 1994. *The Religious Right: The Assault on Tolerance and Pluralism in America*. New York: Anti-Defamation League.

Chan, Raymond W., Risa C. Brooks, Barbara Raboy, and Charlotte J. Patterson. 1998. "Division of Labor among Lesbian and Heterosexual Parents: Associations with Children's Adjustment." *Journal of Family Psychology* 12:402–19.

Chan, Raymond W., Barbara Raboy, and Charlotte J. Patterson. 1998. "Psychosocial Adjustment among Children Conceived Via Donor Insemination by Lesbian and Heterosexual Mothers." *Child Development* 69:443–57.

Dunne, Gillian A. 2000. "Opting into Motherhood: Lesbians Blurring the Boundaries and Transforming the Meaning of Parenthood and Kinship." *Gender and Society* 14:11–35.

Falk, Patrick J. 1994. "The Gap Between Psychosocial Assumptions and Empirical Research in Lesbian-Mother Child Custody Cases." Pp. 131–56 in *Redefining Families: Implications for Children's Development*, edited by A. E. Gottfried and A. W. Gottfried. New York: Plenum.

Flaks, David K., Ilda Ficher, Frank Masterpasqua, and Gregory Joseph. 1995. "Lesbians Choosing Motherhood: A Comparative Study of Lesbian and Heterosexual Parents and Their Children." *Developmental Psychology* 31:105–14.

Gallagher, Maggie. "The Gay-Parenting Science." *New York Post*, March 30, p. 3.

Golombok, Susan, Ann Spencer, and Michael Rutter. 1983. "Children in Lesbian and Single-Parent Households: Psychosexual and Psychiatric Appraisal." *Journal of Child Psychology and Psychiatry* 24:551–72.

Golombok, Susan and Fiona Tasker. 1996. "Do Parents Influence the Sexual Orientation of Their Children? Findings From a Longitudinal Study of Lesbian Families." *Developmental Psychology* 32:3–11.

Green, Richard, Jane Barclay Mandel, Mary E. Hotvedt, James Gray and Laurel Smith. 1986. "Lesbian Mothers and Their Children: A Comparison with Solo Parent Heterosexual Mothers and Their Children." *Archives of Sexual Behavior* 15:167–84.

Harris, Mary B. and Pauline H. Turner. 1986. "Gay and Lesbian Parents." *Journal of Homosexuality* 12:101–13.

Herek, Gregory M. 1998. "Bad Science in the Service of Stigma: A Critique of the Cameron Group's Survey Studies." Pp. 223–55 in *Stigma and Sexual Orientation: Understanding Prejudice against Lesbians, Gay Men, and Bisexuals*, edited by G. M. Herek. Thousand Oaks, CA: Sage.

————2000. "Paul Cameron Fact Sheet" (Copyright 1997–2000 by G. M. Herek). Retrieved (http://psychology.ucdavis.edu/rainbow/html/facts_cameron_sheet.html).

Hoeffer, Beverly. 1981. "Children's Acquisition of Sex-Role Behavior in Lesbian-Mother Families." *American Journal of Orthopsychiatry* 51:536–44.

Hotvedt, Mary E. and Jane Barclay Mandel. 1982. "Children of Lesbian Mothers." Pp. 275–91 in *Homosexuality, Social, Psychological, and Biological Issues*, edited by W. Paul. Beverly Hills, CA: Sage.

Huggins, Sharon L. 1989. "A Comparative Study of Self-Esteem of Adolescent Children of Divorced Lesbian Mothers and Divorced Heterosexual Mothers." Pp. 123–35 in *Homosexuality* and *the Family*, edited by F. W. Bozett. New York: Haworth.

Jenny, Carole, Thomas A. Roesler, and Kimberly L. Poyer. 1994. "Are Children at Risk for Sexual Abuse by Homosexuals?" *Pediatrics* 94:41–44.

Kweskin, Sally L. and Alicia S. Cook. 1982. "Heterosexual and Homosexual Mothers' Self-Described Sex-Role Behavior and Ideal Sex-Role Behavior in Children." *Sex Roles* 8:967–75.

Lerner, Robert and Althea K. Nagai. 2000. "Out of Nothing Comes Nothing: Homosexual and Heterosexual Marriage Not Shown to be Equivalent for Raising Children." Paper presented at the Revitalizing the Institution of Marriage for the 21st Century conference, Brigham Young University, March, Provo, UT.

Lynch, F. R. 1992. "Nonghetto Gays: An Ethnography of Suburban Homosexuals." Pp. 165–201 in *Gay Culture in America: Essays from the Field*, edited by G. Herdt. Boston, MA: Beacon.

McLanahan, Sara S. 1985. "Family Structure and the Reproduction of Poverty." *American Journal of Sociology* 90:873–901.

McNeill, Kevin F., Beth M. Rienzi, and Augustine Kposowa. 1998. "Families and Parenting: A Comparison of Lesbian and Heterosexual Mothers." *Psychological Reports* 82:59–62.

Miller, Judith Ann, R. Brooke Jacobsen, and Jerry J. Bigner. 1982. "The Child's Home Environment for Lesbian vs. Heterosexual Mothers: A Neglected Area of Research." *Journal of Homosexuality* 7:49–56.

Mitchell, Valory. 1998. "The Birds, the Bees . . . and the Sperm Banks: How Lesbian Mothers Talk with Their Children about Sex and Reproduction." *American Journal of Orthopsychiatry* 68:400–409.

O'Connell, Ann. 1994. "Voices from the Heart: The Developmental Impact of a Mother's Lesbianism on Her Adolescent Children." *Smith College Studies in Social Work* 63:281–99.

Patterson, Charlotte J. 1994. "Children of the Lesbian Baby Boom: Behavioral Adjustment, Self-Concepts and Sex Role Identity." Pp. 156–75 in *Lesbian and Gay Psychology: Theory, Research, and Clinical Applications*, edited by B. Green and G. M. Herek. Thousand Oaks, CA: Sage.

————— 1995. "Families of the Lesbian Baby Boom: Parents' Division of Labor and Children's Adjustment." *Developmental Psychology* 31:115–23.

Polikoff, Nancy D. 1990. "This Child Does Have Two Mothers: Redefining Parenthood to Meet the Needs of Children in Lesbian-Mother and Other Nontraditional Families." *Georgetown Law Journal* 78:459–575.

Rand, Catherine, Dee L. R. Graham and Edna I. Rawlings. 1982. "Psychological Health and Factors the Court Seeks to Control in Lesbian Mother Custody Trials." *Journal of Homosexuality* 8:27–39.

Steckel, Alisa. 1987. "Psychosocial Development of Children of Lesbian Mothers." Pp. 75–85 in *Gay and Lesbian Parents*, edited by F. W. Bozett. New York: Praeger.

Tasker, Fiona L. and Susan Golombok. 1997. *Growing Up in a Lesbian Family*. New York: Guilford.

Wald, Michael S. 1999. "Same-Sex Couples: Marriage, Families, and Children, An Analysis of Proposition 22, The Knight Initiative." Stanford

Institute for Research on Women and Gender, Stanford University, Stanford, CA.

Wardle, Lynn D. 1997. "The Potential Impact of Homosexual Parenting on Children." *University of Illinois Law Review* 1997:833–919.

Weeks, Jeffrey, Brian Heaphy, and Catherine Donovan. 2001. *Same Sex Intimacies: Families of Choice and Other Life Experiments.* New York: Rutledge.

Woodruff, Robin. 1998. Testimony re: "Subcommittee Meeting to Accept Empirical Data and Expert Testimony Concerning Homosexual Foster Parents." Hearing at the Office of the Attorney General, September 9, 1998. Little Rock, AK. Available from the authors on request.

QUESTIONS

1. Describe the authors' ideological position on lesbian and gay rights. Why is it important for researchers to acknowledge their personal beliefs on issues relevant to their research?

2. What is the hierarchical model of parenting? How does this model influence the interpretation of research findings?

3. According to the authors' analysis of previous research, how does parents' sexual preference affect a child's (a) gender identity, (b) sexual preferences and behavior, and (c) psychological well-being?

4. Which broad developmental outcome most strongly challenges the conclusion that having gay or lesbian parents is *not* in the best interest of the child?

5. Explain what the authors mean when they state that "the effects of parental gender trump those of sexual orientation."

UNIT III

MEASUREMENT

The work of any scientific discipline, as we saw in Unit I, involves the constant interplay between theory and research. What connects theory to research is the process of **measurement.** Theorizing occurs at an abstract level, as theorists relate concepts to one another; research is concrete, as researchers record data based on empirical observation. Measurement moves from the abstract to the concrete.

The measurement process begins with conceptual clarification. To test hypotheses derived from theories, we must clearly understand the meaning of concepts embedded in theories. Consider, for example, a theory about the consequences of democracy: According to Gerhard Lenski's (1966) theory of social stratification, the rights granted in democratic countries enable disadvantaged groups to bring about changes that redistribute material goods more equitably. One hypothesis, derived from this theory, is that as the number of years that countries have been democratic increases, their levels of income inequality decrease (Muller 1988). To test this hypothesis, researchers must first define the meaning of *democracy* and *income inequality*. In one study, Edward Muller (1988) defined democracy as follows:

> The egalitarian political institutions of modern democracy provide all citizens with both the *opportunity* to participate in the governing process, as manifested by universal adult suffrage and free

and fair elections, and the *opportunity* to contest governmental decisions, as manifested by rights of freedom of expression and association. (p. 65)

Also, according to Muller, *income inequality* refers to the extent to which a nation's income is concentrated in the hands of a few.

Having clarified the abstract meaning of one's concepts, the next step in the measurement process, called *operationalization*, is to specify procedures for observing variation in the concepts. With virtually all concepts, there are many possible **operational definitions**. Muller (1988) operationalized democracy as existing when, among other criteria, "at least approximately a majority of the adult population has the right to vote" (p. 54); the point of transition to democracy occurred when "universal male suffrage was instituted giving approximately a majority of the population the right to vote" (p. 56). Muller measured income inequality as "the size of the share of personal income received by the richest quintile [top one-fifth of the population]" (p. 53). When he examined data for a sample of 55 countries, he found a negative association between years of democratic experience (i.e., number of years since democracy was inaugurated) and income inequality: As years increased, inequality decreased.

In social research, there may be disagreement about the theoretical meaning of concepts and the appropriateness of particular operational definitions. An operational definition is considered appropriate or *valid* when it matches the theoretical meaning of the concept it is intended to measure. **Measurement validity** thus depends on the goodness of fit between theoretical and operational definitions. According to Pamela Paxton (2000), one problem with Muller's and others' research is that although their theoretical definitions commonly include universal adult suffrage—that is, the right to vote for every adult—many operational definitions of democracy are limited to male suffrage, thus excluding women as political participants. When she included women's suffrage in Muller's measurement of democracy, the dates when nations transitioned to democracy changed for 12 of the 55 countries Muller examined. As Paxton points out, such changes affect the interpretation of research findings: Muller's results no longer apply to the effects of democratization as universal suffrage, but instead to the extension of male suffrage.

There are several sources of operational definitions. Muller (1988) relied on various *archival records* to determine when a democracy was established; he used data from the World Bank to measure income inequality. In much social research, including the two selections in this unit, investigators use verbal *self-reports* consisting of replies to direct questions posed in interviews or questionnaires. In the first selection, Wendy Roth also uses *observation* of physical appearance based on skin color, hair color and texture, and other attributes to determine a person's "observed race" (i.e., the race that other people assume that a person is).

Both selections in this unit address the issue of measurement validity. Roth examines the validity of the U.S. Census question on race, using qualitative interviews with Hispanic Americans to determine what the question means to them. Yun-Suk Lee and Linda Waite assess the validity of self-report measures of time spent on housework by comparing estimates for both husbands and wives and by comparing survey estimates with a direct measure of time use based on people's logs of what they are doing at randomly selected times of the day.

REFERENCES

Lenski, G. (1966). *Power and privilege: A theory of social stratification*. New York: McGraw-Hill.

Muller, E. N. (1988). Democracy, economic development, and income inequality. *American Sociological Review, 53*(1), 50–68.

Paxton, P. (2000). Women's suffrage in the measurement of democracy: Problems of operationalization. *Studies in Comparative International Development, 35*(3), 92–111.

RESOURCES

Interactive US Census Form (2010):

http://2010.census.gov/2010census/about/interactive-form.php

- The first selection by Wendy Roth questions the use of the U.S. Census racial self-identification question as it applies to Hispanics. The link above will take you directly to an interactive Census 2010 form, which has the same racial identification question as the Census 2000 form to which Roth refers.

The Experience Sampling Program:

http://www.experience-sampling.org/

- In the second selection of this unit, the researchers rely on data collected through the experience sampling method, which prompts people to record their activities at randomly selected times of the day. This website is a link to the type of computer program that is used in this form of research.

General Social Survey Documentation:

http://www3.norc.org/GSS+Website/Documentation/

- The General Social Survey (GSS) is an excellent source of examples of operationalization based on self-reports. At this site, first select Browse Variables, then Subject Index. By clicking on concepts in the

Subject Index, you can see the GSS questions that have been used to operationalize everything from abortion to mental health to welfare.

Guide to Scales and Their Construction:

http://www.utexas.edu/research/pair/data/scalecons.htm

- Many operational definitions combine two or more survey items to create indexes or scales. From the research pages of the PAIR Project, a longitudinal study of marital couples, this link describes measures of love, maintenance, ambivalence, and conflict. Information is provided on the contents of each measure or scale, reliability estimates, and validity statistics.

Selection 5

Given its importance in American society, race is routinely included as a variable in quantitative social research. In much of this research, investigators measure race by using a set of racial categories officially constructed for the U.S. decennial census and other government-sponsored surveys. In the 2000 Census, respondents were asked: "What is this person's race? Mark one or more boxes." The options are "White," "Black, African Am., or Negro," "American Indian or Alaska Native," nine different choices of Asian or Pacific Islander, and "Some other race." (A separate question also asked if the respondent is of "Hispanic, Latino, or Spanish origin.") Recently, the validity of the official set of racial categories has been called into question, especially as it applies to Hispanic Americans. Based on qualitative interviews with Dominican and Puerto Rican migrants, Wendy Roth shows how the Census race question fails to capture Hispanics' lived experience of race. As you read, take note of the different theoretical dimensions of race, how Roth measured them, and how they reflect her respondents' varied interpretations of the Census race question.

RACIAL MISMATCH: THE DIVERGENCE BETWEEN FORM AND FUNCTION IN DATA FOR MONITORING RACIAL DISCRIMINATION OF HISPANICS

WENDY D. ROTH

Source: "Racial Mismatch: The Divergence Between Form and Function in Data for Monitoring Racial Discrimination of Hispanics," by Wendy D. Roth, 2010, Social Science Quarterly, 91, 1288–1311. Copyright 2010 by Blackwell Publishing—Journals. Adapted with permission.

Recent scholarship shows that the concept of race is far from the static, self-evident reality it has long been assumed to be. Scholars have come to see race as a fluid and multifaceted concept. In fact, there are numerous aspects to what we currently think of as race, including self-identification, racial appearance, how we are classified by others, how we believe we are classified by others, and how we present ourselves to conform to other people's expectations. For many populations, such as Hispanics, multiracial individuals, Native Americans, and Asians, these aspects of race frequently do not correspond (Campbell and Troyer, 2007; Harris and Sim, 2002; Hitlin, Brown, and Elder, 2007; Itzigsohn, Giorguli, and Vazquez, 2005; Rockquemore and Brunsma, 2002; Rodriguez and Cordero-Guzman, 1992). Understanding how race is interpreted in different contexts is important theoretically, but it also has implications for the type of data we collect and what we interpret them to mean.

One of the primary justifications for collecting racial statistics in the United States is the need to monitor racial inequalities and discrimination (Snipp, 2003; Wallman, Evinger, and Schechter, 2000). The OMB [U.S. Office of Management and Budget] explains that a major purpose of setting standards for data collection stems from responsibilities to enforce civil rights legislation: "Data were needed to monitor equal access in housing, education, employment, and other areas, for populations that historically had experienced discrimination and differential treatment because of their race or ethnicity" (1997:2). Discrimination is frequently determined statistically by analyzing the returns to education for different races or the difference between the racial composition of an economic sector from what would be expected in the absence of discrimination (Hirschman, 2004; Telles and Murguia, 1990). Previously, Census data were gathered by interviewers who classified the respondent's race (Anderson, 1988), but today racial statistics are drawn from self-identification questions.

The use of racial self-identification for monitoring discrimination is unproblematic as long as individuals identify and are identified by others in the same way. Most social surveys assume this to be the case. As the Census shifted to self-completion mode, beginning in 1960, there was little aggregate change in racial statistics because interviewer classifications do tend to be highly consistent with self-reports for Whites and Blacks (Hirschman, 2004; Smith, 2001). However, studies of Hispanics, Asians, Native Americans, and multiracial populations show much lower rates of consistency. A comparison between self-reports in the 2000 Census and interviewer observation in the 2000 General Social Survey found 97–98 percent agreement for Whites and Blacks, but only 58 percent agreement for people of other races (Smith, 2001).

The discrepancies between different aspects of race are particularly problematic for Hispanics, the fastest-growing minority group in the United States. Although the OMB stipulates that "Hispanic" is not a race, studies often treat non-Hispanic Whites, non-Hispanic Blacks, and Hispanics as mutually exclusive groups, with no further attention to racial differences among Hispanics. In other cases, information from the self-reported race and Hispanic origin questions is combined, to compare the outcomes of White Hispanics and Black Hispanics, for instance. In such studies, how Hispanics identify their race is typically used as a proxy for their appearance.

Both these approaches fail to capture an important aspect of racial discrimination for Hispanics—discrimination on the basis of phenotype or racial appearance. There is considerable phenotype diversity among Hispanics, who span the color spectrum from White to Black, and experience discrimination based on their racialized appearance (Arce, Murguia, and Frisbie, 1987; Espino and Franz, 2002; Murguia and Telles, 1996; South, Crowder, and Chavez, 2005; Telles and Murguia, 1990). "Racial" discrimination against Hispanics, then, occurs in at least two forms: discrimination based on Hispanic origin, and discrimination based on phenotype. This article focuses on the latter of these types. Although Census data can be used to monitor discrimination based on Hispanic origin,

I argue that racial self-classification is not an adequate proxy for racial appearance in order to monitor discrimination based on phenotype or color.

Scholars have argued that the Census race question does not capture how Hispanics think of race. Many Hispanics identify racially with their ethnic group or identify panethnically as Hispanic or Latino (e.g., Bailey, 2001; Itzigsohn, Giorguli, and Vazquez, 2005; Rodriguez, 2000). Yet nearly half (48 percent) classify themselves solely as White, and 2 percent classify themselves solely as Black (U.S. Census, 2000). This article illustrates why even these racial self-classifications, the ones that supposedly do conform to the Census classification system, often fail to match how respondents are seen by others, and will therefore not represent what scholars intend them to measure when using them to monitor racial discrimination.

RACE AND THE U.S. CENSUS

The original purposes of racial enumeration were hardly intended to benefit minorities. It was necessary to count people of different races to determine taxation and representation. Native Americans were not taxed and were excluded from representation, while slaves were counted as three-fifths of a person to determine the number of House representatives. However, the purpose of racial enumeration shifted over time to ameliorate rather than perpetuate historic inequalities. As Snipp writes: "The civil rights movement and its pursuit of equal access to education, housing, employment, and public services underscored the need for a careful record of conditions among the races. Social scientists brought their expertise to bear on these problems, and the result was the vast expansion of the federal statistical system" (2003:583). Today, racial data are used for such purposes as determining the effectiveness of the Voting Rights Act, the Home Mortgage Disclosure and the Equal Credit Opportunities Act, and other civil rights legislation.

The formulation of the race question in the U.S. Census has changed considerably over time. In early Censuses, federal marshals and, later, enumerators, who were often local residents, traveled from house to house asking the questions and identifying the respondent's race by observation. In 1960, the Census Bureau decided to mail an advance Census form to 80 percent of households, with instructions for respondents to complete it and wait for an enumerator to pick it up (Snipp, 2003). The use of a mail Census expanded to 86 percent of households in 1970 and 96 percent in 1980 (Anderson, 1988). At the same time that racial statistics were increasingly being used to enforce civil rights legislation, the data silently shifted from interviewer-observed race to internal self-identification. Little attention was paid to this shift because it rested on the assumption that these two measures were effectively the same.

The change toward racial self-identification has created a new interpretation for the Census race question—that it provides an avenue for self-expression, and that individuals have a right to recognize their own identity among the options provided. But permitting self-expression is a very different function than monitoring racial discrimination, and a different type of data is needed for each. To the extent that self-identifications match the observations that lead to discrimination, this difference is unproblematic, but, as described below, for many populations these components often do not correspond.

THEORETICAL DIMENSIONS OF RACE

A race can be understood as a group seen as distinct because of common physical or biological characteristics that are believed to be inherent, although which characteristics are seen to define the race is shaped by social conventions (Cornell and Hartmann, 1998). Yet the lived experience of race cannot be understood as a single, static identity (Rockquemore and

Brunsma, 2002; Rodriguez, 2000). As illustrated in Figure 5.1, there are several theoretical components to how race is experienced by oneself and others. Drawing on the work of earlier scholars (e.g., Campbell and Troyer, 2007; Cooley, 1902; Harris and Sim, 2002; Nagel, 1994), I identify *internal race*, or subjective self-identification; *expressed race*—the race you say you are, especially to fit into a society's official classifications; *reflected race*—the race you believe others assume you to be; *observed race*—the race other people actually assume you to be; and *phenotype*—physical appearance related to characteristics that are socially understood as relevant to racial classification. A person's phenotype influences most of the other aspects of race, but is not synonymous with any. There is considerable phenotype variation in many socially defined racial groups, yet how one's appearance leads to designation into racial categories is culturally determined.

I also specify two notable subtypes of the *observed race* dimension. *Appearance-based* (AB) *observed race* is a classification made by others based only on readily observable characteristics such as phenotype, clothing, style, or obvious status markers. *Interaction-based* (IB) *observed race* is a classification made by others based on characteristics revealed through interaction, such as accent, language ability, name, knowledge of family members, or comments about background, as well as appearance.

Police officers, security guards, waiters, salespeople—those most likely to engage in racial profiling or provide poorer service—are more likely to form impressions of AB *observed race* based on initial observations. Teachers, employers, landlords, and lending agents—those with greater access to the resources associated with social mobility—tend to have greater interaction and make assessments from what it reveals.

Yet despite the complexity of how these aspects of race are lived and negotiated, most studies continue to subsume them all under a single word—"race"—that ignores their potential

FIGURE 5.1 Dimensions of Racial Identification

Aspect of Race	Description	Typical Measurement
INTERNAL	Subjective self-identification	Open-ended self-identification
EXPRESSED	The race you say you are to others	Close-ended self-identification
REFLECTED	The race you believe others assume you to be	Questions such as "What race do most people think you are?"
OBSERVED	The race others actually assume you to be	Closed-ended interviewer classification
Appearance-Based	Observed race based on readily observable characteristics	Interviewer instructions for classification on first observation
Interaction-Based	Observed race based on characteristics revealed through interaction	Interviewer instructions for classification after interaction
PHENOTYPE	Physical appearance	Ratings of skin color or features, coded by interviewer

for divergence. This also reinforces the belief that one of these measures is the "real" race while others are misclassifications. None of these measures is more or less authentic than another and together they all contribute to how people experience race.

Hispanics in the United States illustrate the lack of correspondence between racial statistics and how race is experienced. In 2000, 42.2 percent of U.S. Hispanics checked only "Some Other Race" on the Census, suggesting that official systems of racial classification do not correspond well with their self-concept (U.S. Census, 2001). Those from the Hispanic Caribbean are particularly likely to be classified by others in ways they may not classify themselves. U.S. observers often classify those with darker skin as Black, an identity many Dominicans and Puerto Ricans reject (Itzigsohn, Giorguli, and Vazquez, 2005; Rodríguez, 2000).

METHODOLOGY

This article draws on data from a recent study of how migration to the mainland United States influences Dominicans' and Puerto Ricans' conceptions of race. I conducted qualitative interviews with 60 Dominican and Puerto Rican migrants in the New York metropolitan area who were born in Puerto Rico or the Dominican Republic, who came to the United States at age 14 or older, and who had lived in the United States for at least seven years. I used purposive quota sampling to stratify each group roughly evenly by age, sex, occupational status, and skin color. I also sought variation in respondents' age at arrival in the mainland United States and the amount of time spent there. The samples were not intended to be statistically representative, but were drawn to qualitatively examine theoretical hypotheses about what would influence Puerto Ricans' and Dominicans' racial identification across these sampling measures.

I generated quota samples meeting these criteria by combining several recruitment methods. Some respondents were referred by

participants in the Longitudinal Study of Second Generation Immigration to New York (Kasinitz, Mollenkopf, and Waters, 2002). That study included large random samples of second-generation Puerto Ricans and Dominicans, who were asked for the names of friends or relatives in the first generation. I found some respondents by canvassing neighborhoods and passing out flyers in public locations. Some respondents were referred by personal contacts, and others were located through forwarded emails. To find respondents with high occupational status, I approached some professional organizations, which contacted their membership on my behalf. I did not interview more than one respondent referred by any individual or organization. Interviews were conducted in Spanish, with both myself and a native Spanish-speaking research assistant present.

I included several measures of race to provide a rich understanding of respondents' identities. To capture *internal race*, I asked respondents to identify their own race in open-ended terms. I also asked them to complete the race and Hispanic origin questions from the 2000 Census; as their closed-ended options are based on U.S. classifications, I treat this as a form of *expressed race*. Also in open-ended terms, I asked respondents: "What do most Americans think your race is?" *(reflected race)*. Before each interview began, I determined how I would describe the respondent's skin color and other physical characteristics, and immediately after the interview I completed a form to describe the respondent's appearance *(phenotype)* in detail. Respondents also rated their own skin color with the same scale I had used and that they had used to rate a series of photographs during the interview.

Before each interview, I classified the respondent's AB *observed race*, to represent an observer's impression of an unknown individual based on appearance. I classify AB *observed race* with White, Black, and Hispanic as mutually exclusive appearance-based categories within a Hispanic population.

A criterion for inclusion in this study was that all respondents were born in Puerto Rico or the

Dominican Republic and identified ethnically as Puerto Rican or Dominican. Based on my knowledge of this information the IB *observed race* was "Hispanic" for all respondents. Because the IB *observed race* did not vary in this study, I focus here on AB *observed race.*

INTERPRETING THE CENSUS RACE QUESTION

Many have noted that the Census race question does not represent well how Hispanics subjectively understand their race, leading large proportions to reject the categories offered and check "Other" (e.g., Duany, 2002; Hitlin, Brown, and Elder, 2007; Rodriguez, 2000). In other words, *internal race* and *expressed race* often do not correspond. Many of those who check "Other" identify racially with and write in panethnic identities like Hispanic or specific ethnic groups (Bailey, 2001; Itzigsohn, Giorguli, and Vazquez, 2005).

Many treat the Census race question as an (imperfect) measure of *internal race,* but in fact the question does not specify what dimension of race it is measuring. By simply asking "What is this person's race?" the question is ambiguous, leading different respondents to answer with different aspects of race. Figure 5.2 identifies several patterns for interpreting the Census race question, as well as the different aspects of race for several respondents who illustrate these patterns. As the first group shows, some do respond by writing in their *internal race*, even if it is not a listed option. This reaction is illustrated by Hernando, a young Dominican who recently received a degree in business administration but is working in construction until he can find a business job. Reading aloud the Census race question, he explained: "'What is this person's race?' This question is very interesting because, one, I'm not totally Black, and then I'm not White. So I'm in the middle. And I'm not Indigenous. So in this case I have to put Hispanic . . . It's the mixture—I'm the product of a cosmic mixture . . . which is the Latino

mixture." Ethnic and panethnic labels have largely come to represent the racial mixture Hernando describes.

Other respondents, as illustrated in the second group in Figure 5.2, mark how they believe they are seen by others, their *reflected race*, even if it differs from their *internal race*. Bolivar, a retired taxidriver and factory worker from Puerto Rico with very light skin and European features, explains that although he considers himself White, most Americans do not: "I know that for me I'm White, the same as them, but they don't think that. They say that we're of Hispanic race, that's what they think . . .They don't care about the color . . .You speak Spanish, you're Hispanic race . . . And the White is of White race, it doesn't matter if he's Jewish, Italian, whatever he is." Bolivar wrote in "Puerto Rican" on the Census race question, recognizing the double standard that only non-Hispanics are seen by others as really White.

Another pattern, represented by the third group in Figure 5.2, is for respondents to offer an *expressed race* that differs from both their *internal* and *reflected race* yet is their best attempt to make sense of how they think the question intends them to answer. These respondents typically feel they have to check one of the boxes—generally White or Black—even if it does not represent how they see themselves. Hugo, a Puerto Rican IT manager with medium-light skin, describes his *internal race* as *trigueño,* a term indicating wheat-colored or brown skin. He believes that most White Americans see him as non-White. Yet he checks "White" on the Census question. He explains:

> Yes, I am Puerto Rican but I don't consider myself White. Obviously, the options that the questionnaire gives don't have anything like mixed. Don't have anything like *trigueño,* which is what I consider myself. And the options that are given me make me fill out what is closer to what I consider myself . . .

Often, respondents justify their choice by explaining that they are closer to one box than another. Many explain that they feel they must check a box because these are what the United

FIGURE 5.2   Conflicting Aspects of Race in Illustrative Cases

	Internal	*Expressed*	*Reflected*	*Observed (AB)*	*Phenotype*
1. Interprets Census race question as INTERNAL RACE					
Ursula, long-term unemployed, PR	Hispanic	Hispanic	White	White	Light, European
Hernando, construction temp, Dom.	Hispanic	Hispanic	Black	Black	Dark, mostly European
Raquel, assistant principal, Dom.	Black	Black	Dominican	White	Light, European
2. Interprets Census race question as REFLECTED RACE					
Anibal, maintenance worker, PR	White	Puerto Rican	Puerto Rican	Hispanic	Medium, European
Mario, fitness trainer, Dom.	Human Race	Hispanic	Hispanic	Black	Dark, African
3. Feels need to check a box, although it does not represent INTERNAL or REFLECTED RACE					
Marco, doorman, Dom.	Indio	White	Hispanic	Hispanic	Medium, European
Josefa, home aide, Dom.	Hispanic	Black	Puerto Rican	Black	Medium, mostly African
Salvador, restaurant worker, PR	Puerto Rican	White	Hispanic	Black	Dark, Indigenous

States considers to be races, while "Hispanic" is not officially a race. Others check "White" if they were considered White in their country of origin, even though they know this standard does not apply in the United States. Angela, a Dominican investment banker with light skin and European features, marked "White" on the Census question, albeit reluctantly. "[I'd prefer a category other than White, but what that] other category would have been, I don't know. 'Latino', but Latino isn't a race. It's more like a race [than not]. So if they give me three options:

White, Black, Indian, I am not Black or Indian . . . And in my country I am White. But here I'm not White . . . If the difference is between 'Are you Caucasian or Latina?' I'll say Latina."

Respondents interpret the Census race question in a variety of ways. Even when these Hispanics answer in a way intended by the Census Bureau, the race question does not necessarily represent how they identify or their acceptance of U.S. classifications. In fact, it is rarely clear from their response to this question alone which aspect of race they are referring to in their answer.

DISCRIMINATION BY PHENOTYPE

Discrimination does occur on the basis of Hispanic origin, but additional layers of inequality are caused by phenotype discrimination. Yet discrimination by racial appearance within Hispanic groups has been largely overlooked in efforts to enforce civil rights legislation and prevent differential treatment on the basis of race or ethnicity. Research provides evidence of significant socioeconomic inequalities between light and dark Latinos within the same ethnic groups that cannot be explained by differences in human capital or resources (e.g., Espino and Franz, 2002; South, Crowder, and Chavez, 2005; Telles and Murguia, 1990). These studies measure phenotype from interviewer observations, and attribute inequalities in outcomes such as occupational status, income, and residential segregation to phenotype discrimination.

Most of my respondents described experiences they believed to be discriminatory—in their work or school, their search for apartments, or the service they receive in shops and restaurants. Many felt they were watched or followed by security guards more than other shoppers. Several, particularly men, described being harassed or violently apprehended by the police for no apparent reason. Those with dark skin described the most experiences with discrimination. For example, Tomás has repeatedly experienced discrimination in different realms of his life. A young Puerto Rican actor with medium-brown skin, tightly curled hair, and a mix of African and European facial features, many Americans would perceive Tomás as Black, although he wrote "Latino" for his race on the Census question. In restaurants, waiters often ignore him while catering to other clients. When security guards follow him around a shop, he has learned to make a game of it, picking up items and ducking behind different aisles to force them to keep up. The police are a steady presence in his Bronx neighborhood and on more than one occasion have violently stopped him at gunpoint in their search for someone matching his profile. Discriminatory experiences have also affected his career choices. After finishing high school, he pursued becoming a police officer. Despite passing the test with flying colors, the investigator assigned to his case repeatedly discouraged him from applying. He concluded: "[They] don't want to be around people of color. One guy actually said, 'I arrest people of color because I don't want to hang out with them when I have a drink.'" After failing the psychological exam, a test he was sure he had passed, and appealing his case for several years, he lost interest in joining the police.

Many respondents attributed what they perceived as discriminatory treatment to being Hispanic, but many others claimed that even among Hispanics, those with darker skin experienced more discrimination. Hugo, the IT manager with medium-light skin, notices how his wife, whom he describes as *negra*, receives the brunt of racial bias when they enter a high-end establishment. He personally has never received worse service than other clients in a shop, he claims, "but my wife has . . . We went into a jewelry store and my wife wanted to see a watch and the Indian guy didn't really want to. He thought that if he gave us the watch we were going to run away with the watch. And the guy was real nasty. My wife got very offended and she cursed him out."

In the workplace, many migrants observe how European phenotypes provide advantages among Hispanics. Octavio, a Puerto Rican parking garage attendant with very light skin and European features, who would easily be seen as White, believes that Hispanics with lighter skin color, such as himself, do better in the job market than those with darker skin. "It's true," Octavio says, "because I have a brother who is *indio, trigueñito,* and one time we went to look for a job, and they told him that there wasn't a job for him and they told me to come the next day." Racism is partly visual, and even when someone's Hispanic ethnicity is known, it may not matter as much if he or she looks White. Rafaela, a Dominican accountant, claims: "My friend that works with the Italians, . . . she's light-skinned and has straight hair. She would easily pass as a White American person . . . I think that at least Italians, they pay attention a lot to the physical appearance and those things. Maybe with them she'd have more advantage. I've never seen a *negro* employed by Italians." Others note that light Hispanics also have more residential options and can move into White neighborhoods.

More of the dark respondents reported experiencing workplace discrimination than those with medium or light skin. Within my sample, 39 percent of those with dark skin reported workplace discrimination, compared with 32 percent with medium skin, and 24 percent with light skin. Although not representative of a larger population, this pattern is noteworthy because it occurs in a context where one's ethnicity is known by colleagues and employers. The pattern was particularly pronounced among professional respondents. Among respondents who attended college, 75 percent of those with dark skin reported workplace discrimination, compared with 63 percent with medium skin, and 50 percent with light skin. Being Hispanic may affect your opportunities, but color adds an extra layer of barriers to confront.

TREATING EXPRESSED RACE AS A MEASURE OF PHENOTYPE

Some studies do break down the outcomes of Hispanics by their self-identified race on the Census. Because Hispanics span the range from Black to White, the Census race question is often treated as a proxy for whether they "look White" or "look Black" in a U.S. framework. Prominent scholars have used racial self-identification as an indicator of appearance to measure racial inequalities in income, occupation, and residence within their ethnic group (e.g., Denton and Massey, 1989; Rodriguez, 1989), but can Hispanics' self-identification be taken as an accurate measure of how they are seen by others? Here, I use two examples—the individuals highlighted in Figure 5.2—to illustrate the problems with treating Hispanics'

expressed race as an indication of how those with the power to discriminate see them.

Salvador usually finds jobs as a kitchen worker in restaurants throughout New York, particularly his home borough of the Bronx. In open-ended terms, he identifies his race as "Puerto Rican." With his dark skin and indigenous-influenced features, many Americans observing him would consider him to be Black. Yet on the U.S. Census race question, Salvador checks his race as White. He is aware that his skin color is not very light and describes himself as *trigueño*. Yet in his outlook toward race, as in many of his habits, he is more accustomed to Puerto Rican than U.S. standards. Many Puerto Ricans believe that "If you're not Black, you're White," in contrast to the U.S. legacy from the one-drop rule that "If you're not White, you're Black." Salvador does not really consider himself White, but given the options on the Census question, this is the answer that fits best with his understanding of race.

Raquel moved to New York from the Dominican Republic as a young teen. Now in her mid-30s, she works as an assistant principal in the Dominican enclave of Washington Heights. Raquel has very light skin and looks primarily European. I thought most Americans would view her as White. Yet Raquel identifies her race as Black on the Census. She explains how she came to identify this way.

There was a confusion, at least for [me] . . . about what race is, what ethnicity is, what nationality is. So, for me, it was an experience like an epiphany one day when I found out that there are only three races . . . and you have to decide which you belong to. So not only by the color of the skin, but there are a lot of other factors . . . There would be your ancestry—you need to look at your grandparents, your great-grandparents. You need to look at the shape of your mouth, the size of your ears, how your nose is, the texture of your hair. There are a lot of other things: the color of your eyes, the color of your hair, all those things. But in the Dominican Republic, as soon as you're a little light or medium light, already, you can't say that you're Black. No, that's like a sin. So, after you educate yourself and after you accept that there are either three or . . . four [races] but you need to choose one of these three or four. You can't invent a new one. So I don't have any other option than choosing Black because I'm not White or Asian. So I must be whatever is left.

[Raquel's] experience of coming to identify as Black is atypical; most respondents do prefer a national or panethnic identification to a Black one. However, her "epiphany" illustrates the fluid and subjective nature of racial identification and how far it may diverge from the observations of others.

As these cases show, social processes like education and cultural orientation can influence both *internal* and *expressed race.* Most important for the purposes of monitoring discrimination, Salvador and Raquel both complete the Census race question in a way that defies its ability to serve as a proxy for racial appearance, as viewed in a U.S. context. Based on phenotype alone, we would expect Salvador to be at greater risk of racial discrimination, and in fact he does describe more frequent and more significant experiences he believes are discriminatory than does Raquel. Yet his *expressed race* on the census is White, while Raquel describes hers as Black. If phenotype discrimination is pervasive, analyzing it with Census race data will likely underestimate the extent to which "Black" Latinos experience it if many of them look more like Raquel than like Salvador.

DISCUSSION AND CONCLUSIONS

In efforts to monitor and fight against differential treatment due to race or ethnicity, it is crucial to focus on discrimination on the basis of Hispanic origin. Yet this is only one type of differential treatment that Hispanics may experience. Discrimination along color lines can also cause differential treatment within ethnic and racial groups, and this aspect of race is lost in Census measures. Statistical analyses tend either to ignore racial variation among Hispanics

altogether—by treating White, Black, and Hispanic as mutually exclusive categories—or to treat racial self-identification as an indication of appearance, assuming that Hispanics identify themselves as they are seen by others. This study shows that Dominicans and Puerto Ricans interpret the Census race question in a variety of ways, to represent different dimensions of the lived experience of race. There is considerable mismatch between their racial self-identification and how they appear racially to others, illustrating the problems with treating Census measures of race as an indicator of phenotype.

The Civil Rights Act of 1964 and subsequent equal employment legislation prohibit discrimination based on race or color. However, U.S. legal structures primarily focus on discrimination between racial and ethnic groups, while claims of discrimination based on color within these groups are often unsuccessful. In a study of employment discrimination cases involving Hispanics, Hernández (2007) argues that judges inappropriately view the fact of any racial or ethnic diversity in a workplace as evidence that employers have not discriminated, while failing to see other characteristics—such as color—as legally relevant. By this logic, if there are Dominicans in the workplace, the employer cannot be discriminating against Dominicans, even if all those employed are light skinned. For color discrimination to be recognized within our legal system, inequalities on the basis of phenotype need to become a focus of our data collection and monitoring efforts.

On a theoretical level, this exploration of the lived experience of race illustrates the need to break down the concept of race into its various components. Despite recent recognition that race is fluid and complex, there is still an overwhelming tendency to use a single term to represent this complexity. This can give way to the misleading interpretation that people are "misclassified" by observers, or that observations that do not correspond with self-identification represent measurement error. Self-identification and observation are simply different processes and neither is objectively correct. The tendency to group multiple theoretical concepts under the single term of race also carries the risk of perpetuating outdated connotations, such as biological or essentialized meanings, which social scientists rarely intend to convey. Discussions of race should adopt language that communicates the multiplicity of social processes involved, and detail whether they are talking about *internal race, expressed race, reflected race, observed race,* or *phenotype* in different contexts. Such specificity also illustrates the social character of these components, and may do more to convince readers that the notion of race is not inherent than merely asserting that this is the case.

We must also develop the tools to accurately measure the different concepts and ensure that the most appropriate measures are used for different functions. For monitoring color discrimination or racial inequalities within Hispanic groups, measures of phenotype are most appropriate, but *internal race* is better suited for other purposes, such as estimating political power or determining community resource apportionment.

The American Sociological Association (2003), publicly stating its support for collecting racial statistics, asserts that failing to collect racial data does not eliminate racism or discrimination while it does eliminate a valuable tool for understanding and addressing social injustices. We tend to find it more acceptable to measure racial categories than phenotype, which perhaps associates racial categorization a little too closely with biology for comfort. Yet to deal with the way that color influences social stratification, phenotype, too, has to be acknowledged and understood. To accurately monitor phenotype discrimination, the form of race data that are gathered need to represent the way that discrimination functions as a social process. Survey measures of race need to be closely linked to the theoretical concepts they represent and the purposes for which they are used. Only then can we address the false assumptions that we each have one static race and that our current racial statistics are valid measures of what we think they are.

REFERENCES

American Sociological Association. 2003. *The Importance of Collecting Data and Doing Social Scientific Research on Race.* Washington, DC: American Sociological Association.

Anderson, Margo J. 1988. *The American Census: A Social History.* New Haven, CT: Yale University Press.

Arce, Carlos H., Edward Murguia, and W. Parker Frisbie. 1987. "Phenotype and Life Chances Among Chicanos." *Hispanic Journal of Behavioral Sciences* 9:19–32.

Bailey, Benjamin. 2001. "Dominican-American Ethnic/Racial Identities and United States Social Categories." *International Migration Review* 35:677–708.

Campbell, Mary E., and Lisa Troyer. 2007. "The Implications of Racial Misclassification by Observers." *American Sociological Review* 72:750–65.

Cooley, Charles Horton. 1902. *Human Nature and the Social Order.* New York: Charles Scribner's Sons.

Cornell, Stephen, and Douglas Hartmann. 1998. *Ethnicity and Race: Making Identities in a Changing World.* Thousand Oaks, CA: Pine Forge Press.

Denton, Nancy A., and Douglas S. Massey. 1989. "Racial Identity Among Caribbean Hispanics: The Effect of Double Minority Status on Residential Segregation." *American Sociological Review* 54:790–808.

Duany, Jorge. 2002, *The Puerto Rican Nation on the Move: Identities on the Island and in the United States.* Chapel Hill, NC: University of North Carolina Press.

Espino, Rodolfo, and Michael M. Franz. 2002. "Latino Phenotypic Discrimination Revisited: The Impact of Skin Color on Occupational Status." *Social Science Quarterly* 83:612–23.

Harris, David R., and Jeremiah Joseph Sim. 2002. "Who Is Multiracial? Assessing the Complexity of Lived Race." *American Sociological Review* 67:614–27.

Hernández, Tanya Katerí. 2007. "Latino Inter-Ethnic Employment Discrimination and the 'Diversity' Defense." *Harvard Civil Rights Civil Liberties Law Review* 42:259–316.

Hirschman, Charles. 2004. "The Origins and Demise of the Concept of Race." *Population and Development Review* 30:385–415.

Hitlin, Steven, J., Scott Brown, and Glen H. Elder Jr. 2007. "Measuring Latinos: Racial Classifications and Self-Understandings." *Social Forces* 86: 587–611.

Itzigsohn, José, Silvia Giorguli, and Obed Vazquez. 2005. "Immigrant Incorporation and Racial Identity: Racial Self-Identification Among Dominican Immigrants." *Ethnic and Racial Studies* 28:50–78.

Kasinitz, Phillip, John Mollenkopf, and Mary C. Waters. 2002. "Becoming American/Becoming New Yorkers: Immigrant Incorporation in a Majority Minority City." *International Migration Review* 36:1020–36.

Murguia, Edward, and Edward E. Telles, 1996. "Phenotype and Schooling Among Mexican Americans." *Sociology of Education* 69:276–89.

Nagel, Joane. 1994. "Constructing Ethnicity: Creating and Recreating Ethnic Identity and Culture." *Social Problems* 41:152–76.

Rockquemore, Kerry Ann, and David L. Brunsma. 2002. *Beyond Black: Biracial Identity in America.* Thousand Oaks, CA: Sage Publications.

Rodríguez, Clara E. 1989. *Puerto Ricans: Born in the U.S.A.* Boston, MA: Unwin Hyman.

———. 2000. *Changing Race: Latinos, the Census, and the History of Ethnicity in the United States.* New York: New York University Press.

Rodríguez, Clara E., and Hector Cordero-Guzman. 1992. "Placing Race in Context." *Ethnic and Racial Studies* 15:523–42.

Smith, Tom W. 2001. *Aspects of Measuring Race: Race by Observation vs. Self-Reporting and Multiple Mentions of Race and Ethnicity.* GSS Methodological Report 93. Washington, DC: National Opinion Research Center.

Snipp, C. Matthew. 2003. "Racial Measurement in the American Census: Past Practices and Implications for the Future." *Annual Review of Sociology* 29:563–88.

South, Scott J., Kyle Crowder, and Erick Chavez. 2005. "Migration and Spatial Assimilation Among U.S. Latinos: Classical Versus Segmented Trajectories." *Demography* 42:497–521.

Telles, Edward E., and Edward Murguia. 1990. "Phenotypic Discrimination and Income Differences Among Mexican Americans." *Social Science Quarterly* 71:682–96.

U.S. Census Bureau. 2001. "Overview of Race and Hispanic Origin." Census 2000 Brief.

U.S. Office of Management and Budget. 1997. "Revisions to the Standards for the Classification of Federal Data on Race and Ethnicity." *Federal Register Notice* October 30. Available at (http://www.whitehouse.gov/omb/fedreg/1997/standards.html).

Wallman, Katherine K., Suzann Evinger, and Susan Schechter. 2000. "Measuring Our Nation's Diversity: Developing a Common Language for Data on Race/Ethnicity." *American Journal of Public Health* 90:1704–08.

QUESTIONS

1. Before 1960, census enumerators classified each person's race based on personal observation. Since 1960, the Census has used self-identification as the means of racial measurement for most households. How has this shift affected the racial classification of Blacks, Whites, and Hispanics? That is, what are the differences between *observed* and *expressed* race, according to Roth?

2. Roth identifies several different theoretical dimensions of race. Explain the difference between (a) *internal* and *observed race* and (b) *expressed* and *reflected race*.

3. For which of Roth's theoretical dimensions of race did she use the 2000 Census question as the measure? How did she measure *observed race*?

4. Describe two distinct patterns of interpreting the Census race question that Roth found among her respondents.

5. The measurement of race is included in the Census and many other federal surveys for the purpose of monitoring racial discrimination. How has the shift to self-identification as the means of racial measurement affected the ability to assess discrimination against Hispanic Americans?

Selection 6

Sparked by changing gender roles and the dramatic increase in women's participation in the paid labor force, over the past three decades there has been a great deal of research on the household division of labor. Researchers have examined trends, theorized about the determinants of time spent on housework, and raised questions about the consequences of continued inequities. As with any line of inquiry, this research is cumulative, as each study builds on those that preceded it. To advance knowledge, however, it is important that investigators use comparable or equally valid measures. A problem with research on the gender gap in housework, as Yun-Suk Lee and Linda Waite point out, is that researchers have used different measures and methods of estimating time spent on housework. Lee and Waite compare time estimates based on two distinct methods. As you read this selection, note how these estimates are affected by who provides them and the method of obtaining them.

HUSBANDS' AND WIVES' TIME SPENT ON HOUSEWORK

A Comparison of Measures

YUN-SUK LEE

LINDA J. WAITE

Wives spend substantially more time than their husbands on family work, even though women do less and men do slightly more now than 20 years ago (Bianchi, Milkie, Sayer, & Robinson, 2000). Researchers from a wide range of disciplines have attempted to isolate the causes and consequences of this division of household labor for men and women

Source: "Husbands' and Wives' Time Spent on Housework: A Comparison of Measures," by Yun-Suk & Linda Lee J. White, 2005. *Journal of Marriage and Family*, 67, 238–336. Copyright 2005 by Blackwell Publishing—Journals.

and for family functioning (Coltrane, 2000; Shelton & John, 1996) but have used different measures and methods. This raises multiple problems for investigators, especially when comparing their results to other studies (Shelton & John).

Most researchers define household labor as unpaid work that contributes to the well-being of family members and the maintenance of their home (Shelton & John, 1996). Most research focuses on the more restricted category of *housework*, which consists of physical activities such as cleaning, laundry, and cooking. Few studies include the other components of household labor—child care, emotional labor such as providing encouragement or advice, and mental labor such as planning or household management (Coltrane, 2000), although these are clearly important.

To estimate the amount of time spent on housework, most previous studies use either survey questions or time diaries (Coltrane, 2000; Shelton & John, 1996). In surveys, respondents are asked to estimate the number of hours they or their spouses spend on housework or on selected household tasks. In time diary studies, participants are asked to report all their activities, usually for the previous day (Robinson & Godbey, 1997). Time on housework activities is then added up across the day for each respondent. Previous attempts to compare measures of time spent on housework obtained from time diary studies with survey reports (e.g., Marini & Shelton, 1993) have been hampered by the absence of both types of estimates in a single study. Because *both* the samples and approaches differ in these comparisons, the contribution that each makes to discrepancies in estimates of time spent on housework cannot be distinguished.

In addition, both surveys and time diaries generally obtain information from a single member of a married couple. As a result, comparisons of time spent by husbands and wives rely on reports by one respondent on the time spent by self and spouse or on information from male respondents versus information from female respondents. One important exception, the National Survey of Families and Households,

asked both members of married couples similar questions on time spent on housework but has no time-use data with which to compare the answers.

Scholars have developed a number of measures of the division of housework, and each has strengths and weaknesses. One commonly used measure is the *share* of housework done by the husband (Presser, 1994). This has the advantage of providing a simple and direct summary measure but may change over time or differ across couples because of changes in the husband's time, changes in the wife's time, or both. Bianchi et al. (2000) suggest using instead the difference between the hours spent by the wife and the hours spent by the husband. The two measures sometimes tell different stories about the division of housework, as we see later.

This study addresses some of these limitations of previous research. It contributes to the debate about the gender gap in housework through a detailed and careful comparison of key measures of housework time for the same respondents. This article addresses five key questions about the measures and methods used for studying time spent on household chores by husbands and wives and the gender gap in housework. First, do estimates depend on which spouse is asked? Second, does the data collection method affect the estimates obtained? Third, do estimates depend on how one treats secondary activities— two activities done simultaneously? Fourth, are estimates sensitive to the inclusion of mental labor, such as household management, planning, and organization? Fifth, do conclusions about the gender gap in household labor depend on whether one measures the gap as the difference in the number of hours of housework done by the husband and the number of hours done by the wife or as the percentage of household labor done by the husband?

METHOD

Data

The data used here are drawn from a sample of married couples with children aged 5–18 years participating in the Sloan 500 Family Study, which was carried out in 1999 and 2000. The Sloan Study obtained information from three family members—mother, father, and child—in each family using multiple methods—in-depth interviews, questionnaires, and the ESM (described in detail below). Most are non-Hispanic Whites, in their mid-40s. The families in this sample are economically advantaged compared to married parents in the United States as a whole, with high levels of education completed. This paper examines information from the 265 married-couple families in which both the husband and wife completed the survey and the ESM.

Experience Sampling Method

The Sloan 500 Family Study collected data from both spouses using the ESM [Experience Sampling Method] (Csikszentmihalyi, 1997), often described as a *diary-like* method (Coltrane, 2000). The ESM is a unique time study process of data collection in which respondents are given specially programmed wristwatches to wear for 1 week, during which time the watches "beep" during waking hours at a random time within each 2-hour block, producing eight signals a day with no two signals being less than 30 minutes apart. When beeped, ESM respondents are asked to report their primary activity ("What was the main thing you were doing?") and their secondary activity, if any ("What else were you doing at the same time?"). ESM participants are asked to report what they are thinking about when signaled ("What was on your mind?"). Responses to the ESM can be used to estimate time spent by respondents during the sampled week on a wide range of activities, including time spent on housework.

Measures

Household tasks. Most researchers agree that major household tasks include (a) cooking, (b) cleaning, (c) shopping for groceries and household goods, (d) doing dishes, and (e) laundry (Coltrane, 2000, p. 1210). These tasks are included in our estimates of time spent on housework. According to Coltrane, this *routine housework* consists of tasks that are the most time consuming and most frequently done, with little flexibility in scheduling. There is an additional set of tasks that researchers may or may not include in their definition of household labor: driving, financial paperwork, yard maintenance, and repairing tasks. Coltrane calls these *occasional* or *other* household tasks. We include all these tasks except driving, which we exclude because of idiosyncratic features of the Sloan data.

Survey measures of own time and spouse's time spent on housework. In the survey, respondents were asked, for each task, "How many hours per week do you personally spend on the following tasks?" They were also asked, "How many hours per week does your spouse spend on the following tasks?" The tasks and response categories were identical on these two questions. Response categories included *0 hours, 1–2 hours, 3–5 hours, 6–10 hours, 11–15 hours, 16–20 hours,* and *21+ hours.* Each person provided estimates of hours spent on each task for self and, separately, for spouse.

To estimate the number of hours spent on housework from the response categories above, we assigned the value of the midpoint of the response category for each task. For the open-ended category, we assigned the value 21 hours because very few respondents report spending more than that number of hours on a single task. We calculate the number of hours each individual reported spending on housework per week by summing the hours for the seven tasks in Table 6.1. We create a measure of the individual's estimate of own time spent on housework, and another measure of the individual's estimate of spouse's time spent on housework.

ESM time-use measures of own time on housework activities. In the ESM, signals occur at random, providing a representative sample of time use by each respondent. Participants are typically signaled eight times during their waking hours each day for 7 consecutive days, resulting in a total of 56 signals per week. The time spent on household labor is measured by the ratio of the number of beeps for which the respondent reports doing household tasks to the total number of beeps the individual responds to multiplied by the number of waking hours per week. The most restrictive and conservative measure of time spent on housework is based only on beeps for which respondents indicate that housework was the primary activity. A more liberal measure of time spent on housework includes beeps at which respondents report doing housework either as a primary or as a secondary activity. This more liberal (or latter) measure adds 2 hours to housework time for each hour spent doing the laundry while cooking dinner, for example, one for laundry and one for cooking. Clearly, this measure provides an upper-bound estimate of housework time.

The ESM data also provide a measure for how often respondents think about the eight household tasks included in our measure, which allows for the calculation of time spent on the mental labor of housework, excluding the times during which respondents were doing household tasks.

RESULTS

Table 6.1 presents estimates based on responses to survey questions about self and spouse and estimates based on responses to the ESM. Table 6.2 compares the various estimates and presents the gap in the number of hours spent by husband and wife and the husband's share of housework implied by each.

Table 6.1 shows the mean number of hours that husbands (Column 1) and wives (Column 3) reported in response to survey questions that they spent on various housework tasks per week. Table 6.1 also shows the mean number of hours that each reported that their spouse spent on each task per week (Columns 2 and 4). This table indicates that husbands and wives agree that wives spend more time on household labor than husbands do. Husbands estimate that their wives spend, on average, 24.9 hours per week on housework (Column 4 [total]). Wives estimate that they spend 26 hours on the sum of these

tasks (Column 3 [total]). Note that these estimates do not differ significantly.

Table 6.1 also shows that although spouses agree on the approximate amount of time that wives spend on housework, they differ significantly and much more on the amount of time husbands spend (Column 1 [total] vs. Column 2 [total]). On average, husbands report that they spend about 18 hours per week on household chores, but wives estimate that their husbands spend only 13 hours per week on domestic tasks, a statistically significant difference. Previous studies suggest that this 5-hour discrepancy may come from husbands' overestimation of their time on household labor (Press & Townsley, 1998). A comparison of survey and ESM estimates allows us to test this reasoning.

Table 6.1 also provides ESM estimates of the time that husbands and wives in the sample devote to household labor, separately for each task and for the total of all tasks. Column 5 gives estimates of time spent on housework as a primary activity by husbands, given in Column 8 for wives. Columns 6 and 9 present estimates of time spent on housework while doing something else as a primary activity. Columns 7 and 10 present time spent thinking about household tasks.

ESM measures of time spent on housework that include only the primary activity show that husbands and wives spend about 10 and 15 hours, respectively, on household labor per week. The estimate for married men is similar to that from time diary studies that count only the primary activity (Bianchi et al., 2000). The estimate for married women, however, is significantly lower than time diary estimates based only on the primary activity (Bianchi et al.). We discuss possible reasons for this difference in a later section of the paper.

The ESM data in Table 6.1 show that, in this sample, husbands spend approximately 3 hours per week and wives spend about 6 hours per week performing household tasks while engaged in another activity that they consider *primary.* Self-reported hours of both husbands and wives differ significantly from ESM measures of their total housework hours that include time spent on housework as a secondary activity.

TABLE 6.1 Estimates of Number of Hours Spent on Housework per Week: Survey and the ESM ($N = 256$)

	Survey				The ESM					
	Husbands		Wives		Husbands			Wives		
	Reported by									
	Self	Spouse	Self	Spouse	Primary	Secondary	Mental Labor	Primary	Secondary	Mental Labor
	1	2	3	4	5	6	7	8	9	10
Washing the dishes	2.9_a	2.0	3.4_a	3.1	0.9_b	0.1	0.0	1.2_b	0.5	0.0
Cleaning the house	2.4_a	1.3	4.4	4.1	1.8_b	0.8	0.3	3.3_b	1.7	0.4
Laundry	1.6_a	1.1	4.3	4.2	0.7_b	0.4	0.1	1.4_b	1.1	0.2
Cooking	3.0_a	2.0	6.3_a	5.9	2.9	0.8	0.3	5.2_b	1.7	0.9
Shopping for household	1.9_a	1.5	3.1_a	3.4	0.5_b	0.0	0.2	0.9_b	0.2	0.4
Family paperwork	2.3_a	2.1	2.2_a	2.5	0.9_b	0.3	0.7	0.8_b	0.3	0.5
Yard and home maintenance	3.6_a	2.8	2.4_a	1.9	2.3_b	0.6	0.8	2.2	0.8	0.7
Total	$17.7_{a,b,c,d}$	12.8_c	$26.0_{b,c,d}$	$24.9_{e,f}$	10.0_b	3.0	2.3	15.0_b	6.3	3.1

Note: Subscript a indicates significant difference between self-report and spouse's report at $p < .05$; b, significant difference between self-report and ESM primary at $p < .05$; c, significant difference between self-report and ESM primary + secondary at $p < .05$; d, significant difference between self-report and ESM primary + secondary + mental at $p < .05$; e, significant difference between spouse's report and ESM primary at $p < .05$; f, significant difference between spouse's report and ESM primary + secondary at $p < .05$; g, significant difference between spouse's report and ESM primary + secondary + mental at $p < .05$. ESM = Experience Sampling Method.

Table 6.1 indicates that wives and husbands spend between 2 and 3 hours per week on the mental labor of housework, thinking about household labor when they are not performing household tasks. Consistent with the expectation of several researchers (Coleman, 1988; Thompson, 1991), the gender gap in time spent on mental labor is similar to the gap in time spent on housework itself. In addition, the kinds of tasks that married men and women think about are as gender typed as their actual performance of household tasks, which is consistent with the argument that women are held accountable for the success of these tasks but not for those less gender typed (Twiggs, McQuillan, & Ferree, 1999).

Comparisons of Survey and ESM Time-Use Estimates

Table 6.1 shows the statistical significance of differences between survey self-reports of time on each housework task and the three ESM estimates discussed above. We see that survey self-reports of husbands differ significantly from ESM estimates for the total of all tasks and for all separate tasks except cooking. For wives, survey self-reports differ significantly from ESM estimates of the total of all tasks and from ESM estimates of all separate tasks except yard and home maintenance.

The bottom row of Table 6.1 gives estimates of total housework hours obtained from survey (self and spouse) and ESM (primary, primary plus secondary, and primary plus secondary plus mental). It also shows tests of the statistical significance of differences between the measures. We see that husbands' hours of housework reported on the survey differ significantly both from wives' survey estimates of husbands' time and from all ESM estimates of his time—those including only primary activity, primary plus secondary activity, and primary plus secondary plus mental labor. Wives' survey reports of their hours spent on housework do not differ significantly from husbands' reports of wife's hours but do differ significantly from all ESM estimates of wives' hours.

Table 6.2 shows the difference between husbands' and wives' time spent on housework and the share of housework done by the husband for each of the five estimates. The first row of Table 6.2 gives wives' survey reports of their own time on housework and their husbands' time on housework. The second row gives husbands' survey reports of their own and their wives' time. The next three rows give estimates from the ESM, using primary activities only, primary plus secondary activities, and primary and secondary activities plus mental labor, for husbands and wives. Column 3 gives the difference in hours spent on housework (wives' hours minus husbands' hours), and Column 4 gives the proportion of housework done by the husband for each of the measures. Note that for all estimates, husbands' hours differ significantly from wives' hours.

The Gender Gap in Housework

Husbands and wives have different perceptions of the gap in their contributions to household labor, as Table 6.2 shows, even though they agree that wives spend more time on housework

TABLE 6. 2 Estimates of Number of Hours Spent on Housework per Week, Difference in Hours Between Husband and Wife, and Proportion Done by Husband: Survey and the ESM ($N = 265$)

	Wives	Husbands	Difference	Proportion Done by Husband (%)
Survey				
Wives' report on self and spouse	26.0	12.8	13.2**	33
Husbands' report on self and spouse	24.9	17.7	7.2**	42
The ESM				
Primary	15.0	10.0	5.0**	40
Primary + secondary	21.3	13.0	8.3**	38
Primary + secondary + mental labor	24.4	15.3	9.1**	39

*$p < .05$. **$p < .01$.

than husbands do. On average, the difference in husbands' reports of their own and their spouse's time on housework is 7.2 hours, whereas for wives the difference is 13.2 hours. In both cases, the difference between estimates of own time and estimates of spouse's time is statistically significant.

Various estimates differ in the conclusions they would suggest about husband's share of housework, as Column 4 of Table 6.2 shows. The lowest estimate of husband's share—33%—comes from the wife's responses on both her time on household tasks and her husband's time on those same tasks. The highest estimate—42%—comes from the husband's responses for both himself and his wife. Estimates of husband's share based on ESM data fall between those based on answers to survey questions. All three ESM measures of the husband's share are virtually identical.

CONCLUSIONS

Using data collected through surveys and the ESM for husbands and wives from the same families in the Sloan 500 Family Study, we develop and compare a series of estimates for the division of household labor, which range from restrictive to inclusive. These estimates differ in the method of data collection, in who answers the questions and about whom they are asked, and what activities are included as housework. These estimates allow us to address our research questions.

First, to what extent are estimates of husbands' and wives' housework time affected by who provides the information? Our results suggest that the answer is *quite dramatic.*

We find that husbands and wives provide similar estimates of wives' time on household labor but divergent estimates of husbands' contributions. Previous studies often assume that husbands overestimate their own contribution (Press & Townsley, 1998) but that both husbands and wives make accurate assessments of the wife's time (Kamo, 2000). We find little support

for this view. Analyses of the data from surveys and the ESM support the argument that wives make accurate estimates of husbands' time on housework, whereas husbands overestimate their own time. But these same analyses also suggest that both wives and husbands may substantially overestimate the amount of time wives spend on housework. These biases lead men and women to have different perceptions about the size of the gender gap in household labor. Our results suggest that, on average, wives in the Sloan Study think that they do 13 hours more housework per week than their husbands do. But husbands see the gap in hours as only about half as large. These different perceptions of each spouse's contribution may lead to marital conflict (Hochschild, 1989), regardless of the actual amount of time that husbands and wives allocate to household labor (Wilkie, Ferree, & Ratcliff, 1998).

Second, does the data collection method affect the estimates obtained? Our results suggest that it does, and that the differences between survey measures and ESM time-use measures are statistically significant and—for some estimates—quite substantial. Our ESM estimates of *primary activities only* show that wives in our sample spend 15 hours per week on housework. Survey estimates based on the wives' responses on their own time on housework show 26 hours per week. This large and statistically significant difference in estimates between methods for the same individuals points to a substantial challenge for measurement of time spent on household labor.

Third, does inclusion of secondary activities matter? Our results suggest that it does, although the effect is modest. Estimates of housework time for wives increase from 15 to 21.2 hours, with the inclusion of secondary activities. ESM data show that wives are more likely than husbands to report performance of household tasks as their secondary activity, so that adding secondary activities increases the housework gender gap from 5 to 8.2 hours and reduces the share of housework done by the husband slightly from 40% to 38%.

Fourth, to what extent are estimates of housework time and the housework gender gap affected by inclusion of time spent thinking about household tasks? Again, our results suggest that the effect is modest. We find that husbands and wives spend 2–3 hours per week thinking about household labor even when they are not performing household tasks, which supports Mederer's (1993) argument that these tasks are an important component of household labor. We also find that wives spend about 1 hour more per week on this mental labor than their husbands do, so including time spent thinking about housework raises our estimates of the housework gender gap slightly to 9.4 hours per week and decreases husband's share of housework modestly from 40% to 37%.

Fifth, do conclusions about the size of the gender division of labor depend on whether one uses absolute differences in hours or the proportion of housework done by the husband? This is a complicated question to answer. Hours provide a convenient metric, easily translated into dollars given a wage rate or into days lost to work or leisure. So, a gender gap of 13 hours, which we estimate if we use the wife's report of her own and her husband's time on housework, suggests that women are working almost 2 full days more than their husbands, on average. Interpreting the proportion of housework done by husbands is more complicated because this measure depends on both how much time the husband spends cleaning, shopping, and doing yard work *and* how much time the wife spends on similar tasks. Husband's share can go up because either he does more or his wife does less, as Bianchi et al. (2000) point out.

We find that the proportion of housework done by the husband varies from 33% to 42% over our various estimates. The absolute gap varies from 5.0 to 13.2 hours. Note that both the largest absolute gaps and the smallest proportion done by the husband come from the wife's estimates of her time and her husband's time. The smallest absolute gap in hours comes from ESM estimates that include primary activity only.

Implications of these findings are clear: Conclusions about the size of the gender gap in housework depend substantially on who provides the information about time spent on housework, what information that person is asked to provide, and how housework is defined. Results show large and statistically significant differences between survey self-reports of housework time and those estimated from the ESM collected in response to random signals over the course of a week for primary activities. This suggests that researchers should be quite cautious in their use of measures that simply add together respondent reports on the amount of time spent in a typical week on a series of housework tasks. This method of assessing total hours spent on housework seems to provide an upper-bound estimate. Comparison of survey and ESM estimates suggests that wives inflate their own time substantially more than they inflate their husbands', whereas husbands overestimate both their own time and their wives' time more consistently. This means that studies that use both the wife's report of her own time on housework and her report of her husband's time on housework (Goldscheider & Waite, 1991) contain substantial bias that differs for the husband and wife.

Results reported here also suggest that researchers should give considerable thought to the treatment of housework done as a secondary activity. A sizable proportion of time spent on housework is done in conjunction with other activities, often other housework tasks.

Consideration of housework done as a secondary activity gives us a way to reconcile the very large differences between survey responses and time-use data in estimates of own time in household labor. Tasks done frequently, in small blocks of time, seem to be difficult for respondents to summarize into a number of hours a week spent on that task. Thus, they may think of the task as taking the whole block of time during which it was done, rather than as 10 minutes here and there within that block while other activities consumed the remainder.

This study has a number of limitations that must be kept in mind. First, the data used in this study are limited in ways that may affect the results. The married couples in the sample were selected from a small number of communities, so the sample is not nationally representative. The married couples that agreed to participate in this study may also differ from those in the nation as a whole in the amount of time they spend on housework. A larger and perhaps more important issue is that most husbands and wives in the sample are drawn from middle-or upper-middle-class communities, with relatively high levels of education and income compared to the population of the United States as a whole. These families purchase more services to replace spouses' time in housework than most families in the United States (Spitze, 1999). Highly educated men and women also tend to hold more liberal attitudes than others toward the appropriate role for men and women and toward the division of household labor, which tends to increase husband's participation. For these reasons, with a more nationally representative sample, the housework gender gap may be more pronounced. Second, we treat all housework tasks equally, although some recent research (Coltrane, 2000; Twiggs et al., 1999) suggests that tasks differ both in the extent to which they are done more frequently by one gender and in the frequency with which they are done. Future research might explore the differences in measures of housework tasks for these different types. Third, our comparison focuses on housework rather than on the broader category of *household labor*. Future research should explore measurement issues when time spent on child care and on emotional labor are included.

REFERENCES

Bianchi, S. M., Milkie, M. A., Sayer, L. C., & Robinson, J. P. (2000). Is anyone doing the housework? Trends in the gender division of household labor. *Social Forces, 79,* 191–228.

Coleman, M. T. (1988). The division of household labor: Suggestions for future empirical consideration and theoretical development. *Journal of Family Issues, 9,* 132–148.

Coltrane, S. (2000). Research on household labor: Modeling and measuring the social embeddedness of routine family work. *Journal of Marriage and Family, 62,* 1208–1233.

Csikszentmihalyi, M. (1997). *Finding flow: The psychology of engagement with everyday life.* New York: Basic Books.

Goldscheider, F. K., & Waite, L. J. (1991). *New families, no families? The transformation of the American home.* Berkeley: University of California Press.

Hochschild, A. R. (1989). *The second shift.* New York: Avon Books.

Kamo, Y. (2000). "He said, she said": Assessing discrepancies in husbands' and wives' reports on the division of household labor. *Social Science Research, 29,* 459–476.

Marini, M. M., & Shelton, B. A. (1993). Measuring household work: Recent experience in the United States. *Social Science Research, 22,* 361–382.

Mederer, H. J. (1993). Division of labor in two-earner homes: Task accomplishment versus household management as critical variables in perceptions about family work. *Journal of Marriage and Family, 55,* 133–145.

Press, J. E., & Townsley, E. (1998). Wives' and husbands' housework reporting: Gender, class, and social desirability. *Gender & Society, 12,* 188–218.

Presser, H. B. (1994). Employment schedules among dual-earner spouses and the division of household labor by gender. *American Sociological Review, 59,* 348–364.

Robinson, J. P., & Godbey, G. (1997). *Time for life: The surprising ways Americans use their time.* University Park: The Pennsylvania State University Press.

Shelton, B. A., & John, D. (1996). The division of household labor. *Annual Review of Sociology, 22,* 299–322.

Spitze, G. D. (1999). Getting help with housework: Household resources and social networks. *Journal of Family Issues, 20,* 724–745.

Thompson, L. (1991). Family work: Women's sense of fairness. *Journal of Family Issues, 12,* 184–196.

Twiggs, J. E., McQuillan, J., & Ferree, M. M. (1999). Meaning and measurement: Reconceptualizing measures of the division of household labor. *Journal of Marriage and Family, 61,* 712–724.

Wilkie, J. R., Ferree, M. M. & Ratcliff, K. S. (1998). Gender and fairness: Marital satisfaction in two-earner couples. *Journal of Marriage and Family, 60,* 577–594.

78 • UNIT III: MEASUREMENT

QUESTIONS

1. How did the researchers measure time spent on housework?

2. In addition to indicating whether housework was the "main thing" that respondents were doing when beeped, what else does the Experience Sampling Method (ESM) measure?

3. According to the results reported in Table 6.1, do husbands and wives agree on the amount of time that (a) wives spend on housework and (b) husbands spend on housework? (NOTE:

Unless a difference is statistically significant, you should assume that the estimates do not differ [i.e., they "agree"]).

4. Using Table 6.2, compare survey and ESM estimates of wives' and husbands' hours spent on housework. How do they differ? Which measure results in the *lowest* estimate of husbands' share of housework?

5. What do the results of this study imply about the use of survey questions to estimate the gender gap in housework?

UNIT IV

SAMPLING

Social scientists rarely are able to study all the people, places, and events in which they are interested. Therefore, they resort to sampling. Seeking knowledge about a class of objects or events (called a **population**), they observe a subset of these (called a **sample**), and then they extend the findings to the whole class (Stephan & McCarthy, 1958, p. 22). To assess the generalizability of a study's findings, we need to know how the study sample was drawn.

There are two broad approaches to sampling: probability and nonprobability. In **probability sampling**, cases are selected randomly so that all cases in the population have a known probability of being included in the sample. **Nonprobability sampling** refers to any nonrandom method of case selection. The advantages of probability sampling are that it eliminates bias in case selection and makes it possible to statistically estimate sampling error; however, it is not always possible or preferable. To select cases randomly, for example, it is necessary to identify all members of the population; so, if the population is not identifiable, as with many marginal or deviant groups, one must use nonprobability sampling. Moreover, resources such as time, money, and personnel may preclude random sampling.

Probability sampling is a standard feature of surveys and opinion polls, which typically provide precise estimates of population characteristics. In reporting results, pollsters

indicate the margin of sampling error. For example, based on daily telephone interviews with about 1,500 respondents, Gallup tracks the percentage of Americans who approve or disapprove of the job the president is doing. The weekly average for January 2 through 8, 2012, indicated that 46% approved of the job Barack Obama was doing as president (http://www .gallup.com/poll/116479/barack-obama -presidential-job-approval.aspx). The daily poll results have a margin of error of + or − 3%, meaning that the percent approval for all Americans was likely to fall between 43% and 49%.

Nonprobability sampling is common in laboratory experiments, in which subjects often consist of undergraduates who volunteer or receive course credit for participating. It also is a staple of qualitative research, where small samples and research goals tend to favor nonrandom selection. If one is conducting in-depth interviews with a very small number of cases, for example, it usually is better to use expert judgment (i.e., nonrandom selection) than to rely on chance. And in exploratory studies, where the goal is to become more informed about a group or topic, one need not be concerned about precise statistical generalization.

Within each of these two broad sampling methods, there are various ways to select cases. In probability sampling, the specific method depends on the availability of a list of the population and, when personal interviews are conducted, the geographical dispersion of the population. For example, with relatively small, geographically concentrated populations such as universities, researchers may use **simple random sampling**, in which they select cases randomly from a readily available list of the student population. With larger, dispersed populations for which a complete list does not exist, researchers use **multi-stage cluster sampling** in which the population is broken down into segments or clusters such as states, cities, and blocks, and random selection occurs in stages. Because they wanted to accurately describe the nation's sexual beliefs and habits, the authors of the first selection used multi-stage cluster sampling to select respondents for a personal interview survey.

Likewise, researchers may draw nonprobability samples in various ways. For example, they may select a **convenience sample** by interviewing conveniently available passersby on a street corner or asking for volunteers to participate in an experiment. They may use a process of chain referral, called **snowball sampling**, by first interviewing known members of the population and asking each interviewee to provide the names and contact information of other members of the population, who are then contacted and asked to name others, and so on. Or, researchers may use **purposive sampling** in which they use their expert judgment to draw a sample that is representative of the larger target population. Kathleen Blee, author of the second selection, used purposive sampling to draw a small sample of women who belonged to racist groups.

Both probability and nonprobability sampling have their strengths and limitations. As you read the selections in this unit and others to come, think about whether the particular sampling strategy achieves the goals of the studies.

REFERENCES

Stephan, F. J., & McCarthy, P. J. (1958). *Sampling opinions: An analysis of survey procedure.* New York: Wiley.

RESOURCES

The American Association for Public Opinion Research (AAPOR):

http://www.aapor.org/Bad_Samples1.htm

- This specific link is to what the AAPOR calls "bad samples." Not only is this linked material instructive, it can also be quite humorous. The website, as a whole, is devoted to survey research; more information about sampling can be found at: http://www.aapor.org/What_is_a_Random_Sample_1.htm

How Polls Are Conducted:

http://media.gallup.com/PDF/FAQ/HowArePolls.pdf

- An excerpt from the book, *Where America Stands,* this essay provides an overview of how the Gallup organization conducts public opinion telephone surveys. Gallup poll editors describe the selection of a random sample and the selection of respondents within households.

A Sample of a Sample: How the Typical Respondent Is Found:

http://www.nytimes.com/library/national/110499poll-watch.html

- Many opinion polls these days are based on telephone interviews that use random-digit dialing for sample selection. This brief nontechnical article describes the random-digit dialing sampling procedure of the *New York Times*/CBS News Poll.

Research Randomizer:

http://randomizer.org/

- If you need to draw a random sample for a study, you may want to visit this website. It generates random numbers, which you can then match to names from your (numbered) list of the population. Some commonly used software programs can also do this.

Custom Insight, Talent Management Solutions:

http://www.custominsight.com/articles/random-sample-calculator.asp

- The authors of the first selection discuss the importance of sample *size*. In case you missed the link to this from the AAPOR's general sampling page, this website allows you to calculate the sample size one needs at different levels of sampling error. Needless to say, this website is for the statistically inclined.

Sampling for Qualitative Research:

http://fampra.oxfordjournals.org/content/13/6.toc (see Marshall, 522–526)

- This brief article contrasts quantitative and qualitative approaches to sampling, points out the inappropriateness of random sampling for qualitative research such as Blee's study of women in the hate movement (Selection 8), and describes three broad methods of selecting a sample in qualitative studies.

Selection 7

In 1993, Robert Michael, John Gagnon, and Edward Laumann completed the first methodologically sound survey of American sexual practices and beliefs, the National Health and Social Life Survey (NHSLS). Prior to this time, many other sex surveys had been conducted, but all of them used, as Michael and colleagues bluntly put it, "methods guaranteed to yield worthless results" (Michael et al., 1994, p. 16).

Foremost among the flawed methods were the procedures for selecting respondents, including those used by Alfred Kinsey in his well-known sex survey. In this selection from *Sex in America,* the authors contrast Kinsey's sampling methods with their own research. As you read, note the key differences between Kinsey's methods and the scientific sampling techniques of Michael and colleagues' national survey.

THE SEX SURVEY

ROBERT T. MICHAEL, JOHN H. GAGNON,
EDWARD O. LAUMANN, AND GINA KOLATA

Of all the studies that purport to tell about sex in America, the vast majority are unreliable; many are worse than useless. As social scientists, we found that the well-established survey methods that can so accurately describe the nation's voting patterns or the vicissitudes of the labor force rarely were used to study sexuality. And the methods that were used in many of the popular studies had flaws so deep and so profound that they render the data and their interpretations meaningless.

The era of large sex surveys began with the Kinsey reports.[1] And the story of those reports illustrates what has gone wrong with attempts to study sex in America.

Alfred Kinsey felt that standard sample survey methods were a practical impossibility when it came to the subject of sex, so he compromised. Kinsey's compromise was to take his subjects where he could find them. He and his associates went to college sororities and fraternities, college classes and student groups, rooming houses, prisons, mental hospitals, social organizations of many kinds, and friendship groups in which one interview might lead to others. For a fourteen-year period, he even collared hitchhikers in town.

One looming problem was that the people Kinsey interviewed could not stand in for all Americans. A fraternity here, a college class there, a PTA from a third place, and a group of homosexual men from somewhere else do not, taken together, reflect the population of the United States.

Instead of studying randomly selected members of the population, Kinsey interviewed what is called a sample of convenience, a sample that consisted of volunteers that he recruited or who came to him. This introduced two problems. First, the people he interviewed could not be thought of as representative of anyone in the population other than themselves. They got into the sample because they were relatively convenient for Kinsey to find and persuade to participate, or because they offered to participate on their own. Consequently, while they may have told the truth about their own sex lives, neither Kinsey nor anyone else can know how to generalize from these people to say anything useful or accurate about the whole population or about any particular subset of the population.

It's like interviewing people near the train station at 8:45 in the morning to ask how they usually get to work. If 80 percent of them say they take the train, no one would use that fact to generalize that 80 percent of the people who commute to work in that city take the train.

The second problem was that many of Kinsey's respondents volunteered to be in the study. For a sex survey, it seems likely that those who do volunteer and those who do not have different behavior, different experiences, and different attitudes about sex. If so, the data that are collected from volunteers will give an inaccurate picture of the whole population. By including the sexual histories of those who especially want to be counted in the survey, that survey gives a biased picture. This is true for any survey, not just one on sexual behavior. Many studies have suggested that people who volunteer

for surveys are not like people who do not volunteer,[2] and there is some evidence that people who volunteer for sex surveys have wider sexual experience than those who do not. In addition, there is evidence that people who engage in highly stigmatized behaviors, such as incest, may refuse to be interviewed or would not volunteer to do so.

So, since Kinsey did not select his respondents in a way that permitted generalization, the data he obtained are at best interesting facts about the people he interviewed but are not useful for making statements about the population at large.

Yet though the study was flawed, even by the standards of the time, Kinsey's data shocked the nation and became enshrined as the nation's report card on sexual behavior. The subtext of his books, and what particularly outraged many of his critics, was Kinsey's view that a wide variety of sexual practices were normal and biologically based, part of the animal world as well as part of human society.

Although some statisticians pointed out that Kinsey's methods of sampling were bound to lead to unreliable data, skewed toward an exaggeration of Americans' sexual activities, his data were all we had and their inadequacies went little noticed in the sea of criticism over what they would do to the moral fabric.

Our study, called the National Health and Social Life Survey, or NHSLS, has findings that often directly contradict what has become the conventional wisdom about sex. They are counterrevolutionary findings, showing a country with very diverse sexual practices but one that, on the whole, is much less sexually active than we have come to believe.

There are good reasons, however, to believe that our new data more accurately reflect the behavior of the adult American population. Our survey, in contrast to the "reports" that preceded it, was a truly scientific endeavor, using advanced and sophisticated methods of social science research. These methods had been developed and used in the past for investigations of such things as political opinions, labor force participation and hours of work, expenditure patterns, or migration behavior. Like studies of less emotionally charged subjects, studies of sex can succeed if respondents are convinced that there is a legitimate reason for doing the research, that their answers will be treated nonjudgmentally, and that their confidentiality will be protected.

In our original study design we wanted a sample size of 20,000, which would enable us to analyze separately data from people who are members of small subpopulations. For example, if 4 percent of the population were gay, a sample size of 20,000 men and women would yield about 400 homosexual men and 400 homosexual women, enough for us to analyze their responses separately.

In the process of designing our survey, it was clear that we would not be able to achieve this sample size with the limited resources of the private sector. We received enough money from private foundations to study nearly 3,500 adults, enough to be extremely confident about the accuracy of the data as a whole, but the sample would not be large enough for detailed analyses of small minority groups (most political polls, for example, have a sample size of 1,000 to 1,500, which gives them sampling errors of no more than 3 percent).

We knew, because we used established statistical sampling techniques, that our respondents represented the general population. In addition, we purposely included slightly more blacks and Hispanics so that we would have enough members of these minority groups to enable us to analyze their responses separately, with confidence that they made statistical sense.

We would have liked to have done the same for homosexuals, including more gay men and lesbians so that we could analyze their replies separately. However, homosexuals are not so easily identified, and for good reason, because their preferences for a partner of the same gender should be private if they want them to be. But that means we could not so easily find an expanded representative sample of homosexuals as we could find blacks or Hispanics. And that means that we could not analyze homosexual behavior separately, asking, for example, how many partners gay men and lesbians have in their lifetimes or where they met their partners. But we included homosexual sex as part of sex in general, so when we ask a question such as, "How often do you have sex?" we do not distinguish between homosexuals and heterosexuals.

The most important part of our study was the way we selected the people to be interviewed. It can be tricky, and subtle, to pick out a group that represents all Americans. For example, you might say you will go to every neighborhood and knock on the door of the corner house on each block. But that would not give you a representative sample because people who live in corner houses are different from other people—as a rule, they are richer than their neighbors on the block because corner houses tend to cost more. Or you might say you'll find married couples by taking every couple that got married in June. But then you would end up with too few Jews because there is a proscription in Judaism against marrying in certain weeks that often fall in June.

Of course, the most obvious way might be to randomly select individuals from households across the country. But finding and interviewing people scattered across the United States can be very expensive, so social scientists have found a cheaper, but equally valid, way of identifying a representative sample. Essentially, we choose at random geographic areas of the country, using the statistical equivalent of a coin toss to select them. Within these geographic regions, we randomly select cities, towns, and rural areas. Within those cities and towns we randomly select neighborhoods. Within those neighborhoods, we randomly select households.

This method gave us 9,004 addresses. Naturally, since the addresses were generated by a computer, many of the addresses either did not have a residence on them or had a residence on them that was empty. Others had a household but no one who lived there was eligible for our survey—they were not between the ages of eighteen and fifty-nine or did not speak English. We determined that 4,635 of the original 9,004 household addresses were ineligible for one of those reasons, so that left us with 4,369 households that did have someone living in them who was eligible to participate in the study. Although it may seem that our sample shrank quite a bit from the original 9,004 addresses, that is normal and to be expected. We did not say we wanted a random sample of addresses for our survey. We wanted a representative sample of Americans who were aged eighteen to fifty-nine and who spoke English.

We selected the individual in a household to interview by a random process. In effect, if there were two people living in a household who were in our age range, we flipped a coin to select which one to interview. If there were three people in the household, we did the equivalent of flipping a three-sided coin to select one of them to interview.

[Many "reports" of sexual practices, such as those by *Playboy* and *Redbook* magazines, are based on people who volunteer to fill out a questionnaire. However,] the difference between this method and the method used [in our survey] is profound. [In self-selected opinions surveys,] anyone who wants to be interviewed can be. In our surveys, we did not let anyone be interviewed unless we selected them. If we selected a man who offered his wife in his stead, saying he was too busy to be interviewed, we declined to interview her. And if he adamantly refused to be interviewed, his refusal counted against us. He is a nonrespondent, even though his wife might have been eager to fill in for him.

Of all the eligible households, our interviewers completed 3,432 interviews, so we have the remarkable outcome that nearly four out of every five persons we wanted to interview, across the nation, were willing to sit down and answer a ninety-minute questionnaire about their sexual behavior and other aspects of their sex lives. This response rate is even more remarkable because it includes as nonresponders people who simply could not be found to be interviewed.

Once we had the data, we asked whether the 3,432 respondents, as a group, were representative of the population of those aged eighteen to fifty-nine in the United States. In fact, our sample turned out to be exactly like other highly reputable and scientifically valid national samples.

Table 7.1 shows a few of the comparisons we made, using our unweighted sample that excludes the extra blacks and Hispanics that we added on purpose. We compared our group to the Census Bureau's Current Population Survey of over 140,000 people for 1991 as the benchmark. It is the best information that demographers can get about the characteristics of the population.

The similarities between our sample and the Current Population Survey of the Census Bureau extend to age, education level, and marital status, as Table 7.1 illustrates. This extraordinary similarity of our sample to the U.S. population, from which we randomly selected our respondents, provides assurance that the respondents who were interviewed were representative of the population of all Americans aged eighteen to fifty-nine.

We also looked at the proportions of men and women who answered our questions. We knew from the census data that 49.7 percent of Americans aged eighteen to fifty-nine are men. Among our respondents, 44.6 percent are men. Other surveys that are of high quality, like the General Social Survey and the National Survey of Family and Households, had virtually the same percentages of men and women as we have. The General Social Survey has 43.8 percent men and the National Survey of Families and Households had 43.0 percent men. So we can say with confidence that the people who agreed to participate in our survey of sexual behavior were just like the population at large in their gender. We were not disproportionately interviewing—or failing to interview—either men or women.

Now there are many people in the nation who are not represented in our survey. We can speak with confidence about the behavior of the noninstitutionalized, currently housed population aged eighteen to fifty-nine. We can say nothing about those who currently live in institutions like hospitals or jails or about the homeless or about those who are under age eighteen or older than fifty-nine [or about people who speak a language other than English]. Our sample did not include those groups. But 97.1 percent of [English-speaking] American adults aged eighteen to

TABLE 7.1 Comparison of Social Characteristics in NHSLS and U.S. Population

	U.S. Population	*NHSLS*
Gender		
Men	49.7%	44.6%
Women	50.3	55.4
	100%	100%
Age		
18–24	18.2%	15.9%
25–29	14.3	14.5
30–39	29.5	31.3
40–49	22.7	22.9
50–59	15.3	15.3
	100%	100%
Education		
Less than high school	15.8%	13.9%
High school or equivalent	64.0	62.2
Any college	13.9	16.6
Advanced	6.3	7.3
	100%	100%
Marital status		
Never married	27.7%	28.2%
Currently married	58.3	53.3
Divorced, separated	12.4	16.2
Widowed	1.6	2.3
	100%	100%
Race/ethnicity		
White	75.9%	76.5%
Black	11.7	12.7
Hispanic	9.0	7.5
Other	3.3	3.3
	100%	100%

Notes: NHSLS unweighted cross-section sample of 3,159.

Gender: Bureau of the Census, Current Population Survey, 1991.

Age, Race/Ethnicity: Bureau of the Census, Current Population Survey, 1991.

Education: Bureau of the Census, Current Population Survey, 1990.

Marital Status: Bureau of the Census, Current Population Survey, 1992.

fifty-nine in the nation are represented, and this is the first large-scale study of the broad and inclusive dimensions of the sexual patterns and experiences of this large majority of Americans. All this checking of our data has convinced us that this sample is an excellent one from which we can make generalizations about sex in America and we do so with confidence.

NOTES

1. Alfred C. Kinsey, Wendell B. Pomeroy, and Clyde E. Martin, *Sexual Behavior in the Human Male* (Philadelphia: W. B. Saunders Co., 1948); Alfred C. Kinsey, Wardell B. Pomeroy, Clyde E Martin, and Paul H. Gebhard, *Sexual Behavior in the Human Female* (Philadelphia: W. B. Saunders Co., 1953).

2. Norman M. Bradburn and Seymour Sudman, *Polls and Surveys: Understanding What They Tell Us* (San Francisco: Jossey-Bass Publishers, 1988).

QUESTIONS

1. Kinsey interviewed what the authors call a "sample of convenience," or more simply, a "convenience sample." What are the two major problems associated with this type of sample that make it impossible to use as a basis for generalizing to the larger population?

2. Explain why the researchers were able to separately analyze the survey responses of blacks and Hispanics but not homosexuals.

3. The survey that Michael and colleagues conducted, the National Health and Social Life Survey (NHSLS), used multi-stage cluster sampling. Describe the steps or stages involved in selecting their sample of addresses or households.

4. One indicator of survey quality is the **response rate**: the number of completed interviews divided by the number of sampled or eligible households. What was the response rate of the NHSLS?

5. One way to evaluate the representativeness of a sample is to compare it with other established, scientifically valid samples of the same population. How did selected characteristics of the NHSLS compare with the same characteristics of the Current Population Survey?

Selection 8

Racist groups such as the Ku Klux Klan and Aryan Nations "are routinely condemned and shunned" by mainstream society (Blee, 2002, p. 192), as they should be. Yet, to design effective strategies to combat such groups and the ideas that they espouse, we must understand why people choose to join them. Based on this premise, Blee set out to interview women in a variety of racist groups to learn about their identities, life histories, and beliefs. One of the difficulties in studying groups such as these is identifying and selecting members to interview. Blee describes how she used systematic, albeit nonrandom, methods to select a broad-based, national sample of women in the hate movement. As you read, make note of how she sought to overcome the obstacles to drawing a representative sample of this population.

CROSSING A BOUNDARY

KATHLEEN M. BLEE

Intense, activist racism typically does not arise on its own; it is learned in racist *groups*. These groups promote ideas radically different from the racist attitudes held by many whites. They teach a complex and contradictory mix of hatred for enemies, belief in conspiracies, and allegiance to an imaginary unified race of "Aryans." Women are the newest recruiting targets of racist groups, and they provide a key to these groups' campaign for racial supremacy. "We are very picky when we come to girls," one woman told me. "We don't like sluts. The girls must know their place but take care of business and contribute a lot too. Our girls have a clean slate. Nobody could disrespect us if they tried.

We want girls [who are] well educated, the whole bit. And tough as shit."

The groups and networks that espouse and promote openly racist and anti-Semitic, and often xenophobic and homophobic, views and actions are what I call "organized racism." Organized racism is more than the aggregation of individual racist sentiments. It is a social milieu in which venomous ideas—about African Americans, Jews, Hispanics, Asians, gay men and lesbians, and others—take shape. Through networks of groups and activists, it channels personal sentiments of hatred into collective racist acts. Organized racism is different from the racism widespread in mainstream white

Source: *Inside Organized Racism: Women in the Hate Movement,* by Kathleen M. Blee, 2002, Berkeley: University of California. Copyright 2002 University of California Press.

society: it is more focused, self-conscious, and targeted at specific strategic goals.

When I began my research, I wanted to understand the paradoxes of organized racism. Were, I wondered, the increased numbers of women changing the masculine cast of racist groups? Why, I asked myself, did racist activists continue to see Jews, African Americans, and others as enemies, and why did they regard violence as a racial solution? Convinced that we can defeat organized racism only if we know how it recruits and retains its members, I also wanted to learn why people join organized racism and how being in racist groups affects them.

FOCUSING ON RACIST WOMEN

To understand organized racism from the inside—from the experiences and beliefs of its members—I decided that I needed to talk with racist activists. I chose to interview women for a variety of reasons. On a practical level, I found that I could get access to women racists and develop some measure of rapport with them. More substantively, I wanted to study women racists because we know so little about them. Since 1980 women have been actively recruited by U.S. racist groups both because racist leaders see them as unlikely to have criminal records that would draw the attention of police and because they help augment membership rolls. Today, women are estimated to constitute nearly 50 percent of new members in some racist groups, leading some antiracist monitoring groups to claim that they are the "fastest growing part of the racist movement."[1] Yet this new group of racist activists has been ignored, as researchers have tended to view racism as male-dominated and racist women as more interested in domestic and personal concerns than in its politics.

METHODOLOGY

The women in this study are broadly representative of the range of women racial activists across the country and represent the only relatively systematic sample of racist group members in the contemporary United States. A statistically random sample of racist activists is not possible because there is no comprehensive list of racist activists or even a reliable estimate of their numbers. Except for a few public leaders, most racist activists are interested in keeping themselves hidden from the public, and the scholarly, eye. The few studies that have looked at members rather than leaders of racist groups have drawn on small numbers, generally members known personally to the researcher or referred by known members. They also tend to focus on a single racist group or a single geographic area.

To create a broadly based, national sample of women racist group members, I began by collecting and reading all newsletters, magazines, flyers and recordings of music and speeches, websites, television and radio programs, videotapes, telephone and fax messages, and other communications generated or distributed by every self-proclaimed racist, anti-Semitic, white supremacist, Christian Identity, neo-Nazi, white power skinhead, and white separatist organization in the United States for a one-year period from 1993 to 1994. These were gathered from all groups that I could identify through my contacts with self-proclaimed racist activists, through citations in the primary and secondary scholarly literature, from lists maintained by major antiracist and anti-Semitic monitoring and activist organizations (including the Anti-Defamation League of B'nai B'rith, the Southern Poverty Law Center, and the Center for Democratic Renewal), from archival collections on right-wing extremism at Tulane University and the University of Kansas, and from references in the literature of other racist groups. As a result, I collected publications by more than one hundred different groups, most of which issued items at least two times during that year.

I used these materials to determine which groups had significant numbers of women members or women in visible or leadership roles. I then selected approximately thirty groups from among those with active women members or leaders (overlap makes several of these difficult to differentiate). I selected groups that varied in their ideological emphases and form of organization so that I could assess whether these characteristics affected the recruitment and commitment of women members.

To examine whether racist groups that are remnants of racist activities in rural southern areas differ from those in other regions, I also selected groups from every region of the country, with nine from the South, ten from the West Coast, eight from the Midwest, and three from the East Coast. They were located in fifteen different states, with the greatest concentrations in Georgia (four), Oklahoma (three), Oregon (four), and Florida (four). Such geographical dispersion reflects the landscape of organized racism today. Racist groups can be found in almost every area of the country, but they are particularly concentrated in the Pacific Northwest and the northern sections of the West Coast, in part because many racist group members from various parts of the country have migrated to this region in search of a pristine "white homeland."[2]

After identifying a sample of racist groups, I still faced the problem of identifying women to be interviewed. Most racist publications do not publish the actual names of members other than those who are public spokespersons for the group. Many racist activists and even some spokespersons use aliases or code names, such as "Viking Mary." Thus, finding women to be interviewed was a protracted process. I was able to contact a few women through their groups, but generally this direct approach was inadvisable: racist activists are highly suspicious of and hostile to unknown outsiders. I relied most often on a more indirect approach, using personal referrals and contacts to break through layers of evasion, deception, and political and personal posturing. To find racist women, I drew on contacts that I had established in my earlier research. I also located women racists through parole officers, correctional officials, newspaper reporters and journalists, other racist activists and former activists, federal and state task forces on gangs, attorneys, and other researchers. Although they might seem to be an unlikely source of referrals, police and criminal

investigators were valuable contacts for some young racist skinheads, who both hate such authorities and find themselves occasionally dependent on them for protection from abusive peers and the dangers of life on the streets.

To ensure a variety of experiences and perspectives, I selected all the women from my target groups. This method provides a more representative look at organized racism than does a reliance on snowball samples (in which interviewees are referred by prior interviewees) or samples of convenience (in which interviewees are selected based on their accessibility to the researcher), techniques commonly used in studies of difficult-to-locate populations. Even when one interviewee was likely to know women in a group that I was interested in contacting, I rarely made use of this connection because I did not want the women to have the opportunity to slant their narratives to fit, or perhaps to contradict, stories told by earlier interviewees from related or antagonistic groups. Word of my research project spread quickly among networks of racist activists, at once putting me in the awkward position of declining to interview some women who wanted to be part of the study and helping me gain the confidence of others. The knowledge that I had interviewed someone in the past who did not immediately become the target of criminal investigation added credibility to my claim that I was not feeding information to prosecutors.

To explore whether women at different levels of racist group hierarchies vary in their racist identification or commitment, I searched for women in various positions in their groups. I selected four who were leaders known both in and outside the movement, ten who were leaders but who were not known publicly, and twenty who were rank-and-file members of racist groups. I also sought women of disparate ages in an effort to assess whether the appeal of racist groups might be understood differently by those at different ages or with different levels of family responsibilities.

Eventually, I persuaded thirty-four women from a variety of racist and anti-Semitic groups across the country to talk to me at length about themselves and their racist activities. Fourteen women were in neo-Nazi but not skinhead groups, six were members of Ku Klux Klans, eight were white power skinheads, and six were in Christian Identity or related groups.

Why were these racist women willing to talk to me? They had a variety of reasons. Some hoped to generate publicity for their groups or themselves—a common motivation for granting interviews to the media. Many saw an opportunity to explain their racial politics to a white outsider, even one decidedly unsympathetic to their arguments. In a racist variant on the religious imperative to "bear witness" to the unconverted,[3] they wanted the outside world to have an accurate (even if negative) account to counter superficial media reports. As one young woman put it, "I don't know what your political affiliations are, but I trust that you'll try to be as objective as possible." Others wished to support or challenge what they imagined I had been told in earlier interviews with racist comrades or competitors. And, despite their deep antagonism toward authority figures, some young women were flattered to have their opinions solicited by a university professor. They had rarely encountered someone older who talked with them without being patronizing, threatening, or directive.

From the beginning, when I asked women if I could interview them, I made it clear that I did not share the racial convictions of these groups. I explicit said that my views were quite opposed to theirs, that they should not hope to convert me to their views, but that I would try to depict women racist activists accurately. I revealed my critical stance but made it clear that I had no intent to portray them as crazy and did not plan to turn them over to law enforcement or mental health agencies.

I was prepared to elaborate on my disagreements with organized racism in my interviews, but in nearly every case the women cut me short, eager to talk about themselves. What they told me shatters many common ideas about what racist activists are like. Among the women I interviewed there was no single racist type. The media depict unkempt, surly women in faded T-shirts, but the reality is different. One of my first interviews was with Mary, a vivacious Klanswoman who met me at her door with a big smile and ushered me into her large, inviting kitchen. Her blond hair was pulled back into a long ponytail and tied with a large green bow. She wore dangling gold hoop earrings, blue jeans, a modest flowered blouse, and no visible tattoos or other racist insignia. Her only other jewelry was a simple gold-colored necklace. Perhaps sensing my surprise at her unremarkable appearance, she joked that her suburban appearance was her "undercover uniform."

Trudy, an elderly Nazi activist I interviewed somewhat later, lived in a one-story, almost shabby ranch house on a lower-middle-class street in a small town in the Midwest. Her house was furnished plainly. Moving cautiously with the aid of a walker, she brought out tea and cookies prepared for my visit. Meeting her reminded me of the phrase "old country women," which I had once heard from a southern policeman characterizing the rural Klanswomen in his area.

I also interviewed Roseanne, a small, lively white supremacist woman with short-cropped black hair who wore a flowered sundress. We got together in the living room of her government-subsidized apartment in a large, racially mixed housing complex. Her apartment was very small and nearly barren of furniture—making her expensive computer and fax and copy machines dedicated to her work "for the movement" stand out all the more.

My encounters with skinhead women were more guarded, although some were quite animated and articulate. Not one invited me into her home—all I got was a quick glance when I picked her up for an interview in some other location. Most seemed to live at or barely above the level of squatters, in dirty, poorly equipped spaces that were nearly uninhabitable. Their appearance varied. Molly sported five ear piercings that held silver hoops and a silver female sign, an attractive and professionally cut punk hairstyle, fine features, and intense eyes. Others were ghostly figures, with empty eyes and visible scars poorly hidden behind heavy makeup and garish lipstick.

Over a two-year period I spent considerable time with these women, talking to them about their racist commitments and getting them to tell me their life stories. Listening to them describe their backgrounds, I realized that many did not fit common stereotypes about racist women as uneducated, marginal members of society raised in terrible families and lured into racist groups by boyfriends and husbands. Instead, I learned:

- *Most were educated.* Against the idea that racism is the product of ignorance, fourteen of the thirty-four women were in college or held associate or higher degrees. Another fifteen had finished or were currently in high school. Only five had failed to complete high school.
- *Most were not poor.* People generally believe that racism is most intense among poor and lower-working-class people who compete with racial minorities for jobs, housing, and social services. However, most of the women I interviewed had good jobs. They were occupational therapists, nurses, teachers, engineers, librarians, draftspersons, or phone company representatives. Some were attending college; others were not employed but were married to men with decent jobs. Only about one-third were living in more precarious conditions—as waitresses in pizza parlors, as lay ministers in tiny racist churches, as teachers in racist private schools, or as the wives of men who lacked secure employment.
- *For some, poverty was caused by racist activism.* For almost half of those without good jobs (or married to underemployed men), marginal employment was a *consequence,* not a *cause,* of being active in racist politics. Some women (or their husbands) lost their jobs when employers discovered their racist activities, or when they were caught proselytizing racism to customers or fellow employees. Others decided to work in racist enclaves—for example, as teachers in Christian Identity schools—to escape the nefarious influences of the outside world and to contribute to the racist movement.
- *Most did not grow up poor.* Most of the parents of these women had decent jobs. Their fathers

were laboratory technicians, construction workers, store owners, company executives, salesmen, farmers, repairmen, postal workers, architects, doctors, factory foremen, and inspectors as well as Christian Identity "ministers." Their mothers were housewives and Christian Identity schoolteachers as well as nurses, teachers, secretaries, social workers, clerks, computer consultants, corporate executives, real estate agents, and bankers.

- *Most were not raised in abusive families.* Writers often suggest that racist activists are the product of disorganized, uncaring, or abusive families.[4] Yet none of the women I interviewed were raised in foster homes, by relatives, or in institutions. Several grew up in unstable and violent families, ran away from home, or had intense conflicts with parents or stepparents, but it is not clear that such stresses burdened a significantly higher proportion of these women than the population as a whole. In contrast, some women related stories of idyllic family lives, as did the Klanswoman who recalled her "very happy family background [in which] my parents have been married for thirty-two years and all my brothers and sisters and I are very close." Most described their family backgrounds in more mixed terms, as both nurturing and restrictive. In any case, it is difficult to know how childhood experiences are related to racist activism.
- *Not all women followed a man into racism.* Racist women often are seen as compliant followers of the men in their lives. But the women I interviewed described many paths into the racist movement. Several said they and their husbands or boyfriends grew up in the racist movement and followed their family's political path. Four said that they and their husband or boyfriend joined a racist group at the same time, as a mutual decision. Another four said they joined racist groups by themselves and met their current boyfriend or husband at a racist event. Seven said a boyfriend or husband encouraged them to join a racist group. Others followed different patterns, including one woman who followed her son into the racist movement, several who recruited male intimates into racist activism, and a handful whose husbands or boyfriends refused to become involved in organized racism.

NOTES

1. Floyd Cochran, a prominent antiracist activist quoted in Linda Yglesias, untitled in *New York Daily News*, July 27, 1993; clipping in "Aryan Action Line" folder, Anti-Defamation League of B'nai B'rith, New York.

2. "Racists Seek to Form White Homeland in the Northwest," *Albany (Ore.) Democrat-Herald*, June 12, 198

3. On "bearing witness," see Virginia Lieson Brereron, *From Sin to Salvation: Stories of Women's Conversion, 1800 to the Present* (Bloomington: Indiana University Press, 1991). On the perception of researchers as "naïve sympathizers," see Richard G. Mitchell, *Secrecy and Fieldwork* (Newbury Park, Calif.: Sage, 1993), 14.

4. For example, in his study of a racist group in Detroit, *The Racist Mind,* Ezekiel finds family problems and trauma in the background of many of the racist men he interviewed.

QUESTIONS

1. Why did Blee choose to interview female, as opposed to male, racist activists?

2. What prevents researchers from drawing a random sample of racist activists? Prior to Blee's study, how did researchers go about studying members of racist groups?

3. Evaluate Blee's study from the standpoint of generalizability. In what ways did her selection of interviewees constitute a relatively diverse, broadly based, national sample of women members of racist groups?

4. Once she selected a sample of racist *groups*, how did Blee find the women she interviewed?

5. In what ways did the women interviewed by Blee not fit the stereotypes of racist women?

UNIT V

EXPERIMENTS

People unfamiliar with social research may think that any scientific study is an experiment. In fact, however, **experiments** refer to a distinctive approach to social research in which the researcher deliberately alters (or manipulates) some aspect of the environment and then observes the effects of this manipulation. Consider, for example, research on strategies for increasing voter turnout. In one experiment, Donald Gerber and Alan Green (2000) used three strategies to encourage people to vote: (1) personally canvassing one group of registered voters, (2) telephoning a second group, and (3) sending direct mail appeals to a third group. Then, they observed which group was most likely to vote.

Experiments are the most effective approach for determining whether one factor causes another. What makes them so effective is the control that experimenters exert over the conditions of observation. In their voter mobilization study, Gerber and Green (2000) found that people who were personally canvassed were more likely to vote than those who were telephoned or received a direct mail appeal. To gain confidence in such results, experimenters apply procedures to ensure that the only difference between experimental conditions (in this case, the three groups of registered voters) is the manipulated factor (the particular voter turnout strategy). One critical control procedure is **randomization.** To make the three groups

approximately equal in all respects, Gerber and Green randomly assigned registered voters to the experimental conditions; in this way, voters were equally likely to be personally canvassed, to be telephoned, or to receive a direct mail appeal. Another method of control is to make sure that aspects of the environment other than the manipulation are the same throughout the experiment. Thus, Gerber and Green used the same nonpartisan appeals in each condition. In an appeal to civic duty, voters heard or read, "We want to encourage everyone to do their civic duty and exercise their right to vote. Democracy depends on the participation of our country's citizens" (p. 656).

Although experiments provide strong evidence of cause and effect, they have weaknesses that limit their use in social research. Many of the social forces in which social researchers are interested—for example, social movements, residential segregation, poverty—cannot be manipulated. Moreover, because of the need for control, experiments generally examine a very limited set of possible causes and outcomes. A related issue is the extent to which the findings may be generalized beyond the experimental context. Both of the experiments reported in this section address this issue. One study was conducted in the laboratory; the other one in a natural setting. As you read the selections, make note of how the investigators introduce elements of control that strengthen conclusions about cause and effect. At the same time, think about features of the experiments that limit or enhance the generalizability of the findings.

REFERENCES

Gerber, A. S., & Green, D. P. (2000). The effects of canvassing, telephone calls, and direct mail on voter turnout: A field experiment. *American Political Science Review, 94,* 653–663.

RESOURCES

Writing Guide: Experimental and Quasi-Experimental Research

http://writing.colostate.edu/guides/research/experiment/index.cfm

• Part of a site designed as a resource guide for writers at Colorado State University, this page contains a broadly accessible discussion of experimental research. There are links to basic concepts, major steps in planning an experiment, and issues and commentary on doing experiments in educational settings.

Online Social Psychology Studies:

http://www.socialpsychology.org/expts.htm#sinterpersonal

• This page from the Social Psychology Network contains links to more than 200 web-based experiments and other social psychology studies, conducted by both professional and student researchers, as well as web-based experiment resources. Users may participate in a study or add a link to their own study. Resources include how-to guides, software for experimentation, and web-based data collection services.

The Use of Field Experiments for Studies of Employment Discrimination:

http://www.princeton.edu/~pager/publications.htm

• The second selection in this unit describes a field experiment on employment discrimination by Devah Pager. In this article, which can be accessed from Devah Pager's website, she provides a thorough description and critique of this methodology, including an appendix on how to design and implement a field experiment on employment discrimination (called an audit study).

Selection 9

In criminal trials in the United States, prosecuting attorneys are supposed to turn over to the defense any evidence that might pertain to a defendant's guilt or innocence. Not to do so is illegal and is defined as misconduct. Evidence suggests that prosecutorial misconduct may be more prevalent in cases involving severe crimes. Jeffrey Lucas, Corina Graif, and Michael Lovaglia theorize that this may occur because serious crimes exert more pressure on prosecutors to obtain a conviction, making them more inclined to believe that a defendant is guilty. As you read this article, note how the experiment provides a strong test of the investigators' hypotheses while it nevertheless has somewhat limited application to the real world of criminal trials.

MISCONDUCT IN THE PROSECUTION OF SEVERE CRIMES

Theory and Experimental Test

JEFFREY W. LUCAS

CORINA GRAIF

MICHAEL J. LOVAGLIA

The high incidence of procedural errors in the prosecution of serious crimes has caught the attention of legal scholars and social researchers (Gershman 1992; Meares 1995). New investigatory techniques such as DNA testing have led to the overturning of numerous convictions for rape and murder. Bedau and Radelet (1987) found more erroneous convictions in capital murder cases than had been reported in published collections for all other kinds of cases. In an overview, Rattner (1988) found that although homicides represent

---

Source: "Misconduct in the Prosecution of Severe Crimes: Theory and Experimental Test," by Jeffrey W. Lucas, Corina Graif, and Michael J. Lovaglia. 2006, *Social Psychology Quarterly,* 69, 97–107. Copyright 2006 by SAGE Publications.

less than 2 percent of all criminal convictions, they account for 45 percent of known erroneous convictions.

RELEVANT RESEARCH AND THEORETICAL DEVELOPMENT

The discovery of numerous errors in the prosecution of severe crimes raises a question: Do serious criminal cases encourage prosecutorial misconduct (Gross 1996; Meares 1995). Prosecutors theoretically may face increased pressure to convict in trials involving serious crimes, and rewards for high conviction rates in serious cases obtained by prosecutors could lead to higher rates of misconduct in the prosecution of severe crimes. Moreover, if attaining a conviction is more important to prosecutors and if they tend to believe that defendants are guilty in serious cases, then prosecutors could justify their misconduct more easily.

The United States legal system operates under a model of distributive justice based on fault; in this system, it is presumed that severity of crime does not alter perceptions of guilt (MacCoun 1996; Robbennolt 2000). Evidence indicates, however, that more severe crimes may be accompanied by stronger beliefs in a defendant's guilt (Bornstein 1998; Myers 1980). Robbennolt (2000) conducted a meta-analysis of 75 empirical studies on the relationship between outcome severity and perception of responsibility on the part of a potentially accountable individual. The meta-analysis found significantly greater blame attributed to potential perpetrators of more severe crimes. Thus, as the consequences of an act become more severe, the responsibility attributed to the actor becomes greater. In cases involving similar evidence of an individual's guilt, for example, the individual is more likely to be considered guilty by others when the consequences for the victim are more severe (Howe 1991; Sanderson, Zanna, and Darly 2000).

On the basis of this evidence, we propose that when a crime is more severe, prosecutors will be more likely to believe that a suspect is guilty. We further propose that perceptions of guilt may increase the likelihood of misconduct and provide justification. The extensiveness of prosecutorial misconduct in criminal trials in the United States has been well documented (Harmon 2001; Lofquist 2001; Nidiry 1996; Radelet and Bedau 2001), and some observers argue that it is becoming more widespread (Gershman 2001; Lawless and North 1984). It is important to understand the factors that produce this misconduct (Meares 1995); perceptions of a defendant's guilt may be one such factor.

A large body of research demonstrates that individuals develop situation-specific attitudes on the appropriateness of dishonest behavior. Ethical considerations of the situation, for example, are important predictors of such behavior (Birbeck and LaFree 1993; LaBeff et al. 1990). In the case of prosecutorial misconduct, unethical decisions may be tied to "noble cause corruption," in which illegal actions violate citizens' rights for moral reasons (Delattre 1989; Harrison 1999). Because situational factors affect dishonesty, it seems likely that perceptions of the immorality of misconduct decrease as perceptions of a defendant's guilt increase.

HYPOTHESES

Thus we make the following prediction[s]:

Hypothesis 1: Participants prosecuting a murder will be more likely to believe that the defendant is guilty than will participants prosecuting an assault.

Hypothesis 2: Participants prosecuting a murder will view the attainment of a conviction as more personally important than will participants prosecuting an assault.

Hypothesis 3: Participants prosecuting a murder will be more likely to engage in misconduct toward attaining a conviction than will participants prosecuting an assault.

To test these hypotheses, we compare the behaviors and attitudes of individuals prosecuting murders and assaults in contrived criminal trials. Our hypotheses are based on an assumption that participants will view murders as more severe than assaults. If these hypotheses are supported but if participants do not view murders as more severe than assaults, our theoretical propositions will not be supported. Thus we measure participants' perceptions of crime severity through a questionnaire item. In keeping with our theoretical rationale, we expect participants assigned to murder trials to indicate higher perceptions of crime severity than participants assigned to assault trials.

METHODS

Design

We designed a controlled experimental setting that allowed us to compare participants' misconduct when prosecuting a contrived case of severe crime (murder) with their misconduct when prosecuting a less severe crime (assault). The design also allowed us to measure participants' assessments of the defendant's guilt. Each participant was assigned randomly the position of prosecuting a defendant for either murder or assault.

Participants first constructed a case against a defendant. In assembling this case, they had the opportunity to engage in misconduct to increase the likelihood of conviction. Participants then answered a number of questions on their perceptions and behaviors.

Procedure

Participants were recruited from introductory classes at a large Midwestern university and were paid for their participation. Before the beginning of the experiment, each participant was assigned randomly to a criminal case, either murder or assault. In the murder condition, a victim died from injuries sustained during an attack; in the assault condition, the victim recovered fully.

Aside from this difference, the materials given to all participants were identical.

Upon arriving for the experiment, each participant was told that as part of the study, he or she would be acting as a defense attorney, a prosecuting attorney, or a judge in a contrived criminal trial. The participant then was asked to draw one of three slips of paper from a hat to determine his or her role in the study. All the slips, however, contained the word *prosecutor,* so participants always acted as prosecuting attorneys in the study.

The participant then read a packet titled "Police Report," which he or she believed also would be read by the defense attorney and the judge. The report followed a chronological sequence of events, beginning with a call to the police department of Centralia (a fictional city) to report a missing person and ending with criminal charges against a defendant.

By reading the police report, participants learned that police officers traveled to the residence of the individual reported missing. They found the home ransacked and a body in the front hallway. The police report noted that officers then called emergency medical personnel. According to the participant's condition, the medical personnel either pronounced the individual deceased (murder condition) or fully recovered from his injuries in days (assault condition).

Participants learned from the police report that fingerprints on the front door of the victim's home matched those of a convicted felon. After this individual was interviewed, participants read, he left Centralia and was arrested in another city. The police report ended with an indictment against the individual for murder (murder condition) or assault (assault condition).

After reading the police report, participants read a form titled "Facts Relevant to the Case." They believed that both the judge and the defense attorney in the case would read the same form. It described several details of the case; most of these pointed to the defendant as the most likely suspect. Some materials, however, indicated the victim's wife as a possible suspect.

Participants then read a form titled "Your Job—Prosecutor," which explained the duties of the prosecuting attorney during the study. Participants learned that prosecuting attorneys, defense attorneys, and judges would complete the study at different times. Prosecuting attorneys and defense attorneys, they read, assembled cases to present to the judge. The form led participants to believe that if they had been selected as judges, they would have received materials compiled earlier by prosecuting and defense attorneys.

"Your Job—Prosecutor" emphasized that the participants were not to act as detectives: they were not attempting to determine who committed the crimes against the victim. The prosecuting attorney's job, according to the instructions, was only to present the case against the defendant to the best of his or her ability. This would be accomplished by convincing the judge of the defendant's guilt.

Participants also learned that they would be paid on the basis of how well they presented the case against the defendant. They were told that they would receive $10 for participating in the study regardless of the outcome of the trial, but would receive an additional $5 (sent to the participant later) if the judge returned a verdict of "guilty."

The instructions informed participants that as prosecuting attorneys, they would have special responsibilities in the case. Because the defendant had a court-appointed attorney, the prosecution had significantly more resources in collecting evidence than did the defense. Participants read that they, as prosecuting attorneys, would have access to all police interviews. Further, they were obligated by law to turn over to the defense all materials that might point to the defendant's guilt or innocence. If the participant chose not to turn over any such materials, he or she was not likely to be caught. The instructions emphasized, however, that such actions were illegal and were defined as misconduct.

Participants then learned their duties in the trial. First, they were to read through the interviews obtained by police officers. In all, participants read six interviews containing a total of 60 questions, each numbered individually. The first task was to compile a list of questions from the interviews to turn over to the defense. The second task was to select the 10 police interview questions that the participant thought would be most likely to convince the judge of the defendant's guilt. The final task was to write a one-page closing argument to be read by the judge in the case.

Participants then were given a packet containing the interviews. Information in the interviews generally pointed to the defendant's guilt. Four questions, however, contained information identifying the victim's wife as a potential suspect. In one question, for example, a neighbor identified the car of the victim's wife's boyfriend as present in the victim's driveway on the day of the attack.

Participants read through the interviews and completed their three duties. First, they indicated pieces of relevant evidence that they wished to turn over to the defense attorney. To complete this task, they were given a form titled "Questions for Defense," which contained the identifying number of each interview question. Participants circled each question on the form that they wished to submit to the defense; they were permitted to circle all, none, or any number of these questions. We determined misconduct by noting the number of the four questions pointing to the victim's wife as a suspect that participants chose not to turn over to the defense attorney.

The participants' second and third duties in the study (described above) were not relevant to our hypotheses; we included them only to decrease suspicion about the purposes of the list of questions for the defense.

After completing the three duties, participants filled out a post study questionnaire. Items on the questionnaire measured how much prison time the participant believed the perpetrator of the crime deserved, how personally important it was to the participant to attain a conviction in the case, how generally important the participant believed it was to convict the defendant, the extent to which the participant believed that the defendant was guilty, and how likely the participant believed it was that the defendant would be convicted. Participants then were debriefed and paid.

RESULTS

Eighty participants completed the study, 40 in each experimental condition.

Effectiveness of Our Experimental Design

We proposed that severity of crime would affect participants' perceptions of guilt or innocence and their degree of misconduct. In particular, we expected that participants would be more likely to view a suspect as guilty and to engage in misconduct in a murder trial than in an assault trial. That is, we assumed that participants would perceive murder as a more serious crime than assault.

We asked participants to rate the severity of the crime (1 = very severe; 7 = not at all severe). The mean score for participants in the murder condition was 1.28 (sd = .85); for those in the assault condition, 3.03 (sd = 1.44). This difference is in the expected direction; participants regarded murder as more serious than assault. A t-test of the difference is significant (t = 6.62, one-tailed p of difference in predicted direction < .001). Thus we conclude that the participants perceived murder to be more severe than assault.

Tests of Hypotheses

Perceptions of guilt.

Hypothesis 1 predicted that participants in the murder condition would be more likely to view the defendant as guilty than would participants in the assault condition, although identical evidence pointed to the defendant. We tested this hypothesis with a questionnaire item that asked participants to rate on a scale of 1 (definitely not

guilty) to 7 (definitely guilty) how strongly they believed that the defendant was guilty. The mean score on the guilt question for the murder condition was 5.25 (sd = 1.33); for the assault condition, 4.40 (sd = 2.09). This difference is in the predicted direction and is significant (t = 2.17, one-tailed p = .017), and supports Hypothesis 1. Table 9.1 displays mean differences and the results of our hypothesis tests.

Personal importance of attaining a conviction.

Hypothesis 2 predicted that participants in the murder condition would view attaining a conviction as more important than would participants in the assault condition. A posttest questionnaire item asked participants to indicate how strongly they felt that attaining a conviction was personally important (1 = not at all important; 7 = very important). The mean answer on the scale for participants in the murder condition was 5.63 (sd = 1.61); for the assault condition, 4.75 (sd = 1.94). This difference is in the predicted direction: participants in the murder condition viewed a conviction as more personally important. This result is significant (t = 2.19, one-tailed p = .031) and supports Hypothesis 2.

Misconduct.

In Hypothesis 3 we predicted that participants in the murder condition would be more likely to engage in misconduct than participants in the assault condition. We measured misconduct by the number of the four questions pointing to an individual other than the defendant as a potential suspect that participants withheld from the defense. The mean number of these questions withheld from the defense by participants in the murder condition was 2.15 (sd = 1.51); by participants in the assault condition, 1.50 (sd = 1.45). This difference is in the predicted direction: participants in the murder condition were more likely to withhold relevant evidence. A t-test of this difference is significant (t = 1.96, one-tailed p = .027) and supports Hypothesis 3.

TABLE 9.1 Mean Differences and Results of T-tests for Hypotheses

	Mean (SD)	t	p^a
Perceptions of Guilt (7 = high perceptions)			
Murder condition	5.25 (1.33)		
Assault condition	4.40 (2.09)		
Hypothesis 1: Murder condition > assault condition		2.17	0.17
Personal Importance of Conviction (7 = very important)			
Murder condition	5.63 (1.61)		
Assault condition	4.75 (1.94)		
Hypothesis 2: Murder condition > assault condition		2.19	.031
Number of Exculpatory Questions Withheld From Defense			
Murder condition	2.15 (1.51)		
Assault condition	1.50 (1.45)		
Hypothesis 3: Murder condition > assault condition		1.96	.027

aOne-tailed probability values reflect differences in predicted directions.

In addition to behavioral measures on participants' misconduct behavior, a posttest questionnaire item asked participants whether they had withheld relevant material from the defense. Participants were asked to rate the extent to which they believed they had turned over all relevant facts to the defense (1 indicated that they had turned over all relevant information; 7 indicated that they had not done so). The mean score on this scale for participants in the murder condition was 2.70 (sd = 1.91); for participants in the assault condition, 1.93 (sd = 1.31). This difference is in the direction indicating that participants in the murder condition were more likely to withhold relevant information, and is significant ($t = 2.116$, one-tailed $p = 0.19$). This finding is consistent with our behavioral

measures of misconduct, and indicates that participants in the murder condition made conscious decisions to withhold exculpatory evidence.

DISCUSSION AND CONCLUSION

Results of a carefully conducted randomized experiment supported all three hypotheses based on our theory, increasing our confidence in that theory. Generalizing the results of basic experiments to naturally occurring situations is not advisable, however. We cannot assume that the processes found to encourage misconduct in the laboratory operate similarly for working prosecutors or exert similar effects.

We have not learned anything new about the extent or severity of misconduct among working prosecutors except where to look for it in future research of actual criminal cases. The naturally occurring situation contains many other factors with the potential to alter the propensity for misconduct. These may interact with the process we have identified to mitigate or aggravate the extent of wrongdoing.

We have discovered a process capable of increasing misconduct in the prosecution of more severe crimes. Whether that process produces more misconduct when working prosecutors handle more serious cases is an open question. One can argue that the legal system has safeguards in place to counter the process or that the rigorous training of prosecutors limits its effect. Nonetheless, the results of this study shift the research burden of proof to those who think that working prosecutors avoid misconduct when the stakes are high. New research can be designed to investigate how the legal system or the training of prosecutors might limit misconduct in the prosecution of severe crimes.

For example, our study did not include potential punishments for prosecutors who engaged in misconduct. In naturally occurring trials, fear of punishment may make misconduct less likely in cases involving more severe crimes. The opposite effect also could occur: the greater rewards and opportunities for advancement earned by obtaining convictions in serious, high-profile cases may increase pressure to engage in wrongdoing. Moreover, evidence indicates that prosecutors are unlikely to incur sanctions for engaging in misconduct in naturally occurring trials (Chineson 1986; Gershman 1992; Kurcias 2000; Meares 1995). It would be worthwhile to determine how the potential rewards and penalties for prosecutorial misconduct affect its prevalence.

This research supports the theoretical propositions that presumptions of guilt and actions of misconduct will be greater for more serious crimes. Because the consequences of misconduct in the prosecution of serious crimes are potentially much more severe than for minor crimes, future research could address these issues in diverse populations and settings. It will be difficult to determine precisely how strongly severity of crime affects misconduct in natural settings. Perhaps the main contribution of this research is to provide a compelling reason to investigate misconduct among working prosecutors of serious cases.

REFERENCES

Bedau, Hugo Adam and Michael L. Radelet. 1987. "Miscarriages of Justice in Potentially Capital Cases." *Stanford Law Review* 40:21–179.

Birbeck, Christopher and Gary LaFree. 1993. "The Situational Analysis of Crime and Deviance." *Annual Review of Sociology* 19:113–17.

Bornstein, Brian H. 1998. "From Compassion to Compensation: The Effect of Injury Severity on Mock Jurors' Liability Judgments." *Journal of Applied Social Psychology* 28:1477–1502.

Chineson, Joel. 1986. "Do the Courts Encourage Prosecutorial Misconduct?" *Trial* (June):78–81.

Delattre, Edwin. 1989. *Character and Cops*. Washington, DC: American Enterprise Institute.

Gershman, Bennett L. 1992. "Tricks Prosecutors Play." *Trial* (April):46–50.

———. 2001. *Prosecutorial Misconduct*, 2nd Ed. St. Paul: West Group.

Gross, Samuel R. 1996. "The Risks of Death: Why Erroneous Convictions Are Common in Capital Cases." *Buffalo Law Review* 44:469–79.

Harmon, Talia Roitberg. 2001. "Predictors of Miscarriages of Justice in Capital Cases." *Justice Quarterly*, 18:948–68.

Harrison, Bob. 1999. "Noble Cause Corruption and the Police Ethic." *FBI Law Enforcement Bulletin* 68:1–7.

Howe, Edmund S. 1991. "Integration of Mitigation, Intention, and Outcome Damage Information by Students and Circuit Court Judges." *Journal of Applied Social Psychology* 21:875–95.

Kurcias, Lisa M. 2000. "Prosecutor's Duty to Disclose Exculpatory Evidence." *Fordham Law Review* 69:1205–29.

LaBeff, Emily E., Robert E. Clark, Valerie J. Haines, and George M. Dieckoff. 1990. "Situational Ethics and College Student Cheating." *Sociological Inquiry* 60:190–98.

Lawless, Joseph F. and Kenneth E. North. 1984. "Prosecutorial Misconduct: A Battleground in Criminal Law." *Trial* (October):26–29.

Lofquist, William S. 2001. "Whodunit? An Examination of the Production of Wrongful Convictions." Pp. 174–98 in *Wrongly Convicted: Perspectives on Failed Justice*, Edited by Saundra D. Westervelt and John A. Humphrey. New Brunswick: Rutgers University Press.

MacCoun, Robert J. 1996. "Differential Treatment of Corporate Defendants by Juries: An Examination of the 'Deep-Pockets Hypothesis.'" *Law and Society Review* 30:121–61.

Meares, Tracey L. 1995. "Rewards for Good Behavior: Influencing Prosecutorial Discretion and Conduct With Financial Incentives." *Fordham Law Review* 64:851–919.

Myers, Martha A. 1980. "Social Context and Attribution of Criminal Responsibility." *Social Psychology Quarterly* 43:405–19.

Nidiry, Rosemary. 1996. "Restraining Adversarial Excess in Closing Argument." *Columbia Law Review* 96:1299–1334.

Radelet, Michael L. and Hugo Adam Bedau. 2001. "Erroneous Convictions and the Death Penalty." Pp. 269–80 in *Wrongly Convicted: Perspectives on Failed Justice*, Edited by Saundra D. Westervelt and John A. Humphrey. New Brunswick: Rutgers University Press.

Rattner, Arye. 1988. "Convicted but Innocent." *Law and Human Behavior* 12:283–94.

Robbennolt, Jennifer K. 2000. "Outcome Severity and Judgments of Responsibility: A Meta-Analytic Review." *Journal of Applied Social Psychology* 30:2575–609.

Sanderson, Catherine A., Adam S. Zanna, and John M. Darly. 2000. "Making the Punishment Fit the Crime and the Criminal: Attributions of Dangerousness As a Mediator of Liability." *Journal of Applied Social Psychology* 30:1137–59.

QUESTIONS

1. In experiments, the independent (or causal) variable is manipulated. What is the independent variable in all three hypotheses? How is it manipulated?

2. To assess whether a manipulation worked or validly operationalized the independent variable, experimenters sometimes perform **manipulation checks**. Describe the manipulation check used in this experiment. What are the results?

3. The experimenters measured several dependent variables or outcomes, one for each hypothesis. What is the dependent variable in Hypothesis 2? How is it measured?

4. What procedures (common to all true experiments) were applied to make sure that differences between experimental conditions were due to the manipulated variable and nothing else?

5. Briefly describe the results of the experiment with respect to each hypothesis.

6. **Internal validity** is a matter of whether a study provides sound evidence of a causal relationship; **external validity** is a question of generalizability, or the extent to which the results may be applied beyond the context of the experiment. Evaluate the experiment in terms of internal validity and external validity.

Selection 10

An important contemporary institution in producing inequality is the criminal justice system. Evidence indicates, for example, that having a criminal record reduces one's chances of getting a job. Devah Pager asks whether this may be due to the stigma of having a criminal record. Because blacks are far more likely to be incarcerated than whites and are more likely to experience job discrimination, Pager also asks if race compounds the negative impact of a criminal record. As you read this selection, note how her field experiment (more specifically, audit study) effectively separates the effect of the stigma of a criminal record from the effects of other characteristics of job applicants.

THE MARK OF A CRIMINAL RECORD

DEVAH PAGER

While stratification researchers typically focus on schools, labor markets, and the family as primary institutions affecting inequality, a new institution has emerged as central to the sorting and stratifying of young and disadvantaged men: the criminal justice system. With over 2 million individuals currently incarcerated, and over half a million prisoners released each year, the large and growing numbers of men being processed through the criminal justice system raises important questions about the consequences of this massive institutional intervention.

This article focuses on the consequences of incarceration for the employment outcomes of black and white men. While previous survey research has demonstrated a strong *association* between incarceration and employment, there remains little understanding of the mechanisms by which these outcomes are produced. In the present study, I adopt an experimental audit approach to formally test the degree to which a criminal record affects subsequent employment opportunities. By using matched pairs of individuals to apply for real entry-level jobs, it becomes possible to directly measure the extent

Source: "The Mark of a Criminal Record," by Devah Pager, 2003, *American Journal of Sociology,* 108(5), 937–975. Copyright 2003 by University of Chicago Press.

to which a criminal record—in the absence of other disqualifying characteristics—serves as a barrier to employment among equally qualified applicants. Further, by varying the race of the tester pairs, we can assess the ways in which the effects of race and criminal record interact to produce new forms of labor market inequalities.

PRIOR RESEARCH

Existing research has been instrumental in demonstrating the possible aggregate effects of incarceration on labor market outcomes. Unfortunately, however, there are several fundamental limitations of survey data that leave the conclusions of this research vulnerable to harsh criticism. First, it is difficult, using survey data, to rule out the possibility that unmeasured differences between those who are and are not convicted of crimes may drive the observed results. Figure 10.1 presents one possible model of the relationship between incarceration and employment outcomes, with a direct causal link between the two. In this model, an individual acquires a criminal record, which then severely limits his later employment opportunities. But what evidence can we offer in support of this causal relationship? We know that the population

FIGURE 10.1   Model of Direct Causation

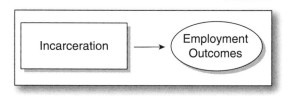

of inmates is not a random sample of the overall population. What if, then, the poor outcomes of ex-offenders are merely the result of preexisting traits that make these men bad employees in the first place? Figure 10.2 presents a model of spurious association in which there is no direct link between incarceration and employment outcomes. Instead, there are direct links between various preexisting individual characteristics (e.g., drug and alcohol abuse, behavioral problems, poor interpersonal skills), which increase the likelihood of both incarceration and poor employment outcomes. In this model, the association between incarceration and employment is entirely spurious—the result of individual predispositions toward deviance.

A second, related limitation of survey research is its inability to formally identify mechanisms. Survey researchers have offered numerous hypotheses regarding the mechanisms that may produce the observed relationship between

FIGURE 10.2   Model of Spurious Effects

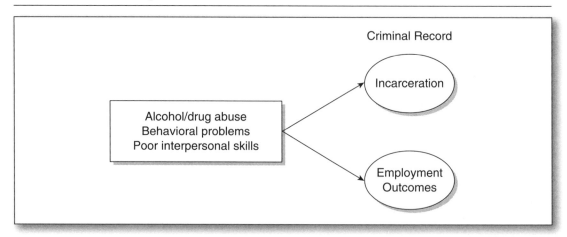

incarceration and employment. These include the labeling effects of criminal stigma (Schwartz and Skolnick 1962), the disruption of social and familial ties (Sampson and Laub 1993), the influence on social networks (Hagan 1993), the loss of human capital (Becker 1975), institutional trauma (Parenti 1999), legal barriers to employment (Dale 1976), and, of course, the possibility that incarceration effects may be entirely spurious (Kling 1999; Grogger 1995; Needels 1996). Without direct measures of these variables, it is difficult, using survey data, to discern which, if any, of these causal explanations may be at work.

The uncertainty surrounding these mechanisms motivates the current project. Before addressing some of the larger consequences of incarceration, it is essential to first establish conclusively the mechanism—or at least one of the mechanisms—driving these results. In the present study, I focus on the effect of a *criminal record* on employment opportunities. While incarceration may in fact additionally transform individuals (and/or their social ties) in ways that make them less suited to work, my interest here is in what might be termed the "credentialing" aspect of the criminal justice system. Those sent to prison are institutionally branded as a particular class of individuals—as are college graduates or welfare recipients—with implications for their perceived place in the stratification order.

In order to investigate this question, I have chosen an experimental approach to the problem, a methodology best suited to isolating causal mechanisms. By using an experimental audit design, this study effectively isolates the effect of a criminal record, while observing employer behavior in real-life employment settings. Further, by using in-person application procedures, it becomes possible to simulate the process most often followed for entry-level positions, as well as to provide a more direct test of the effects of race on hiring outcomes.

RESEARCH QUESTIONS

There are three primary questions I seek to address with the present study. First, we need to ask whether and to what extent employers use information about criminal histories to make hiring decisions. This study formally tests the degree to which employers use information about criminal histories in the absence of corroborating evidence. It is essential that we conclusively document this effect before making larger claims about the aggregate consequences of incarceration.

Second, this study investigates the extent to which race continues to serve as a major barrier to employment. While race has undoubtedly played a central role in shaping the employment opportunities of African-Americans over the past century, recent arguments have questioned the continuing significance of race, arguing instead that other factors—such as spatial location, soft skills, social capital, or cognitive ability—can explain most or all of the contemporary racial differentials we observe (Wilson 1987; Moss and Tilly 1996; Loury 1977; Neal and Johnson 1996). This study provides a comparison of the experiences of equally qualified black and white applicants, allowing us to assess the extent to which direct racial discrimination persists in employment interactions.

The third objective of this study is to assess whether the effect of a criminal record differs for black and white applicants. Most research investigating the differential impact of incarceration on blacks has focused on the differential *rates* of incarceration and how those rates translate into widening racial disparities. In addition to disparities in the rate of incarceration, however, it is also important to consider possible racial differences in the *effects* of incarceration.

THE AUDIT METHODOLOGY

The basic design of an employment audit involves sending matched pairs of individuals (called testers) to apply for real job openings in order to see whether employers respond differently to applicants on the basis of selected characteristics. The appeal of the audit methodology lies in its ability to combine experimental methods with real-life contexts.

This combination allows for greater generalizability than a lab experiment and a better grasp of the causal mechanisms than what we can normally obtain from observational data.

STUDY DESIGN

The basic design of this study involves the use of four male auditors (also called testers), two blacks and two whites. The testers were paired by race; that is, the two black testers formed one team, and the two white testers formed the second team (see Figure 10.3). The testers were 23-year-old college students from Milwaukee who were matched on the basis of physical appearance and general style of self-presentation. Objective characteristics that were not already identical between pairs—such as educational attainment and work experience—were made similar for the purpose of the applications. Within each team, one auditor was randomly assigned a "criminal record" for the first week; the pair then rotated which member presented himself as the ex-offender for each successive week of employment searches, such that each tester served in the criminal record condition for an equal number of cases. By varying which member of the pair presented himself as having a criminal record, unobserved differences within the pairs of applicants were effectively controlled. No significant differences were found for the outcomes of individual testers or by month of testing.

Job openings for entry-level positions (defined as jobs requiring no previous experience and no education greater than high school) were identified from the Sunday classified advertisement section of the *Milwaukee Journal Sentinel*. In addition, a supplemental sample was drawn from *Jobnet*, a state-sponsored web site for employment listings, which was developed in connection with the W-2 Welfare-to-Work initiatives.

The audit pairs were randomly assigned 15 job openings each week. The white pair and the black pair were assigned separate sets of jobs, with the same-race testers applying to the same jobs. One member of the pair applied first, with the second applying one day later (randomly varying whether the ex-offender was first or second). A total of 350 employers were audited during the course of this study: 150 by the white pair and 200 by the black pair. Additional tests were performed by the black pair because black testers received fewer callbacks on average, and there were thus fewer data points with which to draw comparisons. A larger sample size enables me to calculate more precise estimates of the effects under investigation.

Immediately following the completion of each job application, testers filled out a six-page response form that coded relevant information from the test. Important variables included type of occupation, metropolitan status, wage, size of establishment, and race and sex of employer. Additionally, testers wrote narratives describing

FIGURE 10.3 Audit Design: "C" refers to criminal record; "N" refers to no criminal record

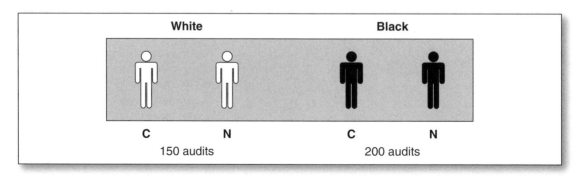

the overall interaction and any comments made by employers (or included on applications) specifically related to race or criminal records.

One key feature of this audit study is that it focuses only on the first stage of the employment process. Testers visited employers, filled out applications, and proceeded as far as they could during the course of one visit. If testers were asked to interview on the spot, they did so, but they did not return to the employer for a second visit. The primary dependent variable, then, is the proportion of applications that elicited callbacks from employers. Individual voicemail boxes were set up for each tester to record employer responses. If a tester was offered the job on the spot, this was also coded as a positive response. The reason I chose to focus only on this initial stage of the employment process is because this is the stage likely to be most affected by the barrier of a criminal record. In an audit study of age discrimination, for example, Bendick et al. (1999) found that 76% of the measured differential treatment occurred at this initial stage of the employment process. Given that a criminal record, like age, is a highly salient characteristic, it is likely that as much, if not more, of the treatment effect will be detected at this stage.

TESTER PROFILES

In developing the tester profiles, emphasis was placed on adopting characteristics that were both numerically representative and substantively important. In the present study, the criminal record consisted of a felony drug conviction (possession with intent to distribute, cocaine) and 18 months of (served) prison time. A drug crime (as opposed to a violent or property crime) was chosen because of its prevalence, its policy salience, and its connection to racial disparities in incarceration. It is important to acknowledge that the effects reported here may differ depending on the type of offense.

More than 70% of federal and nearly 90% of state prisoners have no more than a high school

degree (or equivalent). The education level of testers in this study was chosen to represent the modal category of offenders (high school diploma).

There is little systematic evidence concerning the work histories of inmates prior to incarceration. Overall, 77.4% of federal and 67.4% of state inmates were employed prior to incarceration (Bureau of Justice Statistics 1994). There is, however, a substantial degree of heterogeneity in the quality and consistency of work experience during this time (Pager 2001). In the present study, testers were assigned favorable work histories in that they report steady work experience in entry-level jobs and nearly continual employment (until incarceration). In the job prior to incarceration (and, for the control group, prior to the last short-term job), testers report having worked their way from an entry-level position to a supervisory role.

DESIGN ISSUES

There are a number of complexities involved in the design and implementation of an audit study. Dilemmas posed in the development of the current study required substantial deliberation. First, in standard audit studies of race or gender, it is possible to construct work histories for test partners in such a way that the amount of work experience reported by each tester is identical. By contrast, the present study compares the outcome of one applicant who has spent 18 months in prison. It was therefore necessary to manipulate the work histories of both applicants so that this labor market absence did not bias the results. The solution opted for here was for the ex-offender to report six months of work experience gained while in prison (preceded by 12 months out of the labor force, representing the remainder of the total prison time). The nonoffender, on the other hand, reported graduating from high school one year later (thereby accounting for 12 months) and, concurrent to his partner's six months of prison work time, worked for a temporary agency doing a similar kind of low-skill work. Thus, the actual amount of work experience was equivalent for both testers.

A second major difference between audit studies of race or gender and the present study is that criminal status is not something that can be immediately discerned by the employer. The information had to be explicitly conveyed, therefore, in order for the interaction to become a "test." In most cases, the tester was given the opportunity to communicate the necessary information on the application form provided, in answer to the question "Have you ever been convicted of a crime?" However, in the 26% of cases where the application form did not include a question about criminal history, it was necessary to provide an alternate means of conveying this information. In the present study, testers provided two indirect sources of information about their prior criminal involvement. First, as mentioned above, the tester in the criminal record condition reported work experience obtained while in the correctional facility. Second, the tester listed his parole officer as a reference (calls to whom were recorded by voicemail). These two pieces of evidence provided explicit clues to employers that the applicant had spent time in prison.

Study Context and Descriptives

The fieldwork for this project took place in Milwaukee between June and December of 2001. During this time, the economic condition of the metropolitan area remained moderately strong, with unemployment rates ranging from a high of 5.2% in June to a low of 4% in September. It is important to note that the results of this study are specific to the economic conditions of this period. It has been well-documented in previous research that the level of employment discrimination corresponds closely with the tightness of the labor market (Freeman and Rodgers 1999). Since the completion of this study, the unemployment rate has continued to rise. It is likely, therefore, that the effects reported here may understate the impact of race and a criminal record in the context of an economic recession.

Similar to other metropolitan labor markets, the service industry has been the fastest growing sector in Milwaukee, followed by retail and wholesale trade, and manufacturing (Pawasarat and Quinn 2000). Likewise, the sample of jobs in this study reflects similar concentrations, though quite a range of job titles were included overall.

The most common job types were for restaurant workers (18%), laborers or warehouse workers (17%), and production workers or operators (12%). Though white-collar positions were less common among the entry-level listings, a fair number of customer service (11%), sales (11%), clerical (5%), and even a handful of managerial positions (2%) were included.

In this sample, roughly 75% of employers asked explicit questions on their application forms about the applicant's criminal history. Generally this was a standard question, "Have you ever been convicted of a crime? If yes, please explain." Even though in most cases employers are not allowed to use criminal background information to make hiring decisions, a vast majority of employers nevertheless request the information.

The Effect of a Criminal Record for Whites

Figure 10.4 shows the percentage of applications submitted by white testers that elicited callbacks from employers, by criminal status. As illustrated below, there is a large and significant effect of a criminal record, with 34% of whites without criminal records receiving callbacks, relative to only 17% of whites with criminal records. A criminal record thereby reduces the likelihood of a callback by 50%.

Clearly, the results here demonstrate that criminal records close doors in employment situations. Many employers seem to use the information as a screening mechanism, without attempting to probe deeper into the possible context or complexities of the situation. As we can see here, in 50% of cases, employers were unwilling to consider equally qualified applicants on the basis of their criminal record.

FIGURE 10.4   The Effect of a Criminal Record on Employment Opportunities for Whites

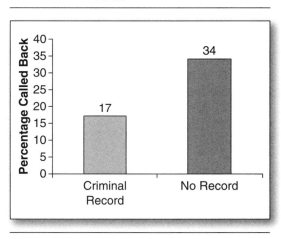

Note: The effect of a criminal record is statistically significant ($P < .01$).

FIGURE 10.5   The Effect of a Criminal Record for Black and White Job Applicants

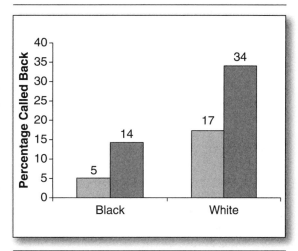

Note: The main effects of race and criminal record are statistically significant ($P < .01$). The interaction between the two is not significant in the full sample. Dark gray bars represent criminal record; light gray bars represent no criminal record.

THE EFFECT OF RACE

A second major focus of this study concerns the effect of race. Figure 10.5 presents the percentage of callbacks received for both categories of black testers relative to those for whites. The effect of race in these findings is strikingly large. Among blacks without criminal records, only 14% received callbacks, relative to 34% of white noncriminals ($P <.01$). In fact, even whites *with* criminal records received more favorable treatment (17%) than blacks *without* criminal records (14%). The rank ordering of groups in this graph is painfully revealing of employer preferences: race continues to play a dominant role in shaping employment opportunities, equal to or greater than the impact of a criminal record.

RACIAL DIFFERENCES IN THE EFFECTS OF A CRIMINAL RECORD

The final question this study sought to answer was the degree to which the effect of a criminal record differs depending on the race of the applicant. Based on the results presented in Figure 10.5, the effect of a criminal record appears more pronounced for blacks than it is for whites. While the ratio of callbacks for nonoffenders relative to ex-offenders for whites is 2:1, this same ratio for blacks is nearly 3:1. The effect of a criminal record is thus 40% larger for blacks than for whites.

DISCUSSION

There is serious disagreement among academics, policymakers, and practitioners over the extent to which contact with the criminal justice system— in itself—leads to harmful consequences for employment. The present study takes a strong stand in this debate by offering direct evidence of the causal relationship between a criminal record and employment outcomes. This finding provides conclusive evidence that mere contact with the criminal justice system, in the absence of any transformative or selective effects, severely limits subsequent employment opportunities. With over 2 million people currently behind bars and over 12 million people with prior felony convictions, the consequences for labor market inequalities are potentially profound.

Second, the persistent effect of race on employment opportunities is painfully clear in these results. Blacks are less than half as likely to receive consideration by employers, relative to their white counterparts, and black nonoffenders fall behind even whites with prior felony convictions. The powerful effects of race thus continue to direct employment decisions in ways that contribute to persisting racial inequality.

Finally, in terms of policy implications, this research has troubling conclusions. In our frenzy of locking people up, our "crime control" policies may in fact exacerbate the very conditions that lead to crime in the first place. Research consistently shows that finding quality steady employment is one of the strongest predictors of desistance from crime (Shover 1996; Sampson and Laub 1993; Uggen 2000). The fact that a criminal record severely limits employment opportunities—particularly among blacks— suggests that these individuals are left with few viable alternatives.

As more and more young men enter the labor force from prison, it becomes increasingly important to consider the impact of incarceration on the job prospects of those coming out. No longer a peripheral institution, the criminal justice system has become a dominant presence in the lives of young disadvantaged men, playing a key role in the sorting and stratifying of labor market opportunities. This article represents an initial attempt to specify one of the important mechanisms by which incarceration leads to poor employment outcomes. Future research is needed to expand this emphasis to other mechanisms (e.g., the transformative effects of prison on human and social capital), as well as to include other social domains affected by incarceration (e.g., housing, family formation, political participation, etc.); in this way, we can move toward a more complete understanding of the collateral consequences of incarceration for social inequality.

At this point in history, it is impossible to tell whether the massive presence of incarceration in today's stratification system represents a unique anomaly of the late 20th century, or part of a larger movement toward a system of stratification based on the official certification of individual character and competence. Whether this process of negative credentialing will continue to form the basis of emerging social cleavages remains to be seen.

REFERENCES

Becker, Gary. 1975. *Human Capital*. New York: Columbia University Press.
Bendick, Marc, Jr. 1999. "Adding Testing to the Nation's Portfolio of Information on Employment Testing." Pp. 47–68 in *A National Report Card on Discrimination in America: The Role of Testing*, edited by Michael Fix and Margery Turner. Washington, D.C.: Urban Institute.
Bureau of Justice Statistics. 1994. *Comparing Federal and State Prison Inmates 1991*, by Caroline Harlow. Washington, D.C.: NCJ-145864.
Dale, Mitchell. 1976. "Barriers to the Rehabilitation of Ex-Offenders." *Crime and Delinquency* 22:322–37.
Grogger, Jeffrey. 1992. "Arrests, Persistent Youth Joblessness, and Black/White Employment Differentials." *Review of Economics and Statistics* 74:100–106.
———1995. "The Effect of Arrests on the Employment and Earnings of Young Men." *Quarterly Journal of Economics* 110:51–72.
Hagan, John. 1993. "The Social Embeddedness of Crime and Unemployment." *Criminology* 31 (4): 465–91.
Kling, Jeffrey. 1999. "The Effect of Prison Sentence Length on the Subsequent Employment and Earnings of Criminal Defendants." Discussion Paper no. 208. Princeton University, Woodrow Wilson School.
Loury, Glenn C. 1977. "A Dynamic Theory of Racial Income Differences." Pp. 153–86 in *Women, Minorities, and Employment Discrimination*, edited by P. A. Wallace and A. M. La Mond. Lexington, Mass.: Heath.

Moss, Philip, and Chris Tilly. 1996. "Soft Sills' and Race: An Investigation of Black Men's Employment Problems." *Work and Occupations* 23 (3):256–76.

Neal, Derek, and William Johnson. 1996. "The Role of Premarket Factors in Black-White Wage Differences." *Journal of Political Economy* 104 (5):869–95.

Needels, Karen E. 1996. "Go Directly to Jail and Do Not Collect? A Long-Term Study of Recidivism, Employment, and Earnings Patterns among Prison Releases." *Journal of Research in Crime and Delinquency* 33:471–96.

Pager, Devah. 2001. "Criminal Careers: The Consequences of Incarceration for Occupational Attainment." Paper presented at the annual meetings of the American Sociological Association, Anaheim, August.

Parenti, Christian. 1999. *Lockdown America: Police and Prisons in the Age of Crisis*. New York: Verso.

Pawasarat, John, and Lois M. Quinn. 2000. "Survey of Job Openings in the Milwaukee Metropolitan Area: Week of May 15, 2000." University of Wisconsin—Milwaukee, Employment and Training Institute, University Outreach.

Sampson, Robert J., and John H. Laub. 1993. *Crime in the Making: Pathology and Turning Points through Life*. Cambridge, Mass.: Harvard University Press.

Schwartz, Richard, and Jerome Skolnick. 1962. "Two Studies of Legal Stigma." *Social Problems* 10:133–42.

Shover, Neil. 1996. *Great Pretenders: Pursuits and Careers of Presistent Thieves*. Boulder, Colo.: Westview.

Uggen, Christopher. 2000. "Work as a Turning Point in the Life Course of Criminals: A Duration Model of Age, Employment, and Recidivism." *American Sociological Review* 65 (4):529–46.

Wilson, William Julius. 1987. *The Truly Disadvantaged: The Inner City, the Underclass, and Public Policy*. Chicago: University of Chicago Press.

QUESTIONS

1. According to Pager, what advantages do experiments have over surveys in investigating the effects of incarceration on employment outcomes?

2. Identify the three research questions addressed in this experiment.

3. Which two variables are manipulated? How are they manipulated? (Be sure to describe *all* the procedures used by Pager to make sure that employers could discern that applicants possessed the manipulated characteristics.)

4. What is the dependent variable? Why did Pager choose to measure this particular outcome?

5. Briefly describe how Pager made sure that the only differences between job applicants were the manipulated variables.

6. Briefly describe the results of the experiment with respect to each of Pager's research questions.

7. Evaluate this study from the standpoint of generalizability.

UNIT VI

SURVEYS

A survey interview is like a "conversation with a purpose" (Schaefer, 1991). This means that **surveys** are like ordinary conversations, expressed in language we use in everyday life. It also means that surveys are administered with a specific goal in mind: namely, to obtain answers (data) from respondents.

Although couched in ordinary language, surveys differ from everyday conversations in a couple of important ways. First, surveys tend to follow a relatively strict script of questions and potential answers that allow for little spontaneity in the conversation. To get standardized data, survey researchers ask the same questions and provide the same possible responses to many people over and over again, which is the essence of a **structured interview** (Fowler & Mangione, 1990). One example of a survey question is the following, which comes from the General Social Survey (GSS) (Smith, Marsden, Hout, & Kim, 2011):

> We are faced with many problems in this country, none of which can be solved easily or inexpensively. I'm going to name some of these problems, and for each one I'd like you to tell me whether you think we're spending too much money on it, too little money, or about the right amount.
>
> Are we spending too much, too little, or about the right amount on welfare?

Second, unlike conversations among friends, surveys are largely conversations between strangers—for example, between a survey interviewer and a random sample of people (s)he is interviewing.

There is a relatively common process to conducting surveys: The process typically entails developing a survey questionnaire; generating a sample list; contacting the potential respondents, following up, asking questions, and recording responses; coding the data; and, entering the data into a spreadsheet or a statistical software program. After this is done, researchers are usually interested in doing one or both of the following: First, they may be interested in describing how many or what percentage of people gave particular answers to questions, such as what percentage of people said that the federal government is spending too much on welfare. These percentages can then be generalized to the larger population from which a random sample was drawn. Second, researchers may be interested in analyzing the relationship between survey responses and people's characteristics (e.g., gender, race, age, socioeconomic status). For example, do men or women differ in what they believe about government spending on welfare?

There are, however, important differences in how survey research is conducted. The first has to do with the mode of survey administration: Surveys may be administered via mail, face-to-face, over the telephone, and increasingly, online and via computers. The first selection in this unit, on college drinking, illustrates the use of mail surveys; the second selection, on attitudes toward homosexuality, is based on GSS data gathered through face-to-face interviews (see the GSS website in the Resources section).

The selections in this unit also highlight the difference between a **cross-sectional survey design** and a **longitudinal survey design**. A cross-section simply refers to a (randomly selected) group of people at a single point in time. In the first selection, the researchers use a cross-sectional survey design to examine the reported drinking behavior of a group of college students in 1993. A longitudinal design examines changes in populations or a group of people over time. In one type of longitudinal survey design, called a **repeated cross-sectional design,** *different* groups of people at *different* points in time are asked the same survey questions. The GSS, discussed above, has long been an example of a repeated cross-sectional survey, whereby random samples of Americans are asked many of the same questions over time. This design allows for the analysis of trends in Americans' attitudes, which Jeni Loftus undertakes in the second selection.

Despite their potential for discovering new patterns, relationships, and trends, surveys are plagued by some of the same problems that plague everyday conversations: people—or, respondents—lie, give only "socially acceptable" answers, misreport, misremember, and so forth. These problems can undermine the **validity**, or accuracy, of survey responses.

Another issue with surveys is that even slight changes in question wording can change the meaning and responses. For example, the GSS question on welfare above was part of a **split-ballot experiment**, whereby some people in the original sample were randomly selected to answer this question. Another random selection of people was asked the same question, but with the words *the poor* replacing the word *welfare* so that the question read: "Are we spending too much, too little, or about the right amount on *the poor?*" (Smith et al. 2011, emphasis added). Tom Smith (1987) found that people are much more supportive of spending on "the poor" than spending on "welfare." This is because welfare is seen as a governmental program that encourages laziness among recipients who are not entitled to the program (Gilens, 1996).

Both selections in this unit discuss the limitations of surveys in some detail. They also reveal the utility of survey research in discovering patterns, uncovering relationships between variables, and detecting trends and social change. As you read these selections, note all of the elements involved in the survey research process. These are especially highlighted in the first selection, which uses mail questionnaires and a cross-sectional survey design. The second selection makes use of GSS data between 1973 and 1998 to describe trends in Americans' attitudes.

REFERENCES

Fowler, F. J., Jr., & Mangione, T. W. (1990). *Standardized survey interviewing: Minimizing interviewer-related error.* Newbury Park, CA: Sage.

Gilens, M. (1996). *Why Americans hate welfare: Race, media, and the politics of anti-poverty policy.* Chicago: University of Chicago Press.

Schaeffer, N. C. (1991). Conversation with a purpose—or conversation? Interaction in the standardized survey. In P. P. Biemer, R. M. Groves, L. E. Lyberg, N. A. Mathiowetz, & S. Sudman (Eds.), *Measurement errors in surveys* (pp. 367–391). John Wiley.

Smith, T. W. (1987). That which we call welfare by any other name would smell sweeter: An analysis of the impact of question wording on response patterns. *Public Opinion Quarterly, 51*(1), 75–83.

Smith, T. W., Marsden, P., Hout, M., & Kim, J. (2011). *General social surveys, 1972–2010* [machine-readable data file]. Principal Investigator, Tom W. Smith; Co-Principal Investigator, Peter V. Marsden; Co-Principal Investigator, Michael Hout; Sponsored by National Science Foundation.

NORC ed., Chicago: National Opinion Research Center [producer]; Storrs, CT: The Roper Center for Public Opinion Research, University of Connecticut [distributor].

RESOURCES

The American Association for Public Opinion Research (AAPOR):

http://www.aapor.org/Question_Wording1.htm

- Previously, we directed you to an AAPOR link on sampling. Using the link above will give you much more information about survey questions, how to word them, and how *not* to word them.

StatPac's Survey Design Tutorial:

http://www.statpac.com/surveys/index.htm#toc

- This is an excellent, brief resource on all of the important steps and issues in the process of conducting surveys, including some topics not explicitly covered in this reader, such as cost considerations and missing survey data.

Survey Monkey™ :

https://www.surveymonkey.com/

- If you decide to create your own (Internet) survey, you can use Survey Monkey™ for free to do so, but note that its free account allows you to ask only a limited number of questions (10) of a limited number of respondents (100).

The General Social Survey (GSS) website:

http://www3.norc.org/GSS+Website

- Here, you can download and analyze existing survey data on virtually all elements of social life in the United States, look at question wording, read methodological reports, and more.

The American National Election Survey (ANES):

http://www.electionstudies.org/

- Like the GSS website, this survey provides a great deal of useful information, which primarily focuses on Americans' *political* attitudes and behaviors.

Selection 11

In 1993, researchers at the Harvard School of Public Health launched the first in a series of national surveys of American college students' drinking habits. Focusing on heavy episodic drinking, the first survey included a controversial new measure of binge drinking subsequently applied in numerous studies. In this selection, the researchers answer the question: Who is most likely to binge-drink and with what consequences? The selection illustrates the use of multi-stage cluster sampling, a mail questionnaire survey, and a cross-sectional survey design, while also discussing the limitations of survey research.

HEALTH AND BEHAVIORAL CONSEQUENCES OF BINGE DRINKING IN COLLEGE

A National Survey of Students at 140 Campuses

HENRY WECHSLER, ANDREA DAVENPORT, GEORGE DOWDALL, BARBARA MOEYKENS, AND SONIA CASTILLO

Heavy episodic or binge drinking poses a danger of serious health and other consequences for alcohol abusers and for others in the immediate environment. Alcohol contributes to the leading causes of accidental death in the United States, such as motor vehicle crashes and falls.[1] Alcohol abuse is seen as contributing to almost half of motor vehicle fatalities, the most important cause of death among young Americans. Unsafe sex—a growing threat with the spread of acquired immunodeficiency syndrome (AIDS) and other sexually transmitted diseases—and unintentional injuries have been associated with alcohol intoxication.[3-5] These findings support the view of college presidents who believe that alcohol abuse is the No. 1 problem on campus.[6]

Despite the fact that alcohol is illegal for most undergraduates, alcohol continues to be widely used on most college campuses today. Since the national study by Straus and Bacon in 1949,[7] numerous subsequent surveys have documented the overwhelming use of alcohol by college students and have pointed to problem drinking among this group.[8-10] Most previous studies of drinking by college students have been conducted on single college campuses and have not used random sampling of students.[9-12] While these studies are in general agreement about the prevalence and consequences of binge drinking, they do not provide a national representative sample of college drinking.

A few large-scale, multicollege surveys have been conducted in recent years. However, these have not selected a representative national sample of colleges, but have used colleges in one state[3] or those participating in a federal program,[5] or have followed a sample of high school seniors through college.[13]

In general, studies of college alcohol use have consistently found higher rates of binge drinking among men than women. However, these studies used the same definition of binge drinking for men and women, without taking into account sex differences in metabolism of ethanol or in body mass.[3,5,9-12,14-17]

The consequences of binge drinking often pose serious risks for drinkers and for others in the college environment. Binge drinking has been associated with unplanned and unsafe sexual activity, physical and sexual assault, unintentional injuries, other criminal violations, interpersonal problems, physical or cognitive impairment, and poor academic performance.[3-5]

This study examines the nature and extent of binge drinking among a representative national sample of students at 140 U.S. 4-year colleges and details the problems such drinking causes for drinkers themselves and for others on their college campus. Binge drinking is defined through a sex-specific measure to take into account sex differences in the dosage effects of ethanol.

METHODS

The Colleges

A national sample of 179 colleges was selected from the American Council on Education's list of 4-year colleges and universities accredited by one of the six regional bodies covering the United States. The sample was selected using probability proportionate to enrollment size sampling. All full-time undergraduate students at a university were eligible to be chosen for this study, regardless of the college in which they were enrolled. This sample contained few women-only colleges and few colleges with less than 1000 students. To correct for this problem, an oversample of 15 additional colleges with enrollments of less than 1000 students and 10 all-women's colleges were added to the sample. Nine colleges were subsequently dropped because they were considered inappropriate. These included seminary schools, military schools, and allied health schools.

One hundred forty (72%) of the final sample of 195 colleges agreed to participate. The primary reason stated for nonparticipation by college administrators was inability to provide a random sample of students and their addresses within the time requirements of the study. The 140 participating colleges are located in 40 states and the District of Columbia. They represent a cross-section of US higher education. Two thirds of the colleges sampled are public and one third are private. Approximately two thirds are located in a suburban or urban setting and one third in a small town/rural setting. Four percent are women-only, and 4% are predominantly black institutions.

Sampling Procedures

Colleges were sent a set of specific guidelines for drawing a random sample of students based on the total enrollment of full time undergraduates. Depending on enrollment size, every *x*th student was selected from the student registry using a random starting point. A sample of undergraduate students was provided by each of the 140 participating colleges: 215 students at each of 127 colleges, and 108 at each of 13 colleges (12 of which were in the oversample). The final student sample included 28,709 students.

The Questionnaire

The 20-page survey instrument asked students a number of questions about their drinking behavior as well as other health issues. Whenever possible, the survey instrument included questions that had been used previously in other national or large-scale epidemiological studies.[13,14] A drink was defined as a 12-oz (360-mL) can (or bottle) of beer, a 4-oz (120-mL) glass of wine, a 12-oz (360-mL) bottle (or can) of wine cooler, or a shot (1.25 oz [37 mL]) of liquor straight or in a mixed drink. The following four questions were used to assess binge drinking: (1) sex; (2) recency of last drink ("never," "not in past year," "within last year but more than 30 days ago," "within 30 days but more than 1 week ago," or "within week"); (3) "Think back over the last two weeks. How many times have you had five or more drinks in a row?" (The use of this question, without specification of time elapsed in a drinking episode, is consistent with standard practice in recent research on alcohol use among this population.[3,5,13,18]); and (4) "During the last two weeks, how many times have you had four drinks in a row (but no more than that) (for women)?" Missing responses to any of these four questions excluded the student from the binging analyses.

Students were also asked the extent to which they had experienced any of the following 12 problems as a consequence of their drinking since the beginning of the school year: have a hangover; miss a class; get behind in school-work; do something you later regretted; forget where you were or what you did; argue with friends; engage in unplanned sexual activity; not use protection when you had sex; damage property; get into trouble with campus or local police; get hurt or injured; or require medical treatment for an alcohol overdose. They were also asked if, since the beginning of the school year, they had experienced any of the following eight problems caused by other students' drinking: been insulted or humiliated; had a serious argument or quarrel; been pushed, hit, or assaulted; had your property damaged; had to "babysit" or take care of another student who drank too much; had your studying or sleep interrupted; experienced an unwanted sexual advance; or had been a victim of sexual assault or date rape.

The Mailing

The initial mailing of questionnaires to students began on February 5, 1993. By the end of March, 87% of the final group of questionnaires had been received, with another 10% in April and 2% in May and June. There are no discernible differences in binging rates among questionnaires received in each of the 5 months of the survey. Mailings were modified to take into account spring break, so that students would be responding about their binge drinking behavior during a 2-week time on campus. Responses were voluntary and anonymous. Four separate mailings, usually 10 days apart, were sent at each college: a questionnaire, a reminder postcard, a second questionnaire, and a second reminder postcard. To encourage students to respond, the following cash awards were offered: one $1000 award to a student whose name was drawn from among students responding within 1 week, and one $500 award and ten $100 awards to students selected from all those who responded.

The Response Rate

The questionnaires were mailed to 28,709 students. Overall, 3082 students were eliminated from the sample because of school reports of incorrect addresses, withdrawal from school, or leaves of absence, reducing the sample size to 25,627. A total of 17,592 students returned questionnaires, yielding an overall student response rate of approximately 69%. The response rate is likely to be underestimated since it does not take into account all of the students who may not have received questionnaires. At 104 of the colleges, response rates were between 60% and 80%, and only six colleges had response rates less than 50%. Response rate was not associated with the binging rate.

Data Analysis

Analyses among students who had a drink in the past year were used to compare nonbinge drinkers, infrequent binge drinkers, and binge drinkers. Binge drinking was defined as the consumption of five or more drinks in a row for men and four or more drinks in a row for women during the 2 weeks prior to the survey. An extensive analysis showed that this sex-specific measure accurately indicates an equivalent likelihood of alcohol-related problems. In this article, the term "binge drinker" is used to refer to students who binged at least once in the previous 2 weeks. Frequent binge drinkers were defined as those who binged three or more times in the past 2 weeks and infrequent binge drinkers as those who binged one or two times in the past 2 weeks. Nonbinge drinkers were those who had consumed alcohol in the past year, but had not binged.

RESULTS

Characteristics of the Student Sample

This analysis is based on data from 17,592 undergraduate students at 140 US 4-year colleges. The student sample includes more women (58%) than men (42%), due in part to the inclusion of six all-women's institutions. This compares with national 1991 data that report 51% of undergraduates at 4-year institutions are women. The sample is predominantly white (81%). This coincides exactly with national 1991 data that report 81% of undergraduates at 4-year institutions are white.

Extent of Binge Drinking

Because of missing responses, there were 496 students excluded from binging analyses (i.e., 17,096 were included). Most students drank alcohol during the past year. Only about one of six (16%) were nondrinkers (15% of the men and 16% of the women). About two of five students (41%) drank but were nonbinge drinkers (35% of the men and 45% of the women). Slightly fewer than half (44%) of the students were binge drinkers (50% of the men and 39% of the women). About half of this group of binge drinkers, or about one in five students (19%) overall, were frequent binge drinkers (overall, 23% of the men and 17% of the women).

Binge Drinking Rates at Colleges

Binge drinking rates vary extensively among the 140 colleges in the study. While 1% of the students were binge drinkers at the school with the lowest rate of binge drinkers, 70% of students were binge drinkers at the school with the highest rate. At 44 schools, more than half of the responding students were binge drinkers.

Colleges located in the Northeast or North Central regions of the United States (compared with those in the West or South) or those that were residential (compared with commuter schools, where 90% or more of the students lived off campus) tended to have higher rates of binging. In addition, traditionally black institutions and women's colleges had lower binge rates than schools that were not traditionally black or were coeducational colleges. Other characteristics, such as whether the college was public or private and its enrollment size, were not related to binge drinker rates.

Drinking Patterns of Binge Drinkers

Table 11.1 indicates that our designations of *binge drinker* and *frequent binge drinker* are

TABLE 11.1 Drinking Styles of Students Who Were Nonbinge Drinkers, Infrequent Binge Drinkers, or Frequent Binge Drinkers[*]

	Nonbringe Drinkers, %[a]		Infrequent Binge Drinkers, %[b]		Frequent Binge Drinkers, %[c]	
	Men	*Women*	*Men*	*Women*	*Men*	*Women*
Drinking Styles	*(n = 2539)*	*(n = 4400)*	*(n = 1968)*	*(n = 2130)*	*(n = 1630)*	*(n = 1684)*
Drank on 10 or more occasions in the past 30 days[d]	3	1	11	6	61	39
Usually binges when drinks	4	4	43	45	83	82
Was drunk three or more times in the past month	2	1	17	13	70	55
Drinks to get drunk[e]	22	18	49	44	73	68

[*]Chi-square comparisons of students who were nonbringe drinkers, infrequent binge drinkers, and frequent binge drinkers and each of the four drinking styles were significant for men and women separately at $P < .001$. Sample sizes vary slightly for each question because of missing values. Binging is defined as four or more drinks for women and five or more drinks for men.

[a]Students who consumed alcohol in the past year, but did not binge.

[b]Students who binged one or two times in a 2-week period.

[c]Students who binged three or more times in a 2-week period.

[d]Question asked, "On how many occasions have you had a drink of alcohol in the past 30 days?" Response categories were 1 to 2 occasions, 3 to 5 occasions, 6 to 9 occasions, 10 to 19 occasions, 20 to 39 occasions, and 40 or more occasions.

[e]Says that to get drunk is an important reason for drinking.

strongly indicative of a drinking style that involves more frequent and heavier drinking. Furthermore, intoxication (often intentional) is associated with binge drinking in men and women.

Alcohol-Related Health and Other Problems

There is a strong, positive relationship between the frequency of binge drinking and alcohol-related health and other problems reported by the students (Table 11.2). Among the more serious alcohol-related problems, the frequent binge drinkers were seven to 10 times more likely than the nonbinge drinkers to not use protection when having sex, to engage in unplanned sexual activity, to get into trouble with campus police, to damage property, or to get hurt or injured. A similar comparison between the infrequent binge drinkers and nonbinge drinkers also shows a strong relationship.

Men and women reported similar frequencies for most of the problems, except for damaging property or getting into trouble with the campus police. Among the frequent binge drinkers, 35% of the men and 9% of the women reported damaging property, and 16% of the men and 6% of

TABLE 11.2 Risk of Alcohol-Related Problems Comparing Students Who Were Infrequent Binge Drinkers or Frequent Binge Drinkers With Students Who Were Nonbinge Drinkers Among College Students Who Had a Drink in the Past Year[*]

Reporting Problem	Nonbinge Drinkers, % (n = 6894)	Infrequent Binge Drinkers, % (n = 4090)	Frequent Binge Drinkers, % (n = 3291)
Have a hangover	30	75	90
Do something you regret	14	37	63
Miss a class	8	30	61
Forget where you were or what you did	8	26	54
Get behind in school work	6	21	46
Argue with friends	8	22	42
Engage in unplanned sexual activity	8	20	41
Get hurt or injured	2	9	23
Damage property	2	8	22
Not use protection when having sex	4	10	22
Get into trouble with campus or local police	1	4	11
Require medical treatment of alcohol overdose	<1	<1	1
Have five or more alcohol related problems since the beginning of the school year[a]	3	14	47

[*]Problem occurred not at all or one or more times. Chi-square comparisons of nonbinge drinkers infrequent binge drinkers, and frequent binge drinkers and each of the problems are significant at $P < .001$, except for alcohol overdose ($P = .009$). Sample sizes vary slightly for each problem because of missing values. See Table 11.1 for explanation of drinking classification.

[a]Excludes hangover and includes driving after drinking as one of the problems.

the women reported getting into trouble with the campus police.

Drinking and Driving

There is also a positive relationship between binge drinking and driving under the influence of alcohol (Table 11.3). A large proportion of the student population reported driving after drinking alcohol. Binge drinkers, particularly frequent binge drinkers, reported significantly ($P < .001$)

higher frequencies of dangerous driving behaviors than nonbinge drinkers.

Secondary Binge Effects

Table 11.4 reports on the percentage of nonbinging students who experienced "secondary binge effects," each of eight types of problems due to other students' drinking at each of the three different school types (i.e., schools with high, middle, and low binge levels). For seven of

TABLE 11.3 Alcohol Related Driving Behavior for a 30-Day Period Comparing Students Who Were Infrequent Binge Drinkers or Frequent Binge Drinkers With Students Who Were Nonbinge Drinkers[*]

	Nonbinge Drinkers		Infrequent Binge Drinkers		Frequent Binge Drinkers	
	Men, %	Women, %	Men, %	Women, %	Men, %	Women, %
Driving Behavior	*(n = 2531)*	*(n = 4393)*	*(n = 1975)*	*(n = 2132)*	*(n = 1630)*	*(n = 1684)*
Drove after drinking alcohol	20	13	47	33	62	49
Drove after having five or more drinks	2	1	18	7	40	21
Rode with a driver who was high or drunk	7	7	23	22	53	48

[*]Chi-square comparisons of nonbinge drinkers, infrequent binge drinkers, and frequent binge drinkers and each of the three driving behaviors were all significant for men and women separately at $P < .001$. Sample sizes vary slightly for each question because of missing values. See Table 11.1 for explanation of drinking classification.

the eight problems studied, students at schools with high and middle binge levels were more likely than students at schools with low binge levels to experience problems as a result of the drinking behaviors of others.

The odds of experiencing at least one of the eight problems was roughly 4:1 when students at schools with high binge levels were compared with students at schools with low binge levels.

COMMENT

To our knowledge, this is the first study that has used a representative national sample, and the first large-scale study to measure binge drinking under a sex-specific definition. Forty-four percent of the college students in this study were classified as binge drinkers. This finding is consistent with the findings of other national studies such as the University of Michigan's Monitoring the Future Project, which found that 41% of college students were binge drinkers,[13] and the Core Alcohol and

Drug Survey, which found that 42% of college students were binge drinkers.[5]

A possible limitation of surveys using self-reports of drinking behavior pertains to the validity of responses; however, a number of studies have confirmed the validity of self-reports of alcohol and substance use.[22-24] Findings indicate that if a self-report bias exists, it is largely limited to the heaviest use group[25] and should not affect such a conservative estimate of heavy volume as five drinks.

The results confirm that binge drinking is widespread on college campuses. Overall, almost half of all students were binge drinkers. One fifth of all students were frequent binge drinkers (had three or more binge drinking occasions in the past 2 weeks) and were deeply involved in a lifestyle characterized by frequent and deliberate intoxication. Frequent binge drinkers are much more likely to experience serious health and other consequences of their drinking behavior than other students. Almost half of them have experienced five or more alcohol-related

TABLE 11.4   Students Experiencing Secondary Binge Effects (Based on Students Who Were Not Binge
Drinkers and Living in Dormitories, Fraternities, or Sororities)

	School's Binging Level		
	Low, %	Middle, %	High, %
Secondary Binge Effect	*(n = 801)*	*(n = 1115)*	*(n = 1064)*
Been insulted or humiliated	21	30	34
Had a serious argument or quarrel	13	18	20
Been pushed, hit, or assaulted	7	10	13
Had your property damaged	6	13	15
Had to take care of drunken student	31	47	54
Had your studying/sleep interrupted	42	64	68
Experienced an unwanted sexual advance[a]	15	21	26
Been a victim of sexual assault or date rape[a]	2	1	2
Experienced at least one of the above problems	62	82	87

[a]Based on women only.

problems since the beginning of the school year, one of three report they were hurt or injured, and two in five engaged in unplanned sexual activity. Frequent binge drinkers also report drinking and driving: Three of five male frequent binge drinkers drove after drinking some alcohol in the 30 days prior to the survey, and two of five drove after having five or more drinks. A recent national report that reviewed published studies concluded that alcohol was involved in two thirds of college student suicides, in 90% of campus rapes, and in 95% of violent crime on campus.[26]

Almost a third of the colleges in the study have a majority of students who binge. Not only do these binge drinkers put themselves at risk, they also create problems for their fellow students who are not binge drinking. Students who did not binge and who reside at schools with high levels of binge drinkers were up to three times as likely to report being bothered by the drinking-related behaviors of other students than students who did not binge and who reside at schools with lower levels of binge drinkers. These problems included being pushed, hit, or assaulted and experiencing an unwanted sexual advance.

Effective interventions face a number of challenges. Drinking is not typically a behavior learned in college and often continues patterns established earlier.

References

1. US Dept of Health and Human Services. *Alcohol and Health*. Rockville, Md: National Institute on Alcohol Abuse and Alcoholism: 1990.
2. Robert Wood Johnson Foundation. *Substance Abuse. The Nation's Number One Health Problem, Key Indicators for Policy*. Princeton, NJ: Robert Wood Johnson Foundation: October 1993.
3. Wechsler H, Isaac N. Binge' drinkers at Massachusetts colleges: prevalence, drinking styles, time trends, and associated problems. *JAMA*. 1992:267: 2929–2931.

4. Hanson DJ, Engs RC. College students' drinking problems: A national study, 1982–1991. *Psychol Rep*. 1992:71:39–42.

5. Presley CA, Meilman PW, Lyerla R. *Alcohol and Drugs on American College Campuses: Use, Consequence, and Perceptions of the Campus Environment, Volume 1: 1989–1991*. Carbondale, Ill: The Core Institute: 1993.

6. The Carnegie Foundation for the Advancement of Teaching. *Campus Life: In Search of Community*. Princeton. NJ: Princeton University Press: 1990.

7. Straus R, Bacon SD. *Drinking in College*. New Haven, Conn: Yale University Press: 1953.

8. Berkowitz AD, Perkins HW. Problem drinking among college students: a review of recent research. *J Am Coll Health*. 1986: 35:21–28.

9. Saltz R, Elandt D. College student drinking studies: 1976–1985. *Contemp Drug Probl*. 1986:13:117–157.

10. Haworth-Hoeppner S, Globetti G, Stem J, Morasco F. The quantity and frequency of drinking among undergraduates at a southern university. *Int J Addict*. 1989:24:829–857.

11. Liljestrand P. Quality in college student drinking research: conceptual and methodological issues. *J Alcohol Drug Educ*. 1993:38:1–36.

12. Hughes S, Dodder R. Alcohol consumption patterns among college populations. *J Coll Student Personnel*. 1983:20:257–264.

13. Johnston LD, O'Malley PM, Bachman JG. *Drug Use Among American High School Seniors, College Students, and Young Adults, 1975–1990. Volume 2*. Washington, DC: Government Printing Office: 1991. US Dept of Health and Human Services publication ADM 91–1835.

14. Wechsler II, McFadden M. Drinking among college students in New England. *J Stud Alcohol*. 1979:40:969–996.

15. O'Hare TM. Drinking in college: consumption patterns, problems, sex differences, and legal drinking age. *J Stud Alcohol*. 1990:51:536–541.

16. Engs RC, Hanson DJ. The drinking patterns and problems of college students: 1983. *J Alcohol Drug Educ*. 1985:31:65–83.

17. Brennan AF, Walfish S, AuBuchon P. Alcohol use and abuse in college students, I: A review of individual and personality correlates. *Int J addict*. 1986:21:449–474.

18. Room R. Measuring alcohol consumption in the US: Methods and rationales. In: Clark WB, Hilton ME, eds. *Alcohol in America: Drinking Practices and Problems*. Albany: State University of New York Press, 1991:26–50.

20. US Dept of Education. *Digest of Educational Statistics*. Washington, DC: National Center of Educational Statistics. 1993:180–205.

21. *Barron's Profiles of American Colleges*. Hauppauge, NY: Barron's Educational Series Inc: 1992.

22. Midanik L. Validity of self-reported alcohol use: A literature review and assessment. *Br J Addict*. 1988:83:1019–1030.

23. Cooper AM, Sobell MB, Sobell LC, Maisto SA. Validity of alcoholics' self-reports: Duration data. *Int J Addict*. 1981:16:401–406.

24. Reinisch OJ, Bell RM, Ellickson PL. *How Accurate Are Adolescent Reports of Drug Use?* Santa Monica. Calif: RAND: 1991. RAND publication N-3189-CHF.

25. Room R. Survey vs sales data for the US. *Drink Drug Pract Surv*. 1971:3:15–16.

26. CASA Commission on Substance Abuse at Colleges and Universities. *Rethinking Rites of Passage: Substance Abuse on America's Campuses*. New York, NY: Columbia University: June 1994.

QUESTIONS

1. Technically, these researchers used a sampling method known as **two-stage cluster sampling**, first selecting a sample of colleges and then selecting students within selected colleges. How did they select colleges? How were students selected?

2. The researchers used a mail questionnaire. Describe two advantages of using a mail survey, as opposed to a face-to-face interview, for this research, given the researchers' topic and sample.

3. What two methods did the researchers use to increase the response rate—the percentage of sampled students who completed the survey?

4. How do the authors define (and measure) non-binge drinking, binge drinking, infrequent binge drinking, and frequent binge drinking?

5. At the end of the selection, the authors discuss a potential limitation of surveys of alcohol use. How do they defend their results in light of this limitation?

Selection 12

Using General Social Survey (GSS) data between 1973 and 1998, Jeni Loftus describes trends in Americans' attitudes toward homosexuality over time. These survey data are based on face-to-face interviews of multiple, or repeated, cross-sections of people over time. As you read this selection, pay attention to survey question wording, Loftus's descriptive findings, and her discussion of the strengths and limitations of GSS data.

AMERICA'S LIBERALIZATION IN ATTITUDES TOWARD HOMOSEXUALITY, 1973–1998

JENI LOFTUS

Since the Stonewall riots in 1969, there have been many steps both forward and backward for gays and lesbians in the United States. They have gained social acceptance among certain subgroups of the populations while facing increased hostility from others (Werum and Winders 2001). But what major gains, if any, have been made in Americans' attitudes toward homosexuality?

Recent research suggests that Americans have become increasingly liberal in their opinions about civil liberties (Brooks 2000), especially those regarding African Americans (Farley 1997; Firebaugh and Davis 1988) and females (Mason and Lu 1988). Research suggests that this liberalization is beginning to be extended to gays and lesbians (Brooks 2000). Yet the research on attitudes toward homosexuality is contradictory and has not systematically explored the causes and patterns of opinion change over time.

[This selection addresses one main question:] Over the past 25 years, what has been the

Source: "America's Liberalization in Attitudes toward Homosexuality: 1973-1998," by Jeni Loftus, *American Sociological Review* Vol. 66, No. 5 (Oct., 2001), pp. 762-782. Copyright 2001 by Sage Publications and the American Sociological Association.

pattern of change in attitudes toward homosexuality?

PRIOR RESEARCH ON ATTITUDES TOWARD HOMOSEXUALITY

Several studies have examined changes in attitudes using the National Opinion Research Center General Social Surveys (GSS), the best data available for studying shifts in these attitudes. Analyzing data from 1973 to 1977, Glenn and Weaver (1979) find a small but significant increase in positive attitudes regarding the morality of homosexuality. Dejowski (1992) finds a decline from 1973 to 1988 in American's willingness to restrict the civil liberties of homosexuals, which he partially attributes to increasing levels of education. Smith (1992) reports a decline from 1973 to 1991 in the willingness of respondents to restrict the civil liberties of homosexuals but he finds an increase in the belief that homosexuality is always wrong.

Yang (1997), using data from 1973 to 1996, finds that attitudes toward the morality of homosexuality remained steady until the 1990s, but liberalized thereafter. Willingness to restrict the civil liberties of homosexuals has declined steadily since 1973.

METHODS

Data

To examine changing attitudes toward homosexuality in the United States, I use data from the General Social Survey (GSS) between 1973 and 1998. The GSS is a national area probability sample of noninstitutionalized adults 18 years of age or older. Until 1994, approximately 1,500 people were sampled in each survey year; the 1994, 1996, and 1998 samples are of approximately 3,000 respondents. Questions concerning homosexuality were asked in 17 survey years over this period.

Measures

The GSS consistently includes four items concerning attitudes toward homosexuality. The first concerns the morality of homosexuality:

> What about sexual relations between two adults of the same sex—do you think it is always wrong, almost always wrong, wrong only sometimes, or not wrong at all?

Respondents could answer "always wrong" (coded 4), "almost always wrong" (coded 3), "sometimes wrong" (coded 2), and "not wrong at all" (coded 1).

Three variables concern the civil liberties of homosexuals:

> And what about a man who admits that he is a homosexual? Suppose this admitted homosexual wanted to make a speech in your community. Should he be allowed to speak or not?

> Should such a person be allowed to teach in a college or university, or not?

> If some people in your community suggested that a book he wrote in favor of homosexuality should be taken out of your public library would you favor removing this book, or not?

Respondents could answer either "yes" (coded 0) or "no" (coded 1).[1] I combined the responses to the last three variables to create an index of restriction of the rights of homosexuals. Values on the index range from 0 (opposition to restrictions) to 3 (support for all three restrictions).

Problems exist with the wording of these questions, primarily the negative slant and the focus on male homosexuals in the civil liberties questions. The negative wording of the questions may lead respondents to acquiesce to more negative attitudes. In addition, respondents may react differently to male and female homosexuals, and this is not captured by these questions. Nonetheless, the GSS is the only nationally representative data set to consistently ask questions concerning homosexuality over a long period of time. Moreover, wording of the questions cannot be changed, as that would prohibit year-to-year comparisons. Thus, this data set is the best, and only, way to explore how attitudes toward homosexuality have changed since 1973.

RESULTS

Trends in Attitudes Toward Homosexuality

Figure 12.1 summarizes trends in attitudes toward homosexuality. A majority of Americans in each year view homosexuality as "always wrong." Americans became more conservative in the 1980s, then became increasingly liberal. The most liberal year was 1998, with 31 percent reporting homosexuality as "not wrong at all,"

and 56 percent reporting homosexuality as "always wrong," compared to 13 percent and 75 percent, respectively, in 1987, the most conservative year for the morality question.

The trend is different for civil liberties of homosexuals. In each year, more people were against than were in favor of restricting the civil liberties of homosexuals. While the general pattern shows a decrease in the willingness to restrict civil liberties, conservativism increased in the 1980s, similar to but much weaker than the conservative trend toward the morality of homosexuality during this time. The most liberal year for civil liberties was 1998 with 65 percent reporting they would not restrict any civil liberties, and only 12 percent reporting they would restrict all three civil liberties. These figures were 39 percent and 30 percent, respectively, in 1973 when negative attitudes toward the civil liberties of homosexuals were at their peak.

FIGURE 12.1   Percentages Responding That Homosexuality Is "Always Wrong" and "Not Wrong at All," and Percentages Responding That They Would Restrict "Zero" and "Three" Civil Liberties of Homosexuals: GSS, by Year, 1973 to 1998

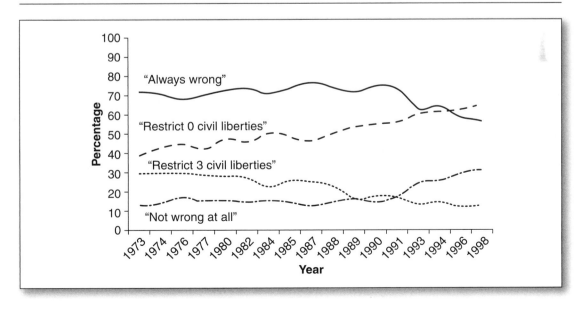

DISCUSSION AND CONCLUSION

Attitudes toward the morality of homosexuality and the willingness to restrict the civil liberties of homosexuals have changed in the last quarter century. Americans' attitudes regarding the morality of homosexuality became slightly more liberal from 1973 to 1976, became increasingly conservative through 1990, and have become more liberal since 1990. Over the same 25-year period, willingness to restrict the civil liberties of homosexuals declined steadily, the only departure being a brief increase in negative attitudes in the late 1980s. Why are the trend lines different for the judgment of the morality of homosexuality and the willingness to restrict the civil liberties of homosexuals?

The American public clearly makes a distinction between whether homosexuality is morally wrong and whether homosexuals should be allowed certain civil rights. While the public still overwhelmingly views homosexuality as wrong, the majority is unwilling to restrict the civil liberties of homosexuals. Two possibilities help explain this distinction.

First, the "morality" question of the GSS concerns homosexuality as a practice, while the "civil liberties" questions concern gays and lesbians as a group. Thus, the morality question focuses directly on homosexual behavior, particularly sexual behavior, while the civil liberties questions focus on issues of minority group status. The morality question may be picking up Americans' puritanical attitudes concerning sexuality, and gay sexuality in particular, while the civil liberties questions do not call up these puritanical attitudes.

Strategies to evoke or avoid this sexual image of gays have been used by both sides of the debate on homosexuality. How political arguments are framed has a profound impact on their reception in the public (Bernstein 1997; Nelson and Kinder 1996). Gay activists often have found it easier to gain public support by focusing political campaigns on their rights as a minority group (Seidman 1993). By likening themselves to other disadvantaged groups, they encourage the public to think of gays and lesbians as disadvantaged and discriminated against. Those on the religious right often try to vilify gays and lesbians by calling forth images of gay sexuality and portraying them as hypersexualized, predatory, and deviant. This frame separates gays and lesbians from other minority groups, portraying them as somehow morally suspect.

Questions about morality also call forth images of "free will" and "choice" with regard to homosexuality. Research indicates that people who believe that homosexuality is a choice are more likely to condemn it than do those who believe that gays and lesbians are born that way (Herek and Capitanio 1995). The religious right argues that gays and lesbians are not like other minority groups because they have *chosen* their lifestyles, therefore other groups genuinely deserve civil rights protections while gays and lesbians do not. The religious right has profiled a number of "ex-gays"—individuals who have chosen to become straight—as a way of reasserting that homosexuality is a freely chosen, and sinful, behavior.

Second, examining the distinction made by Americans between the morality of homosexuality and civil liberties for homosexuals, it is useful to compare the situation of homosexuals with that of other minority groups. Since World War II, an increasing number of Americans have supported equal opportunity for African Americans; however, although in 1990 the majority of white Americans believed that African Americans should have equal opportunity, whites still held many negative stereotypes about African Americans (Farley 1997). This suggests that the distinction between morality and civil liberties is not unique to the situation of gays and lesbians. This distinction emphasizes the definition of "tolerance" in political sociology, whereby an individual grants rights to a particular group even though he or she *dislikes* that group (McClosky and Brill 1983; Stouffer 1955).

Research is, of course, limited by the data available. While the GSS provides the best data set with which to study these issues, there are problems with it. The wording of the questions may have affected the trend lines. Research suggests that the attitudes reported by the respondent may be influenced by whether the homosexual in the question is male or female. The morality question asked about sex-unspecified homosexuals. Research indicates that there is little difference between attitudes expressed toward sex-unspecified homosexuals and those expressed toward gay men (Kite and Whitley 1996), suggesting that when sex is unspecified, respondents assume that the homosexual is male. In the civil liberties questions, the sex of the homosexual was specified to be male. If both questions had been worded so they included gay men and lesbians, the trend lines might have been different. Research suggests that men report more positive attitudes toward lesbians than they do toward gay men, while women report slightly more negative attitudes toward lesbians than they do toward gay men (Kite and Whitely 1996). This suggests that attitudes would have been more positive overall and the trend lines would have shifted down slightly. However, my interest was in the patterns of change over time, and those should not have changed with different wordings of the questions unless attitudes toward gays and lesbians changed differently.

Previous research has not systematically examined the change in attitudes Americans hold toward the morality of homosexuality and the civil liberties of homosexuals. An increasing number of individuals are unwilling to restrict the civil liberties of homosexuals, and a decreasing number of individuals believe that homosexuality is always wrong. Americans appear to be gradually becoming more accepting of homosexuality. It is possible that these changes in attitudes are due largely to the gay and lesbian liberation movements.

NOTE

1. Coding regarding removal of a pro-homosexual book from a library was reversed so that 1 = favors removal, 0 = does not favor removal.

REFERENCES

Bernstein, Mary. 1997. "Celebration and Suppression: The Strategic Uses of Identity by the Lesbian and Gay Movement." *American Journal of Sociology* 103:531–65.

Brooks, Clem. 2000. "Civil Rights Liberalism and the Suppression of a Republican Political Realignment in the United States, 1972 to 1996." *American Sociological Review* 65:483–505.

Dejowski, Edmund F. 1992. "Public Endorsement of Restrictions on Three Aspects of Free Expression by Homosexuals: Socio-Demographic and Trend Analysis 1973–1988." *Journal of Homosexuality* 23:1–18.

Farley, Reynolds. 1997. "Racial Trends and Differences in the United States 30 Years after the Civil Rights Decade." *Social Science Research* 26:235–62.

Firebaugh, Glenn and Kenneth E. Davis. 1988. "Trends in Antiblack Prejudice, 1972–1984: Region and Cohort Effects." *American Journal of Sociology* 94:251–72.

Glenn, Norval D. and Charles N. Weaver. 1979. "Attitudes toward Premarital, Extramarital, and Homosexual Relations in the U.S. in the 1970s." *The Journal of Sex Research* 15:108–18.

Herek, Gregory M. and John P. Capitanio. 1995. "Black Heterosexuals' Attitudes toward Lesbians and Gay Men in the United States." *Journal of Sex Research* 32:95–105.

Kite, Mary E. and Bernard E. Whitley Jr. 1996. "Sex Differences in Attitudes toward Homosexual Persons, Behaviors, and Civil Rights: A Meta-Analysis." *Personality and Social Psychology Bulletin* 22:336–53.

Mason, Karen and Yu-Hsia Lu. 1988. "Attitudes toward Women's Familial Roles: Changes in the United States." *Gender and Society* 2:39–57.

McClosky, Herbert and Alida Brill. 1983. *Dimensions of Tolerance: What Americans Believe about Civil Liberties*. New York: Russell Sage Foundation.

Nelson, Thomas E. and Donald R. Kinder. 1996. "Issue Frames and Group-Centrism in American Public Opinion." *Journal of Politics* 58:1055–78.

Seidman, Steven. 1993. "Identity and Politics in a 'Postmodern' Gay Culture: Some Historical and Conceptual Notes." Pp. 105–42 in *Fear of a Queer Planet: Queer Politics and Social Theory*, edited by M. Warner. Minneapolis, MN: University of Minnesota Press.

Smith, Tom W. 1992. "Attitudes toward Sexual Permissiveness: Trends, Correlates, and Behavioral Connections." Pp. 63–97 in *Sexuality Across the Life Course*, edited by A. S. Rossi. Chicago, IL: University of Chicago Press.

Stouffer, Samuel A. 1955. *Communism, Conformity, and Civil Liberties.* New York: Doubleday.

Werum, Regina and Bill Winders. 2001. "Who's 'In' and Who's 'Out': State Fragmentation and the Struggle over Gay Rights, 1974–1999." *Social Problems* 48:386–410.

Yang, Alan S. 1997. "The Polls—Trends: Attitudes toward Homosexuality." *Public Opinion Quarterly* 61:477–507.

QUESTIONS

1. Throughout the selection and particularly in the conclusion, Loftus consistently describes what "Americans" think about this or that. How can she make such claims if the GSS does not interview *all* Americans?

2. If you were to develop a prediction on the basis of Loftus's analysis as well as prior research, would attitudes toward homosexuality become more liberal, more conservative, or not change at all over time?

3. Loftus discusses both advantages and disadvantages of using GSS data to study attitudes toward homosexuality. List one advantage and one disadvantage. On balance, do these data provide more advantages or disadvantages?

4. Why is the wording of survey questions so important, according to Loftus?

UNIT VII

QUALITATIVE FIELD RESEARCH AND INTERVIEWS

Social scientists often distinguish between quantitative and qualitative research. In **quantitative research**, typified by experiments and surveys, data are transformed into numbers, hypotheses are tested, and in the case of many surveys, characteristics of the population are estimated. **Qualitative research,** by contrast, is designed to explore the meanings that people attach to their experiences and yields data that usually take the form of rich descriptions and verbatim statements by informants or interviewees. There is often a trade-off between generalizable data, as is true of much survey data, versus in-depth data, as is more often the case with qualitative data.

A variety of research may be considered qualitative. Here we are concerned with its two most common forms: **field research** and **qualitative interviews.** Regardless of which of these forms is taken, direct observation generally plays a more central role in qualitative research than in quantitative research. For example, field researchers watch people in their *natural settings*, which is different than the kind of controlled observation that takes place in a laboratory experiment (Bailey, 1995; Lofland, Snow, Anderson, & Lofland, 2006, p. 3). Qualitative researchers may also take greater notice of *how* people respond to interview questions. Thus, they tend to prefer **unstructured interviews** or

semistructured interviews over the standardized, and sometimes rigid, **structured interviews** that survey researchers use.

Of these two common forms of qualitative research, field research is probably the most encompassing: It generally combines observations of the *setting* with qualitative interviews. For example, in her study of how class background affects parenting styles, Annette Lareau (2003) and her assistants spent countless hours in the field observing children at school and interviewing families in the midwestern and northeastern United States. As a first step, Lareau gained access to third-grade classrooms in which some of these families' children were enrolled. Lareau then used a combination of purposive/theoretical and **quota sampling** to choose comparable numbers of black and white families of middle-class, working-class, and poor backgrounds for in-home observations. After securing families' permission, Lareau had to decide how to act so that families would not change their (natural) behaviors, while also maintaining professional standards and ethics. For example, Lareau (2003: 9) writes,

When we [Lareau and her research assistants] introduced ourselves to each family, we said that, following a famous study, we wanted to be treated like "the family dog" . . . [and] the rule of thumb was not to criticize and not to intervene unless a child was in imminent danger.

As this suggests, qualitative research is neither quick nor easy. In fact, Lareau's research took more than 10 years to complete from the time it was started until it was published.

Despite the challenges of qualitative research, it has the advantage of providing more in-depth data *on social processes*. Based on her field research, Lareau (2003) argues that middle-class parents adopt a strategy of "concerted cultivation," which entails negotiating with their children, teaching them to feel comfortable with authority figures, reasoning with their children, and encouraging their children to participate in formal organized extracurricular activities (p. 31). Illustrating some of these processes are Lareau's (2003, p. 119) observational data on a black middle-class family—Christina (a manager and the mother), Terry (a lawyer and the father), and Alex (their 10 year-old child). After Alex's parents ask Alex to find a riddle in a book in order to help him complete his homework assignment of writing five riddles,

> Alex [says] smiling, "Yeah. That's a good idea! I'll go upstairs and copy one from out of the book." Terry turns around with a dish in hand, "That was a joke—not a valid suggestion. That is not an option." . . . Christina says, looking at Alex: "There is a word for that you know, plagiarism." Terry says (not turning around), "Someone can sue you for plagiarism. Did you know that?" Alex: "That's only if it is copyrighted." (Lareau, 2003, p. 119).

By contrast, working-class and poor parents tend to emphasize "the accomplishment of natural growth," which entails teaching their children deference to authority and to follow directions, and encouraging their children to play informally and autonomously (p. 31). An example of the latter characteristic comes from an interview with Ms. Taylor—a black, working-class mother of Tyler—who at least initially did not see formal organized extracurricular activities, such as football, as important for

Tyler's development. According to Lareau (2003), Ms. Taylor said,

> He [Tyler] wanted to play last year, but we wouldn't let him. We thought he was too young and he was very upset . . . And then I think he went to one of the practices with someone around here, one of his friends, and he wanted to sign up. He told me that he wanted to play football, and I said, "No, I don't think so." (p. 77)

Just as Lareau's rich data highlight social processes, so too do the selections in this unit. The process by which women "cool out"—or, "let down"—men in singles bars and nightclubs is the topic of the first selection, which is based on field research (observations and semistructured interviews, specifically). The second selection focuses on how mothers on welfare and in low-wage jobs try to pay their bills, as well as how it affects them and their families. In this selection, notice that the researchers use qualitative interviews to gather both qualitative and quantitative data. As you read these selections, pay attention not only to the substantive process being investigated, but also to the field research and qualitative interview processes themselves.

REFERENCES

Bailey, C. A. (1995). *A guide to field research.* Thousand Oaks, CA: Sage/Pine Forge.

Lareau, A. (2003). *Unequal childhoods: Class, race, and family life.* Berkeley: University of California Press.

Lofland, J., Snow, D. A., Anderson, L., & Lofland, L. H. (2006). *Analyzing social settings: A guide to qualitative observation and analysis.* Belmont, CA: Wadsworth.

RESOURCES

The Qualitative Report (through Nova Southeastern University and maintained by Dr. Ronald J. Chenail):

http://www.nova.edu/ssss/QR/web.html

- This website has links to a number of other websites that focus on qualitative research approaches (as well as qualitative analyses, discussed in Unit X). One of these websites is noted below. On the Qualitative Report site and elsewhere on the Web, you can also find information on qualitative research not explicitly covered in this reader, including feminist research, discourse analysis, conversation analysis, phenomenological research, and more.

The Center for Urban Ethnography, University of California at Berkeley:

http://cue.berkeley.edu/

- This site provides a number of resources, including references to important articles in qualitative research; a journal that the center publishes, *Ethnography*; and even an internship program for undergraduates. This website is especially related to the first selection in this unit, as the researchers write that they are doing an urban ethnography; the second selection in this unit is also focused on urban areas.

- *Qualitative Research Guidelines Project* (through the Robert Wood Johnson Foundation and developed by Cohen D. Crabtree B.):

http://www.qualres.org/index.html

- On this website, you can obtain further information on qualitative research in general, as well as types of interviews (structured, semistructured, unstructured, etc.) more specifically (see: http://www.qualres.org/HomeInte-3595.html).

Field Research Project by Nathan Light:

http://homepages.utoledo.edu/nlight/english/fieldworkproj.htm

- A brief but helpful guide for students doing field research projects involving interviewing and participant observation.

US Department of Health and Human Services, Administration for Children & Families:

http://www.acf.hhs.gov/programs/ofa/tanf/about.html

- The second selection in this unit discusses a program known as Temporary Assistance for Needy Families (TANF). If you are interested in learning more about this program, this website contains information on the program, resources, and data.

Selection 13

How do women reject men's advances in singles bars and nightclubs? David Snow, Cherylon Robinson, and Patricia McCall, drawing from the work of Erving Goffman, argue that women "cool out" men using a variety of strategies, ranging from "polite refusal" to avoidance, depending on how assertive the men are. This "cooling out" process is also important to understand because we often encounter requests in other, everyday interactions, and we have to figure out a way of saying no. As you read this selection, note the range of techniques that the researchers use to collect in-depth, qualitative data and how these data provide validity to the overall argument.

"COOLING OUT" MEN IN SINGLES BARS AND NIGHTCLUBS

Observations on the Interpersonal Survival Strategies of Women in Public Places

DAVID A. SNOW, CHERYLON ROBINSON, AND PATRICIA L. MCCALL

Urban areas provide numerous public places with the potential for interaction between unacquainted and semi-acquainted men and women. One of the characteristic features of interaction in public places is that it is laden with a range of threats to the bodies and selves of those individuals who frequent them (Goffman 1963, 1971; Lofland 1973). These threats are not randomly experienced, however. Women, it has been argued, are particularly vulnerable to being hassled in one form or another (Blair 1974; Damrosch 1975; Enjeu and Save 1974; Goffman 1977; Wekerle 1980). Such hassling can occur at

Source: "'Cooling Out' Men in Singles Bars and Nightclubs: Observations on the Interpersonal Survival Strategies of Women in Public Places," by David A. Snow, Cherylon Robinson, and Patricia McCall. 1991. *Journal of Contemporary Ethnography,* *19*(4):423-449. Copyright 1991 by SAGE Publications and the American Sociological Assocation.

a distance—as when women are monitored by construction workers (Feigelman 1974)—or face-to-face—as when women are approached directly by males in some public or quasi-public setting (Brooks-Gardner 1981; Rochford 1985). It thus follows that the successful negotiation of public places by women is frequently contingent on their ability to fend off men and parry their advances, whether direct or indirect. It is clear that many women are indeed accomplished at this. But how it is done and the reasons underlying the manner in which it is done are not well understood. Our aim in this article is to further empirical and theoretical understanding of these two interconnected questions by examining the strategies and practices employed by women in dealing with the unwanted advances of men in singles bars and other nightclub settings. Our focus is on neither the structure or culture of these settings nor on the range of encounters that occur in them involving men and women but, rather, on those encounters which women seek to avoid or from which they attempt to extricate themselves. We thus attend to the interpersonal lines and practices employed by women for such purposes.

We conceptualize these strategic activities in relation to the "cooling out" process initially outlined by Goffman (1952) and applicable to most settings wherein individuals find themselves either involved in actual encounters from which they seek to disengage or confronted with prospective encounters which they wish to avoid. We ask, in short, how do women "cool out" men in singles bars and nightclubs, and what factors shape the nature of this cooling-out process?

THE COOLING-OUT PROCESS AND ITS RELEVANCE TO WOMEN

As part of the lexicon of the world of criminal fraud, the cooling-out concept traditionally has referred to the interactional process wherein individuals who have been conned into taking a financial loss are consoled after the "blow off" or "sting." Since falling for a con entails not only a financial loss but a loss of face, the aim of the cooling-out process, at least initially, is to help the "mark" adapt to the blow to self so that s/he will not be too humiliated or angry.

Finding metaphorical utility in the concept, Goffman (1952) suggested its extension to any domain of social life where individuals suffer involuntary loss or failure that reflects unfavorably on either their capacity to perform a particular role or their claim to a particular self or identity. In these situations, the individual is not conceptualized as a mark but simply as a person who has lost face because of rejection or failure. Thus the cooling-out process, as conceptualized by Goffman, can be broadly conceived as an interactional strategy that may be invoked in a range of situations to soften the humiliation and dampen the prospect of aggressive compensatory behavior that often follows on the heels of rejection or failure.

The task of cooling out others is not especially desirable. Telling people that they are incompetent, unqualified, unattractive, dishonest, and the like is neither easy nor gratifying, particularly for more sensitive individuals given to empathetically taking the role of others. There are certain informal relationships in which the role of "cooler" looms almost constantly on the interactional horizon, as with the termination of dating or courting relationships. Yet there are some individuals who rather frequently find themselves in the cooler role because they are incumbents of a master status (Hughes 1945) or basic role (Banton 1965) that define them, in part, as objects of solicitation and predation. Such is the case with women.

Consistent with this aspect of the characterization of women, traditional gender role norms not only prescribe that the male initiate contact with the female in many situations but they implicitly legitimate, and perhaps even encourage, various types of hassling. Although gender roles are changing, these normative understandings, be they explicit or implicit, are still operative in many contexts.

The successful negotiation of public places by women is, in part, contingent on their ability to cool men out. Men play a role in this process, too, not only by activating it through their advances but by being normatively obligated to respond to the cooling-out lines directed toward them in a cooperative manner. They are expected, in other words, to leave the encounter without too much fuss and thereby help preserve the "interaction order" (Goffman 1983).

But this microlevel order is highly vulnerable to being fractured, as when individuals who have been cooled out press forward, failing to accept their rejection and the chance to save face. When confronted with such interactional deviance, the cooler can be expected to assume a more defensive posture aimed at terminating the encounter without attending to the inconsistency between the aggressor's self-definition and social definition. This, too, may be regarded as a form of cooling-out behavior.

Because of the interactional uncertainties associated with cooling out people in either of the preceding senses, individuals who expect to find themselves cast in the cooler role may seek to reduce the likelihood of that happening by employing various avoidance tactics that signal unavailability and disinterest in being approached interactionally. This can also be construed as a type of cooling-out behavior but in a preemptive sense.

Each of the foregoing variants of the cooling-out process was readily discerned during the course of our examination of the interpersonal tactics which women employ in order to fend off and parry the unwanted advances of men in one sector of public life.

CONTEXT AND PROCEDURES

Although the female-to-male cooling-out process can occur in most public places, there are few, if any, public settings in which it occurs as frequently and can be observed as readily as in singles bars, cocktail lounges, and other night spots. One of the distinctive features of these settings in American society, as Goffman (1963, 134–35) observed, is that they "tend to be defined as open places" where, among other things, men are free to engage women, even more so than in other public places.

The generalized public accessibility of women is even heightened in drinking establishments and nightclubs frequented by both males and females. From the vantage point of men, women in such settings, whether in the role of patron or employee, constitute "fair game." As one male informant asked rhetorically, "Why else would women be there if they didn't want to be picked up?" Obviously, some do, others are selectively interested, and some are indifferent or disinterested.

By pursuing a female in this environment, the male places his assessment of self at risk, since rejection may signify that he has miscalculated and is less desirable than he had assumed. Rejection in these situations thus represents a loss of face which can elicit hostile and aggressive behavior on the part of the male. In order to avoid embarrassing or hostile reactions to these rejections, females could be expected to invoke the cooling-out strategy. Consequently, the cooling-out process ought to be abundantly evident in singles bars and other night spots. We thus chose such settings as the primary locus for our research.

The data were collected by three means: participant observation in a number of different nightclubs, informal conversational interviews with patrons and employees in those settings, and semistructured interviews with a small nonrandom sample of bar patrons and employees and university students. The participant observation was conducted during the course of a 3-month period in which two of the authors visited, on one or more occasions, nine different nightclubs and drinking establishments. Four of the establishments were singles bars, two were country-western dance clubs, another two were disco and rock clubs, and one was a topless club.

On each occasion, the participant observer always stood or sat where she could hear or see other women. Such strategic positioning enabled the researcher to simultaneously observe and eavesdrop. The eavesdropping tactic was frequently impeded by the din of the music in several settings. As a consequence, it was often necessary to engage in informal, conversational interviews as a supplemental strategy. These interviews were typically occasioned by the observation of a cooling-out exchange that could not be overheard. In such instances, the researcher would attempt to elicit commentary from the female cooler by asking direct questions, such as "What was going on with that guy?", or by interviewing by comment, that is, by making declarative statements, such as "That guy sure is persistent!" Every now and then, their conversations were continued or initiated in the women's restroom. Interestingly, the restroom was found to be a particularly fruitful context for drawing out detailed commentary on cooling-out episodes, particularly when the exchange preceded the restroom excursion.

To supplement and complement the ethnographic data, we also conducted semi-structured interviews with 6 bar patrons, 6 bar employees, and 21 university students. While the majority of respondents were female (70%), we did interview 10 males in order to acquire some sense of the male perspective on the cooling-out process. Following a brief explanation of our research interests to each respondent, we asked them a number of questions aimed at getting them to discuss the cooling-out process as they had experienced it. We were particularly interested in learning about the cooling-out tactics which they had either employed or encountered, and the degree to which their experiences dovetailed with our observations. These data thus provided a kind of "validity check" for our ethnographic observations.

WOMEN'S PROTECTIVE STRATEGIES

Our research found abundant evidence of the three previously mentioned sets of strategic practices associated with actual or anticipated cooling-out encounters. The first set includes all cooling-out lines or tactics typically triggered by initial face-to-face requests or overtures. The second set comprises more defensive and assertive tactics activated by the more persistent and obstinate males. And the third set consists of various practices employed in hopes of avoiding the cooling-out role and encounter altogether.

Initial Cooling-Out Tactics

Initial cooling-out tactics constituted the first line of defense employed by females when confronted by unsolicited or undesired advances by males. They comprised any combination of verbal and nonverbal lines employed in dyadic face-to-face encounters with men for the purpose of expressing disinterest in dancing, conversing, or continuing the encounter, at least for the moment. These tactics were typically elicited by initial advances and tended to be relatively unoffensive, as if the aim were "to let the man down easily."

Polite Refusal

Since male advances in nightclubs were most often initiated by questions—such as "Would you like to dance?" or "Can I buy you a drink?"—women who were the objects of such interrogative overtures had little choice but to respond. They might choose to ignore the initial inquiry by acting as if they did not hear it, but such a response only invited repetition of the question. Thus an answer was socially obligated.

The most frequently observed response was the polite refusal, the generic form being "No, thank you." Nearly all the women with whom we spoke considered such a response to be quite appropriate, especially in the face of initial advances that were courteous and inoffensive. In such instances, one 25-year-old female noted, "I try not to embarrass them or humiliate them. I just let them know very honestly and try not to lead them on."

Our conversations and observations revealed further that polite and cordial cooling-out lines were often accompanied by a conscious attempt to soften or mute the rejection. One way this appeared to be done was by smiling and maintaining eye contact during the encounter. As one cocktail waitress noted when commenting about her dealings with the suggestive advances of a male customer:

> I'd go to his table to see if he needed a drink and say, "Would you like another drink?" and he'd say, "No, but I'd like something else," and I'd say, "Sorry, that's all I sell" and then smile my plastic smile.

Polite refusals were also softened on occasion by articulating them in a fashion that did not imply finality or a permanent lack of interest, as reflected in the comment "not right now, but maybe another time." By leaving the door ajar, so to speak, the female cooler provided the male with some psychic elbowroom so that while he returned to his table or bar stool empty-handed, he was at least left with a ray of hope that things would turn out differently the next time.

Excuses

Excuses comprise a second set of commonly observed cooling-out lines. Over and over again, we heard women disengage themselves from nascent encounters with men by making excuses. The most common excuse entailed the verbalization of commitment to extant personal relationships, particularly to husbands and boyfriends.

The following comments are illustrative:

> "I'm married!"

> "I'm waiting for my boyfriend."

> "No, I really can't. My date will be back in a minute."

> "I'm with someone."

Excuses were also invoked that involved commitments to other responsibilities, such as work and family. One topless dancer explained that her work provided her with a handy excuse: "It's easy for me. I just look them in the eye and tell them that I don't date customers." A cocktail waitress was overheard responding to a male customer in a similar fashion: "I have to work and I really don't have time to socialize. I can't make any money sitting here, and you probably don't want to tip me anyway." On occasion, children were even used as an excuse. And sometimes, a challenged female would parry advances by invoking multiple commitments, as in the case of one female patron who was overheard saying during a cooling-out encounter: "You don't want to pick me up. I'm a married woman and I've got kids, and I'm too busy working."

Normative constraints were also employed as excuses, including references to race, size, and age differences. An especially tall female, who reported using her size to cool out men, recalled the following episode: "We were sitting down, and these guys kept coming over to talk with us and bother us. . . . They were all really short, so I just stood up. That's all I had to do." Age stereotypes were also employed, as when one 38-year-old respondent recalled cooling out a 19-year-old by simply saying, "Hey, I'm an older woman. I'm much older than you."

Finally, some women were heard to invoke excuses based on physiological considerations, such as refusing a drink by pleading, "I've had my limit." Physiological excuses were also useful in refusing a dance. For example, when queried about why she did not want to dance, one 19-year-old female simply said, "[B]ecause I can't dance in these shoes." Other excuses of this same genre included "I'm too tired" and "I can't dance to this song."

Joking

In addition to polite refusals and excuses, we also overheard cooling-out lines that had something of the flavor of jokes. The following comments are illustrative of this jocular banter:

> "You've got to be kidding. You wanta dance with me?"

> "No way! We'd both look like fools."

> "No, I can't dance. My feet are too big, and I'd step all over you."

> "Sorry, but I don't drink, and if I did, I'd probably get sick. You probably wouldn't like that! So you better find someone else."

While such comments sounded a bit like excuses, they were more appropriately conceptualized as jokes in that they made light of the encounter and humorously brushed aside the serious intent of the overture. By redefining the encounter as a humorous misunderstanding, the man's advance was reframed as a deliberate but nonserious overture. Although such a cooling-out tactic ran the risk of offending the initiator of the encounter, it was equally likely to prevent or diffuse tension by transforming a situation of seriousness into one of levity. And, in doing so, the man was allowed to bow out without a serious loss of face, for the failed approach could be seen as a humorous misunderstanding or as the jocular contrivance of the clever man. In either case, the rebuffed suitor was likely to leave, shrouded with the illusion that he had not suffered an unmistakable rejection. It was perhaps because of these considerations that some women employed joking almost routinely as a cooling-out tactic. As one 20-year-old informant noted after having successfully parried an advance by reframing it as a joke, "I usually try to make these situations into a joke. Ya know, I just joke around."

Defensive, Nonempathetic Cooling-Out Tactics

Not all men left the encounters quietly or as inconspicuously as possible. Some simply refused to be cooled out. As one male bartender observed, "They don't get violent about it, but some get pretty irritated" and become more aggressive. The question thus arises: How did women deal with men who refused to be cooled out, at least initially? In other words, how did they counter the persistence of men who failed to acknowledge or accept their initial rejection and the opportunity to leave the encounter with their face intact, thus creating a scene or violating, however momentarily, the interaction order?

Our observations suggest that such interactionally "deviant" persistence invited tactics of defensive assertiveness that showed little of the earlier regard for salvaging the aggressor's initial presentation of self. More specifically, humor was displaced by studied seriousness, politeness gave way to a kind of defensive incivility, and excuses were either embellished and strengthened or jettisoned in favor of justifications. Although these tactical responses were hardly mutually exclusive, we consider them separately for analytical purposes.

Studied Seriousness

By studied seriousness, we refer to the focusing of attention and energy on an immediate, pressing task. In contrast to the initial exchange, typically characterized by seemingly ritualized civility and playfulness, this form of exchange was decidedly somber and potentially combative, as indicated by the interactants' stiffened postures, sharpened voices, and seriousness of expression. This transformation or reframing of the encounter was typically "keyed" by questions or comments offered by the male in response to initial cooling-out lines. Overheard comments and questions that served this keying function included the following:

> "Why not?" (in response to a polite refusal to dance)
>
> "You've gotta be kiddin'!" (in response to a jocular refusal to accept a drink)
>
> "Oh, come on . . . you can dance with me!" (in response to an excuse about being attached)
>
> "No! What do you mean, no?" (in response to a polite refusal)

Such questions and comments not only begged for further response but, coming on the heel of parried advances, they seemed to invite interpersonal lines that resonated with and reflected the new ethos of the encounter and that were thus different from the initial cooling-out lines.

Defensive Incivility

The generic response seemed to be characterized by a kind of defensive incivility. Gone was the earlier apparent concern with softening the blow of rejection. Far more salient was the woman's concern with extricating herself from the now menacing encounter by making unmistakably clear her lack of interest in the man's advance. If she appeared rude and he was personally embarrassed in the process, so be it. Sometimes, the response was bold and straightforward, as illustrated in the case of one respondent who described how she finally cooled out a man who persisted in asking her to dance: "I finally pointed my finger at him as if I was scolding him and said, 'Listen to what I'm saying. I do not want to dance.'" She added that "there were some men standing at the bar nearby who could overhear the encounter" and that the persistent man left immediately when he realized this, "probably to avoid further embarrassment."

Self-Evident Justifications

A sense of this more defensively assertive and nonempathetic attitude is reflected further in the following cooling-out lines that we overheard:

> "Look, I don't want to dance with you!"
>
> "Just leave me alone!"
>
> "I just told you, I'm not interested!"
>
> "Back off!!"
>
> "I don't want anything to do with you!"
>
> "Get control of yourself!"

Such cooling-out lines constituted almost pure forms of self-evident justifications (Scott and Lyman 1968). There was no reference to some external constraint or countervailing agency as in the case of an excuse. The female cooler accepted responsibility for rejecting the overture. She was just plainly uninterested. Moreover, she acted as if there were nothing inappropriate or pejorative about her defensive incivility. After all, she had been pushed into a corner. Her initial cooling-out lines had been rejected themselves in an act of incivility by her prospective suitor. Consequently, her more defensive and assertive posture was situationally commanded. As one informant mused when explaining this switch in frame and attendant action:

> If men come up nicely, you know, I try to be as nice as I can. But if somebody comes up and they really think they're Casanova . . . and they just are overbearing in their attitude and do not accept no

for an answer . . . I just spurt out something like "I wouldn't want to dance with you" . . . to put him down, ya know, put him in his place.

While this general response seemed to be most commonplace in the face of persistent males, we sometimes overheard women laminate their self-justified incivility with an embellished excuse, as if to strengthen the force and credibility of their claim of disinterest. To illustrate, a topless dancer explained how she had used an embellished excuse to drive off a particularly persistent client:

> I had one guy last week who wanted to follow me home [after work] and I said, "Well, you can go ahead and follow me home, but I'm not responsible for the actions of all six bikers that live with me."

Avoidance Tactics

[One] possibility for women was to employ safeguards and strategies that signaled unavailability or disinterest, thereby lessening the likelihood of being drawn into cooling-out encounters. Three such sets of avoidance tactics were discernible during our research.

Tie Signs

Our informants reported that the best way to avoid cooling-out encounters was to be in the company of a male friend or several female friends and to provide unmistakable evidence of involvement or bondedness. Such "tie signs," as Goffman (1971) called these indicators of "anchored relationships," took the form of hand and arm holding, occasional embracing and kissing, continuous conversation, mutual orientation, and greater spatial proximity than was typically the case among unattached, noninvolved patrons.

Direct experiential validation of the reliability of ties with copresent others was provided on a number of occasions when one of the female authors was accompanied by a male friend during several field observations. When the male friend was visibly present, the female researcher received no overtures from other males. But when the friend drifted off from time to time, so that there was no clear-cut evidence of interactional commitment to some proximate other, then the woman became the object of advances by other male patrons.

In the absence of the protective shield provided by proximate others to whom there was indication of some attachment, conspicuously worn or placed jewelry, such as rings, could serve this function. As one 24-year-old female informant noted, "I have a friend who swivels her ring around so it looks like a wedding band. They [the men] really do notice, and when they do, they leave her alone."

The problem with such tie signs in the absence of the signified other is that they frequently went unnoticed. Additionally, they were sometimes ignored or taken to be indicative of a lukewarm relationship at best. Consequently, they were less likely to ensure avoidance of the cooling-out process.

Nonverbal Cues of Disinterest

A second avoidance strategy was to communicate nonverbally a lack of interest in being approached. Since sustained eye contact was perceived as a way to invite an overture, fleeting eye contact was taken as a sign of disinterest. One female respondent reported that she routinely resorted to this ploy. "I look away a lot," she said. "Eye contact is the key." A male informant agreed, noting that he took his cues from a woman's eyes: "[E]yes are very important. If you stare at someone, then it means you're more interested, and vice-versa." Other facial gestures, such as a frown, were also consciously used on occasion to signal lack of interest, sometimes in conjunction with fleeting glances and sometimes independently. One female respondent noted that "a lot of times I'll give a mean look. . . . [I]t's not so much aimed at [any one individual], it's just a look like 'I'm a bitch, leave me alone . . . you don't even want to say "hi" to me.'"

Flight

Should tie signs or gestures of disinterest fail to keep men at a distance, then women occasionally resorted to flight or escape. They might leave the premises, relocate themselves in another sector of the club, or frequent the restroom. In commenting on this pattern to a woman who had just evaded an advancing man, one of the researchers suggested that perhaps a lot of movement that takes place in singles bars reflects efforts to escape undesired encounters. "Sure," the informant responded, " . . . there's just so much you can do. You turn your back on some guy, and he doesn't take the hint that you aren't interested. All you can do then is walk away."

The most common refuge for escape from unsolicited encounters appeared to be the women's restroom. One of the authors tested this observation by remarking to a queue of women in a restroom that she guessed she wasn't the only one avoiding a man. She was answered by an affirmative nod by a number of women. This tack was also confirmed by several male informants who noted that they had been the objects of such evasive action on more than one occasion, as well as by a male bartender who referred to this ploy as "the duck out."

SUMMARY AND DISCUSSION

In this article, we examined one variety of encounter that occurs among women and men in public places: those that women are not interested in pursuing and thus seek to avoid or extricate themselves from by cooling out men. It is this genre of encounter that arises because of the differences in the expectancies attached to male and female roles in many domains of social life. Women are confronted with two choices of action: Either they define public places as dangerous and remain at home, becoming "shut-ins" or, more accurately, victims of the threat of being hassled, or they frequent public places, learning, among other things, how to fend off and parry the advances of men.

Three sets of protective strategies were identified and elaborated: (a) initial cooling-out tactics, entailing polite refusals, excuses, and jokes; (b) a combination of studied seriousness, defensive incivility, and self-evident justifications for dealing with the more persistent and interactionally deviant males; and (c) avoidance of cooling-out encounters by exhibiting tie signs, nonverbal displays of disinterest, or fleeing or escaping. We do not presume that these three sets of interpersonal tactics exhaust the repertoire of cooling-out practices employed by women in public life in general. Indeed, we suspect that examination of the process by which women cool out men in other contexts would yield other protective safeguards and techniques. However, we would expect most such strategies to be variants of the categories we observed. That remains an empirical question, however. At the very least, though, the foregoing observations and analysis provide a point of departure for further examination of the female-to-male cooling-out process in public places and for the eventual development of a fully elaborated grounded theory of female interpersonal survival strategies.

REFERENCES

Banton, M. 1965. *Roles: An introduction to the study of social relations*. New York: Basic Books.

Blair, G. L. 1974. Standing on the corner. *Liberation* 18:6–8.

Brooks-Gardner, C. 1981. Passing by: Street remarks, address rights, and the urban female. *Sociological Inquiry* 15:328–56.

Damrosch, B. 1975. The sex ray: One woman's theory of street hassling. *Village Voice* 7 (April): 7.

Enjeu, C., and J. Save. 1974. The city: Off-limits to women. *Liberation* 8:9–15.

Feigelman, W. 1974. Peeping: The pattern of voyeurism among construction workers. *Urban Life and Culture* 3:35–49.

Goffman, E. 1952. On cooling the mark out: Some aspects of adaptation to failure. *Psychiatry* 15:451–63.

———. 1959. *The presentation of self in everyday life*. New York: Anchor/Doubleday.

———. 1963. *Behavior in public places: Notes on the social organization of gatherings*. New York: Free Press.

———. 1971. *Relations in public: Microstudies of the public order*. New York: Basic Books.

———. 1974. *Frame analysis*. New York: Harper & Row.

———. 1977. The arrangement between the sexes. *Theory and Society* 4:301–31.

———. 1981. *Forms of talk*. Philadelphia: University of Pennsylvania Press.

———. 1983. The Interaction order. *American Sociological Review* 48:1–17.

Hughes, E. 1945. Dilemmas and contradictions of status. *American Journal of Sociology* 50:353–59.

Rochford, E. B., Jr. 1985. *Hare Krishna in America*. New Brunswick, NJ: Rutgers University Press.

Scott, M. B., and S. Lyman. 1968. Accounts. *American Sociological Review* 33:46–62.

QUESTIONS

1. Why do the researchers select singles bars, cocktail lounges, and other night spots to study the "cooling out process"?

2. What three means of data collection do the researchers use?

3. How, exactly, do the researchers collect the participant observation data on male-female interaction? The researchers mention one limitation of this method. How do they overcome this limitation?

4. How do the semistructured interviews complement the data obtained from participant observation?

5. Based on the section entitled "Avoidance Tactics," provide one example of how the researchers' participant observation data and semistructured interview data correspond with each other?

Selection 14

Legislation enacted in 1996 ended the governmental program that most people associate with welfare—Aid to Families with Dependent Children (AFDC)—which is for children of single parents or from disadvantaged families, (in contrast to Supplemental Security Income [SSI], which is for aged people, or those with disabilities, with little or no income, see www.ssa.gov/ssi/). Replacing AFDC a program with more stringent work requirements; it does not allow individuals to stay on welfare as long (see website listed in the resources). Before this new program went into effect, Kathryn Edin and Laura Lein asked how mothers on welfare and in low-paying jobs survive. To answer this question, they also collected data on these mothers' budgets. Note especially how telephone or other surveys of random samples of mothers would not have provided the same answers that their methods provide.

WORK, WELFARE, AND SINGLE MOTHERS' ECONOMIC SURVIVAL STRATEGIES

KATHRYN EDIN AND LAURA LEIN

In 1996, federal lawmakers dramatically changed the rules poor people live by and made states responsible for implementing these rules. Twenty-five percent of the mothers on each state's welfare caseload must be working by the end of 1997; by 2002, 50 percent must be working. If this legislation is fully implemented, virtually every single mother who is not disabled will be expected to work after two years on the welfare rolls, regardless of her educational preparation or skill level.

Longitudinal data on welfare dynamics suggest that if states are to comply with these new federal rules, they face an enormous challenge. In recent years, most mothers who entered the welfare rolls exited relatively

Source: "Work, Welfare, and Single Mothers' Economic Survival Strategies," by Kathryn Edin and Laura Lein, *American Sociological Review*, Vol. 62, No. 2 (Apr., 1997), pp. 253-266. Copyright 1997 by Sage Publications and the American Sociological Association.

quickly—60 percent within two years. Most left for a job, but more than half of those who left welfare for work returned for a subsequent spell (Bane and Ellwood 1994; Harris 1993, 1996; Pavetti 1992). Not surprisingly, those mothers most vulnerable to repeated welfare use had the least work experience and education (Edin and Harris 1996; Harris and Edin 1996). Why was the route from welfare to work so difficult under the old federal system, and what do the experiences of single mothers who moved between welfare and work under the old system tell us about how single mothers might fare under the new state-regulated systems?

In this analysis, we first itemize the expenditures for low-income single mothers and show how these mothers supplemented their main income sources with other income (either welfare or a low-wage job). Second, we demonstrate how low-income single mothers' overall economic situations affected their view of the trade-offs between welfare and work.

DATA AND METHOD

We draw our data from multiple and intensive interviews with welfare- and wage-reliant single mothers in four U.S. cities—the Boston area, Chicago, Charleston, and San Antonio. In these interviews we gathered in-depth data on the full range of economic survival strategies both welfare-reliant single mothers and single mothers who relied on low-wage employment used. National-level data indicate that low-income single mothers in both groups report spending far more on average than they receive in benefits or wages (Edin 1993; Edin and Jencks 1992). Our interviews were designed to document how mothers resolve their budget deficits.

In an earlier project in Chicago, Edin attempted to conduct interviews with welfare recipients by telephone, drawing a sample from respondents who had participated in a prior random-sample study of Chicago residents (Edin 1993). While a few respondents were forthcoming, most were unwilling to offer budget information over the phone. When interviewing these respondents in person, she could not construct budgets that balanced—mothers reported spending more than their welfare benefits or earnings covered, but would not reveal the supplementary income sources that allowed them to do this. Lein had similar experiences with a randomly selected group in San Antonio. We believe these difficulties stemmed from the fact that these mothers had no personal introduction to us and feared we would report their income-generating activity to their caseworkers, who would then reduce or even eliminate their benefits.

Because of these difficulties, we recruited welfare-reliant mothers by asking individuals from nongovernmental community organizations and local institutions to introduce us to welfare recipients with whom they had established some rapport and testify to our trustworthiness. We then asked these mothers to introduce us to one or two other mothers whom they thought we would not contact through an organization. We used the same strategies to recruit our wage-reliant subjects. In each of the four cities, we contacted more than 100 low-income single mothers from between 33 to 40 independent networks, and close to 90 percent of the mothers we approached agreed to participate.

We interviewed approximately equal numbers of African Americans and Whites in Chicago, Charleston, and the Boston area, and equal numbers of African Americans, Whites, and Mexican Americans in San Antonio. We recruited roughly equal numbers of welfare-reliant and wage-reliant mothers in each racial/ethnic group. Approximately one-half of the mothers in each subgroup lived in subsidized housing and one-half lived in private housing. We oversampled mothers in public housing because we wanted to maximize our chances of finding mothers who could live on their welfare benefits or their wages. (Nationally, only 23 percent of welfare recipients receive housing subsidies [U.S. House of Representatives 1993:712]).

After contacting each respondent, we arranged several interviews, which usually took place in respondents' homes and lasted from one to three hours. In the initial interview, we gathered topical life histories. In subsequent interviews, we gathered detailed income and expenditure data. To ensure reliability, after each interview we compared the respondent's income and expenditure data with the budget data they had reported in earlier interviews. Using this method, welfare recipients and workers eventually reported enough income (from welfare, wages, and other sources) to cover their expenditures.

We chose the Boston area, Chicago, Charleston, and San Antonio to represent the range of welfare benefits states offered in the late 1980s and early 1990s. Chicago provided cash welfare benefits that approximated the national average, while Boston's benefits were more generous. Charleston and San Antonio, on the other hand, paid benefits that were significantly below average.

Wages varied in these cities as well. We recruited only those wage-reliant single mothers whose hourly wages fit within the range that our welfare-reliant mothers reported earning in the past. In San Antonio, the slackest labor market we studied, we limited our wage-reliant sample to mothers earning $7.00 per hour or less. In Charleston and Chicago, where labor markets were tighter and wages somewhat higher, we interviewed single mothers earning up to $7.50 per hour. In Boston, where a tight labor market during the 1980s had pushed wages among low-skill workers somewhat higher, we included mothers earning up to $8.00 per hour.

Finally, these four cities varied in their living costs. In Boston, rents at the 25th percentile averaged $446 per month in 1990, whereas rents at the 25th percentile were $375 in Chicago, $346 in Charleston, and only $292 in San Antonio.

Although our sample is neither random nor representative, it is heterogeneous. It includes both never-married mothers and divorced mothers; high school dropouts, graduates, and mothers with post-secondary training; mothers from the inner city and the suburbs; African American, White, and Mexican American mothers; mothers living in private housing and public housing; and mothers of different ages.

Our past experiences suggest that the budget information we sought was so sensitive that this study probably could not have been done using conventional survey techniques.

RESULTS

We begin by reporting the economic situations of the welfare mothers we interviewed; we then compare their situations to the economic situations of the low-wage working mothers.

Expenditures

Table 14.1 shows how the average monthly expenses of welfare recipients compared with those of low-wage working mothers. Working mothers spent substantially more each month to keep their families together than welfare recipients did. Working mothers spent more on housing, partly because they purchased slightly better housing and partly because working mothers who had a housing subsidy had more cash income than did mothers who received welfare. Both groups paid about 30 percent of their cash income for rent. The only other large differences in spending between the groups were for work-related expenses.

In sum, [the table shows] that neither welfare recipients nor low-wage working mothers made ends meet on their main income sources alone. Although the working mothers had more income left over after paying for housing and food, their overall budget deficits were larger because working was more expensive than relying on welfare. The welfare recipients had an average budget shortfall of $311 per month as compared to $411 for working mothers. Although the working mothers reported spending about $367 more each month than the welfare recipients spent to keep their families together ($1,243 compared to $876), the welfare recipients we interviewed probably would have needed to spend more than this if they went to work. Most low-wage working mothers had several mitigating circumstances that lowered the cost of working.

TABLE 14.1   Average Monthly Expenses and Income: Welfare-Reliant Mothers and Low-Wage Working Single Mothers in Four U.S. Cities

Average Monthly Expenses/Income	Welfare-Reliant Mothers	Working Mothers	
Total Expenses	$876	$1,243	**
Housing	$213	$341	**
Food	$262	$249	
Total other essential items	$336	$569	**
Childcare	7	66	**
Medical	18	56	**
Clothing	69	95	**
Transportation	62	129	**
Telephone	31	35	
Laundry/toiletries/cleaning	52	53	
Diapers/baby care	18	10	*
School supplies/fees	14	25	
Appliances/furniture	17	22	
Miscellaneous	47	78	**
Total nonessential items	$64	$84	**
Entertainment	20	27	*
Cigarettes and alcohol	22	22	
Lottery	3	1	
Cable TV	6	9	*
Eating out	13	25	**
Total Welfare Income	$565	$60	**
AFDC	307	—	
Food stamps	222	57	**
SSI	36	3	**
Income from Main Job[a]	—	$802	
Budget Deficit			
Welfare/main job income minus total expenses[a]	−$311	−$441	**
Welfare/main job income minus housing and food expenses[a]	$90	$212	**
Number of Mothers	214	165	
Family Size	3.4	2.9	

Note: Income and expenses are in 1991 dollars. Income/expense subcategories may not sum exactly to totals shown because of rounding error.

[a]Welfare/main job income includes monthly earned income tax credit (EITC).

*p < .05 **p < .01 (two-tailed tests for significance of differences in means between welfare-reliant mothers and working mothers)

Welfare Recipients' Supplemental Income

Table 14.2 shows how welfare recipients in each city made up for their monthly budget shortfalls. We divide work into three categories: reported work, unreported work, and underground work. *Reported work* refers to work in the formal sector that recipients report to their caseworkers. Across cities, between 2 and 9 percent of our welfare recipients worked at jobs and reported their earnings, compared to 6.4 percent nationally (U.S. House of Representatives

1993:696). *Unreported work* refers to either formal sector work that is not reported or to cash work in the informal sector. Between 32 and 52 percent of our welfare recipients engaged in such work to supplement their budgets. Finally, between 2 and 19 percent sold sex, drugs, or stolen goods to generate extra money. We call this *underground work* because it violates both the welfare rules and other laws.

In addition, between 25 and 44 percent received cash assistance from a community group, local charity, or other nonwelfare agency. Finally, from 69 to 91 percent of the welfare

TABLE 14.2 Economic Survival Strategies of Welfare-Reliant Mothers in Four U.S. Cities

	Percent[b]				*Average Monthly Income*			
Survival Strategy	*Boston*	*Chicago*	*Charleston*	*San Antonio*	*Boston*	*Chicago*	*Charleston*	*San Antonio*
Total Supplemental Work[a]	44	60	36	41	$101	$180	$108	$111
Reported work	2	2	9	6	16	5	25	29
Unreported work	36	52	32	35	54	133	79	81
Underground work	7	19	2	3**	31	40	3	1
Community Group/ Agency Assistance	44	27	25	30	$26	$58	$49	$15
Total Network Income[a]	69	77	91	71	$126	$157	$253	$114**
Family	53	40	55	40	44	53	106	54*
Boyfriends	31	24	32	29	62	60	78	32
Absent fathers	27	32	41	32	20	45	69	27*
Covert support	24	21	36	16	18	40	60	17*
Formal support	4	13	18	21	2	4	9	10*
Number of mothers	45	62	44	63	45	62	44	63

Note: Percentages for subcategories will not sum to total percentages because women engaged in multiple survival strategies. Average monthly income is in 1991 dollars. Income subcategories may not sum exactly to totals shown because of rounding error.

[a]Some mothers engage in more than one survival strategy within a category.

[b]Percentage participating over a 12-month period.

*$p < .05$ ** $p < .01$ (two-tailed tests for significance of differences in means between cities)

recipients we interviewed in each city used network-based strategies to make extra money. Between 40 and 55 percent of the recipients got cash help from a family member. From 24 to 32 percent received cash assistance from a boyfriend. Finally, between 27 and 41 percent of recipients received cash help from a child's father. Some fathers contributed through the formal child-support system, and some fathers gave money directly to the mothers.

Our cities differed in ways that explain these variations in welfare recipients' strategies. Tight labor markets (as measured by the county unemployment rate) affected welfare recipients' survival strategies in two ways. First, Chicago's tight labor market provided mothers more opportunities for side work. Second, Charleston's and Chicago's favorable labor markets increased recipients' income from network members, presumably because these network members' earnings increased. One Charleston mother compared her network support in the late 1980s to her situation in the early 1980s when the city's unemployment rate was higher:

> For a while, nobody in my family was helping me 'cause nobody was working. Now my mother and my sister got jobs, and neither one of them are raising kids. . . . [Now] they help me with my bills from time to time.

City size affected welfare recipients' survival strategies in two ways. First, in large metropolitan areas like Chicago, recipients who worked at unreported jobs had little chance of being detected. In smaller urban areas, recipients who engaged in unreported work had difficulty hiding this work from their caseworkers or others in their communities who might have reported them. One Charleston recipient told us:

> I could never get away with taking a regular job [without my caseworker knowing]. Let's say I worked at McDonald's. Everybody in my neighborhood would know about it and someone would turn me in. Even if they didn't, I would probably end up taking an order from my caseworker in the drive-through. Everybody know everybody else's business around here.

Welfare caseworkers in small cities were usually as busy as those in larger metropolitan areas, but found it harder to ignore community members who reported blatant violations of welfare regulations. In these cities, welfare recipients who wanted to combine welfare with covert work generally took less visible jobs in the informal sector (i.e., house-cleaning, babysitting, or sewing). Mothers usually found these jobs through trusted family members or friends whom they believed would not report them. The need for anonymity also applied to underground work, which also varied with city size.

The character of each city's informal and underground economy also affected welfare recipients' range of possible survival strategies. Only in Chicago and San Antonio did recipients tell us they knew how to obtain a false ID, probably because the large numbers of illegal immigrants in each city had created a market for false Social Security cards. In Chicago, mothers paid roughly $20 for a Social Security card with another name. They paid up to $70 if they also required a birth certificate and picture ID. Most welfare-reliant mothers could find suppliers through friends or former coworkers. One Chicago recipient told us:

> At the factory [where I worked] there was a lot of foreigners. They was all illegal to this country. Every one of them was doing it. They told me, "Why don't you go out and get a Social Security card in somebody else's name? Then you can get welfare too!" I went down to Madison Avenue, just like they said. I just showed them my money, and the rest was easy.

The practices of local child-support enforcement officials, which varied considerably from place to place, also affected welfare recipients' survival strategies. In Charleston, where enforcement was much stricter than in other cities and county judges routinely jailed absent fathers on contempt charges for failing to meet their child-support obligations, welfare recipients were the most successful in getting contributions from absent fathers. Charleston's strict enforcement rules made mothers' threats of turning fathers who did not pay informally over to the authorities more credible than in other cities. In addition, when Charleston mothers used the formal system, they also received more child support than mothers in other cities did. One mother in Charleston told us:

> I get $100 a month [under the table] from my son's father and $100 a month [informally] from my daughter's father, and that's the way it's been since my babies were born. That's money that welfare would take away from me if I went through the [child-support enforcement] system. If they don't pay, I [will] turn 'em in. Then they will make them pay [even more every month, and] if they get behind, they [will] go to jail.

Working Mothers' Supplemental Income

How did welfare-reliant mothers' survival strategies compare with those of low-wage working mothers? Table 14.3 compares the survival strategies of mothers in the two groups. First, although roughly the same number of welfare recipients and working mothers engaged in side work to supplement their budgets, working mothers who took side jobs made less money than their welfare counterparts did because they worked fewer hours. This in turn was due to the time constraints imposed by their main jobs. Second, virtually none of the working mothers had earnings from the underground economy, while some of the welfare recipients did. Although several workers told us they had taken such jobs in the past (when they were on welfare), they felt that leaving welfare had made them more respectable in the eyes of their friends and neighbors and they weren't willing to forgo this new status by risking incarceration. Third, welfare recipients were somewhat more likely to receive cash help from community groups. Finally, they were just as likely as the working mothers to rely on members of their personal networks, but working mothers received far more generous contributions from their networks than did welfare recipients (especially from absent fathers).

Working mothers also had more noncash resources than welfare recipients had—resources that lowered the costs of working. One Boston-area working mother described her personal safety net as follows:

> My expenses are very low since I live with my parents. That means I have no rent, no electric bill, no housing bills that people out on their own must pay.

A San Antonio mother who lived with her sister and mother in a three-bedroom apartment (there were five children) told us how she managed to stay at her job:

> [We] share all of our expenses in this house, which allows us to afford much more than if were living separately. [All our kids are in school all day]. [I work from] 9:30 a.m. [to 6:30 p.m.]. [My sister] works from 7:00 a.m. to 3:00 p.m. I drop all the children off at school. She pick[s] up the children from school and [takes] them home. We manage to work [our second jobs] on alternate weekends so that someone is always home with these kids. [If] all else fails, we can always ask our mother to baby-sit. And we don't have to pay her either.

Nine of 10 working mothers reported at least one of these noncash resources, two-thirds reported two or more, and nearly half reported three or more. When we asked our welfare-reliant mothers whether they thought they would have access to similar resources if they left welfare and took a job, less than one-third reported that one or more of these resources would likely be available if they went to work immediately.

Because the working mothers had, on average, more cash network support and more access to noncash resources than welfare recipients had, working mothers generally had a much stronger private safety net than welfare recipients. In many cases, this protected them from having to rely on the public safety net (welfare), at least in the short term. For welfare recipients who relied on covert work or charities, taking a full-time reported job generally meant having to forgo much or all of their income from these sources.

TABLE 14.3   Economic Survival Strategies of Welfare-Reliant Mothers and Low-Wage Working Single Mothers in Four U.S. Cities

	Percent[a]		Average Monthly Income	
	Welfare-Reliant Mothers	Working Mothers	Welfare-Reliant Mothers	Working Mothers
Total Earned Side Income	46	39	$128	$88*
Reported part-time job or overtime	5	12**	19	27
Unreported side job or second job	39	28*	90	59**
Underground economy	8	1**	19	2*
Community Group/Agency Assistance	31	22*	$37	$36
Total Network Income	77	82	$157	$253**
Family and friends	46	47	62	65
Boyfriends	29	27	56	60
Absent fathers	33	42	39	127*
Number of Mothers	214	165	214	165

Note: Percentages for subcategories will not sum to total percentages because women engaged in multiple survival strategies. Average monthly income is in 1991 dollars. Income subcategories may not sum exactly to totals shown because of rounding error.

[a]Percent participating over a 12-month period.

*$p < .05$; **$p < .01$ (two-tailed tests for significance of differences in means between cities welfare recipients and workers).

For these welfare recipients, leaving welfare for work would result in a net loss in income. For families already living very close to the economic margin, this prospect posed a serious threat to their material well-being.

Mothers' Perceptions of the Benefits of Welfare and Work

The economic realities described above profoundly affected low-income mothers' perceptions of the relative utility of welfare versus work. Most of the welfare mothers we interviewed were aware of the economic consequences of working

because they had held reported jobs in the past— 83 percent had work experience in the formal sector and 65 percent had worked at a formal sector job within the previous five years. Furthermore, our recipients had an average of 5.6 years of work experience.

Our mothers learned five primary lessons from their low-wage work experience. First, although even a low-wage job paid more than welfare, it also cost more to work. These costs often equaled, and often even outweighed, a job's earnings advantage. Second, taking a job made the pursuit of other work-based strategies more difficult, so that mothers who relied primarily on these strategies would realize a net loss when they went to work. Third, work income was less stable than welfare income—employers who offer low-wage jobs can seldom guarantee their workers full-time hours, and they are more likely to lay them off than other employers are (Danziger and Gottshalk 1987). Furthermore, such workers were seldom eligible for unemployment insurance (Spalter-Roth, Hartmann, and Burr 1993). Fourth, things would probably not improve over time because most low-wage jobs offer virtually no premium on experience (Blank 1995; Burtless 1985; Harris and Edin 1996; Levitan and Shapiro 1987). Fifth, working in the low-wage sector was often not compatible with parenting. Most of the positions mothers had held offered employees no sick leave or paid vacation days to take care of sick children who could not attend school. In addition, employers seldom allowed mothers to make personal calls from work to check on children left home alone.

Despite these hard lessons, most of the welfare recipients we interviewed showed remarkable dedication to the work ethic. They recognized the stigma that their friends, communities, and the larger society imposed on welfare recipients, as well as the boost in self-esteem and social standing they gained from working. This is why they had tried to live off of work in the past and also why they were trying to find a way to do so in the future.

Of the 214 welfare recipients interviewed, only 15 percent had no real plans to get off welfare for work. Of these, more than one-third were receiving disability payments for themselves or a child. About one-half of the rest said they were not planning to leave welfare for work because they worked nearly full-time in the informal or underground economy and believed they were better off combining welfare with unreported work than having to forgo them both for a formal sector job. Of the remaining mothers, one-half planned to marry off of welfare and the other one-half claimed their current situations were simply too unstable to allow them to think about the future (most of these were victims of domestic abuse).

The rest of the welfare recipients we interviewed (85 percent) expressed a strong desire to leave welfare for work, but only 13 percent said they were ready to do so immediately. These mothers had significantly more education and work experience than did the welfare-reliant group as a whole, and none anticipated paying market child-care costs.

However, two-thirds of mothers who had plans to leave welfare thought that even if their child-care difficulties and health insurance problems were solved, they would have difficulty sustaining their families on a low-wage job. For these recipients, the answer was twofold: Find a way to lower their potential work costs, and in the meantime, pursue further education to improve their earnings potential. In fact, most recipients believed that combining welfare with quality training was the best way to achieve the long-term goal of economic self-sufficiency. One welfare recipient with substantial work experience told us:

> The system is all messed up. When people look in from the outside, [welfare] looks good. You don't have to work and you get money. But no one can live on this. I can't see [any way out]. [If] I get a full-time job [I can't get any help from the government] to go back to school. [If I stay on welfare] I can't afford to live on it. So I'm [going to get a part-time job under the table] and [go part-time to] school.

CONCLUSION

We have offered a detailed account of the family economics of the choice between welfare and work low-skill single mothers must make. We have shown that network strategies are conducive to moving from welfare to work, while side work and agency strategies are not. We have argued that mothers do not freely choose the strategies they employ. Rather, their choices are constrained both by the social-structural characteristics of the cities in which they live and by the quality of mothers' social capital and access to noncash resources.

Finally, we have shown that despite the constraints welfare-reliant mothers face, most have worked in the past and want to work in the future. However, many believe that unless their personal circumstances change or their job skills improve, the increased costs of working will make it difficult, if not impossible, for them to meet their financial obligations while working.

REFERENCES

Bane, Mary Jo and David T. Ellwood. 1994. *Welfare Realities: From Rhetoric to Reform.* Cambridge, MA: Harvard University Press.

Blank, Rebecca. 1995. "Outlook for the U.S. Labor Market and Prospects for Low-Wage Entry Jobs." Pp. 33–70 in *The Work Alternative: Welfare Reform and the Realities of the Job Market,* edited by D. Smith Nightingale and R. H. Haveman. Washington, DC: The Urban Institute Press.

Burtless, Gary. 1995. "Employment Prospects of Welfare Recipients." Pp. 71–106 in *The Work Alternative: Welfare Reform and the Realities of the Job Market,* edited by D. Smith Nightingale and R. H. Haveman. Washington, DC: The Urban Institute Press.

Danziger, Sheldon and Peter Gottschalk. 1987. *Uneven Tides: Rising Inequality in the 1980s.* New York: Russell Sage Foundation.

———. 1993. *There's a Lot of Month Left at the End of the Money: How AFDC Recipients Make Ends Meet in Chicago.* New York: Garland Press.

Edin, Kathryn and Kathleen Mullan Harris. 1996. "Getting Off and Staying Off: Race Differences in the Process of Working Off of Welfare." Department of Sociology, Rutgers University, New Brunswick, NJ; and Department of Sociology, University of North Carolina, Chapel Hill, NC. Unpublished manuscript.

Edin, Kathryn and Christopher Jencks. 1992. "Reforming Welfare." Pp. 204–35 in *Rethinking Social Policy: Race, Poverty and the Underclass,* edited by C. Jencks. Cambridge, MA: Harvard University Press.

Harris, Kathleen Mullan. 1993. "Work and Welfare among Single Mothers in Poverty." *American Journal of Sociology* 99:317–52.

———. 1996. "Life after Welfare: Women, Work, and Repeat Dependency. "*American Sociological Review* 61:407–26.

Harris, Kathleen Mullan and Kathryn Edin. 1996. "From Welfare to Work and Back Again." Department of Sociology, Rutgers University, New Brunswick, NJ: and Department of Sociology, University of North Carolina, Chapel Hill, NC, Unpublished manuscript.

Levitan, Sar A. and Isaac Shapiro. 1987. *Working but Poor: America's Contradiction.* Baltimore, MD: Johns Hopkins University Press.

Pavetti, LaDonna A. 1992. "The Dynamics of Welfare and Work: Exploring the Process by which Young Women Work their Way off Welfare." Paper presented at the APPAM Annual Research Conference, October, Denver, CO.

Spalter-Roth, Roberta, Heidi Hartmann, and Beverly Burr. 1993. *Income Insecurity: The Failure of Unemployment Insurance to Reach Working AFDC Mothers.* Washington, DC: Institute for Women's Policy Research.

U.S. House of Representatives, Committee on Ways and Means. 1993. *Overview of Entitlement Programs: Green Book.* Washington, DC: U.S. Government Printing Office.

QUESTIONS

1. How did the authors select their sample? In what ways does their sampling strategy resemble Blee's strategy in drawing a sample of women who were members of racist groups (see Unit IV, Selection 8)?

2. Why would it have been impossible to obtain the same data from these mothers using a telephone survey of a random sample?

3. Why is rapport so important in gathering data such as these?

4. Provide one example of how the (qualitative) quotes from mothers shed further light on the numbers in one of the tables.

5. Finally, what are the policy implications of this study for welfare?

UNIT VIII

EXISTING DATA ANALYSIS: CONTENT, HISTORICAL, AND COMPARATIVE

Despite their differences, nearly all of the selections in the previous three units have one thing in common: the researchers themselves produced the data. That is, with the exception of the Loftus study (Selection 12), researchers conducted their own experiments, surveys, direct observations and/or qualitative interviews. By contrast, the selections in this unit make use of **existing data**, that is, data that already existed before the study was carried out.

Existing data abound. One form consists of survey or qualitative data collected for a different research purpose. Loftus used data from the General Social Survey, a periodic omnibus survey conducted by the National Opinion Research Center. The **secondary analysis** of surveys is one of the most common types of contemporary social research. Another form of existing data consists of **official statistics** (e.g., birth and death rates) routinely gathered by governments to assist in policy making. But much existing data is produced for non-research purposes. Researchers, for example, may analyze magazines, newspapers, books, television shows, movies, as well as historical and other documents.

Aside from the data used in secondary analysis, three aspects make existing data

particularly valuable for social research. First, because existing data are already available, researchers can sometimes save time and money by analyzing them. Second, unlike the data from surveys, experiments, field research, and qualitative interviews, in which research participants know they are being studied and therefore may react disingenuously, these are **unobtrusive data**. Finally, existing data may be used to investigate social processes that are otherwise inaccessible. For example, in his classic study *Suicide,* first published in 1897, Emile Durkheim (1951) analyzed statistics on suicide compiled by several European nations in the second half of the 19th century. One of his most widely cited findings was that predominantly Roman Catholic countries had lower suicide rates than predominantly Protestant countries.

How existing data are analyzed depends on the form of the data, among other factors. One set of methods called **content analysis** analyzes the symbolic content of communications such as books, documents, mass media, and audio recordings. Usually words or visual images are coded into categories to describe and/or quantify the content of the data. As you will see in the first selection in this unit, Bernice Pescosolido,

Elizabeth Grauerholz, and Melissa Milkie do a content analysis of children's picture books to examine portrayals of African Americans in the United States between 1937 and 1993. Furthermore, they relate these portrayals to variation in interracial conflict in the larger society during this period.

Existing data are the primary means of studying history. Pescosolido and colleagues tested an explanation (interracial conflict) of a particular historical pattern (cultural images of Blacks). Other types of historical analysis use various data and methods to achieve different theoretical aims. To explicate a particular theory, researchers may draw on public documents to conduct an **explanatory case study** of a specific historical event or period. Kai Erikson (1966) sought to understand the usefulness of Durkheim's general theory of deviant behavior—that deviance defines and reinforces community boundaries—in explaining three crises in Puritan New England, including the well-known Salem witchcraft hysteria. For his in-depth analysis of this historical period, he drew largely on court records and the writings of public figures.

Another research strategy, called **comparative-historical analysis**, involves the systematic comparison of multiple cases over time to test theoretical explanations. Theda Skocpol (1979), for example, sought to identify underlying causes of social revolution by intensively analyzing the revolutions in France in 1789, Russia in 1917, and China from 1911 to 1949. As in Erikson's study of Puritan New England, the key theoretical framework for the second selection in this unit, by John Sutton, is Durkheim's theory that the distinction between deviants (criminals in this case) and nondeviants reinforces moral boundaries. To test theoretically derived hypotheses concerning historical increases in imprisonment, Sutton compares five countries using a variety of data gleaned from official statistics.

When you read the selections in this unit, remember that a common theme among them is that they make use of existing data. The data, however, are in different forms and analyzed in

different ways. For example, Pescosolido and colleagues' content analysis of media images is both qualitative and quantitative; Sutton's analysis of official statistics is quantitative. Consider the strengths of these analyses and data, especially compared to other research approaches and data that you have encountered in previous units.

REFERENCES

Durkheim, E. (1951). *Suicide: A study in sociology* (J. A. Spaulding & G. Simpson, Trans.). Glencoe, IL: Free Press.

Erikson, K. T. (1966). *Wayward Puritans: A study in the sociology of deviance.* New York: Wiley.

Skocpol, T. (1979). *States and social revolutions: A comparative analysis of France, Russia, and China.* Cambridge, UK: Cambridge University Press.

RESOURCES

Writing Guide: Content Analysis:

http://writing.colostate.edu/guides/research/content/index.cfm

- This Colorado State University website is an excellent resource for content analysis, as it discusses its theoretical and historical background, different forms, and methodological strengths and weakness. It also provides examples to illustrate the use of content analysis and an annotated bibliography for further research.

Philipp Mayring's (2000) "Qualitative Content Analysis" in Forum: Qualitative Research 1 (2):

http://www.qualitative-research.net/index.php/fqs/article/view/1089/2385

- Philipp Mayring's article focuses specifically on *qualitative* content analysis, which Pescosolido and colleagues undertake in their research (Selection 15). Mayring explains the (inductive) logic of qualitative content analysis and also notes a couple of computer programs that can be used to conduct it (for many other computer programs, see: http:// academic.csuohio.edu/kneuendorf/content/ cpuca/ccap.htm, which is a website accompanying Kimberly A. Neuendorf's *The Content Analysis Guidebook)*.

The Comparative and Historical Section of the American Sociological Association:

http://www2.asanet.org/sectionchs/

• Hosted by the national professional organization of sociologists, this website provides a number of resources for historical, comparative, and comparative-historical analyses, including information for further study and sources of existing data. On the left-hand side of this page, you'll see a number of links: The Student Center, Recent Publications, and Research Aids may be

particularly useful to you as you pursue these types of analyses.

Roy Walmsley's World Prison Population List, *8th ed. (through the International Centre for Prison Studies at King's College in London):*

http://www.prisonstudies.org/info/downloads/ wppl-8th_41.pdf

• In the second selection in this unit, Sutton examines imprisonment rates from 1955 to 1985 in five Western democracies. You can examine data through 2008 for many more countries by downloading the *World Prison Population List* above. However, you should be cautious in examining these data because, as Sutton notes, there are difficulties in comparing imprisonment rates across countries. Also pay careful attention to the sources and verify the numbers with data from other sources whenever possible.

Selection 15

In the last half of the 20th century, vast changes occurred in U.S. race relations. One area of change was in the cultural depiction of African Americans. Bernice Pescosolido, Elizabeth Grauerholz, and Melissa Milkie address an interesting sociological question about this change: Is racial conflict in the United States related to the portrayal of blacks in popular culture? Their answer is based on the content analysis of two forms of existing data: portrayals of blacks in children's picture books and stories of racial conflict reported by the *New York Times*. The content analysis is quantitative (measuring the percentage of books that portray black characters, for example) as well as qualitative (describing *how* blacks are portrayed through an analysis of book content, including words and pictures). As you read this selection, pay particular attention to the researchers' coding, measures, and results.

CULTURE AND CONFLICT

The Portrayal of Blacks in U.S. Children's Picture Books through the Mid-and Late-Twentieth Century

BERNICE A. PESCOSOLIDO, ELIZABETH GRAUERHOLZ, AND MELISSA A. MILKIE

One of the most enduring struggles in the United States centers on social relationships between Blacks and Whites. This struggle has produced not only dramatic changes in the legal, social, and economic power of African Americans, but also changes in cultural portrayals of race and race relations. Accompanying the social oppression of Blacks in the United States has been, in Tuchman's (1978) term, their "symbolic annihilation." Blacks have been ignored, stereotyped, or demeaned in cultural images. For example, in the early part of this century, popular cultural objects that degraded Blacks (e.g., Black

Source: "Culture and Conflict: The Portrayal of Blacks in U.S. Children's Picture Books Through the Mid- and Late-Twentieth Century," by Bernice A. Pescosolido, Elizabeth Grauerholz, and Melissa A. Milkie, *American Sociological Review*, Vol. 62, No. 3 (June, 1997), pp. 443-464. Copyright 1997 by Sage Publications and the American Sociological Association.

caricatures on salt shakers) reflected their low social status, served as a mechanism of social control, and alleviated status anxiety among Whites (Dubin 1987). As the civil rights movement began to unravel the tripartite system of economic, political, and personal oppression (Morris 1984), it also challenged the symbolic embodiments of domination.

We examine how race relations are manifest in one cultural form over time and how power struggles, reflected in racial conflict in the larger society, relate to patterns of symbolic representation. We focus on the portrayal of Blacks in U.S. children's picture books from 1937 to 1993. First we describe, using quantitative and qualitative methods, the extent and character of the portrayal of Blacks and of Black-White interaction over time. Second, we link these portrayals to tensions in U.S. race relations. This examination of changing images in popular culture provides a dynamic view of how social relations and ideological challenges to them are represented in simple yet powerful tales for children.

CULTURE AND SOCIAL CHANGE: BLACK-WHITE RELATIONS AND CHILDREN'S PICTURE BOOKS

Schudson (1989) argues that the study of cultural objects, while not an exhaustive account of culture, provides a key and privileged access to it. Children's picture books, by his definition, are potent cultural objects—they are readily available, have rhetorical force, resonate with children and adults, and are retained in institutions.

Bettelheim (1977) contends that literature represents one of the most powerful vehicles through which children assimilate their cultural heritage. The depiction of race relations to the newest members of a society via children's picture books subtly colors children's understanding of status arrangements, social boundaries, and power. As social significance is manifest through the presence and varied depictions of a social group, so too can the

devaluation of groups be transmitted through "symbolic annihilation"—absence, stereotyping, and trivialization (Tuchman 1978).

Previous studies of children's books indicate that depictions of African Americans have been stereotyped and narrowly focused (Klein 1985; Larrick 1965; Sadker and Sadker 1977). Blacks tend to be relatively invisible in children's literature, and when they do appear they are depicted in negative ways, especially prior to 1945 (Children's Literature Review Board 1977).

Controversy exists over whether this representation has improved. Claims that the portrayal of Blacks has improved over recent decades are countered by concerns that the number of children's books dealing with Blacks has declined in recent years (Miller 1986; Sims 1985). Rather than a simple depiction of whether images are better or worse, we expect a more complex web of symbolic race relations throughout recent U.S. history.

When the position of Blacks has been less challenged or when relations between Whites and Blacks are more clearly defined by social custom or law, portrayals may not necessarily be fewer or uniformly negative. However, when social norms defining Black-White interactions are contested and unsettled, images may not reflect this decreasing subordination, but rather may depict more qualified or subtle stereotypes or retreat from challenges to norms entirely by limiting portrayals, creating more or continued social distance (Jackman 1994).

We argue that attempts to rearrange power, which are reflected in racial conflict, change the way in which artists and cultural gatekeepers draw from their cultural "tool kits" (Swidler 1986). Periods of contested race relations should exhibit altered symbolic representation of Blacks in U.S. children's literature. Radical changes in race relations during the civil rights era were preceded by legislative, migratory, organizational, and ideological developments in the 1930s. However, World War II dramatically destabilized Black-White relations (McAdam 1982; Morris 1984; Woodward 1974). We expect this period of high uncertainty and radical change, the years of rising Black insurgency from World War II to the mid 1960s, to present a crisis in symbolic representation.

In summary, then, we pose two research questions. First, we examine trends in the visibility of Black characters in children's picture books and the substantive nature of these portrayals over time. We expect that trends in the symbolic representation of Blacks will not be linear in nature but will vary systematically from 1937 to 1993. Second, we seek to explain why images change over time by exploring the role of racial conflict.

DATA AND MEASURES

Data

Our study spans the period from the late 1930s, when major publishing efforts and awards in children's literature began, to the 1990s. We consider three sets of books. (1) One set includes picture books that received the Caldecott Medal or were designated Caldecott Honor books for high quality illustration. These awards have been given annually since 1938 and include 235 books published from 1937 to 1993. Among the most prestigious and influential books in children's literature, they are targeted to a narrow market and are relatively expensive. (2) We selected a sample of picture books from the *Children's Catalog,* a broad compilation of books that is a mainstay among librarians who make book purchases. A stratified random sample of books listed each year from 1937 to 1993 was drawn ($N = 1,190$). (3) We also examined the most popular and readily available set of children's books, the *Little Golden Books*. All books in the "standard" series from its inception in 1942 to the present were included ($N = 1,023$). Reissued books were included *only* if there was a change in length, illustrations, or story.

Data on racial conflict were based on descriptions of events involving African Americans listed in the *New York Times Index,* 1936 through 1993; the *Index* has been used and discussed in previous analyses of ethnic conflict (McAdam 1982; Olzak 1992).

Coding and Measures

Cultural representations.

The coding of over 2,400 children's books involved at least one researcher (and often two) coding each book, with another researcher resolving ambiguities (of which there were few for racial variables). For the Caldecott books, for example, we found high levels of inter-rater reliability (in the 85-percent range) for all relevant variables. Basic information on text and illustrations was recorded through a manifest coding—a strict count of "objective" information (Holsti 1969)—such as whether Blacks, Whites, or others appear in the book. The quantitative measures of the overall visibility of Blacks included the percentage of books each year in which (1) at least one Black character was portrayed in text or illustrations and (2) *only* Black characters were portrayed. The values for both variables theoretically range from 0 (i.e., no books with even a single Black character for that year) to 100 (i.e., at least one Black character in each book that year).

We also recorded how Blacks were portrayed in these books by coding geographical and temporal location (e.g., rural versus urban; United States versus other; past versus contemporary), occupational roles, and whether there was interracial contact. We complemented this with a qualitative analysis of the nature of the images and story lines (i.e., latent content; Holsti 1969). Coders kept notes and attended regular sessions focused on these qualitative data. The *nature* of Black representations and Black-White interactions were targeted, including the centrality of the Black characters and the degree to which interracial contact was central (e.g., whether it involved the main character or background characters), intimate (e.g., brief or sustained interactions), or egalitarian (e.g., similar occupational or other social circumstances).

Racial conflict.

The count of racial conflict events each year measures the struggle for the redistribution of social power between Blacks and Whites. Event summaries (excluding editorials and review articles) listed in the *New York Times Index* under the following categories were examined: Negroes (Blacks starting in 1977), education and schools, colleges and universities, labor, housing, Ku Klux Klan, and assaults/disorderly conduct (starting in 1948), and all related subcategories. Any summary that described an unambiguous instance of public racial strife was counted as an event and coded under the year of occurrence. Events included conflicts (involving violence, physical confrontation, or arrest), protests (actions related to racial tensions that did not involve direct confrontation), and legal actions (particularly Black-initiated lawsuits). An event was counted only if it was "public" (i.e., conventions, conferences, or meetings were omitted), about the United States, took place in the United States, and was clearly a confrontation concerning the racial order. Only the first of multiple entries about a particular event or action was coded.

ANALYSIS

Our analysis encompasses the period from 1937 to 1993. Years are the units of analysis, and each book is considered as part of a set of images for a particular year. To determine the visibility of Blacks, we use both the entire set of books ($N = 2,448$) and the subset of books that eliminates those books that have only animals or inanimate objects as characters ($N = 1,967$). We examine and rely on the consistency between the qualitative analyses [and] graphic presentation of the data. For the graphic presentation of trends, figures show three-year moving averages for book data, and a monthly average for the racial conflict data.

RESULTS

Trends in the Portrayal of Blacks in U.S. Children's Picture Books

Our focus in this paper centers on change over time. Figure 15.1 shows that the visibility of Blacks in children's picture books varies systematically across the time period studied. The non-linear time trend reveals roughly four phases of the dependent variable "visibility of Blacks" in these books. In the earliest phase, from 1938 to about 1957, Blacks are represented in modest percentages, with percentages decreasing significantly throughout this period. The second phase, 1958 through 1964, is marked by a virtual absence of Blacks. In the third phase, from the mid-1960s to the early 1970s, Blacks reappear. In the fourth phase, from 1975 to 1993, the percentage stabilizes, fluctuating between 20 and 30 percent for portrayal of at least one Black.

Depictions in the Early Years

From 1937 through the mid-1950s, Blacks are present in modest though declining proportions. About one-half of Caldecott Award books and one-third of *Little Golden Books* that include at *least* one Black character depict *only one* Black character, and virtually all the books are about Whites, with Blacks playing only minor, peripheral roles. When Blacks do appear in children's books, they usually appear briefly and are depicted in subservient positions such as menial workers, servants, or slaves (e.g., *All Aboard*, a 1952 *Little Golden Book*, depicts a Black train porter dusting off a White girl's doll).

In this early phase, Black-White relations can generally be characterized as depicting "surface contact" (Levinger and Snoek 1972), showing no deep relationships, behavior as role-determined, and emphasizing physical appearance and social status position. Interaction reflects the superior status of whites and the inferior position of Blacks. The text of *They Were Strong and Good* (a 1940 Caldecott Medal book) is illustrative:

FIGURE 15.1   Percentage of Children's Books that Portray Black Characters, by Year: All Three Book Series, 1937 to 1993

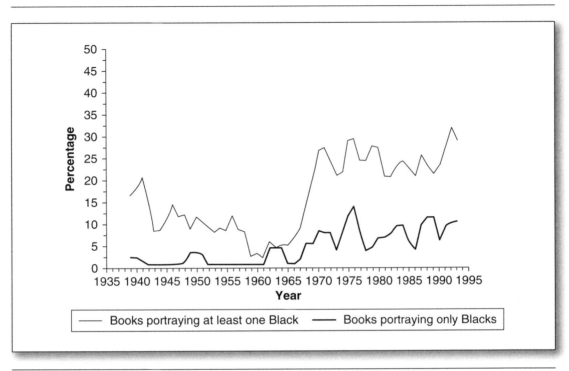

Note: Percentages are three-year moving averages.

When my father was very young he had two dogs and a colored boy. The dogs were named Sextus Hostilius and Numa Pompolius. The colored boy was just my father's age. He was a slave, but they don't call him that. They just called him Dick.

To conclude, however, that these were the only types of portrayals of Blacks in the early phase would be misleading.

A second theme during this phase involved Black characters in multiracial groups of children and occasionally adults, depicting the "family of man" or "all God's children." The latter, characteristic of religious books popular during the 1930s and 1940s, include illustrations of children of different races and cultures, make no specific reference to race, and often have a central White character. In many of these books, the appearance of Black characters reflects only "unilateral awareness"; there is a joint presence but no interaction (Levinger and Snoek 1972). In other books, however, for example *Small Rain: Verses from the Bible* (1944), there is no single, central character, and the inclusion of Black children as part of a group depicted throughout the book and engaged in group activities goes beyond superficial contact.

Other exceptions to the stereotypical and background depiction of Blacks are rare but nonetheless are present. These rare portrayals indicate "mutuality"—egalitarian and intimate relationships that involve the disclosure of unique information and shared experiences (Levinger and Snoek 1972).

The Disappearance of Black Characters

The second phase, from the late 1950s to the mid-1960s, represents the nadir for portrayals of Blacks: Virtually no Blacks appear in children's picture books published from 1958 through 1964. Only one of 24 Caldecott Award books, one of 120 books in the *Children's Catalog* sample, and 10 of 240 *Little Golden Books* depict even one Black character. Representations of Blacks are varied considering their extremely small number and include background images of Blacks, one all-Black book, and another virtually all Black book. One book portrays mutuality between a Black girl and her Brownie troop (*Brownie Scouts,* a 1961 *Little Golden Book*), while others present stereotypes that represent symbolic annihilation. For example, *Boats*, a 1958 *Little Golden Book*, depicts over 200 Whites and 3 Blacks. The Blacks appear on the top deck of a large paddleboat while Whites socialize below—one Black character is asleep, one plays the banjo, and one eats watermelon.

The Reintroduction of Black Characters

From the mid-1960s through the 1970s, the percentage of books depicting Blacks rises dramatically, and portrayals improve considerably from the earlier explicit stereotypic images. What is most curious about this increase is the way Black characters are reintroduced into picture books. The qualitative analysis suggests that this reintroduction occurred differently across particular series. In addition to new titles in which Blacks are included (but rarely as central characters), in several reissued *Little Golden Books*, Blacks simply replace some Whites. For example, *Prayers for Children*, a popular 1952 title by Eloise Wilkin, depicts all White children. When the book was reissued in 1974, two illustrations replaced White children with Black children.

The reappearance of Blacks in the Caldecott Award books is striking. In contrast to *Little Golden Books* and the *Children's Catalog* books, much of the increase in portrayals of Blacks in the Caldecott series occurs because the award panel selected books that featured Black characters only (see Figure 15.2).

The first book written and illustrated by Black authors to be awarded a Caldecott Medal was *Moja Means One* by Tom and Muriel Feelings. This book, as well as all of the Caldecott Award books that featured only Black characters published from 1965 through the mid-1970s, depicts "safe" and distant images of Blacks in Africa. Strong community and family life is depicted in several of the books with African themes—parents interacting with their children, families engaged in work activities, children playing, and groups active in storytelling, dance, and play.

After 1975: Stabilization at New Levels

The increase in representations of Blacks alone or with other races ends after 1975. Since the mid-1970s, the percentage of all children's picture books that portray Black characters has stabilized at about 20 to 30 percent (Figure 15.1) and from 30 to 50 percent in books featuring human characters (data not shown), levels significantly higher than those of the early years.

There is little change in the character of Black-White relations in either the *Little Golden Books* or the *Children's Catalog* books—they continue to portray mainly surface contact, such as "crowd scenes" on city streets, playgrounds, or in classrooms. The *Little Golden Books* series has a smaller percentage of books depicting Blacks in this final phase than in the previous phase, and about the same percentage it had in the earliest years (see Figure 15.3). In the Caldecott series, books featuring only Blacks after the mid-1970s focus on both Africans and African Americans. For most of this phase they continue to focus on historical themes, the depiction of folk tales, or feature social and temporal locations that are difficult to pinpoint

FIGURE 15.2   Percentage of Children's Books in Three Book Series that Portray Only Black Characters, by Year: 1937 to 1993

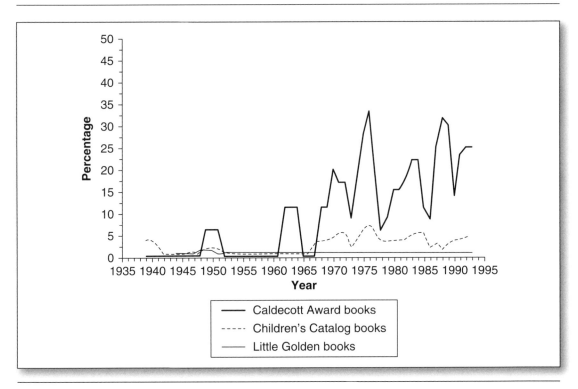

Note: Percentages are three-year moving averages.

(characteristic of other ethnic tales as well). [Also], not until the 1990s do Caldecott books present explicit interracial themes or address political issues.

Standing Back: Neglected Depictions

While each phase has distinctive features, the books as a group display two interesting characteristics that point to a subtle yet telling phenomenon about a lack of improvement in race relations. First, even when Blacks and Whites appear in a book, their interactions show a striking absence of mutuality—intimate, egalitarian relations central to the story line—throughout

the entire period and across series. Second, books that depict Black men and women as central characters, especially contemporary U.S. characters, are extraodinarily rare.

Racial Conflict and the Visibility of Black Characters

We examine whether race relations in the larger society can explain trends in the portrayals of Blacks. Figure 15.4 shows the average number of monthly conflict incidents over the 57-year span. The rise and fall of racial conflict as reported in the *New York Times* offers an inverse image to the greatest change in the visibility of Blacks in U.S. children's picture books. The data

FIGURE 15.3   Percentage of Children's Books in Three Book Series that Portray at Least One Black Character, by Year: 1937 to 1993

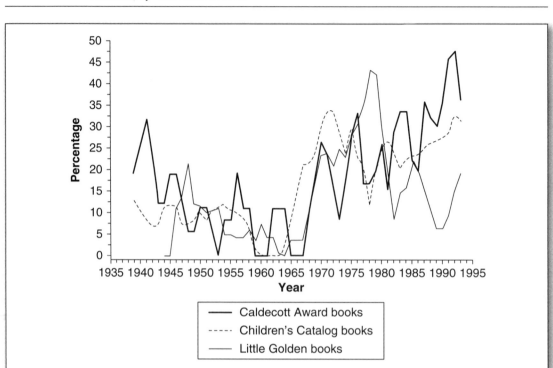

Note: Percentages are three-year moving averages.

indicate a slight rise beginning in 1945 corresponding to a gradual decline in portrayals of Black characters, a sharp rise between 1955 and 1965 corresponding to the disappearance of Blacks in illustrations and story lines, a sharp decline in the late 1960s paralleled by the dramatic reintroduction of portrayals of Blacks in books, and a return to earlier low levels of conflict corresponding to stabilization in the portrayals of Blacks in overall trends. The year 1965 marks the beginning of a dramatic fall in racial conflict (McAdam 1982) and a dramatic rise in the percentage of books with Black characters as well as portrayals of a qualitatively different, more positive nature.

DISCUSSION: SOCIAL CHANGE AND IMAGES OF BLACKS IN U.S. CHILDREN'S PICTURE BOOKS

Racial conflict has cultural as well as social consequences that manifest in the changing portrayals of Blacks in children's picture books. At the time of highest uncertainty in race relations, a period marked by increasing legal and social protests and conflicts, Blacks virtually disappeared from children's books, indicating indecision or unwillingness to portray racial contact in new (and at the time, radical) ways. Two features of the portrayals have remained

FIGURE 15.4   Percentage of Children's Books in Three Book Series that Portray at Least One Black Character and Average Number of Monthly Racial Conflicts, by Year: 1937 to 1993

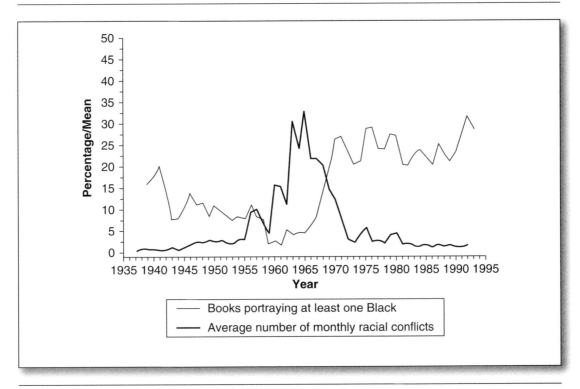

Note: Percentages are three-year moving averages.

relatively stable. First, stories and illustrations in which intimate, interracial relationships are central appear rarely in early and later phases. In books, Black and White characters may stand beside one another; much less often they interact in intimate egalitarian ways central to the story. Second, contemporary Black men and women, more so than Black children, are unlikely to play a central role in the 2,448 children's picture books we examined.

Overall, Blacks were secondary, peripheral, and subordinate characters from the late 1930s through the 1950s. In the late 1950s and first half of the 1960s, Blacks were largely invisible either as central characters or in peripheral roles. In the late 1960s, Black characters reappear in children's books and some positive interracial

contact is depicted, especially in the popular books such as the *Little Golden Books* and books listed in the *Children's Catalog*. Caldecott Award winners show a unique pattern of a large increase in books portraying only Blacks. These books depict distant, historical images of Blacks that are far removed from the contemporary U.S. social scene.

The amount of interracial strife in society is significantly and inversely related to the portrayal of Blacks in children's books. When Black-White relations are stable—before and after the dramatic increase in Black insurgency—Black characters are more visible, whereas during the time of contested Black-White relations, Blacks and Black-White interactions were virtually deleted from children's books.

But why did Blacks reappear in children's books in more positive depictions after 1965, even though some racial conflict persisted? Most likely, it was not the simple decline in racial conflicts, per se, but gains in recognizing Blacks as artists and writers as well as a greater responsiveness among Whites to issues of racial equality. As Morris (1984) documents, by the mid 1960s, Whites (typically Northern liberals) had become increasingly involved in the civil rights movement through financial contributions and active participation. The racial conflict measure used in this study, then, may indicate a shift in social power for Blacks and this redistribution of power among Blacks and Whites drove the changes in images.

In sum, we have shown complex patterns of change in the portrayal of Black characters in a diverse set of children's books that includes both prestigious and popular picture books. We link these patterns to social conflict. In the most unsettled period of U.S. race relations, contested power relations left a void in cultural imagery, as social relations were disturbed and unclear. A rapid rise in Black insurgency directly affected children's picture books during those years and ultimately transformed the representation of Black characters into more positive depictions. However, the dearth of portrayals of contemporary Black adults and of interracial mutuality throughout the twentieth century perhaps captures the persistence of social distance between Blacks and Whites.

REFERENCES

Bettelheim, Bruno. 1977. *Uses of Enchantment*. New York: Vintage Books.

Children's Literature Review Board. 1977. "Starting Out Right: Choosing Books about Black People for Young Children." Pp. 107–45 in *Cultural Conformity in Books for Children: Further Readings in Racism*, edited by D. MacCann and G. Woodard. Metuchen, NJ: Scarecrow Press.

Dubin, Steven, 1987. "Black Representations in Popular Culture." *Social Problems* 34:122–40.

Holsti, Ole R. 1969. *Content Analyses for the Social Sciences and Humanities*. Reading, MA: Addison-Wesley.

Jackman, Mary R. 1994. *The Velvet Glove: Paternalism and Conflict in Gender, Class and Race Relations*. Berkeley, CA: University of California Press.

Klein, Gillian. 1985. *Reading into Racism: Bias in Children's Literature and Learning Materials*. London, England: Routledge and Kegan Paul.

Larrick, Nancy. 1965. "The All White World of Children's Books." *Saturday Review*, vol. 48, September 11, pp. 63–65, 84–85.

Levinger, George and J. D. Snoek. 1972. *Attraction in Relationships: A New Look at Interpersonal Attraction*. Morristown, NJ: General Learning Press.

McAdam, Doug. 1982. *Political Process and the Development of Black Insurgency, 1930–1970*. Chicago, IL: University of Chicago Press.

Miller, James A. 1986. "Black Images in American Children's Literature." Pp. 99–118 in *Masterworks of Children's Literature*, edited by W. T. Moynihan, M. E. Shaner, and J. Cott. New York: Stonehill.

Morris, Aldon D. 1984. *The Origins of the Civil Rights Movement: Black Communities Organizing for Change*. New York: Free Press.

Olzak, Susan. 1992. *The Dynamics of Ethnic Competition and Conflict*. Stanford, CA: Stanford University Press.

Sadker, Myra P. and David M. Sadker. 1977. *Now Upon a Time: A Contemporary View of Children's Literature*. New York: Harper and Row.

Schudson, Michael. 1989. "How Culture Works." *Theory and Society* 18:153–80.

Sims, Rudine. 1985. "Children's Books about Blacks: A Mid-Eighties Status Report." *Children's Literature Review* 8:9–14.

Swidler, Ann. 1986. "Culture in Action: Symbols and Strategies." *American Sociological Review* 51:273–86.

Tuchman, Gaye. 1978. "Introduction: The Symbolic Annihilation of Women by the Mass Media." Pp. 3–38 in *Hearth and Home: Images of Women in the Mass Media*, edited by G. Tuchman, A. K. Daniels, and J. Benet. New York: Oxford University Press.

Woodward, C. Vann. 1974. *The Strange Career of Jim Crow*. New York: Oxford University Press.

QUESTIONS

1. What do the researchers expect to find concerning the relationship between racial conflict and portrayals of blacks in children's books? How is content analysis well-suited to examine this expectation?

2. How did the researchers code (or measure) (a) the representation of blacks in children's picture books and (b) interracial conflict as reported in the *New York Times Index*?

3. In our unit on measurement, we discussed validity, which refers to accurately measuring a concept. Another fundamental aspect of measurement is **reliability**, which refers to obtaining consistent results with multiple measurements of a concept. (a) How do the researchers in this selection ensure that their coding, or measurement, of children's picture books is reliable? (b) In what other way(s) does this selection illustrate the concept of reliability?

4. What are the four distinct phases into which the portrayal of blacks in children's books can be divided? Please note a couple of important characteristics of each phase in your answer.

5. Did the results of the study support the researchers' expectation (from Question 1)? Why or why not?

Selection 16

Over the last 40 years, imprisonment has increased markedly in the United States. As John Sutton points out, this trend is not unique to the United States; moreover, we can best understand it through a comparative analysis. Sutton examines trends in imprisonment between 1955 and 1985 in five countries with similar judicial and political systems. Using quantitative data drawn mostly from official statistics compiled by international organizations, Sutton tests several hypotheses with a statistical technique called **multivariate regression**. This form of quantitative data analysis, which you will learn more about in Unit X, allows Sutton to understand whether changes in the hypothesized factors

(independent variables) are significantly related to changes in the dependent variable (imprisonment rates), controlling for other factors that may affect the dependent variable. To understand the results of this analysis as reported in Table 16.1, keep in mind: (1) an asterisk next to an estimate indicates that an association exists between a given variable and imprisonment rates; and (2) the sign + or - indicates whether increases in the variable are associated with increases in imprisonment rates (+) or with decreases in imprisonment rates (-). As you read this selection, note the usefulness of comparative-historical research to test theoretical explanations, as well as the relationships among theory, hypotheses, and results.

IMPRISONMENT AND SOCIAL CLASSIFICATION IN FIVE COMMON-LAW DEMOCRACIES, 1955–1985

JOHN R. SUTTON

In the post-World War II period, dramatic changes have occurred in the penal regimes of many Western democracies. Most conspicuously, imprisonment rates in the United States declined gradually until the mid-1970s, then rose fourfold over the next two decades.

Source: "Imprisonment and Social Classification in Five Common-Law Democracies, 1955–1985," by John R. Sutton, 2000, *American Journal of Sociology,* 106(2), 350–386. Adapted with permission.

Imprisonment rates have multiplied in the United Kingdom as well, but at a more consistent pace. The trend in most other Western democracies has been toward moderate expansion, and in only a few countries have imprisonment rates remained level or declined. We have a wealth of explanations of the U.S. case (e.g., Beckett 1997; Blumstein 1988; Caplow and Simon 1999; Mauer 1994; Tonry 1999), which focus on both the supply and demand sides of the punishment equation. On the supply side, the maturation of the baby boom generation contributed to a rise in the incidence of some kinds of crime. On the demand side, the structural vulnerability of the American polity to moral panics, the opportunistic use of crime and welfare as "wedge" issues by conservative politicians, and the increasing magnification of crime by the news media have led to the enactment of stricter sentencing policies (especially with regard to drug offenses), tighter restrictions on parole release, and a sharp increase in punishment capacity. Many of these factors are not unique to the United States, however. For example, Canada, New Zealand, and the Netherlands experienced larger baby booms than did the United States, and the United Kingdom's was nearly as large. Crime, along with welfare, race, and immigration, has been politicized elsewhere as well—especially in the United Kingdom (Hale 1989) and even in New Zealand (Pratt 1988)—but with much less apparent effect on inmate populations.

Far from being incomplete, our understanding of punishment trends in the United States is overdetermined: We have too many explanations, some undoubtedly spurious, and too few degrees of freedom to distinguish among them. The appropriate move in this situation is to approach the issue of punishment from a comparative perspective—not to focus on the United States or any other particular country in isolation, but to begin the search for a general explanation of punishment trends in the modern West.

This article moves forward in two steps. First, I outline an institutionalist argument that frames punishment within a more general set of classificatory discourses and practices used in modern societies to manage socially marginal populations. This argument is institutional in the sense that it emphasizes the politics of moral order rather than economic instrumentality as the driving force behind prison expansion. As I will show, the Rusche-Kirchheimer hypothesis [which holds that] prisons in capitalist societies are mechanisms for controlling surplus labor (Rusche and Kirchheimer 1968), can be subsumed under this argument as a special case. Second, I test the hypotheses generated from this argument using data from five Common Law democracies—Australia, Canada, New Zealand, the United Kingdom, and the United States— over the period 1955–1985.

TOWARD AN INSTITUTIONAL ACCOUNT OF IMPRISONMENT

Theoretical Background

The account developed here begins by juxtaposing Durkheim's early argument that crime and punishment are indispensable components of moral order (1982, chap. 3) with his later work on totemic symbolism and classification systems (1965; Durkheim and Mauss 1963) and by reading both through contemporary theories of culture (Bourdieu 1977, 1984; Griswold 1994; Wuthnow 1987). The starting point is the idea that the structure of the moral order arises from a primarily cognitive process of classification.

As Durkheim recognized, the distinction between criminals and noncriminals is the most fundamental classificatory distinction in modern societies. The moral resonance of classification is in this case obvious: crime is constituted as a social fact through public rituals of punishment and exclusion; as such it is not a social pathology, but rather a normal means by which healthy societies reinforce their normative boundaries (Durkheim 1982, chap. 3). We can push a bit farther by recognizing that criminality is only one among several conspicuous criteria of moral distinction. Modern societies support a range of institutions, including mental health systems, welfare agencies, unemployment bureaus, homeless shelters, and substance abuse programs, that constitute and manage more or less specific forms of social marginality. Analysis of the prison should, at the very least, take into account the fact that crime is only one of many possible ways of being deviant. I would argue further that if we take seriously the idea that classification is a generic element of social organization, then what are commonly understood as "social control" agencies turn out to be a subset of a much broader array of institutions that manage individuals' movement through the life course—including families, schools, hospitals, the military, labor markets, and so on. Societies have a finite capacity to produce various kinds of identities, and the production of particular reputable or disreputable selves is dependent on the shape of the institutional terrain (Meyer 1988). The opportunity to become a "professional" depends on the availability of higher education, just as the opportunity to become "insane" depends on the availability of psychiatric expertise. It is consistent with Durkheim to argue that the production of crime is dependent on the capacity to punish.

What determines that capacity? Organizations, professions, and social movements form institutional coalitions—what Bourdieu (1990) terms social "fields"—that compete for jurisdiction over the life course, and particularly over the terrain of social problems. This is fundamentally a discursive process in which competitors seek to expand their domains by adapting their own developmental taxonomies to new forms of social trouble. Whether a particular case of trouble is classified under the criminal code, the public welfare manual, or the Diagnostic and Statistical Manual of the American Psychiatric Association (DSM-IV) is determined not only by the facts of the case, but also by the relative scope and reach of the associated fields. A conspicuous example of cross-societal variation in this regard is hard drug use, which in the United States is classified as a criminal violation to be dealt with (increasingly so) by courts and prisons and in Britain is classified as a medical problem to be treated under the auspices of the National Health Service (Nadelmann 1993).

Hypotheses

I have argued so far that (a) the prison should be viewed as one terminus in the complex classificatory system that makes up the moral order of society and (b) classificatory outcomes—including the rise and fall of imprisonment rates—are influenced by competition for institutional dominance. The most straightforward implication of this argument is that, given finite human and fiscal resources, the expansion of prisons is inversely related to the expansion of other institutionalized means for managing the life course. I explore this empirically at three levels.

Life-course patterns.

Competitive relations should be most obviously apparent in the way bodies flow along alternative life-course paths. Both personal and property crimes are committed disproportionately by young males (Cohen and Land 1987; Gartner and Parker 1990; Hirschi and Gottfredson 1983; Pampel and Gartner 1995), and young males therefore make up a preponderant share of prison inmates (Berk et al. 1983). We can narrow our focus considerably by assuming that young men in modern societies face a limited set of broad life-course alternatives: if they are not in prison, they are likely to be in school, at work, or in the military. Of course this set of alternatives is neither mutually exclusive nor exhaustive. A young man can, for example, work and attend school at the same time. But we can realistically expect that this would reduce his risk of crime and incarceration more than either work or school by itself, thus preserving the logic of the argument.

There is a great deal of evidence—from Hirschi (1969) to Sampson and Laub (1993)—to show that, for any given individual, involvement with legitimate institutions lowers the probability of criminal activity, and probably also incarceration. The implication at the aggregate level is that as opportunities for legitimate attachments expand, rates of crime and incarceration will tend to decline. The institutional orders of work, education, and the military can plausibly be taken as the major defining features of the opportunity space through which young men move, and it is reasonable to suspect that the structure of that space influences the production of criminality.

The allocation argument yields five hypotheses. First, the rate of imprisonment is likely to be influenced by the "supply-side" effect of the age and gender distribution of the population:

> HYPOTHESIS 1. The greater the proportion of young males in the population, the higher the rate of prison growth.

"Young" in this case means ages 15–24, a window that captures peak rates of crime, arrest, and first convictions in Britain and the United States (Hirschi and Gottfredson 1983).

Second, it is also useful to control for the more direct effect of the volume of crime on prison growth. For most crimes, comparable data are not available for all of the countries and years in the sample. Homicide rates, however, are measured with a fair degree of accuracy across modern societies and over time (Monkkonen 1989). Homicide is an attractive candidate for inclusion here for two reasons: (a) because homicides are so conspicuous, they are likely to have an exaggerated influence on public perceptions of crime and on crime-control policies, and (b) such a measure might help account for the U.S. case—U.S. homicide rates, like imprisonment rates, are two to ten times higher than those in the other countries throughout the observation period. The effect here should be positive:

> HYPOTHESIS 2. The higher the homicide rate, the higher the rate of prison growth.

Three other hypotheses identify anticipated trade-offs involving the military, schools, and the labor market. The military recruits disproportionately from the population of young males, and enlistment effectively removes them from the risk of civilian punishment. Evidence from the United States suggests that the military provides a particularly attractive life-course option during economic downturns (Griffin, Wallace, and Devine 1982), especially for the most disadvantaged young men (Mare and Winship 1984). Prior studies using U.S. data by Berk et al. (1981) and Cappel and Sykes (1991) found significant negative associations between military growth and imprisonment, while another by Inverarity and Grattet (1989) yielded mixed results. I expect a negative effect of enlistments on prison growth:

> HYPOTHESIS 3. Expansion in military enlistments reduces the rate of prison growth.

Schooling does not categorically immunize young men from civilian punishment, but it occupies at least some of their energy and provides them with a legitimate identity. To match the expected supply-side effect of the male cohort ages 15–24, the empirical focus here will be on the expansion of enrollments in secondary and tertiary institutions.

> HYPOTHESIS 4. Expansion in young men's secondary and tertiary school enrollments reduces the rate of prison growth.

The final life-course hypothesis focuses on the capacity of the labor market itself:

> HYPOTHESIS 5. Growth in unemployment rates increases the rate of prison growth.

This is the Rusche-Kircheimer hypothesis. In that context, unemployment serves more directly as a measure of slack capacity in the labor market—and particularly in the market for wage labor, which is the most viable port for young men who would otherwise run the greatest risk of imprisonment.

Patterns of policy trade-offs.

The most obvious and measurable expression of institutional competition is government spending in sectors that might be expected to offset prison expansion. I focus on two sectors in particular.

First, there is strong historical evidence to suggest that a trade-off between prison and social welfare is endemic to Anglo-American societies. In the late Victorian period, for example, the British government offered more generous social benefits and moderated the severity of the penal system as means to ease the inclusion of working-class voters into the polity (Garland 1985). At about the same time, the United States made trade-offs of a different sort. Almshouses, which had for much of the 19th century served as all-purpose repositories for the poor, petty criminals and vagrants, the aged and senile, unwed mothers, and homeless children, were gradually closed down. Political opposition precluded a compensating rise in "outdoor relief" payments; instead, the decline of almshouses contributed directly to waves of expansion among juvenile reformatories, prisons, jails, and mental hospitals (Sutton 1987, 1990, 1991).

Modern welfare regimes comprise several different kinds of benefit programs targeted at different groups of citizens. I focus on programs that are targeted at two overlapping groups: wage workers and families with children. Unemployment compensation and work injury benefits provide the primary safety net for working families in the legitimate labor market during times of economic hardship. In addition, Pampel and Gartner (1995) show that more generous spending on benefits targeted at families with children reduces the impact of young male cohorts on homicide rates. This association holds, they argue, because these benefits provide mechanisms to support the transition from youth to adulthood. It is reasonable to suspect that they would influence the imprisonment rate as well. I include two such programs here: public assistance provides benefits on a means-tested basis for the

nonworking poor, and family allowances are benefits payable to families with children, regardless of family income or employment status. Taken together, these four programs provide a rough measure of the level of collective protection available to working and nonworking families. The measure used here is the sum of expenditures on these programs as a percentage of the gross domestic product.

HYPOTHESIS 6. Growth in welfare spending aimed at workers and families with children decreases rates of prison expansion.

The second field that deserves attention is education. Enrollments are likely to be constrained by investments in education, particularly at the tertiary level where schooling is more discretionary, so it is useful to include a measure of spending as a control variable. Education expenditures provide a measure of public commitment to legitimate life-course development, and this effect may be independent of the allocative effects of enrollments. The general expectation is that expansive investments in the field of education tend to narrow the developmental path toward criminality:

HYPOTHESIS 7. Growth in public spending for education decreases rules of prison expansion.

Political domination.

It will also be important [to] examine the political processes that are antecedent to policy commitments. Evidence from the United States suggests that political factors shaped the expansion of prisons, jails, asylums, and reformatories around the turn of the [20th] century (Sutton 1987, 1990, 1991) and that partisan dominance influences spending on criminal justice, the adoption of punitive policies, and ultimately prison admissions (Caldeira and Cowart 1980; Chambliss 1994; Jacobs and Helms 1996). There is cross-national evidence as well. Savelsberg (1994) argues that different structures of political domination account for widely varying rates of imprisonment in the United States and Germany. Hale's (1989) analysis of British politics in the 1970s shows the crucial importance of law and order discourse in Tory campaigns against unions and welfare.

In this analysis, political domination is treated in terms of partisan control of government. The countries in the present sample have roughly parallel sets of party alignments. Left labor parties, which draw their support from working-class, urban, and ethnically marginal voters, tend to define social problems in structural terms and to support tighter regulation of the economy and more expansive programs of social benefits. Right parties attract older, more affluent, rural, and native-born voters; they tend to define social problems in individual moral terms and to promote free-market economics and a law and order approach to social disruption. Thus party rule is not only likely to affect imprisonment directly, but indirectly as well through welfare, labor market, and education policies.

> HYPOTHESIS 8. Prison populations expand more rapidly when right parties are in power than when parties of the left and center are in power.

DATA, MEASUREMENT, AND ESTIMATION

Imprisonment as a Dependent Variable

Quantitative cross-national analysis of punishment raises difficult problems of conceptualization and measurement. This is particularly true for the outcome variable used here, imprisonment rates. Statistical reporting practices in different countries do not reflect natural categories of inmates, but rather the administrative structures of prison systems. These administrative differences can yield inmate counts that are not comparable across countries. U.S.-based studies, for example, typically count only inmates in state and federal penitentiaries, ignoring large numbers of unconvicted inmates and petty criminals in local jails. In studies of European and Commonwealth countries with more centralized prison systems, counts of prison populations typically include less serious offenders, who in the United States would be held in local jails, and sometimes include a substantial proportion of unconvicted prisoners as well.

As a first approach to the problem, this study focuses on trends in aggregate imprisonment rates. The definition of imprisonment used here comprises all inmates, unconvicted as well as convicted, incarcerated in adult prisons and jails administered by national, state, provincial, and local authorities. Imprisonment rates are defined in the conventional way as the proportion of inmates per 100,000 in the general population.

Imprisonment trends in the five sample countries are displayed graphically in Figure 16.1. The graph expresses imprisonment rates in log form to show more clearly the substantial variation that exists among Australia, Canada, New Zealand, and the United Kingdom. Incarceration rates in the United States are higher than in the other four countries by a factor of two to three, depending on the year. But prison *growth* in the United Kingdom was greater in percentage terms than in the United States over the entire 30-year period (104% to about 80%). A key difference is that growth in the United Kingdom was relatively steady from 1955 to 1985, while virtually all prison growth in the United States occurred after 1972. New Zealand shows the third highest rate of growth (26% overall, or 68% if we ignore the steep drop in 1985), followed by Canada (14%). Australia shows a net decline in the imprisonment rate of 5%, mostly the result of a drop that occurred in the early 1970s.

The imprisonment data used in this study were drawn primarily from national statistical yearbooks. Canadian imprisonment data were provided directly by the Canadian Centre for Justice Statistics; for Australia, yearbook data were supplemented with data published by the Australian Institute of Criminology (Mukherjee et al. 1989) and in Biles (1982).

Sources for independent variables, which I have already described, are detailed in Appendix Table 16.A.

FIGURE 16.1 Prison Inmates per 100,000 Population (log)

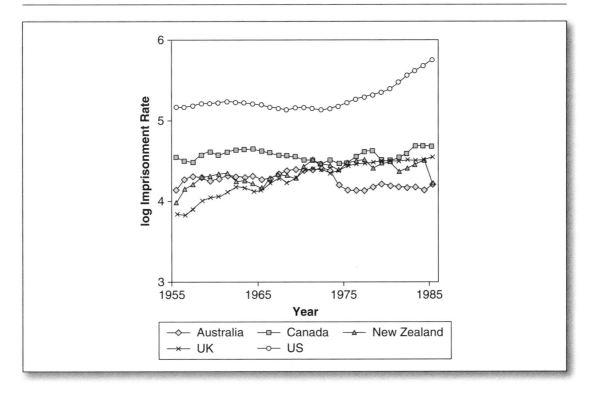

Estimation

The present data comprise 31-year time series for five nations. The approach is [to] analyze variation occurring over both time and space. A lagged value of the dependent variable is used as a predictor in the regression equation. [This is because] the rate of imprisonment in a given year is likely to be heavily dependent on the rate of imprisonment in prior years.

The following analysis uses a lag interval of three years for the lag-dependent variable and most independent variables. The resulting data set contains 28 observations on five countries, yielding a total *N* of 140 observations.

RESULTS

Results from tests of hypotheses 1–8 are presented in Table 16.1. Model 1 presents the simplest and most instrumental account of prison growth, comprising only controls for prior imprisonment rates, the relative size of the young male population, the prevalence of homicide, and stable country-specific effects. Model 2 adds life-course effects of schooling, the military, and labor markets; model 3 adds spending on welfare and education; and model 4 adds right-party dominance. Model 5 is a trimmed model that omits the young males variable.

I begin with some observations about control variables, then discuss results that address substantive hypotheses. Coefficients for the lag-dependent variable are negative and significant in all models. Coefficients for the young males variable in models 1–4 are nowhere near significant. The estimated effect of homicide rates is positive and significant in the first three models.

TABLE 16.1   OLS Estimates of the Effects of Selected Variables on Imprisonment Rates in Five Common-Law Countries, 1955–1985.

	b					β
	1	2	3	4	5	
Log lag dependent	−.302***	−.308**	−.314***	−.306***	−.294***	−1.18
	(.0570)	(.0569)	(.0550)	(.0534)	(.0525)	
Log % young males	−.0882	.00673	.0182	.117		
	(.112)	(.109)	(.106)	(.108)		
Log homicide rates	.170*	.148*	.120*	.0752	.127**	.727
	(.0702)	(.0660)	(.0668)	(.0667)	(.0468)	
Δ male school enrollments		.0968	.0538	.0542	.0398	.0524
		(.0608)	(.0596)	(.0579)	(.0566)	
Δ military enlistments		.181***	.179***	.195***	.186***	.275
		(.0499)	(.0494)	(.0482)	(.0476)	
Δ unemployment rates		.0288**	.0374***	.0362***	.0362***	.221
		(.0120)	(.0118)	(.0115)	(.0116)	
Δ welfare spending			−.122***	−.105**	−.106**	−.214
			(.0349)	(.0344)	(.0345)	
Δ education spending			−.0304	−.0241	−.0332	−.0458
			(.0644)	(.0625)	(.0622)	
Right-party dominance				.0605**	.0535**	.218
				(.0207)	(.0198)	
Canada	.110***	.118**	.123***	.155***	.151***	
	(.0273)	(.0266)	(.0256)	(.0272)	(.0270)	
New Zealand	.105***	.0738**	.0564	.0430	.0572*	
	(.0290)	(.0285)	(.0287)	(.0283)	(.0251)	
United Kingdom ..	.127***	.143***	.139***	.150***	.151***	
	(.0275)	(.0267)	(.0296)	(.0290)	(.0291)	

	b					*β*
	1	*2*	*3*	*4*	*5*	
United States of America ...	.164	.207*	.247*	.308**	.234**	
	(.103)	(.0977)	(.0976)	(.0970)	(.0697)	
Constant	1.30***	1.14***	1.18***	.932***	1.08**	
	(.262)	(.259)	(.262)	(.268)	(.230)	
χ^2.................	49.65***	77.02***	96.10***	110.5***	108.4***	

Note—Metric coefficients, with panel corrected SEs given in parentheses and standardized coefficients given for model 5.

*$p < .05$; ** $p < .01$; *** $p < .001$.

Country dummy variables allow each country in the sample to have a different [constant or intercept, which can be interpreted as the average difference in imprisonment growth races between that country and] the omitted category, Australia, [controlling for other factors]. As we might expect, the U.S. intercept is consistently the largest: while the coefficient is nonsignificant in model 1, it becomes significant and grows larger in the more complex models.

I turn now to results concerning substantive variables in models 2–5. In model 2, unemployment growth is the only life-course variable that performs as expected. The coefficient is positive and significant, showing that a 1% rise in unemployment rates corresponds to about .03% growth in imprisonment rates. Male secondary and tertiary school enrollment rates have no apparent association with prison growth. The association between prison growth and military enlistments is unexpectedly *positive* and clearly significant—on average, when military enlistments grow 1%, imprisonment grows nearly two-tenths of a percent. This not only fails to support the hypothesis that military expansion drains the pool of likely prison inmates, it points to quite the opposite association.

Model 3 includes measures of changes in social welfare and education spending. The welfare effect is significant, and the coefficient is in the anticipated negative direction, supporting the hypothesis that higher welfare spending translates into lower rates of prison growth. But the coefficient for education spending is effectively zero: economic investments in education seem to have no more bearing on imprisonment than do school enrollments.

In model 4, we see that the coefficient for right-party dominance is positive and significant, supporting the hypothesis that prison growth accelerates during periods of conservative rule.

Model 5 drops the % young males variable but retains the two education variables. It would be useful at this point to draw some conclusions about the relative impacts of the broader set of variables tested here. Control variables predominate: prison growth is constrained most severely by the prior size of the prison population ($\beta = -1.18$) and next by the incidence of homicide ($\beta = 0.727$). Setting aside school enrollments and education spending, the standardized effects of other substantive variables are roughly similar in absolute value. In particular, the coefficient for military enlistments is still the largest, but not remarkably so, and that for unemployment rates is far from trivial.

SUMMARY AND INTERPRETATION

This article was motivated by two problems in the existing research on imprisonment, one empirical and one theoretical. The empirical problem is that we lack rigorous analyses of the glaring differences in recent imprisonment trends among Western societies. More specifically, past research explained the divergence between the United States and other countries mostly with exceptionalist accounts that are so far untested, and perhaps untestable, using cross-national data. The theoretical problem arises from the limitations of the venerable Rusche-Kirchheimer hypothesis. Results supporting the hypothesis are suspect, but until recently there was little apparent interest in searching for a more comprehensive explanation of imprisonment trends.

In this analysis, I have sought to bridge that gap by outlining a theoretical framework that nests the labor market/imprisonment association within a broader system of social classification and by testing hypotheses derived from that framework on a sample of countries observed over time.

Results supported hypotheses at all three levels of analysis. Confirming much past research, the dominant life-course effect comes from fluctuations in labor markets: when opportunities for legitimate employment expand, prison growth slows.

There is strong evidence of one policy trade-off: declines in welfare spending are associated with growth in imprisonment rates. The welfare/imprisonment trade-off is much stronger in the United States, but it remains significant across the rest of the sample. Finally, there is convincing evidence that politics matters. The consistently positive effects of right-party rule offer grounds for generalizing Jacobs and Helms's (1996) findings about the punitive tendencies of conservative politics beyond the borders of the United States.

The observed effect of military enlistments is a conspicuous anomaly, suggesting that military expansion contributes to the expansion of prisons. If this is a real effect, it must operate in diffuse and long-term ways because enlistment and imprisonment trends are not parallel.

These findings add considerable depth to our understanding of imprisonment trends, at least in the five countries under examination: net of the effects of supply-side factors, prisons grow more rapidly during economic downturns, when social spending is constrained, when conservative parties control the policy agenda, and perhaps under conditions of long-term military mobilization. Moreover, these results are fairly theoretically coherent: taken together they undercut an instrumental account of imprisonment and move us decisively toward an account that emphasizes the politics of moral order. But there is also persistent evidence of American exceptionalism—the analysis has whittled away at it, but it has not eliminated it. Can this "U.S. effect" be theoretically housebroken?

We can gain some leverage on the problem by revisiting the analysis of interaction effects [not presented in this abridgment], since it tells us something about *how* the United States is different. The effect of welfare spending is exaggerated in the United States; so are the effects of education spending and right parties, though in the end not significantly so. These findings fit a pattern that was predicted early on: under the administratively fragmented and decentralized structure of American government, social policy tends to be highly politicized, localized, and particularistic. More specifically and concretely, police functions in the United States are organized locally, policy-making authority is dispersed among the states, and judges and prosecutors must constantly renew the approval of voters—structural conditions that create a chronic vulnerability to moral panics (Beckett 1997; Caplow and Simon 1999; Tonry 1999). From this perspective, a weak state makes moral order precarious.

APPENDIX TABLE 16.A   Variable Descriptions and Sources

Variable	Description	Source
Dependent...............	Total inmates per 100,000 population (proportional change from *t–3 to t*)	Various (see text)
Lag dependent............	Total inmates per 100,000 population (log, at *t – 3*)	Various (see text)
Homicide rates	Number of homicides per 100,000 population (log, at *t – 3*)	WHO (1951–64; 1962–88)
Military enlistments	Active-duty military personnel as percent of total population (proportional change from *t –3 to t*)	Faber (1989), with updates from IISS (1983–85)
Male school enrollments ...	Males enrolled in secondary and tertiary schools as percent of total population (proportional change from *t – 3 to t*)	UNESCO (1955–90)
Unemployment rates	Unemployed persons as percent of total working population (proportional change from *t – 3 to t*)	JLO (1955–90)
Welfare spending	Sum of expenditures on unemployment compensation, work injury benefits, family allowances, and public assistance as a percentage of GDP (proportional change from *t – 3 to t*)	ILO (1961–92)
Education spending	Total government expenditures on education as percentage of GDP (proportional change from *t – 3 to t*)	UNESCO (1955–90)
Right-party dominance....	Proportion of total cabinet seats held by right parties (running average from *t – 4 to t*)	Hicks and Swank (1992)

Note. Denominators for ratio variables (population, working population, GDPs) are from Summers and Heston (1991). Monetary variables are 1985 $U.S. using PPP exchange rates. WHO = World Health Organization: ILO = International Labour Organization.

REFERENCES

Beckett, Katherine. 1997. *Making Crime Pay: Law and Order in Contemporary American Politics.* New York: Oxford University Press

Berk, Richard A., Sheldon L. Messinger, David Rauma, and John E. Berecochea. 1983. "Prisons as Self-Regulating Systems: A Comparison of Historical Patterns in California for Male and Female Offenders." *Law and Society Review* 17:547–86.

Berk, Richard A., David Rauma, Sheldon L. Messinger, and Thomas F. Cooley. 1981. "A Test of the Stability of Punishment Hypothesis: The Case of California, 1851–1970." *American Sociological Review* 46:805–28.

Biles, David. 1982. "Crime and Imprisonment: An Australian Time Series Analysis." *Australian and New Zealand Journal of Criminology* 15:133–53.

Blumstein, Alfred. 1988. "Prison Populations: A System Out of Control?" Pp. 231–66 in *Crime and Justice: A Review of Research,* edited by

Michael Tonry and Norval Morris. Chicago: University of Chicago Press.

Bourdieu, Pierre. 1977. *Outline of a Theory of Practice.* Cambridge: Cambridge University Press.

———. 1984. *Distinction: A Social Critique of the Judgement of Taste.* Cambridge, Mass.: Harvard University Press.

———. 1990. *The Logic of Practice.* Stanford, Calif.: Stanford University Press.

Caldeira, Greg A., and Andrew T. Cowart. 1980. "Budgets, Institutions, and Change: Criminal Justice Policy in America." *American Journal of Political Science* 24:413–38.

Caplow, Theodore, and Jonathan Simon, 1999. "Understanding Prison Policy and Population Trends." Pp. 63–120 in *Crime and Justice*: *A Review of Research,* edited by Michael Tonry and Joan Petersilia. Chicago: University of Chicago Press.

Cappel, C., and G. Sykes. 1991. "Prison Commitments, Crime, and Unemployment: A Theoretical and Empirical Specification for the U.S., 1933–1983." *Journal of Quantitative Criminology* 7: 155–95.

Chambliss, William J. 1994. "Policing the Ghetto Underclass: The Politics of Law and Law Enforcement." *Social Problems* 41:177–94.

Chiricos, Theodore G., and Miriam A. DeLone. 1992. "Surplus Labor and Punishment: A Review and Assessment of Theory and Evidence." *Social Problems* 39:421–46.

Cohen, Lawrence E., and Marcus Felson. 1979. "Social Change and Crime Rate Trends: A Routine Activity Approach." *American Sociological Review* 44:588–608.

Cohen, Lawrence E., and Kenneth C. Land, 1987. "Age Structure and Crime: Symmetry Versus Asymmetry and the Projection of Crime Rates through the 1990s." *American Sociological Review* 52:170–83

Durkheim, Emile. 1965. *The Elementary Forms of the Religious Life.* New York: Free Press.

———. 1982. *The Rules of the Sociological Method.* New York: Free Press.

Durkheim, Emile, and Marcel Mauss, 1963. *Primitive Classification.* Chicago: University of Chicago Press.

Faber, Jan. 1989. *Annual Data on Nine Economic and Military Characteristics of 78 Nations.* Amsterdam: Europa Institut.

Garland, David. 1985. *Punishment and Welfare: A History of Penal Strategies.* Brookfield, Vt.: Gower.

Gartner, Rosemary, and Robert Nash Parker. 1990. "Cross-National Evidence on Homicide and Age Structure of the Population." *Social Forces* 69:351–71.

Griffin, L. J., M. Wallace, and J. A. Devine. 1982. "The Political Economy of Military Spending: Evidence from the U.S." *Cambridge Journal of Economics* 6:1–14.

Griswold, Wendy. 1994. *Cultures and Societies in a Changing World.* Thousand Oaks, Calif.: Pine Forge Press.

Hale, Chris, 1989. "Economy, Punishment and Imprisonment." *Contemporary Crises* 13:327–49

Hicks, Alexander M., and Duane H Swank. 1992. "Politics, Institutions, and Welfare Spending in Industrialized Democracies, 1960–82." *American Political Science Review* 86:649–74.

Hirschi, Travis. 1969. *Causes of Delinquency.* Berkeley: University of California Press.

Hirschi, Travis, and Michael Gottfredson. 1983. "Age and Explanation of Crime." *American Journal of Sociology* 89:552–84.

IISS (International Institute for Strategic Studies). 1983–85. *The Military Balance.* London: IISS.

ILO (International Labour Office). 1955–1990. *Year Book of Labour Statistics.* Geneva: ILO.

———. 1961–92. *The Cost of Social Security.* Geneva: ILO.

Inverarity, James, and Ryken Grattet. 1989. "Institutional Responses to Unemployment: A Comparison of U.S. Trends, 1948–1985." *Contemporary Crises* 13:351–70.

Jacobs, David, and Ronald E. Helms. 1996. "Toward a Political Model of Incarceration: A Time-Series Examination of Multiple Explanations for Prison Admission Rates." *American Journal of Sociology* 102:323–57.

Mare, Robert D., and Christopher Winship 1984. "Racial Inequality and Joblessness." *American Sociological Review* 49:39–55.

Mauer, Mark. 1994. *Americans behind Bars: The International Use of Incarceration, 1992–1993.* Washington D.C.: Sentencing Project.

Meyer, John W. 1988. "Levels of Analysis: The Life Course as a Cultural Construction." Pp. 49–62 in *Social Structures and Human Lives,* edited by Matilda White Riley. Newbury Park, Calif.: Sage.

Monkkonen, Eric H. 1989. "Diverging Homicide Rates: England and the United States, 1850-1857." Pp. 80–101 in *Violence in America.* Vol. 1, *The History of Crime,* edited by Ted Robert Gurr. Newbury Park, Calif.: Sage.

Mukherjee, S. K., A. Scandia, D. Dagger, and W. Matthews. 1989. *Source Book of Australian Criminal and Social Statistics, 1804–1988.* Canberra: Australian Institute of Criminology.

Nadelmann, Ethan A. 1993. *Cops across Borders: The Internationalization of U.S. Criminal Law Enforcement.* University Park: Pennsylvania State University Press.

Nielsen, François, and Michael T. Hannan. 1977. "The Expansion of National Educational Systems: Tests of a Population Ecology Model." *American Sociological Review* 42:479–90.

Pampel, Fred C., and Rosemary Gartner. 1995. "Age Structure, Socio-Political Institutions, and National Homicide Rates." *European Sociological Review* 11:243–60.

Pratt, John. 1988. "Law and Order Politics in New Zealand 1986: A Comparison with the United Kingdom 1974–79." *International Journal of the Sociology of Law* 16:103–26.

Rusche, Georg, and Otto Kirchheimer, 1968. *Punishment and Social Structure.* New York: Russell & Russell.

Sampson, Robert J., and John H. Laub. 1993. *Crime in the Making: Pathways and Turning Points through life.* Cambridge, Mass.: Harvard University Press.

Savelsberg, Joachim. 1994. "Knowledge, Domination, and Criminal Punishment." *American Journal of Sociology* 99:911–43.

Summers, Robert, and Alan Heston. 1991. "The Penn World Table (Mark 5.5): An Expanded Data Set of International Comparisons, 1950-1988." *Quarterly Journal of Economics* 106:327-68.

Sutton, John R. 1987. "Doing Time: Dynamics of Imprisonment in the Reformist State." *American Sociological Review* 52:612–30.

———. 1990. "Bureaucrats and Entrepreneurs: Institutional Responses to Deviant Children in the United States, 1890–1920s." *American Journal of Sociology* 95:1367–400.

———. 1991. "The Political Economy of Madness: The Expansion of the Asylum in Progressive America." *American Sociological Review* 56:665–78.

Tonry, M. 1999. "Why Are U.S. Incarceration Rates So High? *Crime and Delinquency* 45:419–37.

UNESCO. 1955–90. *Statistical Yearbook.* Paris: UNESCO.

World Health Organization. 1951–64. *Statistiques Epidemiologiques et Demographiques Annuelles.* Geneva: WHO.

———. 1962–88. *World Health Statistics Annual.* Geneva: WHO.

Wuthnow, Robert. 1987. *Meaning and Moral Order: Explorations in Cultural Analysis.* Berkeley and Los Angeles: University of California Press.

QUESTIONS

1. Sutton notes that "the distinction between criminals and non-criminals" is only one of the ways in which people are classified in modern society. What are some of the other ways, according to Sutton's argument? And, how are these other ways reflected in the hypotheses that he develops (especially 3 through 5)?

2. In addition to "life course patterns" that may influence imprisonment (noted in the previous question), Sutton discusses three "policy trade-offs." As one example of these, what is the trade-off between prison and *social welfare* (Hypothesis 6)?

3. According to Sutton, how does the use of existing data across countries challenge researchers?

4. How is Sutton's analysis both comparative and historical?

5. Do Sutton's results support (a) his fourth hypothesis (about the relationship between men's school enrollments and prison growth) and (b) his sixth hypothesis (concerning the relationship between welfare spending and prison growth)?

UNIT IX

MULTIPLE METHODS

Previous units have illustrated a variety of approaches to social research. Much of the time, investigators use only one of these approaches. In the long run, though, the best strategy is to address a research question with multiple methods.

The wisdom of this strategy is conveyed by the concept of **triangulation,** a term social scientists have borrowed from the field of navigation. To understand its conventional usage, imagine that you are lost deep in the woods of Maine and need to pinpoint your location for the local rescue team. Assume you have an old cell phone *without* GPS. Using your phone, you could call members of the team stationed at two different places, A and B. The team member at each position would then use a directional antenna to get a bearing on your location, which is represented by each of the dashed lines running from A and B in Figure IX.1. Neither direction by itself would provide enough information because you could be located anywhere along the A or B lines. But the point where the lines intersect would pin down your location. (Incidentally, GPS is based on a more sophisticated form of triangulation from satellites: see Resources.)

Triangulation in social research refers to the use of two or more dissimilar methods to address the same research question. Each method is analogous to the different vantage points in Figure IX.1. All methods are subject to error or bias, but dissimilar methods are not likely to share the same weaknesses. Therefore, we become more confident in a result when the methods separately zero in on the same findings. In effect, the strengths of one method offset the weaknesses of the other.

An example of how triangulation can strengthen research findings is an experiment to assess the health benefits of writing about a traumatic event. The psychological stress of a traumatic experience can increase one's susceptibility to illness; confronting the experience, such as by openly expressing one's thoughts and feelings, may reduce stress. To test this idea, James Pennebaker, Janice Kiecolt-Glaser, and Ronald Glaser (1988) asked undergraduates to write about either traumatic, upsetting experiences (e.g., death of a loved one, sexual abuse, parental problems) or trivial topics. Triangulation occurred in measuring the healthful effects of the writing exercise. Rather than rely on a single measure, the experimenters used three divergent indicators: (1) number of health center visits, (2) participants' self-reports of their level of psychological distress, and (3) immunological data based on blood samples. Although the three indicators reveal markedly different aspects of "physical health," all of them pointed to the same outcome: a positive impact of writing about traumatic experiences.

The logic of triangulation applies to many different research activities, including the use of multiple survey questions to measure the same underlying concept, two or more observers to

FIGURE IX.1 Triangulating the Location of a Cell Phone From Two Points, A and B.

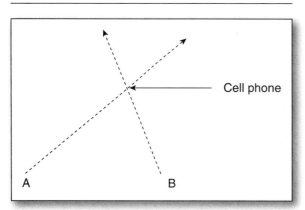

record observations in the same field setting, and two or more studies or approaches to test the same hypothesis. Comparing experimental and survey data, the first study in this unit shows how attitudes expressed in a survey may provide misleading evidence of racial discrimination in practice.

Aside from validating research findings, which is the aim of triangulation, multiple methods may provide complementary information. For example, in-depth interviews sometimes are used to probe the meaning of survey responses. In the second selection, the investigators describe how they used an iterative process of gathering and analyzing data that integrated survey and field research. Survey data provided useful leads that were explored through field research; in turn, a deepened understanding from fieldwork led to hypotheses that were tested with the survey data.

REFERENCES

Pennebaker, J. W., Kiecolt-Glaser, J. K., & Glaser, R. (1988). Disclosure of traumas and immune function: Health implications for psychotherapy. *Journal of Consulting and Clinical Psychology, 56,* 239–245.

RESOURCES

Why Triangulate?:

http://blogs.ubc.ca/qualresearch/files/2008/01/why-tirangulate.pdf

- In this brief article from *Educational Researcher*, Sandra Mathison traces historical origins of the term in social research, outlines the various forms that it can take, and then presents an alternative conception of triangulation. Because data sources and methods do not always converge, she argues that triangulation should not be construed merely as a means of *increasing validity*. Rather, when data are inconsistent or contradictory, triangulation "provides more and better evidence" to "*construct meaningful propositions* about the social world."

Multiple Methods in ASR:

http://www.asanet.org/footnotes/dec05/index two.html

- Both of the articles in this unit were published in the *American Sociological Review* (*ASR*) under the editorship of Jerry Jacobs. A proponent of multi-method research, Jacobs points out in this December 2005 essay that one quarter of the papers accepted for publication in *ASR* under his editorship drew on more than one research method. He then "highlights some of the ways" that these papers have provided "a more informative account of the social world."

Understanding GPS Technology:

http://www.beaglesoft.com/gpstechnology.htm

- For those who want to learn more about the triangulation in navigation, this site explains how GPS is based on triangulation from satellites.

Selection 17

Surveys are a very good strategy for measuring what people think and how they feel about something; however, they are less effective in measuring actual behavior. Still, researchers continue to use verbal reports of what people say they would do as indicators for what they actually do. Showing how this may be particularly problematic in studies of discrimination, Devah Pager and Lincoln Quillian compare the results of a field experiment on hiring discrimination, described in Selection 10, with a telephone survey of the same employers. As you read, note the methodological differences in the two approaches.

WALKING THE TALK?

What Employers Say Versus What They Do

DEVAH PAGER

LINCOLN QUILLIAN

In 1930, Richard LaPiere, a Stanford professor, traveled twice across the country by car with a young Chinese student and his wife. The purpose of the trip, unbeknown to his travel companions, was to assess the reactions of hotel and restaurant proprietors to the presence of Chinese customers. During the course of 251 visits to hotels, auto camps, restaurants, and cafes, only once were they refused service. Six months later, LaPiere mailed a survey to each of the proprietors in which one of the questions asked, "Will you accept members of the Chinese race as guests in your establishment?" More than 90 percent of the respondents indicated unequivocal refusal. The discrepancy between these proprietors' responses to the surveys and their actual behavior is indeed striking. Although nearly none of the proprietors expressed a willingness to accept the patronage of Chinese customers, virtually all of them did so when

Source: "Walking the Talk? What Employers Say Versus What They Do," by Devah Pager and Lincoln Quillian, 2005, *American Sociological Review,* 70, 355–380. Copyright 2005 by Sage Publications. Adapted with permission.

confronted with the situation (LaPiere 1934). If we were to make generalizations based on either the survey results or the field study alone, we would develop radically different views on the level of racial hostility toward the Chinese at that time in history.

LaPiere's study provides a much needed reality check for researchers who rely on expressed attitudes for insight into the nature and causes of discriminatory behavior. Unfortunately, there have been very few efforts to provide the kind of comparison offered in LaPiere's study. Measures from surveys often are accepted as an adequate proxy for behaviors, with little effort to validate this assumption.

RACIAL ATTITUDES, DISCRIMINATION, AND CONTEMPORARY LABOR MARKET INEQUALITY

In the years since LaPiere's study, much has changed about race relations in the contemporary United States. In present times, it would be extremely rare to find respondents willing to state racial objections as candidly as those reported in LaPiere's survey. Indeed, trends in racial attitudes demonstrate steady movement toward the endorsement of equal treatment by race and the repudiation of direct discrimination. According to surveys conducted in the 1940s and 1950s, for example, fewer than half of whites believed that white students should go to school with black students or that black and white job applicants should have an equal chance at getting a job. In contrast, by the 1990s, more than 90 percent of white survey respondents endorsed the principle that white and black students and job applicants should be treated equally by schools and employers (Schuman et al. 2001).

Consistent with these trends, many indicators of social and economic status show that African-Americans have made great strides in approaching parity with whites. In fact, these positive indicators have led some prominent academics to proclaim the problem of discrimination solved.

Economist James Heckman, for example, has asserted that "most of the disparity in earnings between blacks and whites in the labor market of the 1990s is due to the differences in skills they bring to the market, and not to discrimination within the labor market." He went on to refer to labor market discrimination as "the problem of an earlier era" (Heckman 1998:101–102). Indeed, for many observers of contemporary race relations, the barrier of discrimination appears to have withered away, leaving blacks the opportunity to pursue unfettered upward mobility.

And yet, despite the many signs of progress, there remain important forms of social and economic inequality that continue to differentiate the experiences of black and white Americans. According to many indicators, blacks, and black men in particular, continue to lag far behind their white counterparts. Some indicators show black men doing steadily worse. African-Americans, for example, experience roughly double the rate of unemployment experienced by whites, with very little sign of change over time. Likewise, rates of joblessness among young black men have been rising over time (Holzer, Offner, and Sorensen 2005).

How can we explain the discrepancies between these varied measures? On the one hand, the progressive trends in racial attitudes may reflect a genuine openness among white Americans to racial integration and equality. On the other hand, traditional survey measures of racial attitudes may not accurately reflect the degree to which race continues to shape the opportunities available to African-Americans. Indeed, a great deal of evidence suggests that racial stereotypes remain firmly embedded in the American consciousness, affecting perceptions of and interactions with racial minorities even among respondents who overtly endorse the principle of equal treatment (Devine and Elliot 1995). Substantial levels of discrimination have likewise been detected by experimental field studies, which find consistent evidence of racial bias against black applicants in housing, credit, and employment markets (Bertrand and Mullainathan 2004; Turner, Fix, and Struyk

1991; Yinger 1995). As a further reflection of lived experience, the large majority of blacks continue to perceive discrimination as routine in matters of jobs, income, and housing (Feagin and Sikes 1994).

Given the available information, it is difficult to evaluate the extent to which direct discrimination plays a role in shaping the opportunities available to blacks in contemporary society. Surveys of racial attitudes portray one optimistic picture, whereas indicators of economic and social inequality present more mixed results. It is only through direct comparisons of these differing measures that we can assess how and why they may project such divergent conclusions.

In this article, we focus on the specific issue of employment discrimination. Substantively, we are interested in assessing the degree to which employer preferences or biases influence the opportunities available to stigmatized workers. Methodologically, we seek to assess the degree to which choice of measurement strategy affects our understanding of these processes. In our analysis of survey data and behavioral outcomes, we engage with LaPiere's central concern about the correspondence between measured attitudes and behaviors.

Explicit Studies of Prejudice-Discrimination Correspondence

The recent literature on the specific attitude-behavior case of prejudice and discrimination (in sociology) is virtually nonexistent.[1] Indeed, we turned instead to research in psychology for guidance in these matters.

Psychological research has provided several important insights into the correspondence between different types of attitudes and behaviors, pointing to, for example, varying relationships between explicit/conscious attitudes, implicit/unconscious attitudes, and various forms of behavior (Dovidio et al. 2002). From a sociological standpoint, however, these studies have some important limitations, most notably those arising from a reliance on behavioral measures obtained in laboratory settings. For instance, the studies Fiske (2004) reviews use outcome behaviors such as ratings of perceived friendliness in interaction with a mock interviewer, subtle behavioral measures such as the number of blinks and the length of eye contact, or the results of role-playing situations. These outcomes often are far removed from the actual decisions made in their social contexts—to hire, to rent, or to move, to name a few—that are most relevant to understanding the behavioral processes that produce disadvantage among members of stigmatized groups.

For our purposes, the most relevant studies comparing prejudice and discrimination are those that assess these factors in realistic social settings, focusing on forms of discrimination that produce meaningful social disparities. Unfortunately, the three studies that fit this description each were conducted more than 50 years ago (Kutner et al. 1952; LaPiere 1934; Saenger and Gilbert 1950). We have very few means by which to assess the correspondence between contemporary racial attitudes and the incidence of discrimination.

Employer Attitudes and Hiring Decisions

The current study provides an opportunity to investigate these processes in a contemporary context. Bringing together a unique combination of data, we present a direct comparison of self-reported attitudes and corresponding behavior in the context of real-world setting with important implications for inequality. The substantive focus of this study is on employers' willingness to hire blacks and/or ex-offenders for an entry-level position in their company. In both cases, the sensitive topics under investigation lead us to question the use of employer reports alone. By calibrating the estimates we received from surveys with behavioral measures from an experimental audit study, we are able to gain insight into the consistency between these two important indicators of group preference.

Measures of attitudes come in many forms, ranging from abstract statements of feelings (e.g., "I don't like members of group X") to more concrete statements of intended action (e.g., "I would not hire members of group X"). The latter, referred to as behavioral intentions, are considered the form of attitude that should most closely correspond to observed behavior, because of their conceptualization in terms of specific measurable action (Fishbein 1967; Fishbein and Ajzen 1975; Schuman and Johnson 1976). Thus a weak relation between behavioral intentions and behavior suggests an even weaker relation between the behavior and more general attitudinal measures. In the current study, we rely on the behavioral intentions expressed by employers as an indicator of their attitudes about blacks and ex-offenders. Comparing what employers said they would do in a hypothetical hiring situation with what we observed them doing in a real hiring situation forms the basis of our current investigation.

METHODS

In the first stage of the study, employers' responses to job applicants were measured in real employment settings using an experimental audit methodology [see Selection 10]. Between June and December of 2001, matched pairs of young men (testers) were sent to apply for a total of 350 entry-level job openings in the Milwaukee metropolitan area. The two white testers (one with a fictional criminal record and one without) applied for one set of randomly selected jobs ($n = 150$), and the two black testers (using profiles identical to those of the white pair) applied for a second set of jobs ($n = 200$). The preferences of employers were measured based on the number of call-backs to each of the applicants, as registered by four independent voice mail boxes. Additional voice mail boxes were set up for calls to references listed on the testers' resumes. For a more detailed discussion of the research design, see Pager (2003).

The findings of the audit showed large and significant effects of both race and criminal record on employment opportunities. Call-backs were received by 34 percent of whites with no criminal record, 17 percent of whites with criminal records, 14 percent of blacks without criminal records, and 5 percent of blacks with criminal records (Pager 2003). Thus, overall, blacks and ex-offenders were one-half to one-third as likely to be considered by employers, with black ex-offenders suffering the greatest disadvantage.

The second stage of the study provided employers with the opportunity to express their hiring preferences verbally in the context of a telephone survey. Several months after completion of the audit study, each of the 350 employers was called by interviewers from the Michigan State Survey Research Center and asked to participate in a telephone survey about employers' hiring preferences and practices (see Pager [2002] for more detailed discussion of the survey instrument and results). Calls were directed to the person in charge of hiring for each establishment. The final survey sample included 199 respondents, representing a 58 percent response rate.

During the course of this survey, employers were read a vignette describing a job applicant with characteristics designed to match closely the profile of the testers in the audit study. Employers who had been audited by white testers were read a vignette in which the hypothetical applicant was white, and employers who had been audited by black testers were read a vignette in which the applicant was black. In this way, the survey design mirrored the split-ballot procedures used by Sniderman and Piazza (1993) and Schuman and Bobo (1988), avoiding direct racial comparisons within the same survey.

The wording of the vignette was as follows:

Chad is a 23-year-old [black/white] male. He finished high school and has steady work experience in entry-level jobs. He has good references and interacts well with people. About a year ago, Chad was convicted of a drug felony and served 12 months in prison. Chad was released last month and is now looking for a job. How likely would you be to hire Chad for an entry-level opening in your company?

Employers were asked to rate their likelihood of hiring this applicant with the following range of responses: very likely, somewhat likely, somewhat unlikely, and very unlikely.

The vignette presented in the survey was designed to correspond closely to the profile of the testers in the audit study. Chad, the hypothetical applicant, was presented with levels of education, experience, and personal qualifications similar to those on the resumes presented by the testers. The type of crime was identical, although the prison sentence in the vignette (12 months) was shorter than that reported in the audit study (18 months). Thus the vignette aimed to measure employers' self-reports concerning how they would respond to such an applicant, whereas the audit measured how they actually did respond to an applicant with almost identical characteristics. The parallel scenarios of the vignette and audit should maximize the correspondence between the two measures (Schuman and Johnson 1976).

In the current study, the primary outcome of interest represents the employers' willingness to hire an applicant depending on his race and criminal background. As described earlier, in the survey, employers were asked to report how likely they would be to hire the applicant described in the vignette. In the actual employment situations, by contrast, we measured the number of employers who responded positively to testers after they had submitted their application. In most cases, this simply involved the employer inviting the tester to come in for an interview, although in a few cases, the applicant was offered the job on the spot.

RESULTS

Figure 17.1 presents the key results from both data sources. The first two columns represent the percentage of employers who reported that they would be "very likely" or "somewhat likely" to hire the hypothetical applicant, depending on whether he was presented as white or black. We include the "somewhat likely" group here to

correspond to our behavioral measure, which is a call-back rather than an actual hire (see discussion below).

The second two columns represent results from the audit study, illustrating the percentage of call-backs received by each group. In the audit study, call-backs also can be considered a measure of "willingness to hire," given that this represents a first cut in the hiring process. Although a call-back is by no means a guarantee of employment, given that employers typically call back several applicants before selecting their preferred hire, it does indicate a favorable initial review.

The results of the two outcomes, however, are anything but comparable. As Figure 17.1 shows, employers reported a far greater willingness to hire drug offenders in the survey than was found in the audit. In the survey, more than 60 percent of the employers said they were somewhat or very likely to hire a drug offender irrespective of the applicant's race. In the audit, by contrast, only 17 percent of white and 5 percent of black applicants with drug felonies actually received a call-back.

The disparities apparent in these results are extremely consequential for our understanding of the social world. In the survey data, employers' responses present a view of openness to blacks or applicants with drug felonies that is far greater than the reality measured in actual hiring situations. Accepting the survey results as an accurate indicator of the opportunities available to blacks and ex-offenders would grossly understate the barriers to employment they face.

A possible objection to this comparison is that the very framing of the vignette item may artificially exaggerate the difference between survey and audit results. When considering a hypothetical applicant, employers do not have to take into account alternative possibilities among the applicant pool. Thus the hypothetical applicant may exceed the minimum threshold for acceptability even if in actuality there tend to be other applicants who are better qualified. By contrast, the tester in the audit study is competing with a pool of real applicants of varying quality.

FIGURE 17.1 Expressed Willingness to Hire a Drug Offender According to Employer Survey and Audit

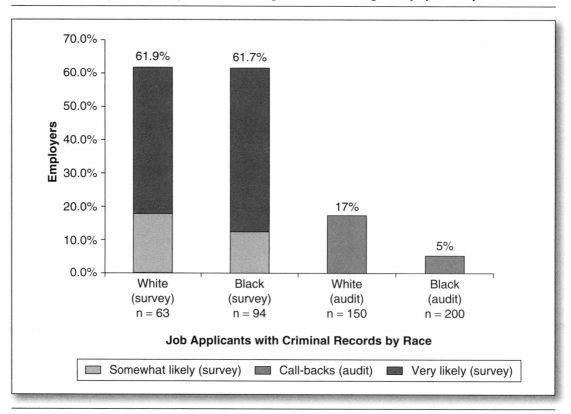

Note: Survey results include employers who said they were "very likely" or "somewhat likely" to hire the hypothetical applicant (with "very" at bottom of columns). Audit results represent the percentage of call-backs for each group. Differences between within-race comparisons of survey and audit results are significant on the basis of a two-sample test of proportions (p < .05).

To the extent that real applicants provide better qualifications than does the tester's profile, the tester will receive few call-backs for reasons unrelated to race or criminal record.

An alternative way of presenting the information that addresses this concern is to calculate the likelihood that a tester with a criminal record will receive a call-back *relative to* a white tester without a criminal record. White testers without criminal records in this case represent a kind of baseline, presenting a given set of qualifications common among all testers, but without the handicaps of minority status or a criminal record. Employers who made call-backs to white testers without criminal records signaled

that this level of education and experience was sufficiently desirable to make the first cut. Relative to this baseline, we can assess the proportion of blacks and whites with criminal records who received call-backs, thereby reducing the effect of employer nonresponses attributable to extraneous factors.

Figure 17.2 displays the results of this procedure, comparing the likelihood of hire based on the survey and audit results with audit results recalculated as a ratio of the percentage of testers in the offender condition who received call-backs to the percentage of white testers with identical qualifications but no criminal background who received call-backs. Overall, 34 percent of white applicants with no criminal records, and with the given set of human capital characteristics presented by all testers, received call-backs. This group serves as our baseline (denominator) for calculating the relative call-back rates for the other groups. Only 17 percent of white testers with identical characteristics plus a criminal record received call-backs, indicating that white testers with a criminal record were 50 percent as likely to receive call-backs as those without a criminal record (Figure 17.2). Black ex-offenders were the least likely to continue in the employment process—only 5 percent received call-backs—indicating that they were just less than 15 percent as likely to receive a call-back as a similar white tester without a criminal record.

The differences between self-reports and behaviors in this comparison, although smaller, remain consistent when call-back frequency is judged relative to that for white non-offenders. In the case of white ex-offenders, the distance between the survey and audit results has narrowed substantially, although it remains

FIGURE 17.2 Expressed Willingness to Hire a Drug Offender According to Employer Survey and Recalibrated Audit

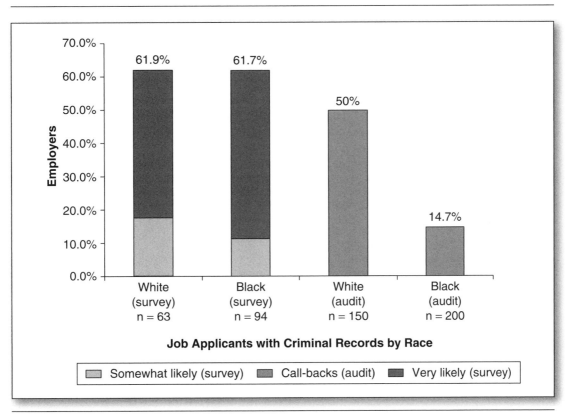

Note: Survey results include employers who said they were "very likely" or "somewhat likely" to hire the hypothetical applicant (with "very" at bottom of columns). Audit results represent the ratio of the percentage of call-backs for each group to the percentage of call-backs for white nonoffenders. Differences in within-race comparisons of survey and audit results are marginally significant for white applicants ($p < .06$) and significant for black applicants ($p < .05$) on the basis of a two-sample test of proportions.

marginally significant statistically. The case for black applicants, on the other hand, maintains a clear and dramatic difference. Even relative to contemporaneous call-back rates for white testers, the call-back rate for black ex-offenders (14.7) remains far short of the survey estimates of hiring likelihoods (61.7). For black ex-offenders, the survey and audit measures provide dramatically different indications of willingness to hire.

Whatever measure is used, two main findings remain clear. First, whereas the survey responses present a rather benign view of the employment barriers facing ex-offenders, the audit results tell a very different story. Employers indicate a high level of willingness to hire drug offenders, but in actual employment situations, they are less than half as likely even to call back such applicants relative to those without criminal records. This result underscores the importance of using great caution in relying on employers' self-reports as an accurate reflection of behavior.

Second, the degree to which race is a factor in hiring decisions is virtually undetectable in the survey results, in sharp contrast to what we find in the audit study. In the survey, although separate employers were asked the vignette in which the hypothetical applicant was white or black, the estimates of hiring likelihoods for both applicants were virtually identical. By contrast, actual behavioral measures in the audit show that white ex-offenders are more than three times as likely to receive consideration from employers as black ex-offenders. These results suggest that employer surveys, even those with split-ballot designs, do not always provide an effective way to gauge the degree to which sensitive characteristics such as race affect actual employment opportunities.

Finally, we turn to the issue of individual-level consistency between survey reports and audit results. Even if the *levels* of openness to hiring ex-offenders are inconsistent between survey and audit, it remains possible that a *correlation* exists between the two: Employers who indicate willingness to hire ex-offenders may be more likely to hire an ex-offender than employers who do not indicate such willingness, even if the overall openness to hiring ex-offenders is strongly overstated in the survey results. This final analysis allows us to compare the survey responses with the audit outcomes at an individual rather than an aggregate level. The results of this cross-tabulation are presented in Table 17.1. Consistent with the results reported

TABLE 17.1   Individual-level Consistency Between Employers' Self-reports and Behavioral Outcomes

Survey Results	Audit Results (for Testers Presenting Drug Felony)	
	No Call-Back	Call-Back
Likely to Hire Drug Offender		
No	56	4
	(93.3%)	(6.7%)
Yes	89	7
	(92.7%)	(7.3%)

Note: This table includes all employers who responded to the survey. Call-backs in the right column above represent calls to the tester in the criminal record condition only.

earlier, we find that the survey responses have very little connection to the actual behaviors exhibited by these employers.

Among those who reported a favorable likelihood of hiring an applicant with a prior drug conviction in the survey, 7.3 percent made calls to the tester with the criminal record in the audit study, relative to 6.7 percent of those expressing an unfavorable likelihood. This difference is in the expected direction, but is only slightly greater than zero (0.6 percent), and far too small to reach statistical significance.

These results cast strong doubt on the accuracy of survey data for indicating relative likelihoods of hiring. Individuals who report a higher likelihood of hiring an ex-offender are only trivially more likely to do so. Confirming the aggregate findings described earlier, the individual-level associations presented here appear to be no better at establishing a relationship between attitudes and behaviors.

RETHINKING THE ROLE OF ATTITUDES

What can we conclude from these results regarding the usefulness of data on attitudes? Should we disregard all employers' self-reports? Certainly, it would be premature to advise such a radical stance. In fact, despite the large discrepancies between the self-reports and behaviors measured in the current study, we believe that survey results remain useful, even if they cannot be viewed as an alternative procedure to the measurement of actual discrimination.

Even in cases in which expressed attitudes have little relationship to measured discrimination, survey data can nevertheless tell us something useful about how employers *think* about important hiring issues. Responses to the survey suggest, for instance, that many employers who discriminate against blacks do not necessarily do so because of a principled belief that black employees should not be hired. In fact, we think it likely that many employers genuinely believe their own responses to surveys, professing the value of equal opportunity, while simultaneously justifying their behavior in hiring situations on grounds other than race (e.g., assumptions about the family/social/educational backgrounds of black applicants; see Kirschenman and Neckerman 1991). In this case, the difference between employers' self-reports and their actual behavior represents a meaningful discrepancy between two legitimate realities. The resolution of these differences represents an important focus of sociological investigation in its own right. Although low correlations between attitudes and associated behaviors often are viewed as a purely methodological test of survey questions, in many cases, these discrepancies actually may provide clues toward a better substantive understanding of the cognitive-emotional basis for action.

Furthermore, it remains possible that survey research may provide a better proxy for behavior in situations that are less complex and subject to fewer contextual influences than hiring. Action in any real social situation is the result of many factors other than the actor's attitude toward the object, including norms, perceived consequences of the action, and implicit or unconscious attitudes toward the object. The many complex influences on hiring decisions make these situations exactly the sort for which survey measures are least likely to be an effective substitute. Indeed, the three "classic" studies that found very weak associations between expressed behavioral intentions and behaviors all were studies of discrimination in social situations (Kutner et al. 1952; LaPiere 1934, Saenger and Gilbert 1950). We believe it possible that survey responses may provide a much more effective proxy for behavior in other contexts, such as those that involve voting (Traugott and Katosh 1979), signing of a petition (Brannon et al. 1973), or patterns of consumer behavior (Day et al. 1991), in which the link between behavioral intentions and actual behavior is less subject to contextual influences apart from the respondent's attitude or intention.

Finally, we have focused on only a few of the many survey techniques that have been developed to measure prejudice and discrimination. Though our measure of behavioral intentions was designed to offer the closest match to the audit context, it remains possible that other more abstracted measures of racial bias may in fact correlate more closely with measures of discrimination. There is an extensive literature that attempts to investigate modern or subtle forms of racial attitudes using survey questions (National Research Council 2004, chapter 8), and certain of these alternative approaches could prove more effective at capturing behavioral outcomes than what we found in this study.

CONCLUSION

LaPiere (1934) showed a striking inconsistency in the way hotel and restaurant proprietors reacted to Chinese customers in person, as compared with how they responded in surveys. The current study notes a similar discrepancy between employers' self-reported likelihood of hiring a particular applicant and their actual hiring behaviors when faced with a nearly identical candidate. We found an especially large and robust disparity between the reported likelihood of employers hiring black ex-offenders and actual rates of hiring. The low correlation between expressed and observed hiring outcomes presents an epistemological worry: our assessments of the degree of disadvantage faced by black ex-offenders would be substantially underestimated on the basis of the survey results alone. Moreover, we found little correlation between greater expressed likelihood of hiring ex-offenders in the survey and actual increased rates of call-backs for ex-offenders in real hiring situations. Given that most research on hiring preferences and practices comes from the self-reports of employers themselves (Downing 1984; Holzer 1996; Husley 1990; Jensen and Giegold 1976; Waldinger and Lichter 2003; Wilson 1996), these results indeed have serious implications.

In terms of the methods used to measure discrimination, these findings suggest that sociologists may need to reevaluate what is learned from studies that use vignettes of hypothetical situations to study behaviors toward stigmatized groups. Although we believe that these vignette studies often do tell us about respondents' abstract beliefs, in some cases these beliefs may have relatively little influence on the behavior of interest. Feelings and evaluations in a concrete social situation may be very different from those in the abstracted situation of the survey, but the two often are treated as nearly identical. An important next step in evaluating the contribution of survey measures for understanding behaviors of interest is to relate these items to actual behavior.

More broadly, these results suggest the limits of survey questions alone for understanding the changing nature of racial inequality. Survey questions indicating a liberalizing of racial attitudes among white Americans have been cited widely as evidence supporting the declining significance of race in American society. But if the items analyzed in this study have any bearing on survey responses more generally, we have reason to question that changing public opinion on matters of race has any necessary correspondence to the incidence of discrimination. Rather, our results support the perspective that there has been a growing gap between the principled statements and beliefs of white Americans in favor of racial equality and their concrete actions. Survey questions provide one important perspective on American race relations, but they must be combined with other information for a complete picture.

NOTE

1. Prejudice refers to negative judgments or opinions about a group (attitudes). Discrimination refers to unfavorable treatment directed toward members of a group (behavior).

REFERENCES

Bertrand, Marianne and Sendhil Mullainathan. 2004. "Are Emily and Greg More Employable than

Lakisha and Jamal? A Field Experiment on Labor Market Discrimination." *American Economic Review* 94:991–1013.

Brannon, Robert, Gary Cyphers, Sharlene Hesse, Susan Hesselbart, Roberta Keane, Howard Schuman, Tomas Viccaro, and Diana Wright, 1973. "Attitude and Action: A Field Experiment Jointed to a General Population Survey." *American Sociological Review* 38:625–36.

Day, Dianne, Boon Gan, Philip Gendall, and Don Esslemont 1991. "Predicting Purchase Behaviour." *Marketing Bulletin* 2:18-30.

Devine, P. G. and A. J. Elliot. 1995. "Are Racial Stereotypes Really Fading? The Princeton Trilogy Revisited." *Personality and Social Psychology Bulletin* 21:1139–50.

Dovidio, John, Kerry Kawakami, and Samuel Gaertner. 2002. "Implicit and Explicit Prejudice and Interracial Interaction." *Journal of Personality and Social Psychology* 82:62–68.

Downing, David. 1984. "Employer Bias toward the Hiring and Placement of Male Ex-Offenders." Ph.D. dissertation, Department of Education, Southern Illinois University, Carbondale, IL.

Feagin, J. and M. Sykes. 1994. *Living with Racism, the Black Middle Class Experience*. Boston, MA: Beacon Press.

Fishbein, M. 1967. "Attitude and the Prediction of Behavior." Pp. 477–492 in *Readings in Attitude Theory and Measurement*, edited by M. Fishbein. New York: Wiley.

Fishbein, M. and I. Ajzen. 1975. *Belief, Attitude, Intention, and Behavior*. Reading, MA: Addison-Wesley.

Fiske, Susan. 2004. "Predicting Discrimination: A Meta-Analysis of the Racial Attitude-Behavior Literature." Working Paper, Department of Psychology, Princeton University.

Heckman, James. 1998. "Detecting Discrimination." *The Journal of Economic Perspectives* 12:101–116.

Holzer, Harry. 1996. *What Employers Want. Job Prospects for Less-Educated Workers*. New York: Russell Sage Foundation.

Holzer, Harry, Paul Offner and Elaine Sorensen. 2005. "What Explains the Continuing Decline in Labor Force Activity among Young Black Men?" *Labor History* 46:37–55.

Husley, Lonnie Freeman. 1990. "Attitudes of Employers with Respect to Hiring Released Prisoners." Ph.D. dissertation, Department of Industrial Education, Texas A&M University, TX.

Jensen, W. and W. C. Giegold. 1976. "Finding Jobs for Ex-Offenders: A Study of Employers' Attitudes." *American Business Law Journal* 14:195–225.

Kirschenman, Joleen and Katherine Neckerman. 1991. "'We'd Love to Hire Them, but . . .': The Meaning of Race for Employers." Pp. 203–232 in *The Urban Underclass*, edited by Christopher Jencks and P. Peterson, Washington, DC: Brookings Institute.

Kutner, Bernard, Carol Wilkins, and Penny Rechtman Yarrow. 1952. "Verbal Attitudes and Overt Behavior Involving Racial Prejudice." *Journal of Abnormal Social Psychology* 47:649–52.

LaPiere, Richard T. 1934. "Attitudes vs Actions." *Social Forces* 13:230–37.

National Research Council, 2004, *Measuring Racial Discrimination*. Panel on Methods for Assessing Discrimination, Committee on National Statistics, Division of Behavior and Social Sciences and Education, edited by Rebecca M. Blank, Marilyn Dadaby, and Constance F. Citro. Washington, DC: The National Academies Press.

Pager, Devah. 2003. "The Mark of a Criminal Record." *American Journal of Sociology* 108:937–75.

———. 2002. "The Mark of a Criminal Record." Doctoral dissertation. Department of Sociology, University of Wisconsin-Madison.

Saenger, Gerhart and Emily Gilbert, 1950. "Custom Reactions to the Integration of Negro Sales Personnel." *International Journal of Opinion and Attitude Research* 4:57–76.

Schuman, Howard and Lawrence Bobo. 1988. "Survey-Based Experiments on White Racial Attitudes toward Residential Integration." *American Journal of Sociology* 94:273–99.

Schuman, Howard and Michael P. Johnson. 1976. "Attitudes and Behaviors." *Annual Review of Sociology* 2:161–207.

Schuman, Howard, Charlottee Steeh, Lawrence Bobo, and Maria Krysan. 2001. *Racial Attitudes in America: Trends and Interpretations*. Rev. ed. Cambridge, MA: Harvard University Press.

Sniderman, Paul M. and Thomas Piazza. 1993. *The Scar of Race*. Cambridge, MA: The Belknap Press of Harvard University Press.

Traugott, Michael W. and John P. Katosh. 1979. "Response Validity in Surveys of Voting Behavior." *Public Opinion Quarterly* 43:359–77.

Turner, Margery, Michael Fix, and Raymond Struyk. 1991. *Opportunities Denied, Opportunities Diminished: Racial Discrimination in Hiring*. Washington, DC: Urban Institute Press.

Waldinger, Roger and Michael Lichter. 2003. *How the Other Half Works: Immigration and the Social Organization of Labor*. Berkeley, CA: The University of California Press.

Wilson, William Julius. 1996. *When Work Disappears: The World of the New Urban Poor*. New York: Vintage Books.

Yinger, John. 1995. *Closed Doors. Opportunities Lost*. New York: Russell Sage Foundation.

QUESTIONS

1. How do previous surveys and field experiments project different conclusions about the present state of racial equality in the United States?

2. Compare the outcome measures in the survey and field experiment. How are they similar and how are they different?

3. Carefully describe how the job applicant in the audit study was similar to the job applicant in the vignette. Why is this similarity an important aspect of the research design?

4. How do the results shown in Figure 17.2 augment the findings in Figure 17.1?

5. Should one conclude from this study that attitudes generally are a poor predictor of behavior? Explain.

Selection 18

To understand the influence of physical and sexual abuse on marriage and cohabitation among low-income women, Andrew Cherlin and associates combined data from a survey and an ethnography (a type of field research). Surveys can describe populations with a high degree of accuracy; however, unless repeated over time, surveys may not provide enough information to trace the history of events or to establish causal direction. Based on small samples, ethnographic findings have limited generalizability. But this type of research is usually carried out over an extended period so that the order of events becomes apparent. As you read this selection, note how the strengths of one method offset the weaknesses of the other.

THE INFLUENCE OF PHYSICAL AND SEXUAL ABUSE ON MARRIAGE AND COHABITATION

ANDREW J. CHERLIN

LINDA M. BURTON

TERA R. HURT

DIANE M. PURVIN

Across all social classes, Americans are more likely to cohabit prior to and after marriage, marry at older ages, divorce more, never marry at all, and have children outside of marriage compared to a half-century ago. In this article, we examine the role of an often overlooked factor in the scholarly and policy discourse on the decline of marriage: the trauma

Source: "The Influence of Physical and Sexual Abuse on Marriage and Cohabitation," by Andrew J. Cherlin, Linda M. Burton, Tera R. Hurt, and Diane M. Purvin, 2004, *American Sociological Review,* 69, 768–789. Copyright 2004 by Sage Publications.

of physical and sexual abuse that some women experience in childhood and adulthood. Although there is extensive literature on abuse and on marriage formation, few studies have explored the connection between them (Macmillan 2001).

Our central claim is that, for many women, the experiences of physical abuse and sexual abuse influence intimate relations in ways that reduce the likelihood of stable, long-term unions. (By a "union," we mean a marriage or a cohabiting relationship.) Physical and sexual abuse may affect union formation in several ways. Exposure to physical abuse by intimate partners in adulthood can create a wariness about relationships with men that leads women to be cautious about making long-term commitments (Edin 2000) and, in some circumstances, to avoid relationships altogether. At the same time, physical and sexual abuse beginning in childhood can predispose women toward more frequent sexual unions and multiple, transient relationships, some of them abusive (Butler and Burton 1990; Loeb et al. 2002; Noll, Trickett, and Putnam 2003). Using both the ethnographic and survey components of a study of low-income families in Boston, Chicago, and San Antonio, we identify patterns of union formation and test hypotheses derived from our collaborative multi-method research and from the literature on physical and sexual abuse.

BACKGROUND

Our exploration of the relationship between union formation and the experience of physical and sexual abuse among low-income women is the result of an iterative collaborative process that integrates demographic and ethnographic approaches. We began by analyzing the survey data to study the empirical relationship between patterns of union formation, on the one hand, and reported experiences of physical and sexual abuse. When an association was found we looked to our ethnographic data to identify detailed patterns of abuse and union formation with the intent of using the ethnographic results to deepen

our understanding and to develop hypotheses that could be tested with the survey data. Generally speaking, our ethnographic analysis suggested that the timing of abuse—whether it occurred in childhood, adulthood, or in both periods—and the form of abuse—whether it was sexual or physical—were strongly related to distinctive union patterns. The extant literature on sexual abuse and physical abuse also guided the development of hypotheses, although not in ways that were as specific as the ethnographic findings.

THEORETICAL MECHANISMS AND HYPOTHESES

Our ethnographic data, as we will discuss, showed that some women seemed to have withdrawn from serious relationships with men altogether, a pattern we will call *abated unions*. Even among women who do have intimate unions, the experience of past abuse could lead to emotional distance from partners and hesitancy to make long-term commitments (Hoff 1990; Kirkwood 1993). Because it is easier to leave a cohabiting relationship than a marriage, women who have experienced abuse and wish to maintain an exit route from relationships may prefer cohabitation to marriage.

In addition, the personal and social resources that women can draw upon may influence union-formation patterns. Women who successfully resist abusive men must be resourceful (Johnson and Ferraro 2000): They must actively solve problems, respond quickly, and negotiate firmly. Those who bring more psychological resources to their adult intimate relationships and who have more social support in adulthood will be more likely to separate themselves from potentially abusive men. Childhood abuse may erode psychological resources by engendering feelings of self-blame, guilt, low self-esteem, and depressive symptoms (Wolfe, Wolfe, and Best 1988). In adulthood, a support network of kin and friends may provide a crucial social resource that allows women to avoid and escape from abusive relationships.

These perspectives and our preliminary analyses led us to expect the following associations between abuse and patterns of marriage and cohabitation in our ethnographic sample:

1. Women who have never been abused will be more likely to show a pattern of sustained, long-term unions than women who have experienced abuse.

2. Women with a history of childhood abuse, particularly childhood sexual abuse, will be more likely to manifest a pattern of frequent, short-term nonmarital relationships, compared to women who have not experienced childhood abuse.

3. Women who were not abused in childhood but encounter abuse in adulthood will be more likely to show a pattern of abated unions, relative to women who were abused in childhood and who also encounter abuse in adulthood.

The survey data we will present is cross-sectional and measures only union status at the time of the survey: married, cohabiting, or single (not cohabiting or married). Nevertheless, the survey data should correspond to the ethnographic data in the following ways: women with a lifetime pattern of sustained unions should be overrepresented among the currently married at the time of the survey; women with a lifetime pattern of frequent, short-term nonmarital unions should be overrepresented among the currently cohabiting; and women with a pattern of abated unions should be overrepresented among the currently single. We therefore formulated three hypotheses that we could test with the survey data:

Hypothesis 1: Women with no history of abuse are more likely to be currently married than to be cohabiting or single, compared to women who have been abused.

Hypothesis 2: Women with a history of childhood abuse, particularly childhood sexual abuse, are more likely to be currently cohabiting than to be married or single, compared to women who have not experienced childhood abuse.

Hypothesis 3: Women who experience physical abuse in adulthood are more likely to be currently single than to be married or cohabiting, relative to women who have not experienced adult physical abuse.

THE THREE-CITY STUDY

Study Design

The data are drawn from a study of the well-being of children and their families in low-income neighborhoods in Boston, Chicago, and San Antonio that included both a random-sample survey of 2,402 children and their caregivers and an ethnographic study of 256 additional children and families, recruited non-randomly, who were not in the survey sample but resided in the same neighborhoods. The survey was conducted as follows. In households in low-income neighborhoods with a child age zero to four or age 10 to 14, with a female primary caregiver, and with incomes below 200 percent of the federal poverty line, interviewers randomly selected one child and conducted in-person interviews with that child's primary caregiver (a mother in over 90 percent of the cases). If the child was in the 10-to-14 year-old age group, he or she also was interviewed. Interviews were conducted between March and November of 1999 with 2,402 families, including an oversample of families receiving benefits from Temporary Assistance for Needy Families (TANF), the main cash welfare program. The response rate was 74 percent. Thirty-seven percent of the families were receiving TANF at the time of the interview, and an additional 20 percent had received TANF in the two years prior to the interview.

Families were recruited into the ethnography between June 1999 and December 2000. Recruitment sites included formal childcare settings (e.g., Head Start), the Women, Infants and Children (WIC) program, neighborhood community centers, local welfare offices, churches, and other public assistance agencies. Of the 256 families who participated in the ethnography, 212 families were selected if they included a child age two to four. The other 44 were recruited specifically because they had a child aged zero to eight years with a moderate or severe disability. To gather ethnographic data on the families the method of "structured discovery" was used, in which in-depth interviews and observations were focused on specific topics but allowed flexibility to capture unexpected findings and relationships (Burton et al. 2001; Winston et. al. 1999). Families were visited an average of once or twice per month for 12 to 18 months and then every six months thereafter through 2003. In addition to these interviews, which were primarily conducted with the biological or adoptive mother or primary caregiver (e.g., grandmother or aunt) of a target child age two to four, ethnographers engaged in participant observation with the family. The latter often involved accompanying the mother and her children to the welfare office, doctor, grocery store, or workplace, and taking note of the interactions and contexts of those places.

Demographic characteristics of the survey and ethnographic samples of families are roughly comparable. Both samples are heavily African American and Hispanic (including, but not limited to, substantial numbers of Mexican Americans in San Antonio and Chicago, Puerto Ricans in Boston and Chicago, and Dominicans in Boston). The survey sample is slightly older and better educated. The ethnographic sample was more likely to be receiving TANF at the start of the study and to be working outside the home. The children in the ethnographic sample tended to be younger. The majority of caregivers in both samples were neither married nor cohabiting at the start of the study, although the ethnography included a greater percentage of cohabiting caregivers than did the survey.

MEASURING ABUSE

Ethnography

Sixty-four percent (N = 147) of the mothers who participated in the ethnography and had complete information disclosed that they had been sexually abused or experienced domestic violence in childhood, adulthood, or both. These disclosures occurred at various times and in varying fieldwork situations during the ethnographers' monthly visits. Approximately 12 percent of these mothers told ethnographers of sexual abuse and domestic violence experiences during the first three months of their involvement in the study. Twenty-nine percent disclosed having experienced abuse during months four through six, 40 percent during months seven through nine, and 19 percent during months 10 through 24. The range in disclosure times reflects variation in what we would call turning points, the moments when participants trusted the ethnographer enough to share intimate, highly sensitive, and often painful information about abuse.

Reports of abuse were obtained under one of three circumstances. Only 10 percent of the disclosures occurred in response to specific questions about abuse in a semi-structured interview on intimate relationships that the ethnographers generally conducted during the third through sixth month of the study. In contrast, 71 percent unexpectedly revealed information about abuse when they were asked about related topics such as health or seemingly unrelated topics such as transportation, family demographics, and intergenerational care-giving. For example, general questions about health, particularly stress and coping, often triggered mothers' disclosures of sexual abuse and domestic violence experiences. During a health interview conducted during the seventh monthly visit, the ethnographer asked Darlene, a 26-year-old Latina mother of four, how she coped with stress. She responded:

> I used to keep a journal of my life, because, when I was younger, I was molested. And so was my sister, so you know, one of our things of therapy was, you know, to write down what we felt for the next time we [would see] our counselor, and I was just like, alright, you know, well, and then I just kept a habit of constantly writing.

Finally, 19 percent disclosed abuse when the ethnographer unexpectedly encountered a violent situation when visiting the participant or when the participant experienced an episode of abuse shortly before the ethnographer's regularly scheduled visit. In both instances, the abuse situation was fresh in the minds of mothers and they chose to discuss it with the ethnographers in great detail. For instance, the ethnographer for Patrice, a 28-year-old European American mother of two, described the circumstances that led to Patrice's crisis-related disclosure:

I arrived at Patrice's house 10 minutes before the interview only to find the streets covered with cops, patrol cars, and an ambulance. "Oh my God," I thought, "What has happened?" They were taking one man out of Patrice's house. He appeared to be shot or stabbed. Patrice was on the porch screaming, her face bloody and cut. The kids were running

around everywhere screaming and crying. . . . When I visited Patrice three weeks later the floodgates opened without me asking. I listened as she told me everything about the incident and about other incidents of physical and sexual abuse that she had experienced since childhood nonstop.

Based on disclosures under all these circumstances, we coded mothers' reports of rape, molestation, parentally enforced child prostitution, and witnessing of incest-acts as sexual abuse. Physical beatings, attacks with weapons, and witnessing consistent physical violence among parents, partners, and children were coded as physical abuse. As Table 18.1 will show, most women who reported sexual abuse also reported physical abuse, suggesting that sexual abuse often occurs in the context of physical violence.

TABLE 18.1   Union Patterns by Abuse Categories: Ethnography Sample

Union Patterns	None	Childhood Only	Adulthood Only	Childhood and Adulthood
A. By Timing of Abuse, %				
Sustained unions	88	54	29	18
Transitory unions	9	31	25	72
Abated unions	4	15	46	10
Total %	101	100	100	100
N	81	13	63	71
	None	*Sexual*	*Physical*	*Sexual and Physical*
B. By Type of Abuse, %				
Sustained unions	88	33	27	24
Transitory unions	9	50	15	72
Abated unions	4	17	58	4
Total %	101	100	100	100
N	81	6	59	82

Note: Percentages may not sum to 100 due to rounding. Ethnography sample total *N* = 228 (28 cases were not included in this analysis because of insufficient data).

Survey

In the survey, specific questions about several sensitive topics, including physical and sexual abuse and sexual activity, were asked using the audio computer-assisted self-interview (Audio-CASI) method: Respondents were given a laptop and provided with earphones. They saw and heard questions that no one else in the room could see or hear. They responded to these questions by pressing number keys on the laptop, as instructed by the program. Studies have shown that this technique raises substantially the reported rates of injection-drug usage, violent behavior, risky sex (Turner et al. 1998b), and abortion (Turner et al. 1998a). Given the possibility that the perpetrators of abuse were in the home during the interview, we viewed this method of improving confidentiality as essential. Nevertheless, it is possible that these reports are incomplete.

Sexual abuse.

Women were first asked the following question: Before you turned 18, did anyone—a stranger, friend, acquaintance, date, or relative—ever try or succeed in doing something sexual to you or make you do something sexual to them against your wishes?

Twenty-four percent said yes. All women were then asked the following:

> Since you turned 18, did anyone—a stranger, friend, acquaintance, date, or relative—ever try or succeed in doing something sexual to you or making you do something sexual to them against your wishes?

Eleven percent said yes. Childhood and adult abuse were correlated: Among women who were sexually abused as children, 37 percent reported being sexually abused as adults and 84 percent reported experiencing serious physical abuse (defined later in this article) as adults.

Physical abuse.

Women also were asked about physical abuse as a child: Before you turned 18, were you ever hit, beaten up, burned, assaulted with a weapon, or had your life been threatened by an adult in your family or household?

Twenty-one percent said yes. Women were also asked a series of questions about physical abuse that they may have suffered as an adult. We use a scale composed of affirmative responses to four questions about the more serious forms of violence.[1] Forty-four percent of the women reported experiencing at least one of these four forms as an adult, and 19 percent had experienced three or four of them.

All told, 52 percent of the women responded that they had been sexually abused or had suffered serious physical abuse as a child or an adult. Thus, a majority of women in the survey reported that they had experienced abuse at some point. Table 18.2 will show that, as in the ethnography, most women who reported sexual abuse also reported physical abuse. Two thirds of the women who reported abuse (sexual or physical) in childhood or adolescence also reported abuse as adults, suggesting continuity through the life course in experiences with abuse.

MEASURING UNION STATUS

Ethnography

The detailed information that the ethnographers obtained allowed us to examine patterns of union formation in adulthood. We attempted to classify these patterns in ways that could capture the fluidity that some women's histories showed. A thorough, systematic analysis of the ethnographic data indicated that many mothers could be classified as showing one of two union-history categories that we expected a priori and a third pattern that emerged from the data during the analysis. The defining characteristic of sustained unions is that the woman has been in long-term unions most of her life with only one or two men. About half of the women had union histories that fit this category. Transitory unions may be sequential unions with different men or they may take the form of a long-term involvement with a man that cycles between living together and breaking up, with the woman living with other men during the break-up periods. Women in this category experience unions as short-term partnerships and rarely

TABLE 18.2   Current Union Status by Abuse Categories: Survey Sample

Current Union Status	None	Childhood Only	Adulthood Only	Childhood and Adulthood
A. By Timing of Abuse, %[a]				
Married	42	24	20	24
Cohabiting	4	11	6	9
Single	54	64	74	67
Total %	100	99	100	100
N	1,139	224	539	494
	None	Sexual	Physical	Sexual and Physical
B. By Type of Abuse, %[b]				
Married	42	32	23	18
Cohabiting	4	9	6	11
Single	54	59	71	72
Total %	100	100	100	101
N	1,139	149	669	439

Note: Percentages may not sum to 100 due to rounding. Survey sample total $N = 2,396$.

[a]$\chi^2 = 133.2$, df = 6; $p < .0001$.

[b]$\chi^2 = 125.9$, df = 6; $p < .0001$.

live without partners for substantial periods of time. About one-third of the women had union histories that fit this category.

In addition, about one-sixth of the women had not lived in a union for at least one year prior to the field period, did not begin a union during the field period, and told the ethnographers that they did not currently want to be involved with a man. We classified them as having *abated unions*. These women indicated that they are not interested in forming another union with a man and have effectively taken themselves off the market.

Survey

As mentioned, in the survey, women could be classified only according to their union status at the date of the interview, because the survey did not include enough life history information to construct complete union histories. Thus, the data allow only for a cross-sectional analysis of the determinants of union status at the interview date. We classify each woman as being married, cohabiting, or single (i.e., not cohabiting or married) at the time of the 1999 survey.

RESULTS

We will present comparable tables from the ethnography and the survey that cross-classify union history (or current union status) by the timing and the type of abuse a woman has experienced.

Ethnography

Panels A and B of Table 18.1 present cross-tabulations of union history patterns by timing of abuse and type of abuse, respectively, for the ethnographic sample. Both panels show strong relationships. Consider Panel A of Table 18.1 first. Eighty-eight percent of women who had never been abused showed a pattern of sustained unions. Women who had been abused in either childhood or adulthood, but not both, were less likely to experience sustained unions, and women who were abused in both childhood and adulthood were the least likely to experience sustained unions. Note also that women who had been abused in adulthood only were substantially more likely to show a pattern of abated unions. Thus, the patterns of union formation differed sharply across the categories of abuse history.

Panel B of Table 18.1 reports union patterns by type of abuse. Note that among women who had experienced sexual abuse, either alone or in combination with physical abuse, the most common pattern was transitory unions. In contrast, among women who had been abused physically but not sexually, the most common pattern was abated unions. To be sure, a modest number of women who had been abused reported a pattern of sustained unions. Further analysis showed that the majority of women in this category were first generation Mexican American immigrants and were distributed fairly equally across the three cities.

Overall, Table 18.1 suggests that the timing and nature of abuse are strongly associated with union patterns. Women who had experienced abuse were much less likely to have sustained unions. Women who experienced abuse beginning in childhood or who reported sexual abuse (alone or in combination with physical abuse) were more likely to develop a transitory union pattern in adulthood. Women who did not experience abuse in childhood but later experienced physical abuse in adulthood were more likely to display the abated union pattern than were other women. Let us illustrate these findings with some brief ethnographic profiles

that show links between mothers' abuse histories and their current intimate relationship patterns.

Sustained union pattern.

Channel, a 27-year-old African American mother of one said that she never would have married her husband, Reginald, if "abuse had been anywhere on the radar screen." She notes,

> I was poor all my life and so was Reginald. When I got pregnant, we agreed we would marry some day in the future because we loved each other and wanted to raise our child together. But we would not get married until we could afford to get a house and pay all the utility bills on time. I have this thing about utility bills. Our gas and electric got turned off all the time when we were growing up and we wanted to make sure that would not happen when we got married. That was our biggest worry. We never worried about violence, like hitting each other because we weren't raised that way. We worked together and built up savings and then we got married. It's forever for us. Fighting and slapping each other around is not how we do business. No matter how hard it is, we just don't roll like that.

Transitory union pattern.

Marilyn is a 45-year-old European American woman with four children—two teenage daughters and a daughter and son in middle childhood. Marilyn's history of abuse is long-standing. She was sexually and physically abused as a child and adolescent and witnessed frequent domestic violence involving her parents. As a young adult and now as a woman in mid-life, Marilyn continually enters and exits relationships with men, moving them into her household only a few days after meeting them and allowing them to stay for a maximum of six to eight months. Most of the men that Marilyn has invited into her home, her life, and the lives of her children have abused her or abused her children. Marilyn appears unable to recognize the pattern of revolving-door relationships and the risks that these relationships create for her children.

Abated union pattern.

Mary, a 33-year-old African American mother of one indicated that she has taken herself "off the marriage market." She divorced her husband after he "went crazy," beating her and causing her to lose the child she was pregnant with. Mary's parents supported her through the divorce, acknowledging that they would not allow "any man to beat on their child." Since the divorce, Mary has moved three doors down from her parents and has adopted a little girl whom she adores. Mary indicated that all her energy and time will be spent mothering her daughter and that there is no room for a man in the "new order" that she was creating in her life.

Survey

Let us now turn to the findings from the survey sample. Panel A of Table 18.2 shows a cross-tabulation that is analogous to Panel A of Table 18.1: current union status by timing of abuse. It shows an association between being currently married and never having been abused. Forty-two percent of women who said that they had not been abused were currently married, compared to 20 to 24 percent of women who reported abuse. Panel B displays a cross-tabulation according to type of abuse. It suggests that women who had experienced physical abuse (alone or in combination with sexual abuse) were most likely to be currently single. The associations in Table 18.2 are consistent with the ethnographic findings, and chi-squared tests reject the null hypotheses at the $p < .0001$ level; nevertheless, the relationships between union status and timing and type of abuse are not as strong as in the ethnographic tables.

DISCUSSION

We have used information from an ethnography and a survey of low-income families in Boston, Chicago, and San Antonio to investigate the relationship between experiencing sexual or physical abuse and patterns of union formation. Both sets of data suggest that women who have been abused are substantially less likely to be in sustained marital or cohabiting unions. Both sets of data also suggest that different forms of abuse have distinctive associations with union formation. Childhood abuse, and particularly childhood sexual abuse, is associated with a pattern in which women are less likely to be in a stable marriage or a long-term cohabiting relationship but are instead more likely to experience multiple short-term unions. Adult abuse, and particularly adult physical abuse, on the other hand, is associated with a reduction in the probability of being in either form of union.

The ethnographic data analysis identified a group of women in the sample who had not been abused as children, for the most part, and who subsequently experienced adult physical abuse and then withdrew from having relationships with men. We called this pattern abated unions. However, women who *had* been abused as children and who then experienced adult abuse were less likely to withdraw from relationships; rather, they tended to have a series of them—a pattern we called transitory unions. Since the distinction between abated and transitory union patterns emerged somewhat unexpectedly from our analysis, we do not presume to have a full understanding of the role of abuse in the formation of these patterns. Nevertheless, our ethnographic observations and the research literature lead us to suggest the following possible explanation: Women who have not been abused as children are more likely to have families, or to be in networks of friends, that they can draw upon for emotional, material, and protective support if, as adults, they are abused by romantic partners. These women are also more likely to have clearer ego boundaries, self-protective capacities, and other psychological resources necessary to recognize and exit from relationships with abusive partners. On the other hand, women who were abused as children often have strained ties with families and friends who have fewer emotional and material resources. These women are also more likely to have weaker, highly permeable relationship boundaries and a greater incidence of undiagnosed depression and other mental health issues, all of which make it more difficult for them to avoid repeatedly abusive romantic entanglements.

NOTE

1. The four questions asked whether a romantic partner had ever "slapped, kicked, bit, or punched you," "beaten you," "choked or burned you," or "used a weapon or threatened to use a weapon on you." We did not include affirmative answers to the categories "thrown something at you" or "pushed, grabbed, or shoved."

REFERENCES

Burton, Linda M., Robin Jarrett, Laura Lein, Stephen A. Matthews, James Quane, Debra Skinner, Constance Williams, William Julius Wilson, and Tera R. Hurt. 2001. "Structured Discovery: Ethnography, Welfare Reform, and the Assessment of Neighborhoods, Families, and Children." Paper presented at the Biennial Meeting of the Society for Research in Child Development, April, Minneapolis, MN.

Butler, Janice R. and Linda M. Burton. 1990. "Rethinking Teenage Childbearing: Is Sexual Abuse a Missing Link?" *Family Relations* 39:73–80.

Edin, Kathryn. 2000. "What Do Low-Income Single Mothers Say about Marriage?" *Social Problems* 47:112–33.

Hoff, Lee Ann. 1990. *Battered Women as Survivors*. London: Routledge.

Johnson, Michael P. and Kathleen J. Ferraro. 2000. "Research on Domestic Violence in the 1990s: Making Distinctions." *Journal of Marriage and the Family* 62:948-63.

Kirkwood, Catherine. 1993. *Leaving Abusive Partners: From the Scars of Survival to the Wisdom for Change*. Thousand Oaks, CA: SAGE Publications.

Loeb, Tamra Burns, John K. Williams, Jennifer Vargas Carmona, Inna Rivkin, Gail E. Wyatt, Dorothy Chin, and Agnes Asuan-O'Brien. 2002. "Child Sexual Abuse: Associations with the Sexual Functioning of Adolescents and Adults." *Annual Review of Sex Research* 13:307–45.

Macmillan, Ross. 2001. "Violence and the Life Course: The Consequences of Victimization for Personal and Social Development." *Annual Review of Sociology* 27:1-22.

Noll, Jennie G., Penelope K. Trickett, and Frank W. Putnam. 2003. "A Prospective Investigation of the Impact of Childhood Sexual Abuse on the Development of Sexuality." *Journal of Consulting and Clinical Psychology* 71:575–86.

Turner, Charles. F., Barbara H. Forsyth, James. M. O'Reilly, Phillip.C. Cooley, Timothy K. Smith, Susan. M. Rogers, and Heather G. Miller. 1998a. "Automated Self-Interviewing and the Survey Measurement of Sensitive Behaviors." Pp. 455–73 in *Computer Assisted Survey Information Collection*, edited by Mick P. Couper, Reginald P. Baker, Jelke Bethlehem, Cynthia Z. F. Clark, Jean Martin, William. L. Nicholls II, and James M. O'Reilly. New York: Wiley.

Turner, Charles F., Leighton Ku, Susan M. Rogers, Laura D. Lindberg, Joseph H. Pleck, and Freya L. Sonenstein. 1998b. "Adolescent Sexual Behavior, Drug Use, and Violence: Increased Reporting with Computer Survey Technology." *Science* 280:867–73.

Winston, Pamela, Ronald J. Angel, P. Lindsay Chase-Lansdale, Andrew J. Cherlin, Robert A. Moffitt, and William Julius Wilson. 1999. *Welfare, Children, and Families: A Three-City Study, Overview and Design*. Retrieved November 14, 2004 (http://www.jhu.edu/~welfare/overviewand design.pdf).

Wolfe, David. A., Vicky V. Wolfe, and Connie L. Best. 1988. "Child Victims of Sexual Abuse." Pp. 157–185 in *Handbook of Family Violence*, edited by Vincent B. Van Hasselt, R. L. Morrison, Alan S. Bellack, and Michel Hersen. New York: Plenum.

QUESTIONS

1. Explain what the researchers mean by *abated unions*. From what data source did they develop this concept?

2. (a) How did the researchers measure abuse in the ethnography? (b) How did they measure it in the survey?

3. *Union status* has different meanings in the field study and survey. How did the methodological approach determine the definition or measurement of union status?

4. How do the effects of child abuse on union formation differ from the effects of abuse in adulthood?

5. Explain how the concept of triangulation applies to: (a) observing or measuring abuse with two different methods; and (b) carrying out the study in three different cities.

UNIT X

DATA ANALYSIS: QUANTITATIVE AND QUALITATIVE

Whereas research begins with a question, it ends, ideally, with answers and theoretical conclusions based on analysis of data. In this way, data analysis is an integral part of the theory-research connection introduced in the first unit of this book. Data analysis proceeds from a deductive logic of inquiry, an inductive logic of inquiry, or both. Whether researchers conduct **quantitative** and/or **qualitative** data analysis depends on the type of data their methodological approaches generate (see Units V–IX). Recall that quantitative data are numerical and are often generated in surveys and experiments. Qualitative data are verbatim statements and/or researchers' observations, which are particularly likely to come from field research and qualitative interviews. While both quantitative and qualitative data analysis may be used to *describe* populations or groups of people and identify patterns in the data, they represent different logics to answering research questions.

Often following the *deductive* mode of inquiry, quantitative data analysis is used to test hypotheses concerning the relationship between two or more variables. In a deductive mode of inquiry, theory and previous research are like lenses, which researchers use to deduce hypotheses, identify concepts, operationalize them as variables, and code or organize the quantitative data they have gathered. The hypotheses are then tested on the data or observations.

In the simplest hypothesis testing in quantitative data analysis, researchers conduct **bivariate analyses,** such as cross-tabulations or correlations, to determine if one variable is related to another. If the variables are related in a manner that could not have occurred by chance, researchers note that there is a **statistically significant relationship** and indicate this in tables with asterisks (*,**, or ***) or other symbols as noted in table footnotes. In **multivariate analyses**, the most common form of which is called Ordinary Least Squares (OLS) regression, researchers conduct hypothesis testing of the relationships among several variables and of the theoretical model as a whole. Specifically, **regression analysis** allows researchers to more precisely determine the relationship between variables (e.g., how a one-unit change in the independent variable is related to a change in the dependent variable). Multiple regression shows how this relationship changes once other theoretically relevant factors are also considered and how well the entire model—all of the factors/variables analyzed—fits the data. In the first selection in this unit, you'll see that Royce Singleton uses both bivariate and multivariate (OLS) analyses to answer the question of how drinking is related to academic performance.

Qualitative data analysis often proceeds from an *inductive* mode of inquiry, where the data are analyzed to uncover empirical patterns. Unlike the deductive model followed by researchers using quantitative data analysis, the inductive model followed by researchers using qualitative data analysis does not typically test a hypothesis. As in quantitative data analyses, data are organized and coded. However, data coding begins in the field and occurs throughout the research process (Lofland, Snow, Anderson, & Lofland, 2006).

Through qualitative data analysis, researchers attempt to detect patterns that *emerge* in their data (Glaser & Strauss, 1967). On the basis of coding, for example, they may identify certain themes, subthemes, and forms from observations and/or interviews. A **theme** is a pattern that runs across, or unites, many pieces of the data. In the second selection in this unit, you'll see that David Snow and Leon Anderson identify three major themes in their data on how the homeless construct their identities. Snow and Anderson also relate these themes, and the forms they take, to how long the homeless have been on the street. Thus, their analysis uncovers patterns in the data and also generates new theoretical concepts for future research.

Both quantitative and qualitative data analysis are means to the ends of answering research questions and informing theory/research, but the answers that each type of analysis provides should not necessarily be judged by the same standard. Given that quantitative data analysis often follows the deductive logic of inquiry, we should ask ourselves if and how the research is informed by theory and/or previous research. Are the results consistent with hypothesized relationships between variables? Can the results be generalized in an empirical and/or theoretical sense? Given that qualitative data analysis often follows an inductive logic of inquiry, we should ask ourselves if and how the research leads to a better understanding of the group or event being studied. Are empirical patterns in the data valid accounts of social processes? Do the findings provide broader theoretical insights? As you read

the selections in this final unit, think about how each type of analysis helps to answer the research question at hand and how each selection may be evaluated by the above respective standards.

REFERENCES

Glaser, B. G.. & Strauss, A. L. (1967). *The discovery of grounded theory: Strategies for qualitative research*. Chicago: Aldine.

Lofland, J., Snow, D. A., Anderson, L., & Lofland, L. H. (2006). *Analyzing social settings: A guide to qualitative observation and analysis* (4th ed.). Belmont, CA: Wadsworth/Thompson Learning.

RESOURCES

Statistics Every Writer Should Know:

http://www.robertniles.com/stats/

- Described as "a simple guide to understanding basic statistics, for journalists and other writers who might not know math," this site explains several basic statistical concepts—such as, measures of central tendency, standard deviation, Student's *t*—"in plain English".

Jacob Cohen's "The Earth is Round (p < .05)"

- There are numerous books, articles, and websites that can introduce you to quantitative data analysis and statistics, but this widely cited and admittedly advanced article (*American Psychologist* [1994] 12: 997–1003) is a true exemplar of the logic (and sometimes lack thereof) of quantitative data analysis in practice. It also references both deductive and inductive forms of logic noted in this unit introduction.

UCLA Academic Technology Services:

http://www.ats.ucla.edu/stat/

- UCLA has put together a wonderful page on statistical computing, which includes a number of resources on one of the most commonly used statistical programs, SPSS (see http://www.ats.ucla.edu/stat/spss/default. htm). Here, you can look at class notes, watch movies on SPSS, and much more. If you're using SPSS for the first time, the "starter kit" page may be a good place to begin (http:// www.ats.ucla.edu/stat/spss/sk/default.htm).

Online QDA: Learning Qualitative Data Analysis on the Web:

http://onlineqda.hud.ac.uk/resources.php

- This website provides a wide variety of links and resources, such as books, articles, and videos on different types of qualitative data analysis, including many not mentioned in this book. It complements a similar website described in the Resources section of Unit VII (on field research and qualitative interviews).

The Grounded Theory Institute:

http://www.groundedtheory.com/

- In the introduction to this unit, we made reference to Glaser and Strauss's seminal work on grounded theory. The site above is Glaser's; on it, you can find a variety of readings, lectures, and seminars on this oft-cited approach of analyzing qualitative data.

Atlas.ti:

http://www.atlasti.com/

- Atlas.ti is a popular qualitative data analysis program. This site provides information about the program itself as well as free training, webinars, and tutorials on how to use the program.

Selection 19

According to findings from the College Alcohol Study, reported in Selection 11, students who drink heavily are more likely than other students to report that they have missed class and gotten behind in schoolwork as a consequence of drinking. Such findings beg the question addressed in this selection: What is the relationship between drinking alcohol and the grades students earn in college? Royce Singleton answers this question through quantitative analyses of survey data collected from randomly selected students at a liberal arts college in the northeastern United States. Singleton found, as expected, that students with higher levels of alcohol consumption tend to receive lower grades. Most important, he tested the relationship between alcohol consumption and grades after statistically controlling for a host of factors that may come causally prior to alcohol consumption, collegiate academic performance, or both. As you read this selection, pay particular attention to the logic of the quantitative analysis, how the process of measurement factors into it, and the differences in the results of the bivariate versus multivariate (regression) analyses.

COLLEGIATE ALCOHOL CONSUMPTION AND ACADEMIC PERFORMANCE

ROYCE A. SINGLETON, JR.

During the past 2 decades, college drinking has become the focus of increasing concern. Spurred by a widely cited national survey of heavy episodic drinking in the early 1990s (Wechsler et al., 1994), researchers have turned their attention to a range of problems connected to student alcohol misuse, including negative effects on the drinkers themselves such as personal injury, physical illness, and death as well as damages to other people and institutional costs. Surveying the adverse consequences of student drinking, Perkins (2002) concluded that

Source: "Collegiate Alcohol Consumption and Academic Performance," by Royce A. Singleton, Jr., 2007, *Journal of Studies on Alcohol and Drugs* 68:548-55. Copyright 2007 by Alcohol Research Documentation, Inc. Adapted with permission.

"at least 10% of students and frequently as much as one third of the population are negatively affected in a given year" (p. 99).

Of particular interest to educators is the association between alcohol consumption and academic performance. This relationship has been inferred from two types of evidence: (1) students' subjective determination that alcohol has impaired their performance (e.g., Wechsler et al., 2000; Presley and Pimentel, 2006) and (2) correlations between self-reported alcohol consumption and grades (Core Institute, 2006).

[Yet] both sets of findings are open to interpretation. People may perceive a connection between drinking and study habits as a way of rationalizing their poor academic performance. In addition, correlation [does not] imply causality. It is possible that poor academic performance is a cause rather than a consequence of heavy drinking. In fact, among adolescents academic failure has been shown to predict subsequent heavy alcohol and illicit drug use (Hawkins et al., 1992); further, high school GPA has been linked—through senior-year substance use—to young adult alcohol and illicit drug use (Schulenberg et al., 1994). It is also possible that the relationship is spurious—that one or more other variables are the cause of *both* problematic alcohol use and academic problems. Recent studies that have addressed these issues have produced inconsistent results.

Examining data gathered at a liberal arts college, the present study rectifies many of the problems with prior studies of the connection between college alcohol consumption and academic performance. In particular, grade data were obtained from official college records rather than self-reports; several key variables, including measures of academic aptitude, prior academic achievement, and parents' education, were controlled in the analysis; and the sample was randomly selected with a high response rate.

Although unique in some ways, the college in the present study also has several characteristics that make it a good site for testing this relationship. As a small (2,700 students), very competitive, residential college in the

northeastern United States, it is among those types of schools and in the part of the United States with the highest rates of heavy drinking (Wechsler et al., 2000). Most typically, students consume alcoholic beverages while "partying" on weekend nights. In addition, using this institution effectively controls for the effects of attrition on the association between alcohol use and academic performance. High attrition may lead to an underestimation of the magnitude of this association because many students who drop out may "experience academic problems due to alcohol misuse/abuse" (Wood et al., 1997, p. 201). However, the college has a very low attrition rate, the 4-year graduation rate annually hovers around 90%, fewer than 10 students per year (less than 1% of each class) are suspended or dismissed for academic reasons, and students who drop out or transfer almost invariably report that they do so for financial or personal reasons. Finally, unlike many other highly selective colleges, where few grades are given below B+ and grade inflation limits grade variability, there has been comparatively little inflation in recent years at the college in this study. In the fall 2003 semester, the mean grade was 3.19 on a 4.0 scale. Thus, the effects of alcohol consumption can be estimated in terms of a relatively wide range of academic performance.

In short, the data presented here should clarify whether poor academic performance is, at least at this type of college, "a product of the drinking lifestyle of students or simply a covariate where both drinking and [academic performance] reflect other influences in one's social background" (Perkins, 2002, p. 98).

Method

Sample

Participants were 754 students at a northeastern U.S. liberal arts college who were interviewed during one of four consecutive semesters between fall 2003 and spring 2005. Each semester a simple random sample of the student body was drawn, with sample sizes varying from 180 in spring 2005 to 220 in spring 2004 to 260 in fall 2003 and fall 2004. Response rates were consistently high, averaging 89.3% and yielding a total of 822 interviews. Some respondents, however, were selected and interviewed in more than one survey. For these respondents, a single interview was randomly selected in compiling the combined data set.

Data Collection

In all four surveys students enrolled in a research methods course conducted structured, face-to-face interviews with fellow students as part of a class project. Each survey provided informed consent to all participants and was approved by the college's institutional review board. Interviewers received thorough training on survey interviewing and were carefully supervised, and all interviews were validated by the supervisor. Fall surveys were conducted in October and early November and the spring surveys in late March and April. Although each survey focused on a different topic (e.g., health issues, politics, friendship), the main questions analyzed here were included in all four surveys. At the conclusion of the interview, respondents were asked for permission to retrieve information from official college records, including grades, high school class rank, and scores on the SAT. No less than 93.8% gave permission during any one semester; overall, 94.4% of the combined sample granted permission.

Measures

Academic performance.

Two measures of academic performance were added to the data file at the end of the semester during which the survey was conducted: a student's average grade during the semester of the survey (semester GPA) and his or her cumulative average grade at that point (cumulative GPA).

Alcohol consumption.

Three questions were asked about alcohol consumption. First, students were asked, "How would you describe your consumption of alcohol? Do you abstain from drinking or would you describe yourself as a light, moderate, or heavy drinker?" Nonabstainers were then asked how often they drink alcoholic beverages, with seven possible responses ranging from "about once a year" to "almost every day." Finally, they were asked, "On a typical weekend night when you choose to drink, about how many drinks do you consume? Consider one drink as a bottle of beer, a glass of wine, a wine cooler, a shot glass of liquor, or a mixed drink." In operationalizing frequency of consumption and amount consumed, abstainers were assigned a code of zero for the second and third questions.

As an alternative measure of alcohol use and partial check on the validity of the latter measures, in the fall 2003 survey students also were asked the CAS standard measure of heavy alcohol use (see, e.g., Wechsler and Nelson, 2001), which varies for men and women respondents. First, all respondents were asked when they most recently drank an alcoholic beverage: within the last week, within the last 2 weeks, 3–4 weeks ago, or more than a month ago. If they had drunk within the last week or last 2 weeks, men were asked, "During the last two weeks, how many times have you had five or more drinks in a row, that is, within a couple hours?" (Women were asked how often they had "four or more drinks.") Frequency of heavy alcohol use was operationally defined as responses to the second question, with abstainers and those not drinking in the previous 2 weeks coded as zero. This measure showed a moderate to high correlation with both frequency of consumption ($r = .59$) and amount consumed ($r = .70$).

Academic aptitude.

Academic aptitude was represented by a student's combined verbal and math scores on the SAT, obtained from student records. SAT scores were available for 680 respondents (90.2% of the sample).

High school class rank.

High school class rank, also obtained from official records, was transformed into a percentile score equal to 100 - (rank divided by graduating class size). Unfortunately, high schools had provided this information for 388 respondents only (51.5% of the sample) with the proportion increasing by academic class, from 45.6% of first- to 56.1% of fourth-year students. In addition to this class bias, students for whom high school rank data were available differed in several ways from those for whom data were not available: They had significantly higher semester and cumulative GPAs and reported a lower frequency of drinking and a lower amount of alcohol consumed. Consequently, the subset of cases with high school rank may underestimate the magnitude of the relation between alcohol consumption and academic performance.

Frequency of partying.

In two semesters (fall 2004 and spring 2005), students reported how often they attended off-campus parties on an 8-point scale ranging from 0 (never) to 7 (nearly every day).

Demographics.

Additional measures were obtained for gender, academic class, race/ethnicity, athletic status, parental level of education, and parents' annual income. Academic class was highly correlated with age at this institution ($r = .88$); therefore, class essentially served as a proxy for age and was treated as an interval-level variable. Given the relatively low proportion of nonwhite respondents and the consistent association between being white and heavy alcohol use found in prior research, race/ethnicity was coded as a white/ nonwhite dichotomy. Athletic status also was coded as a dichotomy based on whether a student was an intercollegiate athlete. Parental education was operationalized as the sum of father's and mother's education, each measured according to 5 categories ranging from 1 (less than high school) to 5 (graduate or professional degree). Parents'

income was measured by asking respondents to estimate their parents' combined income the previous year using 8 categories ranging from 1 (less than $25,000) to 8 ($200,000 or more).

Results

Sample characteristics

In the initial sample of 754 students, 52% were women, 85% were white, 99.5% ranged in age from 18 to 23 years old, and 88% lived on campus. By academic class, 27.1% were first-, 26.5% second-, 20.4% third-, and 26.0% fourth-year students. These figures very closely correspond to characteristics of the college as a whole as well as the subsample of 680 respondents for whom SAT scores were available.

One in eight students reported that they abstained from drinking, and two thirds reported that they drank at least 1 to 2 times a week. The average (SD) number of drinks consumed on a typical weekend night was 5.62 (3.90). Men and women did not differ significantly in frequency of alcohol consumption ($p > .05$), but men consumed significantly more drinks than did women (mean = 7.26 [4.38] vs 4.11 [2.62], respectively; $t = 3.90$, 752 df, $p < .001$).

[Missing Data]

Excluding frequency of partying, measured in two of the four semesters, and variables measured with official records, there were few missing values except for parents' income. For two cases with missing data on amount of alcohol consumed, mean values were imputed from nonmissing data based on the gender of the respondent; for eight cases with missing values on either mother's or father's level of education, missing values were imputed from the value of the nonmissing parent. For the baseline sample, 148 respondents either refused to report their parents' income or, more commonly, did not know. Because eliminating these cases from multivariate analyses would produce a smaller and possibly less representative sample, the mean income of nonmissing cases was assigned to missing values. Correlations with the recoded income variable tended to be slightly lower than correlations with income for nonmissing cases only (e.g., $r = .145$ and $.158$, respectively, with amount consumed); hence, regression models may underestimate the influence of parents' income.

Bivariate Correlations

Overall, the correlations indicated, first, that amount consumed was more strongly associated with academic performance ($r = -.26$ with cumulative GPA) than frequency of consumption ($r = -.16$ with cumulative GPA). This is consistent with cross-sectional surveys from several countries, which show that a range of alcohol-related problems tends to correlate with volume consumed (Bondy, 1996). Second, amount consumed tended to be more strongly associated with other independent variables than frequency of consumption. The only major exception to this pattern was that frequency of consumption related more strongly to academic class ($r = .19$) than amount consumed ($r = .08$; $z = 2.01$, $p < .05$). Third, the pattern of correlations was very similar for semester and cumulative GPA; in fact, none of the differences in correlations between these two measures was statistically significant ($p > .05$). Therefore, multivariate analyses focused on amount consumed and cumulative GPA.

The correlations among other variables also reinforce the need to control for various background factors in examining the relation between alcohol use and academic performance. Every variable except academic class and parents' income correlated significantly with cumulative GPA, and every variable except SAT total score correlated significantly with alcohol consumption.

Multivariate Analysis

Table 19.1 shows the ordinary least squares regressions for amount consumed. Model 1 presents data for the subsample of 680 with SAT scores; Models 2 and 3 present data for the two semesters in which frequency of partying was measured. When amount consumed was regressed on the background variables, excluding high school class rank, for the larger sample, gender, race, academic class, and parents' income were significant predictors. When the same variables were included in the smaller sample in Model 2, the regression coefficients were similar to Model 1 except for race, which was not statistically significant. Model 3 shows, however, that gender and frequency of attending off-campus parties were relatively strong predictors, whereas the direct effects of all other variables were negligible. This model accounted for 43% of the variation in amount consumed. Further, a comparison of Models 2 and 3 suggests that much of the effects of academic class and parents' income on amount consumed occurred because these variables influenced how often students attended off-campus parties. Bivariate correlations showed that frequency of partying was positively associated with both academic class and parents' income.

Table 19.2 presents ordinary least squares regressions on semester GPA and cumulative GPA. Preliminary analyses showed that the semester of the survey had no effect on cumulative GPA; therefore, this variable was excluded from the final models. Model 1 includes all independent variables except amount consumed and high school class rank. SAT total score was positively related to GPA, men received significantly lower grades than did women, white students obtained higher grades than nonwhites, and intercollegiate athletes earned lower grades than other students. When amount consumed is added in Model 2, the beta coefficient for being an intercollegiate athlete was reduced to nonsignificance, and the coefficient for the gender dummy variable also decreased in size, from -.24 to -.15, which indicates that part of the difference in the GPA of men and women may be explained by men's higher level of consumption. In addition, the regression coefficient for amount consumed in Model 2 ($\beta = -.24$) was nearly the same as the bivariate correlation between consumption and grades ($r = -.26$). Thus, although

TABLE 19.1   OLS Standardized Regression Coefficients for Amount Consumed

Variable	Model 1[a]	Model 2[b]	Model 3[b]
SAT total	−.038	−.001	.017
Male	.412[†]	.466[†]	.427[†]
White	.105[†]	.058	.061
Intercollegiate athlete	.061	.027	−.025
Academic class	.084*	.094*	.014
Parents' education	.023	.026	−.020
Parents' income	.131[†]	.179[†]	.089
Frequency of partying	-	-	.448[†]
Adjusted R^2	.211	.256	.434

Notes: OLS = ordinary least squares. [a]Based on subsample of cases for whom SAT scores were available ($n = 680$); [b]based on subsample of cases for whom frequency of partying was measured ($n = 333$).

*$p < .05$ [†]$p < .01$.

SAT was the strongest predictor of academic performance, amount consumed also was a significant predictor, even after controlling for key background variables.

Models 3 and 4 present the regressions of cumulative GPA on the subset of respondents for whom high school class rank was available. Although this is a biased sample, the *pattern* of regression estimates is similar to models excluding this variable. High school class rank was a significant predictor of college cumulative GPA, but when rank was controlled, amount consumed also was a significant predictor. The beta coefficient for amount consumed in Model 4 ($\beta = -.14$) was smaller than in Model 2, reflecting the fact that high school class rank was associated with both consumption and GPA. However, it should be noted that the bivariate correlation between amount consumed and GPA for the subsample of 371 cases in Model 4 ($r = -.20$) was smaller than in the larger sample ($n = 680$) on which Model 2 was based ($r = -.26$).

Except for mostly minor variations in coefficients, the regression models for semester GPA are very similar to those for cumulative GPA. Most importantly, the beta coefficients for amount consumed are nearly identical. Two differences are noteworthy, however. First, academic class was positively related to semester GPA but unrelated to cumulative GPA. Second, SAT total score was a stronger predictor of cumulative GPA than less stable semester GPA; consequently, models explain more of the variation in cumulative GPA.

Because prior studies have focused on first-year students and because academic class may moderate the effects of alcohol consumption on grades, separate regressions were performed for each class. When the variables in Model 2, excluding academic class, were regressed on cumulative GPA, the regression estimates for amount consumed were statistically significant in all 4 years. The beta coefficient for first-year students only ($\beta = -.21$) was slightly lower than for second- through fourth-year students ($\beta = -.25$). Finally, two additional regressions were run for respondents younger than age 21

TABLE 19.2 OLS Standardized Regression Coefficients for Semester GPA and Cumulative GPA

Variable	Cumulative GPA				Semester GPA	
	Model 1[a]	Model 2[a]	Model 3[b]	Model 4[b]	Model 2[a]	Model 4[b]
SAT total	.324[†]	.315[†]	.333[†]	.321[†]	.265[†]	.289[†]
Male	−.244[†]	−.147[†]	−.154[†]	−.106[*]	−.169[†]	−.160[†]
White	.148[†]	.173[†]	.089	.105[*]	.128[†]	.054
Intercollegiate athlete	−.071[*]	−.056	−.052	−.046	−.081[*]	−.050
Academic class	.023	.043	.031	.043	.116[†]	.130[†]
Parents' education	.052	.058	.047	.047	.038	.019
Parents' income	−.044	−.013	.035	.051	.023	.094
Amount consumed	-	−.235[†]	-	−.136[†]	−.229[†]	−.150[†]
High school class rank	-	-	.267[†]	.259[†]	-	.215[†]
Adjusted R^2	.227	.270	.286	.299	.236	.255

Notes: OLS = ordinary least squares; GPA = grade point average. [a]Based on subsample of cases for whom SAT scores were available (*n* = 680); [b] based on subsample of cases for whom high school class rank was available (*n* = 371).

[*]$p < .05$; [†]$p < .01$.

and those 21 and older. Once again, the beta coefficients were nearly identical for these age groups (β = -.24 and -.25, respectively).

Finally, given the popularity of the CAS operational definition of heavy alcohol use (five or more drinks for men; four or more drinks for women), the principal analyses were repeated with frequency of heavy alcohol use as the predictor instead of amount consumed. In general, the results provide further evidence of the utility of "amount consumed." For the fall 2003 survey in which frequency of heavy alcohol use was measured, the bivariate correlation with cumulative GPA was -.18, compared with -.27 between amount consumed and GPA. Model 4 estimates were similar for the two measures, except the beta coefficient for heavy alcohol use was -.15, compared with -.24 for amount consumed. Thus, at this college, the number of

drinks students consumed on a typical weekend night was a stronger predictor of their academic performance than how frequently they engaged in "heavy" alcohol use.

DISCUSSION

Two studies (Wood et al., 1977; Pascall and Freisthler, 2003) concluded that problematic alcohol use has either no effect or a markedly attenuated effect on academic performance among college students when other predictors of academic failure, most notably prior academic achievement and academic aptitude, are controlled. Indeed, Wood et al. (1997) called this finding "highly generalizable" (p. 208). Results from the present study challenge this conclusion but also beg the question of why, in contrast to these two prior studies, the effect of alcohol consumption on grades remained significant when key variables were included in regression models.

One possible answer is that prior studies examined alcohol use in the first year only, whereas the present study included all 4 years. However, the effects of alcohol consumption examined here were similar for every class, from first through fourth year; therefore, class difference does not seem to be the answer. Each of the prior studies also measured more distal effects of alcohol misuse; Wood et al. (1997) tracked the academic problems of students for 6 years after matriculation, at the end of which only 41% of the research participants had graduated. By contrast, the present study examined grade records at the end of the semester in which alcohol consumption was measured, and grades obtained in the semester of the survey produced the same results as a student's cumulative GPA. Thus, these data suggest that alcohol consumption may have both short-and long-term effects on academic performance; moreover, the relationship appears to be relatively stable.

Another important difference between the present and past research is the representativeness of the samples: only the present study employed a random sample with a high response rate. But the crucial difference may be the type of institution. Wood et al.'s (1997) research participants attended a large, midwestern university; Pascall and Freisthler's (2003) participants attended the University of California, Berkeley. These institutions have more diverse student bodies, more diverse student lifestyles, and more varied campus subcultures than the small, liberal arts college studied here. At small colleges, student bodies are more homogeneous, the student culture tends to be monolithic, and students may experience greater pressures to drink. At the present institution, where almost 90% of the students live on campus, the social lives of students outside the classroom, at least on the weekends, revolve around partying and alcohol consumption. More than 80% of the respondents reported that they drank alcoholic beverages at least two to three times a month; 75% reported that they attend off-campus parties this often.

Associations between "background" variables and alcohol consumption in the present study support this conclusion. Men and white students drank more than their counterparts; further, academic class and parent's income were positively associated with how much students consumed. That the effects of race, class, and income were attenuated when frequency of partying was added to the regression model shows that these variables affected how often students partied or, in other words, participated in the dominant subculture of partying/drinking. In addition, the greater their involvement, at least in terms of how much students' drank, the lower their academic performance.

Because the present study was carried out at a single institution, generalizations are hazardous. Still, this college shares many features in common with other colleges; and the evidence strongly indicates that heavy alcohol use—at least at a certain type of institution—has a negative impact on academic performance. In light of this research, it would be premature to discontinue investigations of alcohol's effects on academic performance. Rather, future research on this relationship—and on drinking behavior generally—needs to consider the influence of the campus context. This will require (1) large-scale studies with both institutional and individual units of analysis, and (2) the identification and measurement of key institutional variables, especially drinking norms and residential systems. In addition, other individual-level variables, not included in the present study, such as students' commitment to academic achievement and satisfaction with school, may influence both alcohol use and GPA. Incorporating all of these factors in theoretical models and research designs should provide a more complete understanding of the causes and consequences of problematic alcohol use among college students.

REFERENCES

Bondy, S.J. Overview of studies on drinking patterns and consequences. *Addiction 91:*1663–1674, 1996.

Core Institute. Data from *2005 CORE and Alcohol Drug Survey*, December 2006, Cardondale, IL. Core Institute, Southern Illinois University, 2006.

Hawkins, J.D., Catalano, R.F., and Miller, J.Y. Risk and protective factors for alcohol and other drug problems in adolescence and early adulthood: Implications for substance abuse prevention. *Psychol. Bull.* 112:64–105, 1992.

Paschall, M.J. and Freisthler, B. Does heavy drinking academic performance in college? Findings from a prospective study of high achievers. *J. Stud. Alcohol 64:*515–519, 2003.

Perkins, H.W. Surveying the damage: A review of research on consequences of alcohol misuse in college populations. *J. Stud. Alcohol*, Supplement No. 14, pp. 91–100, 2002.

Presley, C.A. and Pimentel, E.R. The introduction of the heavy and frequent drinker: A proposed classification to increase accuracy of alcohol assessments in postsecondary educational settings. *J. Stud. Alcohol 67:*324–331, 2006.

Schulenberg, J., Bachman, J.G., O'Malley, P.M., and Johnston, L.D. High school educational success and subsequent substance use: A panel analysis following adolescents into young adulthood. *J. Hlth Social Behav.* 35:45–62, 1994.

Weschler, H., Davenport, A., Dowdall, G., Moeykens, B., and Castillo, S. Health and behavioral consequences of binge drinking in college: A national survey of students at 140 campuses. *JAMA 272:*1672–1677, 1994.

Wechsler, H., Lee, J.E., Kou, M., and Lee, H. College binge drinking in the 1990s: A continuing problem. Results of the Harvard School of Public Health 1999 College Alcohol Study. *J. Amer, Coll, Hlth 48:*199–210, 2000.

Wechsler, H. and Nelson, T.F. Binge drinking and the American college student: What's five drinks? *Psychol. Addict. Behav. 15:*287–291, 2001.

Wolaver, A.M. Effects of heavy drinking in college on study effort, grade point average, and major choice. *Contemp. Econ. Policy 20:*415–428, 2002.

Wood, P.K., Sher, K.J., Erickson, D.J., and DeBord, K.A. Predicting academic problems in college from freshman alcohol involvement. *J. Stud. Alcohol 58:*200–210, 1997.

QUESTIONS

1. As pointed out in this article, a fundamental principle of social research is that "correlation does [not imply] causality." Thus, the relationship between alcohol consumption and academic performance may be spurious insofar as "one or more other factors are the cause of both problematic alcohol use and academic problems." How does the quantitative analysis undertaken by Singleton address the problem of spuriousness?

2. Building on your knowledge of measurement in Unit III, how are *alcohol consumption* and *academic performance* operationally defined in this selection? How does Singleton perform a partial check on the validity of the measures of alcohol consumption? Which measure of alcohol consumption does he ultimately use in the analyses?

3. An issue that frequently comes up in quantitative analysis is the handling of missing data. How does Singleton handle missing data for the variable *parents' income*? What are the (acknowledged) consequences of this method for the quantitative analysis?

4. Based on the bivariate correlations among variables, Singleton found that every variable except students' SAT scores was significantly correlated with—or, related to—the number of alcoholic drinks they consumed. Yet, when he conducted multivariate analyses using ordinary least squares regression of alcohol consumption on the same set of variables (see Table 19.1), he found that several of these variables were no longer significantly related to the number of alcoholic drinks students consume. Why is this the case? (Hint: Consider the logic of your answer to the first question.)

5. Table 19.2 presents the results of the multivariate regression of GPA (cumulative and semester) on alcohol consumption and other factors. What is the relationship between GPA and alcohol consumption in these analyses? What other notable relationships change when Singleton introduces alcohol consumption into the statistical model?

6. In general, how does this selection illustrate the deductive logic of inquiry and the role that quantitative data analysis plays in it? (Hint: Refer back to the unit introduction.)

Selection 20

In the 1980s, as homelessness increased and homeless people became more visible on the streets of major cities, social scientists applied their quantitative skills to estimate the extent of the problem and to investigate the conditions that produced it. By contrast, as illustrated in this selection, David Snow and Leon Anderson moved beyond demographic estimates to examine the *meaning* of homelessness for those experiencing it. Through field research and in-depth interviews of homeless people in Austin, Texas, Snow and Anderson discovered the various strategies that the homeless use to construct their personal identities. As you read this selection, pay careful attention to the qualitative data analysis that leads to the various patterns and subpatterns of "identity work."

IDENTITY WORK AMONG THE HOMELESS

The Verbal Construction and Avowal of Personal Identities

DAVID A. SNOW

LEON ANDERSON

Congregated at the bottom of nearly every social order is an aggregation of demeaned and stigmatized individuals variously referred to historically as the *ribauz* (Holmes 1966), the *lumpenproletariat* (Marx and Engels 1967), untouchables (Srinivas and Beteille 1965), the underclass (Myrdal 1962), or superfluous people (Harrington 1984). However

---

Source: "Identity Work Among the Homeless: The Verbal Construction and Avowal of Personal Identities," by David A. Snow and Leon Anderson, 1987, *The American Journal of Sociology,* 92(6), 1336–1371. Copyright 1987 by University of Chicago Press. Adapted with permission.

they come to be situated at the lowest reaches of a status system, whether through political design, structural push, inadvertent slippage, or birth, they tend to be viewed and discussed primarily in terms of the characterological problems they are thought to have (e.g., cultural deprivation, genetic inferiority, and mental depravity), the problems they are thought to pose for the larger community (e.g., crime, contamination, demoralization, and welfare), or the problems associated with their material survival (e.g., food, shelter, and clothing). Their inner life, and particularly the problem of generating and maintaining a sense of meaning and self-worth, is rarely a matter of concern.

This lacuna is also evident in research on America's current wave of homelessness. To date, research has focused almost solely on the demographic characteristics of the homeless, their physiological survival needs, and the problems they have or pose (e.g., alcoholism, mental illness, criminality, and urban blight). That an under-standing of life on the streets and variation in patterns of adaptation may be contingent in part on the webs of meaning the homeless spin and the personal identities they construct has rarely been considered empirically or theoretically. Our primary aim in this paper is to fill this void in part and thereby further understanding of the manner in which a sense of personal significance and meaning is generated and sustained among individuals who have fallen through the cracks of society and linger at the very bottom of the status system. We pursue this objective by ethnographically examining processes of identity construction and avowal among homeless street people. This method of inquiry is consistent with the Blumerian version of symbolic interactionism (Blumer 1969) and the Geertzian strand of interpretive anthropology (Geertz 1973). Both hold, among other things, that an understanding of the social worlds people inhabit requires consideration of the meanings imputed to the objects that constitute those worlds and that these meanings can be apprehended best by intimate familiarity with the routines and situations that are part and parcel of those social worlds.

THE PROBLEM OF IDENTITY CONSTRUCTION AMONG THE HOMELESS

Unlike nearly all other inhabitants of a society, the homeless are seldom incumbents of social roles that are consensually defined in terms of positive social utility and moral worth. As does any highly stigmatized class, the homeless serve various societal functions, such as providing casual labor for underground economies, but these are not the sorts of functions from which personal significance and self-worth can be easily derived. As a consequence, the homeless constitute a kind of superfluous population, in the sense that they fall outside the hierarchy of structurally available societal roles and thus beyond the conventional, role-based sources of moral worth and dignity that most citizens take for granted. As one homeless young man who had been on the streets for only two weeks lamented, "The hardest thing has been getting used to the way people look down on street people. It's real hard to feel good about yourself when almost everyone you see is looking down on you."[1] Homeless street people are thus confronted continuously with the problem of constructing personal identities that are not a mere reflection of the stereotypical and stigmatized manner in which they are regarded as a social category.

To what extent and how do they manage this identity problem? How do they carve out a modicum of self-respect given their pariah-like status? And, What are the implications of the answers to these questions for understanding more generally the relationships among social roles, identity, and the self? What, in short, can we learn from the homeless about identity and identity-construction processes?

PROCEDURES AND CONTEXT

We address these questions with data from a field study of homeless street people in Austin, Texas. While urban homelessness has been associated traditionally with the large industrial cities of the Northeast and Midwest, in recent years the phenomenon has become increasingly common on the streets of Sun Belt cities. Statistics from agencies serving the homeless in such "booming" Sun Belt cities as Phoenix, Dallas, and Austin clearly reflect this increase. In Austin, for example, local Salvation Army figures indicate that the number of different individuals who were served jumped from 4,938 in 1979 to 11,271 in 1984, an increase of 128%. That the majority of these individuals are indeed homeless street people is suggested even more graphically by the quantum jump in lodgings and meals during this same time period, from 16,863 to 156,451, an 828% increase.

[Statistics from samples of the homeless in Austin and elsewhere] . . . suggest that there is nothing strikingly peculiar about the homeless in Austin that should render reasonable generalizations based on them implausible. Not only have many of them come from the different regions of the country, but they are demographically similar to the homeless elsewhere. Moreover, we have learned from many of them that, aside from variations in climate and the availability of free shelter and food, most aspects of life on the street are quite similar from one city to another. We think it is therefore reasonable to expect considerable similarity in basic patterns and process of identity construction and avowal among the homeless.

We pursue the identification of these processes with data gathered during a year-long ethnographic field study conducted among homeless individuals living in or passing through Austin from September 1, 1984, to August 31, 1985. The major research strategy was to "hang out" with as many of these individuals as possible on a daily basis, spending time with them in varied settings (e.g., meal and shelter lines, under bridges, in parks, at day-labor pickup sites), over the course of the 12-month period. The basic task was to acquire an appreciation for the nature of life on the streets and the ways in which the homeless managed street life both experientially and cognitively. We thus followed the homeless we encountered through their daily routines and listened not only to what they told us but also to what they told one another.

We asked questions and probed from time to time and also "interviewed by comment,"[2] but the major task was that of listening to conversations among the homeless to enhance the prospect of securing perspectives that seemed to arise naturally rather than only in response to the researcher's coaxing or intervention. This relatively unobtrusive listening took two basic forms: eavesdropping, which involved listening to others within a bounded interactional encounter without being a part of that encounter, as when waiting in meal lines or in day-labor offices; and a kind of nondirective, conversational listening that occurred when we engaged in encounters with two or more homeless individuals.

Behavioral observations and conversational dialogues were recorded in a stepwise fashion, beginning with mental and jotted notes in the field and culminating in a detailed field narrative based on elaboration of these notes. Since compulsive note taking can deflect attention from the behaviors being observed to the process of recording, as well as give rise to various reactive effects, we chose to make mental and jotted notes instead of fully detailed notes when in the field. What this involved was the memorization or jotted recording of behavioral observations and comments. The jotted recordings typically included key phrases, longer quotes, and behavioral descriptions. These jotted notes, which were taken as inconspicuously as possible while eavesdropping or immediately following the dissolution of conversations, were then elaborated as soon as possible after exiting the field. It is these narrative elaborations that constitute the field notes or data log out of which the analysis presented herein emerged.

Although the ethnographic research role was customarily performed by the second author, it was not enacted in the "lone ranger" (Douglas 1976, pp. 192–93) fashion. Rather, the field researcher's activities, observations, and notes were continuously monitored and responded to by the first author, who assumed the role of a detached observer, functioning much like a sideline coach. Seldom was a day or evening in the field not followed by a debriefing session that included discussion of field experiences, methodological and theoretical implications, and the elaboration of plans for subsequent outings. Conscious and reflective enactment of these two roles enabled us to maintain involvement and detachment at one and the same time, thereby facilitating management of the insider/outsider dialectic characteristic of ethnographic research.

The data derived from our field observations and encounters were supplemented by taped, in-depth, life-history interviews with six homeless individuals who had been on the streets for various lengths of time, ranging from two months to 14 years. All but one of the individuals were key informants with whom we had numerous contacts and who functioned for us in a manner similar to "Doc" in *Street Corner Society* (Whyte 1943) and Tally in *Tally's Corner* (Liebow 1967).

All totaled, 405 hours were spent in 24 different settings (e.g., Salvation Army, city hospital, soup kitchen, plasma center, casual labor corner) with 168 homeless individuals. Field encounters with this nonrandom sample totaled 492, averaging three per person, with a high of 22. Field notes based on these encounters yielded over 600 double-spaced typed pages. From this pool of data, a total of 202 statements by 70 individuals about self and identity were extracted, coded, and analyzed. In order to enhance the probability of coder reliability, all field notes were coded jointly by the two authors. These data were initially coded broadly, as indicated by the 24 different focal settings and 30 different cultural domains that emerge,[3] only one of which was the identity and self-concept domain. In due time, however, it became clear that some of these settings and domains were more central than others to the lives and daily routines of the homeless, as indicated by variation in the number of data entries contained in each respective coding category.[4] In short, some of the files "bulged" with data and others did not. One of these bulging files pertained to self and identity.

VARIETIES OF IDENTITY TALK AMONG THE HOMELESS: FINDINGS AND OBSERVATIONS

Up to this point, we have used the term "identity" in a general and undefined fashion. It is necessary to clarify what we mean by the term "identity" and related concepts before proceeding further. We distinguish among social identities, personal identities, and self-concept. By social identities, we refer to the identities attributed or imputed to others in an attempt to place or situate them as social objects. They are not self-designations or avowals but imputations based primarily on information gleaned on the basis of appearance, behavior, and the location and time of action. In contrast, personal identities refer to the meanings attributed to the self by the actor. They are self-designations and self-attributions brought into play or asserted during the course of interaction. Since personal identities may be inconsistent with imputed social identities, the two need to be kept analytically distinct. Standing in contrast to these two variants of identity is the self-concept, by which we refer to one's overarching view or image of her- or himself "as a physical, social, spiritual, or moral being" (Gecas 1982, p. 3). Following Turner (1968), we view the self-concept as a kind of working compromise between idealized images and imputed social identities. Presented personal identities provide a glimpse of the consistency or inconsistency between social identities and self-concept, as well as indications of the latter.

Our empirical concern here is primarily with personal identities and particularly with the ways in which the homeless construct and utilize such identities. We conceptualize identity construction and assertion as variants of the generic process we call *identity work*, by which we refer to the range of activities individuals engage in to create, present, and sustain personal identities that are congruent with and supportive of the self-concept. So defined, identity work may involve a number of complementary activities; (a) procurement or arrangement of physical settings and props; (b) cosmetic face work or the arrangement of personal appearance; (c) selective association with other individuals and groups; and (d) verbal construction and assertion of personal identities. In this paper, we concentrate on the last variety of identity work, which we refer to as *identity talk*.

Inspection of these conversational data yielded three generic patterns of identity talk: (1) distancing, (2) embracement, and (3) fictive storytelling. Each was found to contain several varieties that tended to vary in use according to the duration of one's street career. We discuss and elaborate in turn each of the generic patterns and their subtypes.

Distancing

Our findings reveal that a substantial proportion of the identity talk of the homeless we studied was consciously focused on distancing themselves from other homeless individuals, from street and occupational roles, and from the institutions serving them. Nearly a third of the 202 identity statements were of this variety.

Associational distancing.

Since one's claim to a particular self is partly contingent on the imputed social identities of one's associates, one way to substantiate that claim, in the event that one's associates are negatively evaluated, is to distance oneself from them. This distancing technique manifested itself in two ways in our research: dissociation from the homeless as a general social category and dissociation from specific groups of homeless individuals.

Categorical associational distancing was particularly evident among homeless individuals who had been on the streets for a comparatively short time. Illustrative of this technique is the following comment by a 24-year-old white male who had been on the streets for less than two weeks: "I'm not like the other guys who hang out down at the 'Sally' [Salvation Army]. If you want to know about street people, I can tell you about them; but you can't really learn about street people from studying me, because I'm different."

Such categorical distancing also occurred among those individuals who saw themselves as on the verge of getting off the street. One 22-year-old white male who had been on the streets for several years but who had just secured two jobs in hopes of raising enough money to rent an apartment indicated, for example, that he was different from other street people: "They have gotten used to living on the streets and are satisfied with it. But not me! Next to my salvation, getting off the street is the most important thing in my life."

Among the homeless who had been on the street for some time and who appeared firmly rooted in that life-style, there were few examples of categorical distancing, Instead, these individuals frequently distinguished themselves from other groups of the homeless. This form of associational distancing was most conspicuous among the homeless who were not regular social service or shelter users and who thus saw themselves as being more independent and resourceful. These individuals not only wasted little time in pointing out that they were "not like those Sally users," but they were also given to derogating the more institutionally dependent. Indeed, while they were among those furthest removed from the middle class in their way of life, they sounded at times much like middle-class citizens berating welfare recipients. Illustrative is the comment of an alcoholic, 49-year-old woman who had been on the streets for two-and-a-half years: "A lot of these people staying at the Sally, they're reruns. Every day they're wanting something, wanting something. People get tired of giving. All you hear is 'give me, give me.' And we transients are getting tired of it." Although associational-distancing provides one means by which some of the homeless set themselves apart from one another and thus develop a somewhat different and more self-respecting personal identity, such distancing varies in scope according to the duration of time on the streets.

Role distancing.

Role distancing was the second form of distancing employed by the homeless in order to buffer the self. As with associational distancing, role distancing manifested itself in two ways: distancing from the basic or general role of street person and distancing from specific occupational roles. The former, which we construe as a variant of categorical distancing, was particularly evident among individuals who had been on the street for less than six months. It was not uncommon for these individuals to make explicitly clear that they should "not be mistaken as a typical street person." Role distancing of the less categorical and more situationally specific type, however, was most evident in day-labor occupational roles, such as painters' helpers, hod carriers, warehouse and van unloaders, and unskilled service occupations, such as dishwashing and janitorial work. Although the majority of the homeless we encountered would avail themselves of such job opportunities, they seldom did so enthusiastically because of the jobs' low status and low wages. This was especially true of the homeless who had been on the streets between two and four years, who frequently reminded others of their disdain for such jobs and of their belief that they deserved better, as exemplified by the remarks of a drunk young man who had worked the previous day as a painter's helper: "I made $36.00 off the labor corner, but it was just 'nigger' work. I'm 24 years old, man. I deserve better than that." Similar distancing laments were frequently voiced over the disparity between job demands and wages: While we were conversing with a small gathering of homeless men on a Saturday afternoon, one of them revealed, for example, that he had turned down a job earlier in the day to carry shingles up a ladder for $4.00 an hour because he found it demeaning to "do that hard of work for that low of pay."

The foregoing illustrations suggest that the social identities lodged in available work roles are frequently inconsistent with the desired or idealized self-conceptions of some of the homeless. Consequently, "bitching about," "turning down," and even "blowing off" such work may function as a means of social identity disavowal, on the one hand, and personal identity assertion, on the other. Such techniques provide a way of saying, "Hey, I have some pride. I'm in control. I'm my own man."

Institutional distancing.

An equally prevalent distancing technique involved the derogation of the very institutions that attended to the needs of the homeless in one way or another. The one agency that was the most frequent object of these harangues was the local Salvation Army. It was frequently typified by many of the homeless who used it as a greedy corporation run by inhumane personnel more interested in lining their own pockets than in serving the needy. The flavor of this negative characterization is captured by such comments as the following, which were heard most often among individuals waiting in the Salvation Army dinner line: "The Salvation Army is supposed to be a Christian organization, but it doesn't have a Christian spirit. It looks down on people. . . . and "If you spend a week here, you'll see how come people lose hope. You're treated just like an animal."

[At the Salvation Army,] clients are processed in an impersonal, highly structured, assembly-line fashion. The result is a leveling of individual differences and a decline in personal autonomy. Bitching and complaining about such settings thus allow one to gain psychic distance from the self implied and to secure a modicum of personal autonomy. Criticizing the Salvation Army, then, provided some regular users with a means of dealing with the implications of their dependence on it. It was, in short, a way of presenting and sustaining a somewhat contrary personal identity.

While this variety of distancing was observable among all the homeless, it was most prevalent among those regular service users who had been on the streets for more than two years. Since these individuals had used street institutions over a longer period of time, their self-concepts were more deeply implicated in them, thus necessitating distancing from those very institutions and the self implied.

Thus far, we have elaborated how some of the homeless distance themselves from other homeless individuals, from general and specific roles, and from the institutions that deal with them. Such distancing behavior and talk represent attempts to salvage a measure of self-worth. In the process, of course, the homeless are asserting more favorable personal identities. Not all homeless individuals engage in similar distancing behavior and talk, however. Categorical distancing tends to be concentrated among those who have been on the street for a comparatively short time, typically less than six months. The only instances of such distancing we heard from those who had been on the streets for more than four years were made by individuals categorized as "mentally ill," as in the case of one 32-year-old white male who expressed disdain for the homeless in general even though he had been on and off the street for 10 years between stays in Texas state mental hospitals. For those who are more firmly entrenched in street life, then, distancing tends to be confined to distinguishing themselves from specific groups of the homeless, such as novices and the institutionally dependent, from specific occupational roles, or from the institutions with which they have occasional contact.

Embracement

By "embracement," we refer to the verbal and expressive confirmation of one's acceptance of and attachment to the social identity associated with a general or specific role, a set of social relationships, or a particular ideology. Embracement involves the avowal of implied social identities rather than their disavowal, as is true of distancing. Thirty-six percent of the identity statements were of this variety.

Role embracement.

The most conspicuous kind of embracement we encountered was role embracement of the categorical variety, which typically manifested itself in the avowal and acceptance of street role identities such as the "tramp" and "bum." Occasionally, we would encounter an individual who would immediately announce that he was a tramp or a bum. A case in point is provided by our initial encounter with a 49-year-old man who had been on the road for 14 years. When we engaged him in conversation on a street corner, he proudly told us that he was "the tramp who was on the front page of yesterday's newspaper." In that and subsequent conversations, his talk was peppered with references to himself as a tramp.

Role-specific embracement was also encountered occasionally, as when a street person of several years referred to himself as an "expert dumpster diver." In street argot, "dumpster diving" refers to scavenging through garbage bins in search of clothes, food, and salable items. Many street people often engage in this survival activity, but relatively few pridefully identify themselves in terms of this activity. For some homeless individuals, [though,] the roles they enact function as a source of positive identity and self-worth.

Associational embracement.

A second variety of embracement used to denote or embellish a personal identity entailed reference to oneself as a friend or as an individual who acknowledges the norm of reciprocity and who thus takes his social relationships seriously. A case in point is provided by the individual alluded to who pridefully acknowledged that he was a bum. On one occasion, he told us that he had several friends who either refused or quit jobs at the Salvation Army because they "weren't allowed to associate with other guys on the streets who were their friends." Such a policy struck him as immoral: "They expect you to forget who your friends are and where you came from when you go to work there. They asked me to work there, and I told them, 'No way.' I'm a bum and I know who my friends are."

Identification of oneself as a person who willingly shares limited resources, such as cigarettes and alcohol, occurred frequently, particularly among avowed tramps and bums. One evening after dinner at the Salvation Army, for example, a 29-year-old white male who had been on the street for several years quickly responded to the researcher's offer of a cigarette with an offer of his own to take a drink from his Coke, commenting, "See, man, I'm all right. I share, man. I don't just take things."

Associational embracement was also expressed in self-identification as protector or defender of one's buddies. Two older drinking partners whom we came to know claimed repeatedly to "look out for each other." When one was telling about having been assaulted and robbed while walking through an alley, the other said, almost apologetically, "It wouldn't have happened if I was with you. I wouldn't have let them get away with that." Similar claims were made to the field researcher, as when two street acquaintances indicated one evening after an ambiguous encounter with a clique of a half-dozen other street people that, "If it wasn't for us, they'd have had your ass." Such [protective claims] functioned not only to cement tenuous ties but also to express something concrete about the claimant's desired identity as a dependable and trustworthy friend.

Ideological embracement.

A third variety of embracement that can provide an individual with a special niche in which to lodge the self and thereby distinguish himself from others entails the acceptance of a set of beliefs or ideas and the avowal of a cognitively congruent personal identity. We refer to this as ideological embracement.

Among the homeless we studied, ideological embracement manifested itself primarily as an avowed commitment to a particular religion or set of religious beliefs. One middle-aged tramp called Banjo provides an example. He routinely identified himself as a Christian, he had painted on his banjo case "Wealth means nothing without God," and his talk was sprinkled with references to his Christian beliefs. When asked whether he was afraid to sleep at the Salvation Army following a murder that had occurred the night before, he replied: "I don't have anything to worry about since I'm a Christian, and it says in the 23d Psalm: 'Yea though I walk through the valley of death, I shall fear no evil, for Thou art with me.'"

An equally powerful but less common functional equivalent of religion as a source of identity is the occult and related supernatural beliefs. Illustrative of this was a 29-year-old male who read books on the occult regularly, identified himself as a "spirit guide," and informed us that he had received "a spiritual gift" at the age of 13 and that he now had special prophetic insights into the future that allowed him to foresee the day when "humans will be transformed into another life form."

We have seen how the personal identities of the homeless may be derived from the embracement of the social identities associated with certain stereotypical street roles, such as the tramp and the bum; with role-specific survival activities, such as dumpster diving; with certain social relationships, such as friend and protector; and with certain religious and occult ideologies or belief systems. While embracement and distancing are not necessarily mutually exclusive means for constructing personal identities among the homeless, we have noted how their usage tends to vary according to the stage or point in one's street career. More specifically, we have found that the longer one has been on the street and the more adapted one is to street life, the greater the prevalence of categorical embracement in particular. That relationship is emphasized even further when it is noted that the only cases of such embracement among those who had been on the streets for less than two years occurred among those categorized as mentally ill, as in the case of a 33-year-old black female who avowed the nonstreet identity of The Interracial Princess, which she said had been bestowed on her by "a famous astrologer from New York."

Fictive Storytelling

A third form of identity talk engaged in by the homeless is what we refer to as fictive storytelling. It involves the narration of stories about one's past, present, or future experiences and accomplishments that have a fictive character to them. We characterize these stories as fictive because they tend to range from minor exaggerations of experience to fanciful claims and fabrications. We thus distinguish between two types of fictive storytelling: embellishment of the past and present and fantasizing about the future. Slightly more than a third of the identity statements we recorded fell into one of these two categories.

Embellishment.

By "embellishment," we refer to the exaggeration of past and present experiences with fanciful and fictitious particulars so as to assert a positive personal identity. Examples of such embellishment for identity construction purposes abound among the homeless. The most common form of embellished storytelling tended to be associated with past and current occupational and financial themes. In the case of financial embellishment, the typical story entailed an exaggerated claim regarding past or current wages.

Illustrative of such embellishment is an encounter we overheard between an inebriated 49-year-old homeless woman passing out discarded burritos and a young homeless man in his early 20s. When he took several burritos and chided the woman for being drunk, she yelled stridently at him: "I'm a floating taper and I make 14 bucks an hour. What the fuck do you make?" Aside from putting the young man in his place, the statement functioned to announce to him, as well as to others overhearing the encounter, the woman's desired identity as a person who earns a respectable wage and must therefore be treated respectfully. Subsequent interaction with this woman revealed that she worked only sporadically and then most often for a temporary day agency at $4.00 per hour. There was, then, a considerable gap between claims and reality.

Disjunctures between identity assertions and reality appear to be quite common and were readily discernible on occasion, as in the case of a 45-year-old transient from Pittsburgh who had been on the streets for a year and who was given to excessive embellishment of his former military

experiences. On several occasions, he was overheard telling tales about his experiences "patrolling the Alaskan-Russian border in Alaskan Siberia" and of encounters with Russian guards, who traded vodka for coffee with him. Since there is no border between Alaska and Siberia, it is obvious that this tale is outlandish. Nonetheless, such identity constructions, however embellished, can be construed as attempts to say something concrete about oneself and how one would like to be regarded in a particular situation.

Fantasizing.

The second type of fictive storytelling that frequently manifested itself during the course of conversations with and among the homeless is verbal fantasizing. Fantasizing involves future-oriented fabrications about oneself. Regardless of the degree of self-deception, the spoken fantasies we were privy to were generally organized around four themes: self-employment, money, material possessions, and the opposite sex, particularly for men. Fanciful constructions concerning self-employment were usually expressed in terms of business schemes. A black 30-year-old male from Chicago told us and others on several occasions, for example, about his plans "to set up a little shop near the university" to sell leather hats and silverwork imported from New York.

An equally prominent source of fanciful identity construction was the fantasy of becoming rich. Some of the homeless would make bold claims about becoming rich, without offering any details. The following is illustrative: "You might laugh and think I'm crazy, but I'm going to be rich. I know it. I just have this feeling. I can't explain it, but I am."

As we previously noted, fanciful identity assertions were also constructed around material possessions and encounters with the opposite sex. These two identity pegs were clearly illustrated one evening while we were hanging out with several homeless men along the city's major nightlife strip. During the course of making numerous overtures to passing women, two of the fellows jointly fantasized about how they would attract these women in the future: "Man, these chicks are going to be all over us when we come back into town with our new suits and Corvettes. We'll have to get some cocaine too. Cocaine will get you women every time."

Although both the embellished and fanciful variants of fictive storytelling surfaced rather frequently during the course of the conversations we overheard, they were not uniformly widespread or randomly distributed among the homeless. Embellishment occurred among all the homeless but was particularly pronounced among those who had been on the street for two to four years. Fantasizing, on the other hand, occurred most frequently among those who still had one foot anchored in the world they came from and who could still envision a future; it occurred least often among those individuals who appeared acclimated to street life and tended to embrace one or more street identities. For these individuals, especially those who have been on the street for four or more years, the future is apparently too remote to provide a solid anchoring for fictive, identity-oriented spinoffs that are of this world.

CONCLUSIONS AND IMPLICATIONS

We have identified and elaborated three generic patterns of identity talk through which the homeless we studied construct and avow personal identities that yield a measure of self-respect and dignity. We have noted that each pattern of talk—distancing, embracement, and fictive storytelling—contains several varieties and that their frequency of use tends to vary with the duration of one's street career. Categorical role and associational distancing and the construction of fanciful identities were found to occur most frequently among those who had been on the streets a comparatively short time. Categorical embracement and embellishment, however, tended to manifest themselves most frequently among those who had been on the streets for two or more years.

Our findings make clear that the personal identities homeless people construct and avow are not static but, instead, change with the passage of time on the streets. The typical progression is from categorical distancing and the assertion of fanciful, future-oriented identities to categorical embracement, distancing from specific types of homeless individuals and street institutions, and the embellishment of past experiences and encounters.

Finally, it is important to emphasize that our research, unlike most research on identity, was based on in situ observations of and encounters with individuals engaged in natural ongoing interaction. The identities discerned and recorded were thus "in use" in an ongoing system of action rather than responses to prestructured questions in purely research-contrived situations. Whatever the limitations of this research tack, we think they are outweighed by the fact that it provides a relatively rare glimpse of the actual construction and use of personal identities in the course of everyday life among individuals at the very bottom of society.

[Our] findings caution against the tendency within sociology to adopt an overly structuralized conception of self and identity, treating the latter as an entity that is routinely assigned or bestowed upon the actor rather than constructed or negotiated on occasion. Clearly, the homeless we came to know provide an empirical counterpoint to that tendency.

NOTES

1. All such spoken material throughout the paper represents verbatim quotes of some of the homeless whom we encountered. They are used for illustrative purposes and are representative of what we heard or were told. The process by which these materials were discerned and recorded will be discussed in detail in the Procedures and Context section following an intentional statement rather than by asking a direct question.

2. Interviewing by comment refers to an attempt to elicit spoken information from a respondent or an informant by making an intentional statement instead of asking a direct question.

3. By "focal settings," we refer to the major institutions or agencies (e.g., city hospital, city police department, and Salvation Army), commercial establishments (e.g., bars, restaurants, and plasma centers) and territorial niches (e.g., particular campsites, bridges, parks, and street corners) that are most relevant to the daily rounds, life-style, and prospects of the homeless living in or passing through Austin. By "cultural domains," we refer to categories of meaning, events, and problems that constitute the social world and life-style of the homeless (e.g., drinking and alcohol, drugs, food and eating, sleeping and shelter, social relationships, and work) and that were discerned by the previously discussed procedures.

4. By "data entries," we refer to single bits of information relevant to any single focal setting, cultural domain, or homeless individual. The focal settings (24), cultural domains (30), and homeless individuals (168) composed the coding categories that emerged over time. The data entries, extracted from the field notes, varied from a single sentence to several pages in length and were assigned to one or more of the coding categories.

References

Blumer, Herbert. 1969. *Symbolic Interactionism: Perspective and Method*. Englewood Cliffs, N.J.: Prentice-Hall.

Douglas, Jack D. 1976. *Investigative Social Research: Individual and Team Field Research*. Beverly Hills, Calif.: Sage.

Gecas, Viktor. 1982. "The Self-Concept." *Annual Review of Sociology* 8:1–33.

Geertz, Clifford. 1973. *The Interpretation of Cultures*. New York: Basic Books.

Harrington, Michael. 1984. *The New American Poverty*. New York: Holt, Rinehart & Winston.

Holmes, Urban Tigner. 1966. *Daily Living in the Twelfth Century: Based on the Observations of Alexander Neckham in London and Paris*. Madison: University of Wisconsin Press.

Liebow, Elliot. 1967. *Tally's Corner: A Study of Negro Streetcorner Men*. Boston: Little, Brown.

Marx, Karl, and Friederich Engels. (1848) 1967. *The Communist Manifesto*. New York: Penguin.

Myrdal, Gunnar. 1962. *Challenge to Affluence*. New York: Pantheon.

Srinivas, M. N., and Andre Beteille. 1965. "The Untouchables of India." *Scientific American* 216:13–17.

Turner, Ralph H. 1968. "The Self-Conception in Social Interaction." Pp. 93–106 in *The Self in Social Interaction*, edited by C. Gordon and K. J. Gergen. New York: Wiley.

Whyte, William F. 1943. *Street Corner Society: The Social Structure of an Italian Slum*. Chicago: University of Chicago Press.

Questions

1. In the introduction to this unit, we noted that the analysis of qualitative data begins "in the field." How does this selection illustrate this?

2. In this selection, the data are based on "*600 double-spaced typed pages*" (*our emphasis*)—an overwhelming number, to be sure! How many statements and individuals is the analysis of *self and identity* specifically based on? Why did Snow and Anderson focus on self and identity?

3. What are the three categories into which data entries are coded? (Hint: Look at endnote 4). Under which of these three categories would the Salvation Army most likely fall?

4. What are the "three generic patterns of identity talk" found among the homeless? Provide an example of how *two* of these forms of identity talk reference one of the researchers' "focal settings" in their data coding.

5. Provide an example of how one of the "three generic patterns of identity talk" varies by time on the street, based on Snow and Anderson's findings and observations.

6. In general, how does this selection illustrate the inductive logic of inquiry and the role that qualitative data analysis plays in it? (Hint: Refer back to the unit introduction.)

GLOSSARY

anonymity: a research condition protecting privacy in which researchers are unable to identify data with particular research participants.

bivariate analysis: statistical analysis of the relationship between two variables; a common bivariate statistic is the correlation coefficient, which describes the strength and direction (positive or negative) of the linear association between two variables.

comparative-historical analysis: the analysis of data representing multiple points in time and/ or multiple nations, states, or other groupings.

confidentiality: an agreement protecting privacy whereby researchers are bound not to divulge information obtained from research participants without their permission.

content analysis: a set of methods for analyzing the symbolic content of communications such as books, documents, and pictures; usually words or visual images are coded into categories to describe and/or quantify content.

convenience sample: a type of nonrandom sample in which the researcher simply selects cases that are conveniently available.

cross-sectional survey design: a research design in which a sample of respondents is surveyed at essentially one point in time.

deception: an act that leads a person to believe something that is not true; although common in experimental research as allowed by federal and other professional ethical guidelines, the use of deception in social research is controversial.

deduction (or deductive logic): a type of reasoning that moves from abstract statements to concrete observations; researchers employ deductive logic in deducing hypotheses from theories and testing hypotheses with observations or data.

dependent variable: the variable that the researcher tries to explain or predict; in terms of cause and effect, the dependent variable is the presumed effect; in relation to independent variables, it is the variable being influence**D**.

existing data: sources of information, or data, that were not produced directly by the researcher who uses them; this may include historical and documentary data, in addition to the type of data examined in content analysis (see above).

experiment: an approach to social research in which the researcher deliberately alters (or manipulates) some aspect of the environment and then observes the effects of the manipulation.

explanatory case study: the application of one or more theories to the in-depth analysis of a single case such as a person, historical event or period, group or community.

external validity: the extent to which research findings generalize beyond a specific study; usually applied to the evaluation of experiments.

field research: an approach to social research in which the researcher directly observes and interacts with others in a natural setting; this may include qualitative interviewing.

hypothesis: a proposed or expected relationship between two or more variables.

independent variable: a presumed influence or cause of the dependent variable; it is the variable that **I**nfluences the dependent variable.

induction (or inductive logic): a type of reasoning that moves from concrete observations to abstract statements; researchers employ inductive logic in discerning patterns in a set of observations and inferring their larger theoretical meaning.

informed consent: an ethical practice, required by federal ethical guidelines, that provides research participants with enough information about a study, especially its potential risks, to make an informed decision about whether to participate.

internal validity: the degree to which a study, usually an experiment, accurately tests a causal relationship between variables.

longitudinal survey design: a research design for understanding social stability and change in which surveys are conducted at multiple times with the same or different samples.

manipulation check: evidence that an experimental manipulation validly measured the independent variable.

measurement: the process by which researchers create the means of recording observations to represent theoretical concepts; sources of measurement in social research include self-reports from surveys and interviews, direct observation, and archival records.

measurement validity: the degree to which an operational definition (or measure) accurately represents the concept it is intended to measure.

multi-stage cluster sampling: a probability sampling technique commonly used in national face-to-face surveys in which sampling is carried out at two or more stages (e.g., a sample of voting precincts followed by a sample of voters leaving the selected precincts).

multivariate analysis: statistical analysis of the simultaneous relationships among three or more variables; in multiple regression, researchers analyze the relationship between each independent variable and the dependent variable, while controlling for the influence of other independent variables.

nonprobability sampling: methods of selecting observations other than random selection; see convenience sample, purposive sampling, and snowball sampling.

official statistics: information such as birth rates, infant mortality rates, and crime rates that are routinely collected by governments to assist in policy making.

operational definitions: the research operations or procedures designed to record data that will represent study concepts or variables.

population: all the members of a defined group of people, objects, or events that the researcher is studying.

probability sampling: methods of selecting observations based on random selection; see simple random sampling, multi-stage cluster sampling.

purposive sampling: a set of sampling techniques often used in qualitative research in which systematic, albeit nonrandom methods are used to select a representative sample of the population.

qualitative interview: an interview found in qualitative research intended to acquire an in-depth understanding of social life; such interviews may be semistructured or unstructured.

qualitative research: social research intended to explore the meanings people attach to their experiences in which recorded data take the form of rich descriptions and verbatim statements.

quantitative research: social research, typified by experiments and surveys, conducted for the purposes of testing hypotheses or estimating population characteristics, in which data are transformed into numbers.

quota sampling: a nonprobability sampling method that involves selecting quotas of cases with specific characteristics (e.g., 10 men and 10 women), which is intended to make the sample representative of, or proportionate to, the frequency of those characteristics in the population.

randomization: the process in well-conducted (or true) experiments by which research participants are assigned to experimental and control groups strictly on the basis of chance.

regression analysis: a set of statistical techniques for estimating how much changes in the dependent variable vary with changes in one or more independent variables.

reliability: the degree to which repeated or multiple measurements yield the same results; a reliable measure is consistent.

repeated cross-sectional design: a survey research design that traces changes in responses to particular questions administered repeatedly to independent samples of the same population; also called a trend study.

response rate: an indicator of survey quality that consists of the proportion of sampled respondents who completed the questionnaire or interview.

sample: a subset of a population, usually selected in social research to be representative of a defined group of people, objects, or events.

secondary analysis: the analysis of survey or qualitative data (e.g., fieldnotes or transcriptions of interviews) by someone other than the researcher or agency that collected them to address research questions beyond the original purpose of gathering the data.

semistructured interview: a type of interview based on a pre-established set of questions that allows interviewers flexibility in meeting study objectives by adding questions as a result of what the interviewee says.

simple random sampling: the simplest form of probability sampling in which cases (e.g., individuals) are randomly selected such that each case and each combination of cases has the same probability of being selected; cases or individuals

are selected randomly from a complete list of the population.

snowball sampling: a sampling technique often used in qualitative research, most notably studies of deviance, that makes use of social networks to select individuals in a process of chain referral—each contact is asked to identify additional members of a group, who are asked to name others, and so on.

social theory: a set of abstract statements describing some aspect of the social world.

split-ballot experiment: an experiment incorporated into surveys that presents two or more versions of the same questions to randomized subsets of respondents.

statistically significant relationship: a relationship between variables that is unlikely to have occurred by chance or random processes; ordinarily, researchers report the likelihood that the relationship could have occurred by chance (e.g., probability [p] $< .05$ or 5 times in hundred) according to statistical tests; may be signified in tables by asterisks (e.g., *, **, or ***) or other symbols.

structured interview: the preferred type of survey interview in quantitative research (i.e., studies designed to test hypotheses or estimate population characteristics); all questions, most of which provide a fixed set of answers, are written beforehand and asked in the same order for all respondents; also called a standardized interview.

survey: an approach to social research that involves asking a sample of respondents predetermined questions in questionnaires or interviews.

theme: a common thread or pattern that emerges through the process of coding in qualitative analysis.

theory: See social theory.

triangulation: in social research, the use of more than one method or approach to address the same research question.

two-stage cluster sampling: See multi-stage cluster sampling.

unobtrusive data: data gathered in such a way that research participants are unaware of being studied.

unstructured interview: a type of interview common to qualitative research with very general research objectives in which the interviewer may have little more than a topical outline, and questions are developed as the interview proceeds.

validity: See measurement validity, external validity, internal validity.

ABOUT THE EDITORS

Jeffrey C. Dixon, Assistant Professor of Sociology at the College of the Holy Cross, received his PhD from Indiana University, Bloomington, and also holds a BS in Secondary Education from Wright State University. His research has appeared in such journals as *Social Forces, Public Opinion Quarterly, British Journal of Sociology, International Migration Review,* and *Teaching Sociology*. His current research focuses on liberal-democratic values and attitudes in Turkey and the European Union (EU), job insecurity in the EU (with Andrew S. Fullerton and Dwanna L. Robertson), and the process of EU enlargement in historical and comparative perspective. He has taught research methods courses for four years, including a graduate course at Koç University in Istanbul and an undergraduate course at Holy Cross.

Royce A. Singleton, Jr., Professor Emeritus of Sociology at the College of the Holy Cross, received his PhD from Indiana University, Bloomington. He is the co-author (with Bruce Straits) of *Approaches to Social Research*, now in its 5th edition (Oxford University Press, 2010). Spanning several methodological approaches, his research has appeared in the *American Sociological Review, Social Forces, Sociological Quarterly, Sex Roles,* and *Teaching Sociology* among other journals. His most recent publications include a chapter on "Survey Interviewing" in *The Sage Handbook of Interview Research* and articles on college drinking and college voluntarism. Before his recent retirement from full-time teaching, he taught both graduate and undergraduate courses in social research methods, including a course offered at Holy Cross for 32 years.